ISSUES IN COGNITIVE MODELING

ISSUES IN COGNITIVE MODELING

a reader edited by
A. M. Aitkenhead and J. M. Slack
at the Open University

LEA LAWRENCE ERLBAUM ASSOCIATES, PUBLISHERS LEA
London   Hillsdale, New Jersey

in association with The Open University

Reprinted 1987

Lawrence Erlbaum Associates Ltd., Publishers
27 Palmeira Mansions
Church Road
Hove
East Sussex BN3 2FA

British Library Cataloguing in Publication Data

Issues in cognitive modeling.—(An Open University set book)
1. Cognition
I. Aitkenhead, A. M.   II. Slack, J. M.
153.4   BF311

ISBN 0-86377-029-0
ISBN 0-86377-030-4 Pbk

Typeset by Tradespools Ltd., Frome
Printed and bound by A. Wheaton & Co. Ltd., Exeter

CONTENTS

SOURCES AND ACKNOWLEDGEMENTS

Chapter

1. **Trends and Debates in Cognitive Psychology,** by G. A. Miller. Extracted by permission of the author and publisher from: *Cognition, 10,* 215–225, 1981. (Published by North Holland.)

2. **Representation of Knowledge,** by D. E. Rumelhart and D. A. Norman. Extracted from: *Representation in Memory. CHIP Technical Report (no. 116).* San Diego: Center for Human Information Processing, University of California, 1983. Copyright John Wiley and Sons, Inc. 1985. Reprinted by permission.

3. **The Medium and the Message in Mental Imagery: A Theory,** by S. M. Kosslyn. Extracted by permission of the author and publisher from: *Psychological Review, 88,* 46–65, 1981. (Copyright 1981, The American Psychological Association).

4. **Mental Models,** by P. N. Johnson-Laird. Extracted by permission of the author and publisher from chapters 1 and 7 of: Johnson-Laird, P. N. (1983). *Mental Models.* Cambridge: Cambridge University Press.

5. **Vision: The Philosophy and the Approach,** by D. Marr. Extracted by permission from: Marr, D. (1982). *Vision.* San Francisco: W. H. Freeman and company. (Copyright ©1982 by W. H. Freeman and company.)

6. **Perceptual Organization in Information Processing,** by J. Pomerantz. Extracted by permission from: Kubovy, M. and Pomerantz, J. (Eds.) (1981). *Perceptual Organization.* Hillsdale, N. J.: Lawrence Erlbaum Associates.

7. **General Constraints on Process Models of Language Comprehension,** by R. de Beaugrande. Extracted by permission of the author and publisher from: Le Ny, J. F. & Kintsch, W. (Eds.) (1982). *Language and comprehension.* Amsterdam: North Holland.

8. **What Does it Mean to Understand Language?,** by T. Winograd. Extracted by permission of the author and publisher from: *Cognitive Science, 4,* 209–241, 1980. (Published by Ablex Publishing Corporation.)

9. **Realistic Language Comprehension,** by C. K. Reisbeck. Extracted by permission from: Lehnert, V. G. & Ringle, M. H. (Eds.) *Strategies for Natural Language Processing.* Hillsdale, N. J.: Lawrence Erlbaum Associates Inc., 1982.

10. **Domains of Recollection,** by A. Baddeley. Extracted by permission of author and publisher from: *Psychological Review, 89,* 708–729. Copyright 1982 by The American Psychological Association.

11. **Reminding and Memory Organization,** by R. C. Schank. Extracted by permission of the author and publisher from: Lehnert, W. G. & Ringle, M. H. (Eds.) *Strategies for Natural Language Processing.* Hillsdale, N. J.: Lawrence Erlbaum Associates Inc., 1982.

12. **Information-Processing Theory of Human Problem Solving,** by H. A. Simon. Extracted by permission of the author and publisher from: Estes, W. (Ed.) *Handbook of Learning and Cognitive Processes* (Vol. 5). Hillsdale, N. J.: Lawrence Erlbaum Associates Inc., 1979.

13. **Analogical Problem Solving,** by M. L. Gick and K. J. Holyoak. Extracted by permission of the author and publisher from: *Cognitive Psychology, 12,* 306–356. (Copyright 1980 Academic Press.)

14. **Twelve Issues for Cognitive Science,** by D. A. Norman. Extracted by permission of the author and publisher from: *Cognitive Science, 4,* 1–33. (Copyright 1980 Ablex Publishing Corporation.)

SOURCES OF FIGURES, TABLES AND QUOTATIONS

Introduction

Psychology has always been open to the influence of other scientific and intellectual disciplines, and this is particularly true of the study of human cognition. Philosophy of the mind, traditional experimental psychology, communication theory, systems theory, computer science, linguistics, and neuroscience, have all played important roles in the shaping of this research area—changing its focus, providing new theoretical concepts and supplying integrative metaphors as explanatory tools. Out of the differing objectives of the contributing disciplines a consensus approach has evolved that is best described by the term *cognitive modeling*. Within this approach, explanations of human cognition are expressed as abstract models based on the conception of the human brain as a physical symbol system consisting of a representation system and the processes which manipulate it. This book outlines the scope of the advances made within the cognitive modeling approach in explaining the numerous facets of cognition.

Throughout its relatively short history, the cognitive modeling approach has followed two related lines of development. Within *cognitive psychology*, modeling involves the formulation of information-processing models which are evaluated with respect to a body of experimental data. The success of such models is determined by the degree to which they match the empirical evidence. In contrast, cognitive modeling within the discipline of *artificial intelligence* (A.I.) involves building computer-based models of performance which are assessed by such criteria as computational efficiency and logical coherence. Given that the basic objective of both forms of modeling is the explanation of human cognition, it is inevitable that the researchers in both fields should draw on each other's ideas. This common ground between artificial intelligence and cognitive psychology has recently been formalized in the establishment of a new multi-disciplinary research area known as *cognitive science*. This subject embraces disciplines as diverse as neuroscience and sociology—in fact any research discipline with an interest in human cognition. Given these origins, it is not surprising that cognitive modeling has become the dominant approach within cognitive science.

In choosing the readings for this volume we have attempted to sketch a realistic picture of the current state of the discipline. Some of the contributions describe seminal work within a particular research area; work which has had a major influence in determining the content and direction of thinking on the underlying problems of cognition. Other papers outline the concepts and ideas which have been generated in response to a particular issue; emphasizing the relationships between them and providing an integrated overview of the associated problems and potential solutions. One or two of the papers also identify new directions for cognitive research, isolating fresh problems, as well as pointing towards possible solutions. It must be stressed, however, that this collection of articles does not attempt to provide a comprehensive account of the field; some important topics have been omitted altogether. Rather, the range of articles is meant to represent the scope of the field, highlighting some of the current issues and advances, while also tracing out their historical and theoretical roots.

This volume serves as an accompanying reader to an Open University course on cognitive psychology (D309), but, given the aims of the book, its content should appeal to anyone with an interest in cognitive modeling. Its overall structure reflects the traditional decomposition of the study of cognition into more manageable areas. These represent the basic faculties of cognition—perception, language, memory, and problem solving. To these we have added a section on representation—a key concept within the cognitive modeling approach. In the conclusion section, Norman argues that while this partitioning of the material is valid it is also incomplete. However, the chosen organization does mirror the present state of cognitive research, and many of the new issues identified by Norman are also foreshadowed within the other articles.

The first reading, by George Miller, tackles the central question of whether human intelligence can be adequately modeled by physical symbol systems. Miller assesses the relevance, testability and completeness of computer simulations of human thought processes and concludes by considering the internal representations by which we make sense of the world we inhabit.

The problem of how information is represented within the cognitive system is fundamental to the endeavor of cognitive modeling. For this reason, a major section of the book is devoted to the representation issue. A model of a particular cognitive ability requires the specification of the representation of the knowledge structures underlying the ability, and a description of the processes which operate on those structures. These two components of a model are interdependent, but the representation problem tends to dominate the initial stages of model building. The chapter by Rumelhart and Norman provides a comprehensive discussion of the issue; specifying the basic problem, clarifying the different debates which have arisen, outlining different solutions to the problem, and showing how the different proposed forms of representation relate to each other. The other articles in this section take up some of the more specific issues in greater detail. The article written by Kosslyn focuses on the *analogical* versus *propositional representation* debate. He briefly describes his general model of mental imagery, specifying both the analogical data structures and the forms of the processes which operate on them. He contrasts his ideas with alternative explanations of the phenomena associated with the experience of mental imagery which are based on a propositional representation format. The Johnson-Laird article introduces the useful notion of a *mental model* and relates it to other forms of representation, such as propositions and images, showing how it amalgamates different features of these lower-level representational formats.

The two papers in the perception section illustrate contrasting approaches to the investigation of human visual processing. The first paper is an extract from Marr's influential book *Vision*, which concentrates on the fundamental question of what constitutes an adequate explanation of how our visual system provides us with a reliable representation of what is "out there" in the real world of solid objects. Marr reviews previous work on vision, showing how different levels of explanation are required within cognitive psychology, and provides a sketch of his computational approach to understanding human vision. In contrast, the Pomerantz reading reviews experimental studies on organizational effects in vision from an information-processing perspective. He views perception as an active process which determines the relationships between whole figures and their constituent parts in deciphering the sensory input.

The three papers comprising the language section each identify a particular problem with the information-processing model of language understanding, and outline alternative approaches which might provide potential solutions. The article by de Beaugrande highlights the shortcomings of basing theories of language understanding on the analysis of single sentences rather than on texts or real-life dialogues. He then goes on to outline the features of a more comprehensive model of language understanding. Whereas de Beaugrande focuses mainly on the linguistic and psycho-linguistic accounts of language, Winograd's article assesses the advances made in attempting to get computers to understand natural language. After pointing out some of the shortcomings of the A.I. approach, the paper considers the question of what it actually means to understand language. This question is really at the heart of all three papers, but Winograd analyses it in the most depth. He isolates four domains of explanation within which the question can be interpreted. Many of the limitations of the A.I. approach to language are inherent in the single domain within which most of the work has been oriented, and Winograd argues that a broader conception of language understanding is required before further significant progress can be made. The researchers into language understanding at Yale University only partly agree with this conclusion. While the goal of their work is to construct computer programs which simulate realistic language comprehension, they believe that this can be achieved within the traditional A.I. approach by utilizing the vast store of knowledge and beliefs that people retain in memory. The Reisbeck article outlines the philosophy of the Yale approach, and demonstrates the extent to which the different programs developed at Yale succeed as realistic language comprehension systems.

The memory section consists of two readings which demonstrate how the goal of cognitive modeling can be pursued both within empirically-oriented cognitive psychology and by constructing testable computer models of memory organization. Baddeley's article represents the growing trend to move outside the psychology laboratory and investigate how human memory functions in everyday life. He reviews the theoretical concepts of *levels of processing* and the *encoding specificity principle*, and after applying them to real-world problem areas, suggests the more workable notion of *processing domains* in memory. Schank's article shows how such experimental studies can influence the development of computer-based models of memory. Schank discusses the shortcomings of his earlier *script*-based model of human memory in the light of experimental findings. He introduces the concept of *Memory Organization Packets* (MOPs) to help explain the possible structure of memory and the dynamic process of reminding.

The two readings in the problem-solving section illustrate contrasting, but complementary, approaches to the question of how to construct testable models of human problem-solving abilities. Simon's article outlines an information-processing theory based on computer simulations of problem-solving behaviour. He discusses the difficulties involved in using people's verbal accounts of how they solve problems as the basis for constructing and testing computer models. The Gick and Holyoak reading shows how such protocol analyses can be used experimentally to investigate the ability to solve problems by using analogies with previously-encountered situations. They stress the crucial role that the mental representations of such problems must play in facilitating "insight" and investigate what factors influence the ability to use analogies.

The concluding section contains an article by Norman in which he argues for a multi-disciplinary approach to the problems of modeling human cognition. He identifies 12 issues that he believes represent a feasible decomposition of cognition. Some of these correspond to the topics which have been used to structure this book. The other issues, however, have received far less attention within cognitive science and reflect the need for new directions of research. Norman stresses that the 12 issues must be regarded as inter-dependent problems; the progress made on one issue is bound to have profound implications for research into other areas. If researchers adhere to Norman's advice then future books on cognitive modeling may well be structured according to the comprehensive set of issues that he specifies.

This book has been prepared in consultation with our Open University course team colleagues and we would like to thank them for their invaluable assistance. Also, Mrs Patricia Vasiliou deserves special mention for her secretarial support in compiling the original manuscript.

A. M. Aitkenhead
J. M. Slack

OVERVIEW

1 Trends and Debates in Cognitive Psychology

George A. Miller

[...]

There are those who object that it diminishes human dignity to compare people to machines. I think the truth is that the comparison now signals a new conception of what machines can be and do. And what is that new conception? Stated abstractly, the modern computer has led to the concept of a *physical symbol system* (Newell, 1980)—"the concept of a broad class of systems capable of having and manipulating symbols, yet realizable in the physical universe" (Newell, 1980, p. 135). A computer *is* a physical symbol system.

The basic assumption of A.I. is that a physical symbol system is capable of intelligent behavior. That is to say, the ability to accept input symbols and generate output symbols, to store and erase them, to compare them and to branch according to the outcome of the comparison are the only kinds of building blocks required for the synthesis of intelligence.

The claim that physical symbol systems can be intelligent seems to have been well established by many examples. However, the further claim that *human* intelligence can be modelled by physical symbol systems takes this basic assumption an important extra step. And some would go still further to claim that the human brain *is* nothing but a physical symbol system. The attempt to explore these further claims has led to the use of computers to simulate the cognitive processes of human beings, and has resulted in many studies that compare human and artificial intelligence.

[...]

The parallels between artificial and natural intelligence have enormously enriched contemporary cognitive psychology. It is not surprising, therefore, that many cognitive psychologists have accepted the claim that all human thinking is information processing and that many theoretical ideas can be transferred more or less directly from A.I. to the description of human intelligence. This assumption has characterized one of the most productive lines of research in cognitive psychology in recent years.

However, the idea that human intelligence can be modelled by physical symbol systems has not been accepted without criticism. Since it often helps clarify a discussion to consider objections to as well as arguments for a hypothesis, I want to discuss three of the many objections that have been raised. For convenience, I shall call them (1) the question of relevance, (2) the question of testability, and (3) the question of completeness.

The question of relevance raises the possibility that artificial intelligence may be achieved in ways completely different from those that evolved with the human brain. Testability leads into basic questions about the relation of language to cognition—can verbal reports of thought processes be used to test the validity of computer simulations of those processes? What, if anything, simulations of mental processes do leave out is the question of completeness. I shall discuss these three questions in turn, and conclude with some comments on problems still outstanding.

RELEVANCE TO HUMAN INTELLIGENCE

The question of relevance is nicely illustrated by chess playing machines, which have been intensively and competitively studied by workers in A.I., probably because the performances of men and machines are so easily compared. As of this writing, the best machines cannot beat international grand masters, but they are sneaking up into the master class. The point ... is that the programs that simulate the thought processes of human players have proved inferior to programs that simply exploit to the limit the sheer speed and power of modern computers.

From studies of chess players (De Groot, 1965) it is known that on any given move in the middle game a grand master will consider only a few hundred alternative lines of play, and some lines may be explored in considerable depth. The most successful computer programs, on the other hand, explore every legal continuation for about three moves ahead— millions of alternative lines, but none in depth. Improvement in the computer's skill has resulted from larger and faster machines, not from cleverer heuristics for solving chess problems. The moral is that, if your goal is to use a computer to perform some function as intelligently as possible, the best solution may not be to imitate expert human beings. [...]

Those who believe that A.I. is relevant to the study of human cognition usually reply to this possibility by pointing out that chess programs are a special case, and that so far most advances in A.I. have been achieved by modeling them on what we know or believe about human performance. Of course, this situation could change. But if A.I. does develop non-anthropocentric kinds of intelligence, the general principles and specific devices that it will generate will still be useful in understanding human intelligence (Pylyshyn, 1978). Indeed, a truly general theory of intelligence will not be achieved until we can characterize human intelligence as a special case.

The outcome of this debate, therefore, is that the goals of artificial intelligence and of cognitive simulation are indeed different, and may become more so. But these differences raise no serious challenge to the central claim that human intelligence can be modelled by physical symbol systems.

TESTABILITY: VERBAL REPORTS AS DATA

The conclusion to the first question indicates the importance of the second question. How is the special case of human intelligence to be recognized? If there are many ways to perform any particular intelligent function, how are we to know which way people perform it? The obvious answer is to ask them, but that turns out not to be as simple as it sounds.

[. . .]

Nisbett and Wilson (1977) reported several situations in which people seemed to be unaware of stimulus factors that determined their responses. For example, passers-by in commercial establishments were asked to evaluate an array of consumer goods. They were asked which item was the best quality and, when they announced a choice, were asked why they had chosen the article they had. The choices showed a strong position effect, such that the right-most item in the array was preferred to the left-most item by a ratio of almost four to one, but nobody ever mentioned position as the reason for the choice. Indeed, when asked directly about position, everyone denied that it had had any influence on their decision.

In this and several other situations Nisbett and Wilson concluded that only the *product* of the mental process was accessible to consciousness; the *process* whereby the choice occurred was not open to introspective report. If this conclusion is correct, verbal reports about how people solve problems and make decisions cannot be used as data to test the psychological plausibility of artificially intelligent systems.

Critics of this conclusion have replied, however, that the distinction between mental processes and mental products has never been clearly drawn (Smith and Miller, 1978). As White (1980) remarks, it is all too easy to fall into the trap of calling anything that appears in consciousness "product" and everything else "process", in which case [Nisbett and Wilson's conclusion] becomes true by definition. Smith and Miller (1978) would drop the question of whether people have access to processes and focus instead on when such access can occur.

[. . .]

Surely, not all verbal reports of mental events are worthless. No doubt many verbal reports should not be taken as complete and veridical descriptions of mental processes, but it seems absurd to claim that intelligent adults cannot say anything true or informative about their own conscious experience. The question is, when can we trust a verbal report? What factors determine the veridicality and usefulness of verbal reports?

Such questions inspired Ericsson and Simon (1980) to undertake a classification of the different kinds of verbal reports. Reports of the outcome of some decision process will normally be accepted as veridical. If you ask me whether I would like an apple and I say "Yes", you will accept my reply as veridical. To reject this kind of verbal report would be to deny the value of language as a medium for effective social interaction. Reports of events leading to such a decision, however, are harder to evaluate. Sometimes they appear to be total fabrications, as when people try to explain why they have conformed to a post-hypnotic suggestion. Others seem veridical, as when people report concurrently on the subgoals they are considering in the course of solving some complicated problem.

Some factors affecting the value of verbal reports are obvious. Concurrent reports are more likely to be accurate than are retrospective reports. Reports about specific mental events are less likely to be fabricated than are comments that require the thinker to draw abstract conclusions about goals or methods.

Based on their review of the literature, Ericsson and Simon concluded that only information in focal attention can be verbalized, and that information appears in focal attention only when information processing is executed under cognitive control, not when it is executed automatically (Shiffrin and Schneider, 1977). Ericsson and Simon list perceptual recognition, retrieval from memory, and skilled motor actions as examples of automatic processes. Information processing that has not become automatized, however, is accessible for verbal report. Since most steps in solving unfamiliar problems will not be automatized, a concurrent verbal report can contain much useful data about the processes that the human thinker is executing and the order in which they occur.

The outcome of this discussion of the second question, therefore, is that even though some kinds of verbal reports cannot be trusted, and even though some automatic mental processes are unavailable for verbal report, under optimal conditions it is possible to test the psychological plausibility of intelligent programs. That is to say, under optimal conditions it is safe to use verbal reports as data. So the claim that human intelligence can be modelled by physical symbol systems need not be abandoned as untestable.

[...]

THE COMPLETENESS OF COMPUTATIONAL THEORIES

If a computer were used to model the weather, no one would fear that a cyclone might destroy the computing center. But using a computer to model cognitive processes is frequently assumed to be different: the brain is itself a computer in a sense in which weather is not. A computer that models an intelligent brain is expected to *be* a brain, to display actual intelligence. This feeling that cognitive simulations are somehow nearer to the real thing they are simulating is probably responsible for a tendency to claim that minds are nothing but information processing systems, and to assume that computational theories of mind are complete in every respect.

A standard objection to this position has always been, "What about consciousness?" Some psychologists believe that consciousness is the constitutive problem for psychology, just as matter and energy are the constitutive problems for physics and life is the constitutive problem for biology. Inasmuch as physical symbol systems draw no distinction between conscious and unconscious states or processes, any psychology phrased in those terms must be incomplete—and incomplete in a respect that is crucially important for psychology.

The nature of consciousness is, of course, one of the most intractable puzzles ever posed. Since psychologists themselves have made so little headway in understanding consciousness, it would be invidious of them to criticize computational theorists for having done no better. I assume that it will be much more difficult to instantiate consciousness than to understand attributions of consciousness to others, but for the moment I will ignore the fact that we lack an adequate theory of either instantiation or attribution. The question for the moment is whether cognitive simulation could contribute to such a theory, or whether it must fail on principle to accommodate the conscious-unconscious distinction.

It would not be surprising if we were to find that a cognitive theory was incomplete. Immanuel Kant popularized the familiar threefold categorization of mental faculties: cognitive, affective, and conative; or knowing, feeling, and willing. The implication is that a theory of cognition could not be a complete theory of the mind, since emotional and intentional dimensions would be excluded. But to ignore feeling and willing is not the same as to ignore consciousness.

What do we know about consciousness? A few fundamental propositions would probably inspire general agreement:

Consciousness Occurs in Living Systems. Some would amend this to, "and only in living systems"—which prejudges the question at issue here.

Consciousness is Associated with Motility. Presumably, rocks and trees are not conscious—which suggests that consciousness is important for volitional aspects of purposive behavior (Langfeld, 1927), and for the control of perception (Powers, 1973).

The Level of Consciousness Depends on Activity in the Limbic System. On the general level of arousal, which suggests that consciousness is important for effective and emotional aspects of mental life (Mandler, 1975).

Consciousness Serves Some Useful Purpose in Cognition. The argument here usually proceeds as follows: Consciousness would not have evolved if it had not had survival value; presumably, consciousness facilitated cognitive processing—made its possessor more intelligent—in some way that we do not yet fully understand, and intelligence had survival value.

But perhaps consciousness is less important for cognition than we had formerly imagined. If it were true that a physical symbol system, for which the conscious-unconscious distinction is not relevant, could perform all the cognitive processes of an intelligent person, would that not imply that consciousness is unnecessary for cognition? Or, to word it more carefully, can one say that to simulate a cognitive function successfully is to prove that consciousness is unnecessary for the performance of that function? In my opinion, that would be a research program of considerable psychological importance. The very fact that complex cognitive processes can be executed unconsciously, assuming it is a fact, should provide an important datum for anyone interested in consciousness.

How might psychological theory accommodate such a generalization? Perhaps consciousness emerged in the evolution of affective and volitional systems, and provides no more of a window on cognition than is required for feelings and for purposive movement. Or—as seems more plausible to me—perhaps A.I. will prove to be an incomplete theory of cognition, a theory of certain lower level processing operations that require conscious attention only when they fail.

I shall not pursue further the question of completeness, except to say that I cannot see how it can be settled until we have a theory of brain function adequate to suggest what else, other than information processing, a brain might do. And I need hardly remind anyone that we are far from having such a theory of brain function at the present time.

PRESENTATION AND REPRESENTATION

The crowning intellectual accomplishment of the brain is the real world. Physicists and chemists long ago demonstrated that the real world of our experience is very different from the inanimate universe of physics and chemistry. The sounds and colors we perceive, the apparent objects that integrate them, the space in which those objects are located, the values we attach to them, the intentions we attribute to others—all these fundamental aspects of the real world of our experience are adaptive interpretations of the really real world of physical science.

I would like to use the word "presentation" to refer to the way the real world presents itself to us or, more precisely, to the awareness we have at any moment of this real world we have constructed (Ward, 1919). All organisms achieve some presentation of their environments adequate for their survival as a species, although they do it in very different ways: the human world is very different from the world of a honey bee, but similar to the world of a chimpanzee. Moreover, categorization is a basic process in the construction of any such representation: at the very least, substances must be categorized as edible or inedible and organisms must be categorized as friend or foe. Insofar as we can discover something about the categories recognized by a species, we can come to appreciate something of the world in which it lives. The work requires great imagination, but I see no reason to conclude that it is impossible.

For human beings, the presentation problem arises at two levels: first, at the level we call the real world; second, at the level of communicable symbols. I find it convenient to distinguish between *perceptual presentations* and *symbolic representations*. The level of symbolic representation not only builds on the cognitive categories established at the level of perceptual presentation, but introduces many conventional categories that our ancestors have found useful. If the level of symbolic representation could be regarded as a simple one-to-one mapping onto presentations at the perceptual level, cognitive theory would be much simpler than it is. But the two levels interact so intimately and pervasively that it might be misleading to try to pull them apart.

I take the problem of characterizing the interactions between these two levels—between the real world and the world of words—to be the central problem in the study of human cognition (Miller and Johnson-Laird, 1976).

Cognitive psychologists recognize that the symbolic representation influences the perceptual presentation in subtle ways—it influences what a person pays attenton to and what perceptual distinctions will be drawn and remembered. Most important, it brings to bear cognitive schemata that enrich the perception and the person's response to it. The symbolic component does not simply label the output of the perceptual analyzer; it also controls the input to it.

Minsky (1975) has proposed frame theory as a possible answer to such problems. A frame is a list of attributes associated with a concept, along with default values for many of those attributes. Recognition is achieved by matching the input to the appropriate frame; where perceptual input is lacking it can be supplemented by adopting the default value—the most likely value that instances of that category have had in the past.

Cognitive theory will need schemata, or frames, just as certainly as it will need categories. And it may need several further insights before it can capture the intentional quality that is so much a part of our mental life. The matter of what a person intends to do can be fruitfully discussed in computational terms (Miller, Galanter, and Pribram, 1960; Powers, 1973; Rosenblueth, Wiener, and Bigelow, 1943). Those of us interested in the relation of language to cognition are constantly reminded of the importance of such intentions; people so seldom say what they really mean that if hearers could not attribute appropriate communicative intentions to them, linguistic communication as we know it would be impossible (Schank and Abelson, 1977). But the more pervasive intentional phenomenon is basically semantic: how do processes in a brain intend (become symbolic of) something beyond themselves?

In general, the adequacy of any computer simulation is related directly to the adequacy of our knowledge of the cognitive process that the system is intended to simulate. For example, linguistic understanding of phonology and grammar is reasonably advanced, and there we have systems of considerable power. Psychological understanding of communicative intentions, on the other hand, is still weak and groping, and there we have only systems of limited scope.

I suspect we will not make rapid progress in these more complex systems until we have solved two basic problems: first, how to organize very large data bases the way people do, and, second, how to characterize the human point of view. The first of these problems has been well enough defined so that we can expect to see considerable progress in the next few years. But the second is a vague and elusive ambition at the present time.

To conclude: cognitive psychology has profited enormously from its interactions with the new data processing technology. Forty years ago psychologists interested in the so-called higher mental processes had few conceptual tools to work with beyond perceptual thresholds and chains of conditioned reflexes. Today we talk seriously about the organization of huge memories and the overall structure of intelligent systems, topics that would have sounded like pure moonshine before they were objectively instantiated by the new technology.

When I feel discouraged about all the difficult problems that remain outstanding, therefore, I comfort myself with the thought of how far we have already come. The test of our progress is not the extent of our ignorance, but the extent to which we have accumulated knowledge that we can act on without fear. If I extrapolate our progress at the same rate I have seen in my own lifetime, the future looks very bright indeed.

REFERENCES

De Groot, A. D. (1965) *Thought and choice in chess.* The Hague: Mouton.

Ericsson, K. A., & Simon, H. A. (1980) Verbal reports as data. *Psychological Review, 87,* 215–251.

Langfeld, H. S. (1927) Consciousness and motor response. *Psychological Review, 34,* 1–9.

Mandler, G. (1975) *Mind and emotion.* New York: Wiley.

Miller, G. A., Galanter, E., & Pribram, K. H. (1960) *Plans and the structure of behavior.* New York: Holt, Rinehart, and Winston.

Miller, G. A., & Johnson-Laird, P. N. (1976) *Language and perception.* Cambridge, Mass.: Harvard University Press.

Minsky, M. L. (1975) A framework for representing knowledge. In P. H. Winston (Ed.), *The psychology of computer vision.* New York: McGraw-Hill.

Newell, A. (1980) Physical symbol systems. *Cognitive Science, 4,* 135–183.

Nisbett, R. E., & Wilson, T. D. (1977) Telling more than we can know: Verbal reports on mental processes. *Psychological Review, 84,* 231–259.

Powers, W. T. (1973) *Behavior: The control of perception.* Chicago: Aldine.

Pylyshyn, Z. (1978) Computational models and empirical constraints. *Behavioural and Brain Sciences, 1,* 93–127.

Rosenblueth, A., Wiener, N., & Bigelow, J. (1943) Behavior, purpose, and teleology. *Philosophy of Science, 10,* 18–24.

Schank, R. C., & Abelson, R. P. (1977) *Scripts, plans, goals and understanding.* Hillsdale, NJ: Lawrence Erlbaum Associates.

Shiffrin, R. M. & Schneider, W. (1977) Controlled and automatic human information processing: II. Perceptual learning, automatic attending, and a general theory. *Psychological Review, 84,* 127–190.

Smith, E. R., & Miller, F. D. (1978) Limits on perception of cognitive processes: A reply to Nisbett and Wilson. *Psychological Review, 85,* 355–362.

Ward, J. (1919) *Psychological Principles.* Cambridge: Cambridge University Press.

White, P. (1980) Limitations on verbal reports of internal events: A refutation of Nisbett and Wilson and of Bem. *Psychological Review, 87,* 105–112.

II REPRESENTATION

2 Representation of Knowledge

David E. Rumelhart and Donald A. Norman

Problems of representation are central issues in the study of memory and of cognition as a whole. Questions of how knowledge is stored and used are involved in nearly all aspects of cognition. In spite of its centrality (perhaps because of it) issues surrounding the nature of representation have become some of the most controversial aspects of the study of cognition. At the same time, representation has become one of its most muddled concepts. For most Cognitive Scientists, it is impossible even to imagine a cognitive system in which a system of representation does not play a central role. But even among those for whom the concept of representation is taken to be central, there are still tremendous debates concerning the precise nature of representation:

What is a representation anyway?

Is it analogical or propositional?

Is it procedural or declarative?

Is there only one kind of representation or are there several?

What does [the] information [stored in memory] look like?

Is the information stored in memory organized so that related information is stored together, or is it stored in packets or records, each independent of the remaining packets?

Is knowledge stored as a collection of separate units or are individual memory traces intertwined over large regions of memory?

[. . .]

Representation as Mappings

Let us ... try to be clear about what kind of a thing a representation really is. ... To begin, a representation is something that stands for something else. In other words, it is a kind of a model of the thing it represents. We have to distinguish between a *representing world* and a *represented world*. The representing world must somehow mirror some aspects of the represented world. Palmer (1978) has listed five features that must be specified for any representational system:

1. What the represented world is;
2. What the representing world is;
3. What aspects of the represented world are being modeled;
4. What aspects of the representing world are doing the modeling;
5. What the correspondences are between the two worlds.

These features are illustrated in [Fig. 2.1]. In this example the represented world consists of two stick figures—one taller than the other. We can imagine that each has the property of having some height and the relationship *TALLERTHAN* holding between the first and second figure. We have illustrated four different possible representing worlds. In the first (I) we have the symbol *A* representing the taller figure and the symbol *B* representing the shorter. We represent the relationship among the height of the two by the formula *TALLERTHAN(A,B)*. There is no direct represen-

Represented World		Representing World			
		I	II	III	IV
Objects:	🧍	A	│	15	7
	🧍	B	│	13	9
Properties:	height	not directly represented	line length	numeric value	numeric value
Relations:	a taller than b	TALLER THAN (A,B)	LONGER THAN	GREATER THAN	LESS THAN

FIG. 2.1. The relationship between the represented world and the representing world showing four different ways the *representing* world might choose to model the physical-relation of *TALLERTHAN* that holds between the two figures in the *represented* world. I shows a propositional representation: *TALLERTHAN(A,B)*. II shows a representation by means of line length. III shows a representation by means of numerical value, and IV shows that the relationship can be arbitrary, as when smaller numbers in the representing world represent larger figures in the represented world.

tation of height in this system. In the second example (II) the figures are represented by lines and height is directly represented by line length. The TALLERTHAN relation is implicitly represented by the physical relation LONGERTHAN among the line segments. In the third example (III), numbers are used to represent the figures and the magnitude of the numbers represent their heights. The TALLERTHAN relation is represented by the arithmetic relation of GREATERTHAN ($>$). Note that the representational format is quite arbitrary. Thus, example IV shows an alternative format for using the magnitude of numbers to represent heights, in this case, with the taller figures represented by smaller numbers; the TALLERTHAN relation is represented by the arithmetic relation of LESSTHAN ($<$). If our only goal were to represent height, then the representational systems of III and IV would be functionally equivalent. These four examples illustrate how the same characteristic in the represented world can be represented very differently in different representing worlds.

[...]

Representation IN Versus Representation OF the Mind. The most important point of a representation is that it allows us to reach conclusions about the thing being represented by looking only at the representing world. When considering how knowledge is represented in the human there are four kinds of things we need to keep in mind:

1. An environment in which there are objects and events;
2. A brain which attains certain states dependent on its current state and the sensory information that impinges on it;
3. Our phenomenal experience, which is assumed to be a function of our brain state;
4. A model or theory of the environment, the brain states, and the experience.

In studying representational systems, it is important to realize that there are several different pairs of representing and represented worlds, and that our *theories* of representation are in actuality representations of a representation: that is, *representations* of the mental activity that in turn is a representation of the environment. Thus, as shown in [Fig. 2.2], within the brain there exist brain states that are the representation of the environment. The environment is the represented world, the brain states are the representing world. Our theories of representation are in actuality representations of the brain states, not representations of the world. Therefore, theories of representation have the brain states as the represented world and the theoretical structures as the representing world. Finally, our phenomenal experience reflects the brain states, and so can be considered a representing world with the brain states as their represented world. When people think of representation, they often think of the relationship between phenomenal experiences and the environment, but in fact, this relationship is a secondary one, with brain states as an intermediary, although this is seldom stated explicitly in psychological theories of representation.

[. . .] Consider the sense in which our phenomenal experience "represents" the external world. There are objects in the world and there are objects of experience. The objects of our experience are not the same as the objects of the world, but they would seem to reflect much of the structure of the world. In this way, it probably does make sense to speak of our experiential "representation" of the world.

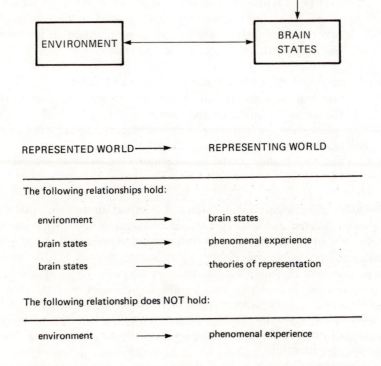

FIG. 2.2. The relationships among the represented world, the brain, and the environment.

Overview of Representational Systems

The representational systems most popular today fall into [three] basic families. These are:

1. The propositionally based systems in which knowledge is assumed to be represented as a set of discrete symbols or propositions, so that concepts in the world are represented by formal statements.

2. Analogical representational systems in which the correspondence between the represented world and the representing world is as direct as possible, traditionally using continuous variables to represent concepts that are continuous in the real world. Examples are the use of electrical voltages in an analog computer to represent fluid flow or shaft rotation, or maps that are analogical representations of some geographical features of the world, or pictures in which three-dimensional space is represented by marks on a two-dimensional medium.

3. Procedural representational systems in which knowledge is assumed to be represented in terms of an active process or procedure. Moreover, the representation is in a form directly interpretable by an action system. Consider how to pronounce the word "serendipitous." The movement made by the vocal apparatus is clearly procedural in that it is tied up in the actual performance of the skill and is not available apart from the ability to do the task, even though one normally does have conscious control and accessibility to many of the components of the task. Thus, to describe the tongue movements made in pronouncing the word, one actually has to perform the task—that is, to say the word "serendipitous"—and then describe aloud the actions performed.

[...]

Most actual representational systems are hybrids that fall into more than one of these ... categories. Nevertheless, these categories form a useful framework within which to describe the various systems that have been proposed.

Representational Systems Include Both Representation and Process

We have introduced several categories of representational systems. There is, however, one more important aspect of a representation system that must be considered: the processes that operate upon the representations. Consider the four different representational formats illustrated in [Fig. 2.1]. The point of this figure was to demonstrate some of the properties of the four formats. But note that the representations within the representing world did not carry their meaning without the assistance of some process that could make use of and interpret the representational structures. Thus, if height is to be represented by line length, there must exist some process capable of comparing line lengths. If height is to be represented by numbers, then there must be some processes that can operate upon those numbers according to the appropriate rules of mathematics and the rules established by the choice of representation (e.g., whether it is type III or IV in [Fig. 2.1]). ... The processes that evaluate and interpret the representations are as important as the representations themselves.

PROPOSITIONALLY BASED REPRESENTATIONAL SYSTEMS

Most of the representational systems that have been developed and evaluated to date fall into the category of propositional representations. These representational systems all share the characteristic that knowledge is represented as a collection of symbols. According to other views, knowledge merely consists of lists of such symbols. According to still other views, knowledge is thought of as highly structured configurations of such symbols with associated procedures for interpreting the symbols.

[...]

Semantic Features or Attributes

Perhaps the simplest of the propositional representation systems is the assumption that concepts are properly represented as a set of semantic features or attributes. This means of representation is a very natural application of the language of set theory to the problem of characterizing the nature of concepts. Variations on this view have been very popular in the study of semantic memory and as assumptions describing the representation of knowledge. According to these views, concepts are represented by a weighted set of features. Thus, concepts can stand in the familiar set relationships: two concepts can be disjoint (have no attributes in common); overlap (have some but not all attributes in common); be nested (all of the attributes of one concept are included in another); or be identical (be specified by exactly the same set of features). The features can have weights associated with them that represent various saliency and importance characteristics for the concepts in question.

Rather than review all of the applications of these ideas here, we choose to describe ... the "feature comparison" model proposed by Smith,

Shoben and Rips (1974). . . . The proposals of Smith et al. were made in the context of a series of studies that began with Collins and Quillian (1969) and Meyer (1970) on simple "semantic verification" tasks. The general procedure followed in these studies was to present a statement that asked whether a member of one semantic category could also be a member of another. Thus, typical sentences would be: *A robin is a bird, A vegetable is an artichoke*, or perhaps, *A rock is a furniture*. Subjects were asked to respond "TRUE" or "FALSE" to the sentences as quickly as possible. The basic representational assumption was that the words representing the two categories to be considered could be represented by a set of semantic features that vary in their relationship to the formal definition of the category. In particular, features could be divided into those that were "defining" (they must hold if an item is a member of the category) and those that were "characteristic" (they usually apply, but are not necessary for the definition). Thus, *has feathers* is a *definitional feature* for the concept bird, whereas *can fly* is a *characteristic feature*; birds characteristically can fly, but flying is not essential to a thing being a bird. In addition, the concept bird might have features specifying that it has a particular size, shape, etc., things that might be true of only the most typical instances of birds. [Fig. 2.3] (from Smith & Medin, 1981) shows an illustrative set of features and weights for the concepts of *robin, chicken, bird,* and *animal*.

In formulating their proposal, Smith et al. had a number of empirical results in mind. Collins and Quillian (1969) found that subjects took less time to verify statements of the form *A canary is yellow*, than statements of the form *A canary has feathers*, which in turn took less than the time to verify *A canary eats food*. From this they deduced that the information is stored hierarchically; properties specific to canaries are stored with the concept canary, properties specific to birds in general are stored with birds, and properties specific to animals are stored with animals. Thus, the further up the hierarchy one has to search to find the relevant information, the longer it takes subjects to answer the question. Smith et al. found that the time to verify a statement does not always conform with the predictions from a hierarchical model. Thus, it might take longer to confirm that *A cat is a mammal* than to confirm that *A cat is an animal*. More interestingly, it was found that it is faster to verify that *A robin is a bird* than to verify that *A chicken is a bird* or that *A penguin is a bird* (Rips, Shoben & Smith, 1973). In general, the more *typical* an instance is of a category, the more quickly it can be verified that it, in fact, belongs to that category.

Smith, Shoben, and Rips (1974) proposed that category membership is not a pre-stored characteristic but rather was computed from the comparison of a set of features. They proposed that the process of verifying a category membership statement consisted of two stages. First, a very quick

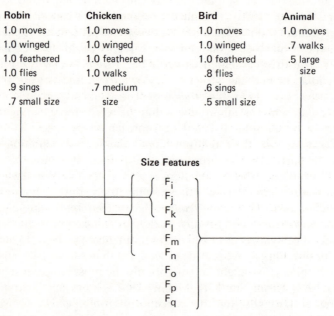

FIG. 2.3.   An illustrative set of features and weights for the concepts of *robin, chicken, bird,* and *animal* (from Smith & Medin, 1981).

comparison of all features (characteristic and defining) was performed. If this comparison was sufficiently good, the question was answered in the affirmative. If the comparison was sufficiently poor, the question was answered in the negative. If the comparison led to an intermediate result, a slower comparison process applied to the defining features was initiated. This model accounts for the basic experimental results: true statements involving highly typical items (e.g., *A robin is a bird*) are affirmed very quickly; false statements involving very distinct items (e.g., *A door is a bird*) are rejected very quickly; statements involving less typical examples of a category (e.g., *A penguin is a bird*) are affirmed relatively slowly; and statements involving things similar to, but not members of, the category (e.g., *A bat is a bird*) are rejected relatively slowly.

A number of different kinds of verification proposals have been made, all somewhat different from one another, but all consistent with the spirit of this general approach. . . . The newer models, of course, usually account for the data better than do the earlier models. The important point, however, is that all of these models assume that conceptual knowledge is represented by a set of features and that these features include necessary and sufficient attributes of the concept being represented as well as attributes that are only characteristic of the concept being represented. [...]

In spite of their relative simplicity, semantic feature models offer remarkably good accounts of a rather wide body of data. [...] Such theories do, however, have their limitations. In particular, almost all of the work has been with simple nominal concepts ... it is not clear how such models would represent simple facts (e.g., *typewriters are used for typing*) or simple events (e.g., *John went to the store*). The semantic feature model does not handle distinctions between the statements that a robin is a bird, a sparrow is a bird, but that a sparrow is not a robin: if category membership were determined solely by defining characteristics, one might very well determine that a sparrow was a robin, or perhaps that a bird was a robin. In similar fashion, these models cannot account for problems of quantification, as represented in the contrast in meaning between the sentences *Everyone kissed someone* and *Someone was kissed by everyone*. In fairness to semantic feature models, they were not intended to solve all of the problems of representation, but rather primarily those of similarity and of definition. In this, they do well.

[...]

[...] Psychologists and workers in Artificial Intelligence have to a large extent explored representations that emphasized what could be thought of as the most salient psychological aspects of knowledge:

The associative nature of knowledge;

The notion of knowledge "units" or "packages", so that knowledge about a single concept or event is organized together in one functional unit;

The detailed structure of knowledge about any single concept or event;

That it is useful to consider different levels of knowledge, each level playing a different organizational role, and with higher order units adding structure to lower order ones;

The everyday reasoning of people, in which "default" values seem to be substituted for information that is not known explicitly, in which information known for one concept is applied to other concepts, and in which inconsistent knowledge can exist.

These beliefs have guided studies of representation towards structures called semantic networks, schemata, frames and scripts. [...] Historically, these approaches to the study of representation started with semantic networks, so let us start there as well.

Semantic Networks and Their Properties

An important step in the representation of the associations within long term memory was Quillian's (1968) development of the "semantic network." The basic notion is that knowledge can be represented by a kind of directed, labeled graph structure in which the basic structural element is a set of nodes interrelated by relations. Nodes represent concepts in memory. A relation is an association among sets of nodes. Relations are labeled and directed. In this view the *meaning* of a concept (represented by a node) is given by the pattern of relationships among which it participates. It is important to note that not all nodes in a semantic memory system have names corresponding to words in natural language. Some nodes represent concepts which have no natural language equivalent, others represent instances (or tokens) of the concepts represented by other nodes. [. . .]

Inheritance Properties. . . . One of the attractive features of the semantic network formalism is the convenience with which the property of *inheritance* is formulated. [Fig.. . .2.4] illustrates a common semantic network representational format for information about animals. The basic structure of a network is illustrated in the figure. Nodes (the dots and angle brackets) stand for concepts: relations (the lines with arrows) stand for the relationship that applies between the nodes. The arrows are important for specifying the direction of the relation. [. . .]

The semantic network, as drawn in [Fig. 2.4] is attractive in suggesting the kinds of inter-relations that occur among the entire set of concepts in memory and suggesting processing strategies. However, the notation becomes clumsy and unwieldy as the network structures become large and complex. Today, it is more usual to list each unit separately, putting it into what amounts to an outline form. Thus, the information in [Fig. 2.4] can be depicted in this way:

animal			person	
eats	food		subset	animal
breathes	air		has-as-part	legs
has	mass		has-as-part	arms
has-as-part	limbs			

The relation-node pairs (e.g., eats food) are called *slots* and *fillers*.

There must exist a basic set of nodes and relations, the fundamental structures that are necessary for the semantic network to work properly. An important class of relations is that of *type*, indicating that one node is an instance of the class pointed to by the relation. The two most important kinds of type relations are *isa* (where *a isa b* means that the concept

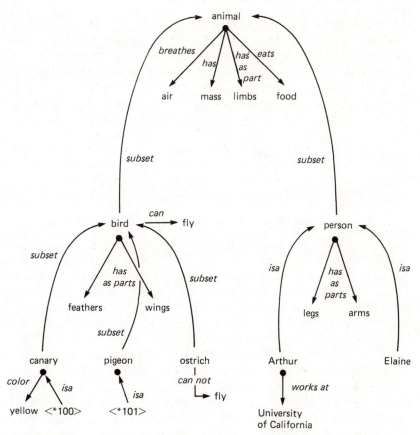

FIG. 2.4.   A simple semantic network, chosen so as to illustrate the use of inheritance.

represented by node *a* is an instance of the concept represented by node *b*) and *subset* (where *a subset b* means that the concept represented by node *a* is a subset of the concept represented by node *b*).

Suppose we wish to represent information about animals, as shown in [Fig. 2.4]. We know that animals breathe, have mass, and eat food. This information is represented by relations from the node named "animal". We know that people are animals, that Arthur and Elaine are instances of people, that birds are animals, and that canaries and pigeons and ostriches are kinds of birds. We also have seen particular birds, indicated by nodes <*100> and <*101> (indicated by angle brackets and arbitrary names). Note that the fact that Arthur eats food is derivable from the triples (Arthur isa person), (person subset animal), and (animal eats food). This derivation illustrates the property of *inheritance; instances and subsets inherit the properties of their types.* [...] Note also that because the node for "bird" indicates that birds have feathers and fly, by inheritance, we know that these properties apply to all birds, including all of the ones in [Fig. 2.4] (canaries, pigeons, ostriches, <*100>, and <*101>). ... in the absence of other knowledge, we assume (deduce) that all birds have feathers and fly. In this case, the defaults for birds is wrong: ostriches don't fly. The solution is to add to the node for ostrich that it doesn't fly (as is done in the figure). But now we have inconsistent data in the data base. In semantic networks, the issue presents no difficulty if the appropriate processing rules are followed:

1. In determining properties of concepts, look first at the node for the concept.
2. If the information is not found, go up one node along the "type" relation and apply the property of inheritance.
3. Repeat 2 until either there is success or there are no more nodes.

This processing rule will always find the lowest (most specific) level relationship that applies to a given concept and will never even notice inconsistencies of the sort illustrated in the figure. The basic principle is that if two pieces of conflicting information appear to apply to a concept, accept the one that is most specific to that concept. [...]

Semantic networks provide a convenient and powerful formalism for representing knowledge, allowing for both inferential mechanisms and processing considerations. The nice thing about the network structure is that it matches many of our intuitions for the representation of a large domain of our knowledge.

The Representation of N-ary Relations in Semantic Networks.   We have shown how the semantic network representation builds upon the node-relation-node triple (*a R b*). Because any node can have an indefinite number of relations from it to other nodes, it is also possible to view the representation as an *n*- place predicate that applies to the concept specified by the node, In particular, if the node specifies an *n*-place predicate (a predicate with *n* arguments), then the node name can be identified with the predicate name. Each of the nodes pointed to by the relations leaving the node can be considered to be the arguments of the predicate. The relations specify the interpretation of each argument. This conceptualization makes it easy to represent complex verbs within the network, and was the scheme adopted by the LNR research group (Norman & Rumelhart, 1975). [...]

Types and Tokens.   In a semantic network it is essential to distinguish between *types* and *tokens* of the concepts being represented. [Fig. 2.5], illustrates the kinds of confusion that arises from failure to make the distinction. This figure is intended to represent the facts that "Cynthia threw the ball" and that "Albert threw the book." Notice that because there is only one node for "threw" we are unable to determine who threw the ball and who threw the book. [Fig. 2.5B] correctly represents the distinction between the events of Cynthia's throwing and Albert's throwing by introducing *token* nodes, illustrated by the ovals in the figure. These token nodes are instances of the type node for "threw," allowing us to distinguish the various incidents in which the action occurs from one another.

A similar situation occurs with concepts, such as "ball." Thus, as shown in [Fig. 2.5C], when both Cynthia and Albert start throwing balls, we

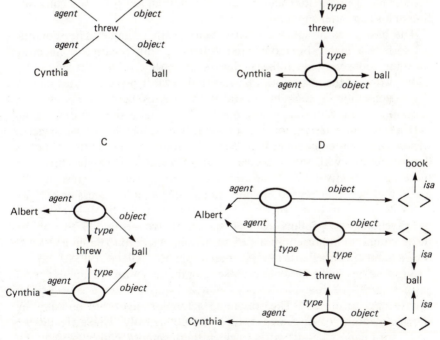

FIG. 2.5.   The need for distinguishing types from tokens. A. Who threw the ball and who threw the book? B. Token nodes for "threw" solve the problem shown in A. C. Did both Albert and Cynthia throw the same ball? D. Token nodes for "ball" solve the problem in C.

cannot tell from the representation whether or not they are throwing the same ball. We need to be able to represent that Cynthia threw a particular ball and that Albert threw some other particular ball. Basically, we use the type relation *isa*, to point from a node that represents a token instance of a concept to the node that represents its more general type concept. (The relation "isa" can be read as "is an instance of.") [Fig. 2.5D] illustrates how this is done, using angle brackets to represent tokens of concepts. (In most actual drawings, the "type" or "isa" relations are not shown, but the use of angle brackets and ovals indicates that the nodes are tokens and that type relations exist, but are not shown.)

Spreading Activation in Semantic Networks. One important processing method that has commonly been associated with semantic networks is that of "spreading activation" in which the network itself conducts activation values among its links. The first description of a spreading activation mechanism was made by Quillian, and the ideas were most fully described and elaborated in a paper by Collins and Loftus (1975). Anderson (1976) has used it as the basis of his modeling of human memory, both for guiding psychological predictions and experimentation and also for the construction of his computer simulation.

The basic idea of spreading activation is rather simple. The semantic network is a highly interconnected structure, with relations connecting together nodes very much like highways and airline routes interlink cities of the world. Much as motor vehicles and aircraft ply the routes among cities, activation is thought to travel the routes between nodes. The concept of activation is a general one. If the model is thought of as being only a functional description, not necessarily dictating the physical system within which it is embedded, then the nodes and relations are thought of as data structures with the relations being pointers between structures. In these cases, "activation" is an abstract quantity, usually represented by a real number, that represents how much information processing activity is taking place on that structure. This is the interpretation usually given by psychologists (Collins & Loftus, 1975; Anderson, 1976), or by those computer representations of spreading activation (Fahlman, 1981; McClelland & Rumelhart, 1981; Rumelhart & McClelland, 1982). [...]

Suppose one had a network representing the structure of animals (much as in [Fig. 2.4]). How would a question such as, "Does a canary have wings?" get answered? The spreading activation algorithm operates by starting at both "canary" and "wings" simultaneously. This activates the nodes for "canary" and "wings," which then, simultaneously, activate all of the relations that leave these two nodes. Activation spreads down the relations, taking time to do so, and reaches the nodes at the end of the relations. These nodes get activated and, in turn, spread activation down all the relations that lead from them. Imagine spreading rings of activation, each ring originating from one of the starting points. Eventually these expanding rings will coincide. When that happens, we know there is a path between the nodes that have originated the colliding rings of activation. That path can then be readily found by following the activation traces, and, depending upon the nature of the path, the question can then be answered.

There are many details left out of this story. There are a large number of possible questions:

How is the fact that two expanding rings of activation have intersected actually detected?

How can the resulting path be followed?

If there are N relations leaving a node, does the amount of activation depend upon N?

Do the expanding rings of activation trace out all of the possible relations, or can they be restricted to a subset of the class of relations?

For how long a period of time does activation leave a trace?

Are there different kinds of activation? That is, is it possible to distinguish the activation left by one process from the activation left by another?

What is the best possible way to model this process?

What is the best possible way to construct a working, simulation model of this process?

These are the kinds of questions that have guided the research in this area. One of the major psychological issues addressed by activation studies has been the time course of activation (e.g. Maclean & Schulman, 1978; Neeley, 1976). A second use of activation has been as a tool to examine the nature of the representation: if activation of one node will activate another, then the secondary activation "primes" any information processing that must make use of the other, thereby speeding its operation. Priming, therefore, is a technique that allows one to study the manner by which the interconnections are constructed. The basic priming study goes like this (after Meyer & Schvaneveldt, 1971): Subjects are asked to read two strings of letters and to decide as rapidly as possible whether each is a word or non-word. Thus, a typical pair of items might be "nurse plame." If the two words are related (as in "bread butter") the judgement that both are words is considerably faster than if the two are not related (as in "bread nurse"). The interpretation is that reading of the first word sends activation to words related to it, thus "priming" the other words and making their detection and judgement easier and faster. Clearly, this kind of result can be used to study the inter-relationships of items within memory by examining the amount of priming effect.

In a similar way, Collins and Quillian (1970) argued for support of their hierarchical organization of memory by demonstrating that prior exposure to the statement *A canary is a bird* reduced the amount of time that it took a person to determine whether it was true that *A canary can fly* more than it reduced the time to decide whether it was true that *A canary can sing*. They argued that to answer the question about flying, the node for "bird" had to be examined, and this was primed by the prior exposure, whereas to answer the question about singing, only the "canary" node was involved, and this was only minimally primed by the prior exposure.

[. . .]

[Another] issue that has been widely investigated is whether or not the number of relations that leave a node affect the speed or amount of activation that goes down the interconnecting links. This is called the *fan effect*, and it has most widely been studied by Anderson and his collaborators. Anderson's model of cognition (ACT: Anderson, 1976) uses activation as one of its central themes, and so in addition to describing the fan effect that he has studied so extensively, let us also review the basic model.

ACT and the Fan Effect.   ACT makes a set of processing assumptions that are used in conjunction with its representational assumptions (which are of the standard form we described for propositional representation) to make predictions about specific experiments. In particular, ACT consists of the following assumptions about memory structure.

1. *Representation.* Information in memory is stored in network structures.
2. *Activation.* Each node and each link in memory can be in one of two states, either *active* or not. The links connecting active nodes need not be active. If a link is active, the nodes it connects with become active; activation spreads from one node to the next through the active interconnecting links.
3. *Strength of Links.* Each link has a strength s associated with it.
4. *Spread of Activation: The fan effect.* The probability that activation will spread through a link is a function of the ratio of the strength of the particular link to the sum of the strengths of all of the links emanating from the node.
5. *Active lists.* Active nodes may be on an *active list*. The number of nodes that can be on the active list at one time is limited, but unless a node is on this list, its activity cannot be sustained for more than a short period.

Anderson assumes that the actual processing and interpretation is performed by an external interpreter that is in the form of a "production system." ... The processor can put nodes on the active list (or remove them) and carry out the specific tasks required of the cognitive system as a whole.

One major set of investigations that have been motivated by the ACT system have been studies of the fan effect. Basically, the "fan" experiments are strong tests of assumption (4) and weaker tests of the other assumptions. In particular, the fan effect refers to the fact that the activation that goes across a link is inversely proportional to the number of links that "fan out" from or leave the node. This results in the somewhat non-intuitive prediction that the more one knows about something, the longer it takes to retrieve that information. This follows because the more links emanating from a particular node the longer, on average, it will take the activation to spread to adjacent nodes. Because the major mechanism for retrieving information makes use of the activation spreading along links, it should be possible to get rather direct information on the pattern of links from observations on retrieval time. The typical procedure for these experiments involves teaching subjects a set of facts arranged so that different numbers of facts apply to different concepts. In a typical experiment, experimental subjects are shown a number of sentences to learn and then tested on their ability to recognize test sentences. The results indicate that subjects are slower to recognize a sentence of the form "The doctor hated the lawyer" if they had learned other factors about the lawyer and the doctor than if they had not. Thus, the more sentences of the form "The doctor loved the actor" and "the lawyer owned a Cadillac," the slower the recognition of the text sentence. The basic result is as predicted: the more facts, the slower the recognition time.

[. . .]

Schank's Conceptual Dependency.   One of the more important applications of the semantic network has been the work of Schank and his colleagues on the representation of concepts (Schank, 1975, 1981; Schank & Abelson, 1977). Schank took seriously the task of creating a plausible representation of the kind of knowledge that underlies language use. He wanted a representation that was unambiguous and unique. He wished to be able to express the meaning of any sentence in any language. The representations were intended to be language independent; if two sentences had the same meaning, they should have the same representation whether they were paraphrases within a given language or translations between languages. Moreover, Schank wished concepts which were similar to have representations which were likewise similar. In order to carry out this process he proposed that all incoming information be stored in terms of a set of conceptual primitives. *Conceptual dependency theory* was designed to interrelate these conceptual primitives in order to represent a wide range of different meanings. The first job with such an enterprise is to be very specific about what the representational primitives are and Schank, more than anyone, has taken this task seriously. He has proposed a list of eleven *primitive acts* which he believes underlie the representation of all concepts. These include five basic *physical* actions of people:

PROPEL which means to apply force to:

MOVE which means to move a body part;

INGEST which means to take something inside of an animate object;

EXPEL which means to take something that is inside an animate object and force it out;

GRASP which means to grasp an object physically.

There are also two basic *change of state* acts:

PTRANS (for physical transition) which means to change the location of something:

ATRANS (for abstract transition) which means to change some abstract relationship (usually ownership) of an object.

Shank lists two *instrumental* acts:

SPEAK which means to produce a sound;

ATTEND which means to direct a sense organ towards some particular stimulus.

Finally, there are two basic *mental* acts:

MTRANS (for mental transition) which means to transfer information such as from one person to another or from one part of the memory, say LTM (long term memory) to STM (short term memory);

MBUILD (for mental build) which means to create or combine thoughts. This is involved in such concepts as thinking, deciding, etc.

In addition to these primitive acts, there are a number of other primitive elements which are combined to represent meanings. For example, there are PPs (picture producers) underlying the meaning of concrete nouns, sets of primitive states, such as HEALTH, FEAR, ANGER, HUNGER, DISGUST, SURPRISE, etc. There are also a set of *conceptual roles* which these various primitive elements can play such as ACTOR, OBJECT, INSTRUMENT, RECIPIENT, DIRECTION, etc. A simple example will suffice to illustrate how the various basic elements combine in Schank's representational system. [Fig. 2.6a] shows the conceptual dependency representation for the sentence:

1. John gave Mary a book.

In this case, the verb "to give" has been represented as the primitive ATRANS, the ACTOR (illustrated by the double arrow) is "John," the time is the past (illustrated by the **p** labeling the double arrow), the OBJECT is "book," and the RECIPIENT goes from "John" to "Mary." Note that the representation is *not* for the particular words of a sentence, but rather for the intended meanings. Thus, the figure represents only one interpretation of the sentence. The point is that in Schank's system, it is not sentences

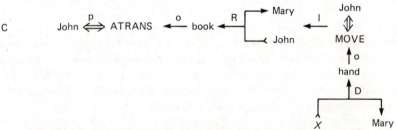

A   John ⟺ ATRANS ← book ← R ⟶ Mary
                                      ⟶ John

B   John ⟺ DO
            ⇑
      Mary ⟺ ATRANS ← book ← R ⟶ Mary
                                    ⟶ John

C   John ⟺ ATRANS ← book ← R ⟶ Mary ← I ⟺ John / MOVE ↑ o hand ↑ D / X ⟶ Mary

FIG. 2.6.   The conceptual dependency representation underlying three interpretations of "John gave Mary a book." *A* shows the most basic interpretation of the sentence. *B* is the case in which John did something which allowed Mary to take the book and *C* shows the representation for John handing Mary the book. (From Schank, 1975, pp. 31–32.)

that have representations, rather it is meanings that are represented. [Fig. 2.6a] represents the case in which John physically gave Mary the book. The same sentence could have been used for the case in which John had carried out some other action which let Mary take the book for herself. In this case, the correct representation would be the one illustrated in [Fig. 2.6b]. Here, we see that "Mary" is now the ACTOR of the ATRANS and the action of "John" is the non-specific DO. [Fig. 2.6c] illustrates the conceptual dependency underlying the case in which the same sentence means that John handed the book to Mary. In this case we see that "John" is again the ACTOR of the ATRANS, and that there is now an INSTRUMENT of the ATRANS specified. Note that the INSTRUMENT is an entire conceptualization which involves "John" MOVEing his hand from some location "X" to "Mary."

[...]

Schemas and Frames

So far, we have covered a variety of representational schemes that focus upon the basic, elementary levels of representation. The semantic feature approaches focussed almost exclusively on the representation of word meanings, ... and the semantic network and the conceptual dependency formalisms strived to include both lexical level and sentential level knowledge. The one thing that all these systems have in common is that they represent all knowledge in a single, uniform format. What is needed is the ability to introduce higher levels of structure. There is a need for representations which represent *supra-sentential knowledge*. In this case the goal is not to remedy the expressive problems of other representational methods, but to change the level of discourse.

The movement towards systems that focused on higher units of knowledge was signaled by the publication, in 1975, of four papers: "A framework for representing knowledge" by Minsky, "Notes on a schema for stories" by Rumelhart, "The structure of episodes in memory" by Schank, and "Concepts for representing mundane reality in plans" by Abelson. Over the next several years, these papers led to the development of a number of related knowledge representation proposals, all aiming at the representation of suprasentential knowledge units. In his paper introducing the concept of the *frame* as a knowledge representation formalism, Minsky put the argument this way:

> It seems to me that the ingredients of most theories both in artificial intelligence and in psychology have been on the whole too minute, local, and unstructured to account—either practically or phenomenologically—for the effectiveness of common sense thought. The "chunks" of reasoning, language, memory, and "perception" ought to be larger and more structured,

and their factual and procedural contents must be more intimately connected in order to explain the apparent power and speed of mental activities (Minsky, 1975, p. 211).

A number of theorists have developed representational systems based on these "larger" units. [. . .]

A theory of schemas as developed by Rumelhart and Ortony (1977) and extended by Rumelhart and Norman (1978) and Rumelhart (1981).

A theory of scripts and plans developed by Schank and Abelson (1977) and further elaborated into MOPS by Schank (1980).
[. . .]

The basic underlying feature of these theories is that the earlier work was useful in providing a foundation for further work, but that it was focussed on the wrong level to be useful in the understanding of understanding. The nodes and relations of semantic networks, . . . and the feature lists of semantic concepts do have a place in the structure of representation, but they do not allow one to structure knowledge into higher-order representational units. The major function of these new approaches is to add such structure, wholistic units that allow for the encoding of more complex inter-relationships among the lower level units. These higher order units were given different names by each of the theorists: frame (Minsky), schema (Rumelhart & Norman), script (Schank & Abelson). . . . Nonetheless, the motivating force and in most cases the underlying themes are similar. We now turn to examine these higher-level structures.

Summary of the Major Features of Schemas.   The notion of the schema finds its way into modern cognitive psychology from the writings of Bartlett (1932) and from Piaget (1952). Throughout most of its history, the notion of the schema has been rejected by main stream experimental psychologists as being too vague. Recently, however, as we have begun to see how such ideas might actually work, the notion has become increasingly popular. In this section, we sketch the basic ideas of the schema, particularly as developed in the papers by Rumelhart and Ortony (1977), Bobrow and Norman (1975), Rumelhart and Norman (1978) and by Rumelhart (1981). For the most part, the characteristics of the schema as developed in these papers is consistent with the work of the other writers on the subject. However, as we will indicate below, there are features which differentiate the ideas as well.

Schemas are data structures for representing the generic concepts stored in memory. There are schemas for generalized concepts underlying objects, situations, events, sequences of events, action and sequences of actions. ... Schemas in some sense represent the stereotypes of these concepts. Roughly, schemas are like models of the outside world. To process information with the use of a schema is to determine which model best fits the incoming information. Ultimately, consistent configurations of schemas are discovered which, in concert, offer the best account for the input. This configuration of schemas together constitutes the *interpretation* of the input. There appear to be a number of characteristics of schemas that are necessary (or at least useful) for developing a system that behaves in this way. Rumelhart (1981) and Rumelhart and Ortony (1977) listed several of the most important features of schemas. These include:

1. Schemas have variables;
2. Schemas can embed, one within another;
3. Schemas represent knowledge at all levels of abstraction;
4. Schemas represent *knowledge* rather than *definitions*;
5. Schemas are active recognition devices whose processing is aimed at the evaluation of their goodness of fit to the data being processed.

Perhaps the central feature of schemas is that they are packets of information that contain *variables*. Roughly, a schema for any concept contains a fixed part, those characteristics which are always (or nearly always) true of exemplars of the concept, and a variable part. Thus, for example, the schema for the concept DOG would contain constant parts such as "a dog has four legs," and variable parts such as "a dog's color can be black, brown, white, ..." Thus, NUMBER-OF-LEGS would be a constant in the schema, whereas COLOR and SIZE would be variables. Similarly, in the GIVE schema the aspects involving a change of possession would be constants, and those aspects involving who the giver or the receiver was would be variables. There are two important aspects of variables for schema-based systems. In the first place, variables have *default values*. That is, the schema contains information about what values to assume for the variables when the incoming information is unspecified. Thus, consider as an example the following story sentences:

2. Mary heard the ice cream truck coming down the street. She remembered her birthday money and rushed into the house.

In processing such a text, people usually invoke a schema for ice cream trucks going through a community selling ice cream to the children. In this schema there is a fixed part involving the relationships among the characters of the ice cream truck drama and a variable part concerning the particular individuals playing the particular roles in this drama. In this case, we tend to interpret Mary as the filler of the BUYER variable in the schema. Although the story tells us nothing about the age of Mary, we tend to think of her as a little girl. Thus, the default value of the age of the BUYER in this schema is childhood, and unless otherwise indicated, we tend to assume that this is the age of the BUYER. Default values can, of course, be overcome by explicit information in the incoming information. [. . .]

A second important characteristic of schemas is that they can embed one within another. Thus, in general, a schema consists of a configuration of sub-schemas. Each sub-schema in turn consists of a configuration of sub-schemas, etc. Some schemas are assumed to be primitive and to be undecomposable. Thus, we might imagine that the schema for a human body consists, in part, of a particular configuration of a head, a trunk, two arms, and two legs. The schema for a head contains, among other things, a face, two ears, etc. The schema for a face contains a particular configuration of two eyes, a nose, a mouth, etc. The schema for an eye contains an iris, an upper lid, a lower lid, etc. The schemas at the various levels can offer each other mutual support. Thus, whenever we find evidence for a face, we thereby have evidence for two eyes, a nose, and a mouth. We also have evidence for a head, and thereby, perhaps for an entire body. Thus, unlike the attribute or featural representational systems in which features are generally viewed as unitary elements, the schema theories propose a whole hierarchy of additional levels.

The third characteristic of schemas is that they represent knowledge at all levels of abstraction. Just as theories can be about the grand and the small, so schemas can represent knowledge at all levels—from ideologies and cultural truths, to knowledge about what constitutes an appropriate sentence in our language, to knowledge about the meaning of a particular word, to knowledge about what patterns of excitations are associated with what letters of the alphabet. We have schemas to represent all levels of our experience, at all levels of abstraction. Thus, the schema theories suppose that the human memory system contains countless packets of knowledge. Each packet specifies a configuration of other packets (sub-schemas) which represent the constituents of the schema. Furthermore, these theories assume that these packets themselves vary in complexity and level of application.

The fourth characteristic involves the kinds of information that schemas are assumed to represent. We believe that schemas *are* our knowledge. All of our generic knowledge is embedded in schemas. When we think of representations for word meanings, we can imagine that we might wish to represent one of two kinds of information. On the one hand, it has been common for representational theorists to assume that word meanings are rather like what one might find in a dictionary—the essential aspects of the word meanings. On the other hand, one might assume that the meaning of a word is represented by something more like an encyclopedic article on the topic. In this case one would expect that in a schema for a concept like "bird," we would have in addition to the dictionary knowledge, many facts and relationships about birds. A third kind of information needs to be represented: our experiences with birds. The first two kinds of knowledge about birds are referred to as *semantic memory*. The third kind of knowledge is referred to as *episodic memory* (the terms were invented by Tulving, 1972). It is generally assumed that schemas must exist for both semantic and episodic memory, and that schemas for semantic memory contain a great deal of world knowledge and are much more encyclopedic than dictionary-like.

Finally, schemas should be envisioned as active processes in which each schema is a process evaluating its goodness of fit, binding its variables, and sending messages to other schemas that indicate its current estimate of how well it accounts for the current data. In this case, it is useful to distinguish between two data sources that a schema can use in evaluating its goodness of fit:

1.   Information provided by the schema's sub-schemas on how well they account for their parts of the input (*bottom-up information*);

2.   Information from those schemas of which the schema is a constituent about the degree of certainty that they are relevant to structuring the input (*top-down information*). The process of interpretation can consist of repeated processing loops as various schema interact with top-down and bottom-up information processing in an attempt to find the best overall fit. Eventually, the process settles down. The set of schemas that has the best goodness of fit to the input constitutes the final interpretation of the input data.

Scripts, Plans and MOPS.   According to schema theory the memory system consists of an enormous number of packets of knowledge. Schank, Abelson and their colleagues (cf., Schank & Abelson, 1977) have developed specific examples of the knowledge one might have stored. This allows us to determine whether the system has practical value, that is, whether such knowledge could really serve as the basis for the kind of interpretations we get of stories we read. Schank and Abelson have developed a number of specific kinds of schemas, the simplest type being the *script*. A script can be thought of as a schema for a frequently occurring sequence of events. Schank and Abelson suggest that there are scripts for very common types of social events. For example, they suggest that there are scripts for a visit to a restaurant, for a visit to a doctor, for a trip on a train, and many other similar frequently occurring event sequences. The script which has received the most attention is that for the *restaurant*. [Fig. 2.7] gives Schank and Abelson's proposal for the restaurant script. A script, like all schema, has a number of variables. These can be divided roughly into two categories, those which require a person to fill them (called *roles*) and those which must be filled by objects of a certain kind (called *props*). Each script contains a number of *entry conditions*, a sequence of *scenes*, and a set of *results*. Script processing, like schema processing in general, allows one to make inferences about aspects of the situation which were not explicitly mentioned. Consider the following example:

Mary went to a restaurant.
She ordered a quiche.
Finally, she paid the bill and left.

Once it is determined that the Restaurant script is the proper account for this little story, it is possible to make a large number of inferences. In the first place, we can assume that when Mary started the episode, she was hungry. We also can assume that she had some money before she went into the restaurant and that she ate the quiche before she paid the bill. We further assume that there was a waiter or waitress who brought her a menu, that she waited for the food to be served, and so on. Thus, among other things, the script provides the structure necessary to understand the temporal order of events. In communicating, we need only provide enough information to be certain that our listener finds the correct script, and we assume the rest follows automatically. The script itself allows the listener to infer many of the details.
    [. . .]
    According to Schank and Abelson, the script is only the simplest of the schema-like knowledge structures. Clearly, not all situations that we wish to understand consist of a sequence of high frequency events. Often, the knowledge structures we have to bring to bear to get an interpretation of the situation must consist of more general and more abstract schemas. One important type of such an abstract schema is what Schank and Abelson have called the *plan*. Plans are formulated to satisfy specific motivations and goals. Future actions can be expected to involve attempts to attain these goals. Consider the following example:

John knew that his wife's operation would be very expensive.
There was always Uncle Harry . . .
He reached for the suburban phone book.

Many people, when they encounter this story, assume that John wants to

Theoretical Restaurant Script (Adapted from Schank & Abelson, 1977)

Name: Restaurant

Props: Tables   *Roles:* Customer
      Menu   Waiter
      Food   Cook
      Bill   Cashier
      Money   Owner
      Tip

Entry Conditions: Customer hungry   *Results:* Customer has less money
                      Customer has money   Owner has more money
                                                       Customer is not hungry

Scene 1: Entering
     Customer enters restaurant
     Customer looks for table
     Customer decides where to sit
     Customer goes to table
     Customer sits down

Scene 2: Ordering
     Customer picks up menu
     Customer looks at menu
     Customer decides on food
     Customer signals waitress
     Waitress comes to table
     Customer orders food
     Waitress goes to cook
     Waitress gives food order to cook
     Cook prepares food

Scene 3: Eating
     Cook gives food to waitress
     Waitress brings food to customer
     Customer eats food

Scene 4: Exiting
     Waitress writes bill
     Waitress goes over to customer
     Waitress gives bill to customer
     Customer gives tip to waitress
     Customer goes to cashier
     Customer gives money to cashier
     Customer leaves restaurant

FIG. 2.7. The Restaurant Script. (From Bower, Black and Turner, 1979, p. 179; adapted from Schank and Abelson, 1977.)

borrow money from Uncle Harry and that he is reaching for the phone book to find Uncle Harry's phone number to ask for the money. Now, we probably don't have a specific script for this particular activity. We do, however, probably know that when people are presented with problems, they attempt to solve them. Thus, having identified the problem in the story (the cost of the wife's operation) we expect to see some problem solving behavior on the part of the protagonist, so that we interpret further activity as an attempt to solve the problem. Moreover, we can assume that subgoals will be generated along the way, and that further activities will be generated toward the solution of the subgoal. In this case, the primary goal is to pay for the operation; the plan is to borrow money from Uncle Harry. Borrowing money involves contacting Uncle Harry, which in turn leads to the subgoal of calling on the telephone, which involves the further subgoal of discovering his phone number, and so on. Rumelhart (1975, 1977) and Wilensky (1978) have shown that many stories can be analyzed by means of problem solving.

. . . Bower, Black and Turner (1979) [have] found that subjects sometimes [recall] events which occurred in one script (say a dentist script) in [recalling a different but similar script]. If different scripts are entirely different data structures, there is no reason to suppose that events from similar scripts would be more often confused than events from quite different scripts. This result prompted Schank to revise the notion of the script so that scripts are not stored in memory as a simple sequence of events, but are derived at the time they are used from smaller, more fundamental data elements (Schank, 1980). Those elements which combine to form scripts, Schank calls MOPS. Thus, the doctor script is not a unitary element. Rather, it is derived from the interrelationship of such MOPS as the fix-problem-MOP, the health-care-MOP, the professional-office-visit-MOP and many other MOPS. [Fig. 2.8] illustrates the configuration of MOPS that Schank assumes might underlie the doctor script.

ANALOGICAL REPRESENTATIONS

Most of the representational systems we have discussed thus far were designed to represent information stored in long term memory. In particular, they were designed to represent *meanings*, which led naturally to propositional representations. But other considerations lead to other classes of representational ideas. Consider the representation of an *image*; how would one represent objects undergoing various transformations? A number of researchers, especially Shepard, Kosslyn, and their colleagues (c.f. Shepard & Cooper, 1982; Kosslyn, 1980), have proposed that the

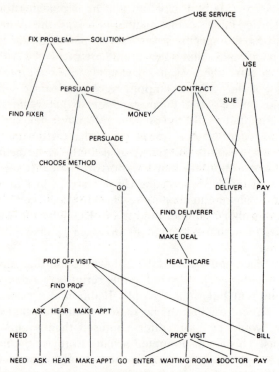

FIG. 2.8. The configuration of MOPS which are assumed to underlie our knowledge of a doctor's visit. (From Schank, 1980, p. 137.)

knowledge underlying images is *analogical* rather than *propositional*. There has been a good deal of debate concerning the nature of analog representations and of how they differ from propositional ones. [...]

Shepard

Shepard and his co-workers have focused primarily on a set of simple mental transformations of mental images. Most of their work has focused on a study of mental rotations. The general procedure is to present a picture of a pair of objects that either are similar or mirror images of one another, but that differ in orientation (see [Fig. 2.9]). The subject's task is to decide, as quickly as possible, whether the objects can be rotated into congruence. . . . the time to respond increases linearly and continuously as the angular difference between the two objects increase, whether they differ in picture plane orientation or in orientation in depth. Subjects often report that they do the task by imagining one of the objects being rotated into congruence with the other.

Based on their experimental findings, Metzler and Shepard (1974) argued that the process of mentally rotating an object involves the use of a *mental analog* of a physical rotation. There are, they argue, two characteristics of such an "analog process." First, an analog process:

> has something important in common with the internal process that would go on if the subject were actually to perceive the one external object physically rotating into congruence with the other.

Second, in an analog process:

> the internal representation passes through a certain trajectory of intermediate states each of which has a one-to-one correspondence to an intermediate stage of an external physical rotation of the object.
> . . .
> To speak of it [a process] as an analog type of process is . . . to contrast it with any other type of process (such as feature search, symbol manipulation,

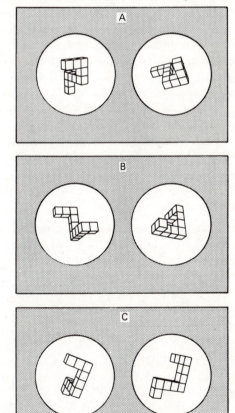

FIG. 2.9. Illustrative pairs of perspective views, including a pair differing by an 80° rotation in the-picture plane (*A*), a pair differing by an 80° rotation in depth (*B*), and a pair differing by a reflection as well as rotation (*C*). (From Metzler and Shepard, 1974.)

verbal analysis, or other "digital computation") in which the intermediate stages of the process have no sort of one-to-one correspondence to intermediate situations in the external world. (From Metzler & Shepard, 1974, pp. 150–151.)

In addition to the claim that the *processes* are analog, Shepard and his colleagues have argued that the *representations* themselves are analog: "The internal representation undergoing the rotation is viewed as preserving some degree of the spatial structure of its corresponding external object" (Cooper & Podgorny, 1976) and in this sense is an *analog* to the object itself (see also Shepard & Cooper, 1982, pp. 12–13).

[...]

Despite the clarity of the empirical results, not everyone has been convinced of the need for an *analog* as opposed to a *propositional* representational system. There are three reasons for this. First, it is possible that a "propositional" system could be constructed which would produce the same results. Second, the kind of analog system envisioned by Shepard and his colleagues is clearly a special case system: it is not at all clear how it might interface with the kinds of propositional representational systems that have been so powerful in other domains. Third, it is not at all clear what the analogical system would look like in detail. How should these analog systems be represented in our theories? What would such a system actually look like? In what ways would it really be different from the representational systems we have discussed thus far? These questions have been addressed and tentative answers have been proposed by Kosslyn and his colleagues, and so we turn now to a discussion of this work.

Kosslyn

The best articulated theory of image representation was put forth by Kosslyn and Schwartz (1978) and refined in Kosslyn (1980). Kosslyn's theory was built around what he called the Cathode Ray Tube (CRT) metaphor for visual imagery. [Fig. 2.10] illustrates the basic aspects of the metaphor. The basic idea is that there are two fundamental kinds of representations of imaginal information. First, there is the *surface representation* corresponding to the visual image itself. This representation is assumed to occur in a "spatial medium" which imposes a number of characteristics on the image:

Parts of the image represent corresponding parts of the imaged object in such a way that, for example, distance between parts of the representation correspond to distance between parts of the imaged object.

Just as a CRT has a limited spatial extent, so an image should have a

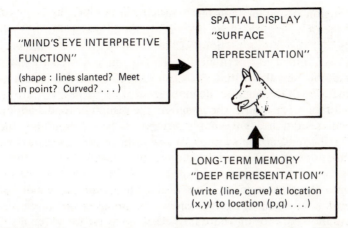

FIG. 2.10.   A schematic representation of the cathode-ray-tube (CRT) metaphor. (From Kosslyn, 1980, p. 6.)

limited spatial extent: images that are too large can not be represented without overflowing.

Surface representations of images, like those of CRTs, are assumed to have a "grain size," so that there is a loss of detail when an object is imaged too small.

Images, like CRT screens, require a periodic "refreshing" without which they will fade away.

In addition to the surface representation, the CRT metaphor suggests that there is a *deep representation* from which the image is being generated. Kosslyn (1980) suggests that images are generated from some sort of propositional representation, so that the underlying memory representation may not have the same spatial properties as the surface image. The third suggestive aspect of the CRT metaphor involves the existence of an *interpreter* or "mind's eye" that processes the surface image and serves as an interface between the surface image and a more abstract "semantic" interpretation of the constructed image. The interpretive processes might involve some of the same processing mechanisms used in general visual processing.

Kosslyn has constructed a computer simulation model that offers plausible accounts of a variety of data on visual imagery. In his model, Kosslyn proposes that the *surface* representation consists of a matrix of points. An image is represented in the matrix by filling in the cells of the matrix. The matrix is of limited *extent*, thus limiting how large an image can be; it has a particular *grain size*, thus limiting how small an image can be and still be seen clearly, and the matrix is organized so that the grain of the central region is smaller than the grain size of the peripheral region (the cells in the outer region of the matrix are not all used). Further, Kosslyn assumes that the representations in the visual matrix *fade* unless the old material is "refreshed" periodically. This is implemented by having the magnitude of the value within each cell of the matrix decrease with time after having been written into the matrix.

As with the CRT model, the images in the computer model are not long term representations, but simply temporary representations that are constructed to aid in the solution of particular problems. The long term representations or *deep* representations contain the knowledge that allows the construction of the images. Consequently, Kosslyn has two kinds of long term representations. He uses a relatively standard *propositional* representation for storing general knowledge and also what he calls a *literal* representation for storing the data necessary to create an image. These literal images are themselves stored as a set of polar coordinates ... with respect to an origin. The polar coordinates allow easy shifting of location of the image (by changing the origin), easy change of size (by multiplying ... by a constant), and easy rotation (around its origin). Figure [2.11] shows the long term memory representations and the major processes of the theory.

There are three major classes of processes proposed by Kosslyn. These are IMAGE, LOOKFOR and various TRANSFORMATIONS. IMAGE is a procedure for generating an image from the stored representation. It constructs a whole image out of the literal representations of their parts and their descriptions. LOOKFOR scans the image, using the surface representation along with the long term memory description of the object and finds the location of the looked for object in the image, if it is in the image. There are also four image transformation operations: SCAN, ZOOM, PAN and ROTATE. SCAN moves the image within the matrix. ZOOM moves all points out from the center, leaving a larger image. PAN moves all of the points toward the center, creating a smaller image. ROTATE moves all points of an image around a pivot, thus rotating the surface image. All of these transformations operate in small steps so that the surface matrix goes through intermediate points as it processes. Thus, in Shepard's sense, Kosslyn's system is truly an analogical system.

[...]

In Kosslyn, then, we have a detailed model of an analogical representation and [he provides a] substantial amount of evidence illustrating many important features of images [Kosslyn, 1980]. Perhaps the strongest single conclusion to be drawn is that people can create images that are surprisingly veridical and that can be processed in the way that an actual picture would be processed. Imagined objects are certainly analogs of the physical objects which they represent. As we will see later, however, the matrix representational format is probably not sufficiently general for use in many cases in which we use our imagination to solve problems. It seems likely that a richer representational format is necessary.

[...]

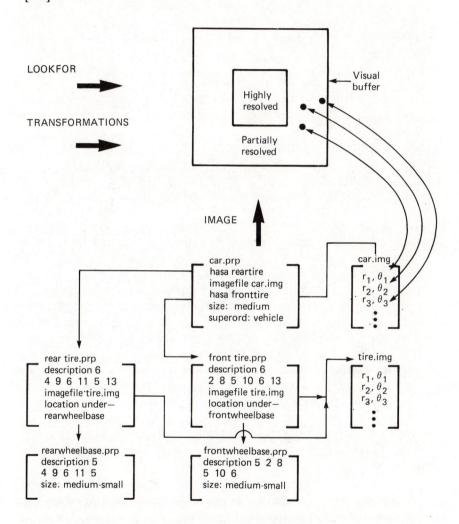

FIG. 2.11. A schematic representation of the structures posited by Kosslyn. The major processes of the model LOOKFOR things in the image, perform TRANSFORMATIONS on the images and create an IMAGE from a long term memory representation. (From Kosslyn, 1980, p. 147.)

Propositional and Analogical Representation

Much has been made of the supposed fundamental differences between analogical and propositional systems of representation. It is our belief that these differences are highly overstated and overemphasized. There are indeed different methods of representation, each with its own virtues and deficits, each good for a particular set of circumstances. Clearly, however, the notion of analogical representation conjures up a particular form of representation. Let us examine these aspects of representation so that we might understand how they fit into the entire spectrum of representational systems.

What does it mean for a representation to be "analogical"? In one sense, the question is meaningless, for the whole point of any representational system is that the represent*ing* world be similar or analogous to the represent*ed* world. [...]

Representation is (purely) intrinsic whenever a representing relation has the same inherent constraints as its represented relation. That is, the logical structure required of the representing relation is intrinsic to the relation itself rather than imposed from outside. Representation is purely arbitrary whenever the inherent structure of a representing relation is totally arbitrary and that of its represented relation is not. Whatever structure the representing relation has, then, is imposed on it by the relation it represents. It is typical of so-called analogical representational systems that the crucial relations of the system tend to be intrinsic in the representational format. It is typical of propositional representations that the inherent characteristics of the representing relations are not characteristics of the objects being represented and thus must be added to the representation as additional, extrinsic, constraints. It should be emphasized, however, that whether a set of constraints is intrinsic or extrinsic makes no difference in the operation of the representational system. The essential feature is that representational systems have the power to express those relationships of the represented world that are being represented.

As we have already seen, the critical thing about a representation is that it maps some selected aspects of the represented world into a representing world. There are two keys to understanding the differences among representations:

1. The selection of *which* dimensions of the represented world are to be captured within the representing world;
2. The determination of *how* the selected dimensions shall be represented.

These two aspects of the decision—the "which" and the "how"—then govern the properties of the representational system. Note that even in the mapping of a single represented world, the questions might have to be answered several times. For each dimension of the represented world that is selected, there could very well be a different determination of how that dimension is to be represented. In some cases, the very choice of a dimension tightly constrains the set of possible ways to do the representation. In other cases, having made the one decision, there are a number of possibilities remaining for the second.

[. . .]

Analogical Does Not Mean Continuous.   One common misconception of the meaning of "analog representation" is that it is continuous whereas propositional representation is digital, or discrete. This can't really be true. . . . Still, the notion of continuity persists, perhaps hedged with the realization that there may be a discrete cellular representation, but it is still analogical if the cells are of fine enough grain. It is easy to see where this belief comes from, for this distinction does characterize many existing systems. But the distinction is a result of the choice of dimensions from the represented world that are to be represented, not from any inherent property of the representational system itself. If we map spatial information into spatial form, then we are apt to use a continuous method of representation. If we map number of objects into either the number system or by a one-to-one map of object to representational symbol, then the most reasonable analogical representation is discrete, either the non-negative integers or finite symbols. That is, if the dimension in the represented world is continuous, then it makes sense for the representing world to be continuous. If the represented dimension is discrete—or if the continuity of the dimension is of no particular interest—then the best analog in the representing world would be a finite representational format. Whether or not we wish to characterize the representation as analogous depends upon how well we have captured the critical features of the represented world.

A discrete representation of a continuous dimension may still be characterized as analogical. Take the mental rotation phenomenon of two-dimensional figures as an example. First, we separate consideration of the representation of the figures to be rotated from the representation of the rotation: either one may be analogical or propositional, regardless of the other. Consider the four possibilities this gives rise to. If the figure is propositionally represented [by statements of the form ONTOPOF(cube1, cube2)] angular position could be represented either by discrete position [POSITION-OF(main-axis, horizontal)], or by continuous position [POSITION-OF(main-axis, 30.267 . . . °)] the difference being whether the position is selected from a finite set of descriptions (such as the integers) or from the real numbers. [. . .] If the figure is analogically represented . . . we still need to determine how to represent the rotation. It is easy to see how we might represent rotation in non-analogical form; we simply jump from the current position to the new position, traversing few or none of the intermediate states. If there is a matrix representation, it is not simple to actually do the rotation: the contents of each cell of the matrix would have to be moved to an appropriate new cell, and the algorithm that might accomplish this in a continuous way is not at all obvious. Yes, one could do the appropriate matrix multiplication, but then, why not just compute the desired end point—there is no need to actually rotate the representation. Moreover, if the representation is a matrix of this form, continuity is not possible in principle, for the same angular rotation covers different numbers of matrix cells at the periphery of the figure than near the center: at some point, intervening cells must either be repeated or skipped. If we try angular rotation on a cartesian grid, the grain size problem is a fundamental limitation. [. . .]

Consideration of what it means for the representation of rotation to be analogous to physical rotation makes it clear that the critical feature is whether or not the rotation passes through intermediate values. Indeed, this is why Shepard and Cooper (1982) place so much stress on the experimental demonstration that their experimental subjects did appear to rotate the test figures through the intermediate states. Their experimental findings allow us to conclude that people do represent rotation in a manner analogous to physical rotation. We can make this statement with confidence, regardless of whether human rotation actually is smooth and continuous, or whether it might be by discrete rotational jumps. . . . The point is that we can separate the determination of something being continuous from the determination of it being analogical.

PROCEDURAL REPRESENTATIONS

There is a classic distinction in representational systems between knowledge about something (called *knowledge of*, or *declarative* knowledge) and knowledge about how to do something (*knowledge how*, or *procedural* knowledge). Some of our knowledge is declarative, in the sense of making a statement about some property of the world. Thus, a statement of the form "George Washington was the first president of the United States" is a prototypical declarative statement. Knowledge of how to kick a football is a prototypical piece of procedural knowledge. Declarative knowledge tends to be accessible; it can easily be examined and combined with other declarative statements to form an inference. Procedural knowledge tends to be inaccessible, being used to guide our actions, but oftentimes offering remarkably little access or ability to be examined. Thus, although we can pronounce a word like "serendipitous," we cannot say what movements our tongue takes during the pronunciation without actually doing the task and noting the tongue movements. We seem to have conscious access to declarative knowledge; but we do not have this access to procedural knowledge.

So far in this chapter we have only discussed declarative systems of representations, systems in which the manner by which knowledge is represented is the critical concern. Procedural representational systems comprise a contrasting class of systems where the concern is *what* they do, not how they do it. Note, however, that the discussion of procedural representation has intermixed two different, but related, concepts. One concern is with how we should represent the knowledge of how to do things: knowledge of how to perform actions upon the world, knowledge of mental strategies that allows us to perform actions upon the representational structures of mind. The other concern is why there is this apparent difference between the accessibility of declarative and procedural knowledge. The two issues need not be related, although in practice, they are. The first issue is actually concerned with the *representation of procedures*. The second issue is concerned with *procedural representation*. To understand the differences between these two concepts, we must first look at some of the properties of an information processing system.

[. . .]

. . . Overall, an information processing system must have five separately identifiable components:

A sensory apparatus;
A motor system;
A memory;
A processing mechanism;
An interpreter.

Note that these five components need not be physically distinct. The processor, memory, and interpreter may use the same physical mechanisms. The sensory and motor apparatus may share mechanisms. The distinctions among these five are conceptual, not physical.

Our interest here is in the interpreter (and the symbol system upon which it operates). An interpreter acts as a translator, going from symbols to actions. An interpreter, therefore, must be capable of examining symbols and executing the actions that they specify. This means that the interpreter itself is composed of procedures. It can perform operations upon the symbols, including getting access to them, comparing them with others, and initiating actions that depend upon the results of the comparisons. Interpreters therefore use symbols in the declarative sense, for they must be able to examine the symbols and perform the operations that they specify.

The Representation of Procedures

When we represent procedures in a form that is to be interpreted, then we are representing procedures in a declarative format. Consider the procedure for answering the question, "Can X fly?":

> *Procedure*: "Can X fly?"
> *If there exists a relation* can fly *leading from X,*
> *then answer "Yes, X can fly" and stop.*
> *If there is no Y such that (X is a Y or X subset Y),*
> *then answer "As far as I can tell, X does not fly" and stop,*
> *otherwise, for each Y such that (X is a Y or X subset Y),*
> *do the procedure "Can Y fly?"*

Note that this procedure can be represented in any of the propositional representational systems that we have examined, and, if the system had an appropriate interpreter, it could then be executed to produce the desired result. Moreover, it would even be possible to modify the representational structure according to the results found by the procedures. Thus, suppose that the representation were a semantic network. The appropriate way to do the modification is to change the first "answer" statement to read:

> *then answer "Yes, X can fly" and*
> *if there exists a relation* can fly *leading from X,*
> *then stop,*
> *otherwise, connect* can fly *to X and stop.*

This method of imbedding procedures within the representation really means that the representational format for the knowledge in the representation (the data) and for the procedures (the programs) that operate upon the knowledge have the same format. [...] This means that the same information structure can be viewed as either data (declarative) or program (procedural)—and that is the key to this method of procedural representation. The power of this system comes from the fact that the interpreter can access procedural information as data, and thus describe it, alter it, and even simulate what would happen were the procedure to be invoked, actually doing the operations. Similarly, the interpreter can follow the procedure, thus doing the operations in the manner specified.

For many aspects of learning, the kind of accessibility provided by imbedding procedures within their own representational structure, accessible to an interpreter, seems critical. Indeed, this is what verbal or written instructions consist of: descriptions of procedures that are to be followed in performing the task that is being learned. The learner is expected to understand the instructions, to convert them into knowledge structures within the representational system, and then to follow them at the appropriate times in the performance of the task.

[...]

Procedural Representation

In one important class of representational systems, data are stored in a procedural representation of the second sense: inaccessible to inspection. This form of representational system has certain efficiencies and other virtues. Suppose we wished a representational system to be able to answer queries of the form "*Do birds fly?*" In the representational systems that we have studied so far, [such] questions would be answered by seeking an explicit declaration of the knowledge, perhaps in the form of ... [a] semantic network structure. In the preceding section we illustrated how one might search for such information within an interpreted, *declarative* system of representation. In a *procedural* representational system, the details of how the information was stored would not be visible. Instead, there would simply be a procedure available that would yield the appropriate response. Thus suppose that "bird" were a procedure (which could be thought of as a program) that could answer questions about itself. When the question "Do birds fly" was asked, the procedure for "bird" would supply the answer: "yes" (or perhaps, "usually"). The rest of the system would have no access to the knowledge structures except through the outputs of procedures: the representational system is opaque in the sense that its contents are not visible.

There are a number of important distinctions between declarative and procedural systems, most dealing with problems of efficiency, of the control processes that are invoked in the use of the system, and with issues of modularity and accessibility of knowledge. For psychologists, it is these last issues that are of most concern—modularity and accessibility. In a declarative system, the manner in which information is represented is of critical importance, and it is essential that the data structures be available for interpretation by other processes. In procedural representations, the data format is hidden away, inaccessible to procedures other than the one in which the knowledge is contained. All one knows is the output of the operations themselves. These differences have led to considerable argumentation and speculation about the most appropriate form of representation (Hewitt, 1975; Winograd, 1972, 1975).

Benefits of procedural representation include efficiency of operation, the ability to encode heuristics, and to readily incorporate both knowledge processing considerations within the same structure. ...Thus many things we know seem difficult to describe in declarative fashion: we know them by the way in which we do the task. Good examples come from our skilled behavior, whether it be speech, motor control, or thought. Procedural representation allows one to tailor the way that knowledge is represented in the manner best suited for the particular task in which it will be needed. Knowledge in a declarative system must in general be useable for a variety of purposes, and it is not apt to be maximally efficient for any particular use. To many people, procedural representations seem appropriate for the knowledge used in skilled human performance; declarative forms seem more appropriate for less skilled performance. The efficiency of procedural representations must be contrasted with the ease of inspection and modification (and thereby the ease of learning) of declarative representations. It is clear that the two different forms of representation each have their strengths and weaknesses, so that any sufficiently general system is apt to contain aspects of both.

[...]

... One important aspect of procedures is how they are to get triggered: what makes them do their actions? There are basically two ways that have been suggested for invoking procedures. One is by direct invocation: some other procedure (or the interpreter) determines just which procedure it should call for the need at hand and causes it to be brought into action. The second is by a triggering mechanism: the procedure itself watches over an appropriate data base of information for data structures that are relevant to it; when the appropriate data structures exist, the procedure is triggered. [...]

Demons.   An attractive processing strategy for modern representational systems is that conceptualized by "demons." Basically, it is as if there were a group of active processing structures all sitting above a data base, looking for patterns relevant to themselves. Whenever a relevant pattern occurs, then the demon is "triggered," going into action and performing its activities. The results of those activities can then cause new data structures to appear in the data base, possibly causing other demons to be triggered. Alternatively, demons may pass messages among one another, or they may directly lead to sensory or motor activity.

The reason that these processing structures are relevant to our discussion of representation is that they combine representational information with control structures. Norman and Bobrow (1976) suggested that these processing structures could be used to direct processing in such tasks as perceptual recognition problem solving, and memory retrieval ..., and Rumelhart (1977) demonstrated how such combined processing/representational systems could lead to an "interactive" system for word recognition. ... These processing schemes are called "interactive" because they combine both data-driven (bottom-up) and conceptually-driven (top-down) processing with the appropriate representational systems. The representational systems that they use are not new; what is new is the combination of processing structure. Each schema detects arriving data that are relevant to it, processes them, and then communicates what it has found to other, higher level, schemas. This represents the bottom-up, or data driven processing. In addition, higher level schemas can direct queries to lower level ones, shaping the course of processing, seeking evidence that would confirm their relevance. [...]

[...]

Production Systems. Production systems are a form of demon system in which all the communication among schemas takes place through a common data structure, usually called the *working memory* (WM). A production consists of an "if→ then" or "condition→ action" statement:

IF *(condition-for-triggering)* → THEN *(do-these-actions)*

If the conditions described on the left-hand side of the arrow are found in WM, then do the actions described on the right hand side of the arrow. Production systems represent a form of processing called *pattern directed processing*, because the processing actions associated with a production (the procedures) are triggered into action whenever the pattern of data represented by the condition side of the production appears within WM. In general, in a production system, the actions operate upon the structures within WM, which triggers other productions to operate.

Because of the way they have been used in representational systems, production systems provide an interesting merger of active processes and control structure with representational issues. The modern use of production systems in psychology and artificial intelligence is largely due to the work of Newell (1973)....

One important property of production systems is *modularity*. That is, because each production is a self contained entity, it is possible to add or subtract productions at will, without worrying about the structure of the system. As a result, new learning is readily incorporated into the system, at least in principle; as new productions are learned, they can simply be added to the existing base of productions. In practice, however, such additions are not so straightforward, and as the system gets too large, strange behavior can result from too many new additions. It seems clear that a good theory of learning is going to be required before production systems (or any other formalism) will be able to meet their apparent promise.

[...]

Problems with Production Systems as Models of Human Process-ing. Not everyone is happy with production systems, however. Their architecture is somewhat arbitrary, and although it is claimed to match that of human processing, most of the structure had to be created in advance of good psychological theory and evidence. Working memory may corres-pond to human short-term memory, but the size of working memory needed to get production systems to work correctly far exceeds even the largest estimate for human short-term memory. The handling of variables seems arbitrary; we do not yet know how human processing structures manage this feat. The structure of productions is homogeneous, and does not yet match the power of the other forms of representational systems that we have studied. There are oftentimes conflicts when a number of productions simultaneously match the information within working memory, and special rules must be developed to handle these issues. [...] Not all these objections are fundamental. Most will be overcome as production systems are integrated within other forms of representational systems.... Moreover, some of the problems of productions may actually be virtues; the conflicts that arise when several productions simultaneously match the conditions in working memory may be similar to conflicts that are observable in human behavior. . . .

CONCLUSION

The problem of representation is one of determining a mapping between the concepts and relations of the *represented* world and the concepts and relations of the *representing* world. The problem for the psychologist, of course, is to find those representational systems that cause the behavior of our theories to correspond to the behavior of the human. In developing a theory of representation, it is important to be aware of exactly what it is that is being represented: in particular, much of cognitive psychology and artificial intelligence is concerned with attempts to represent the mental activity of the human. To quote the earlier portion of this chapter: "Within the brain, there exist brain states that are the representation of the environment. The environment is the represented world, the brain states are the representing world. Our theories of representation are in actuality representations of the brain states, not representations of the world."

In many ways, the "representation problem" is, in truth, a "notation problem." That is, in establishing a representation for our theories, we wish to discover a notation:

1. That is rich enough to represent all of the relevant data structures and processes;

2. In which those processes which we wish to assume are natural (i.e., are easily carried out) are, in fact, easily carried out.

Three Major Controversies

Traditionally, the problem of representation has had a number of different components that have led to long debate. Three major debates have arisen over the distinctions between representational formats: propositional versus analogical, continuous versus discrete, and declarative versus procedural. The position that we have taken in this chapter is that these debates do not reflect fundamental distinctions about representational systems, but rather reflect differences in the way that representational systems meet the two criteria for such systems stated above. Let us review each issue briefly.

The Propositional—Analogical Controversy.   Propositional representations are ones which consist of formal "statements" that reflect the represented world, either in the form of networks, schema-based structures, or logical formulae. Analogical representations attempt to determine a "direct" mapping between the characteristic of the represented world of primary importance and the representing world. Thus, spatial or temporal properties of the represented world might be mapped onto spatial properties of the representing world, and ordered properties of the represented world are mapped onto ordered properties of the number system in the representing world. All representational systems are, of course, to some extent analogs of the represented world; after all, that is what a representation is all about—to capture the essence of the represented world. Whatever the mapping, a key feature of representations that we are willing to call *analogical* is that if the thing being represented undergoes change or modification, then the structure in the representing world should undergo the corresponding change or modification, passing through the same intermediate states as the original. Thus, if we have a picture of a star above a cross and move the star closer to or further from the cross, an analogical representation of that movement will have to represent the same set of intermediate states as the physical movement. This could be accomplished with a representation that consisted of a manipulable "picture" of the star and cross, perhaps ... it could be represented by using a two-dimensional coordinate system within a set of propositions, specifying location by values on the real numbers.
[...]

The Continuous—Discrete Controversy.   Oftentimes, continuous representations are confused with analogical, and discrete with propositional representations. However, the two distinctions are actually independent of one another. What is involved here is the "grain size" or "acuity" that one wishes to have in the represented world. Thus, if the things to be represented are discrete in nature, then even the most analogical representation in the representing world is likely to be discrete. Alternatively, one might choose a continuous (real-number) representation within a propositional structure. The real point is that one is attempting to capture aspects and relations that are considered important in the represented world within the structures of the representing world, and the choice of a discrete or continuous representation simply reflects the choice of what features are important. Thus, if one represented a moving object by a matrix representation of the object, where the movement was represented by small, discrete changes in the representing location, this would qualify as an analogical representation as long as the discrete steps within the representing movement were small relative to the step size of interest. In this case, a discrete representation of a continuous event would still be considered analogical.

The Declarative—Procedural Controversy. The difference between representations called "declarative" and representation called "procedural" really reflect differences in the *accessibility* of the information to the interpretive structures. In the case of declarative representations, the information is represented in a format that can be examined and manipulated directly by the interpretive processes. Thus, the information is accessible for inspection, for use by multiple processes, and for that matter, for the interpreter simply to announce whether or not the information is known to be present within the representational system. In the case of procedural representations, the information is not available in a form that can be accessed by the interpreter. Rather, one must "execute" the procedure and examine the results. Information that is procedural is therefore "encapsulated" for this level of representation, not available for inspection, not easily available for multiple processes (unless their use has been explicitly provided for), and it is not possible for the interpreter to make announcements regarding the presence or absence of information that is procedurally encoded. Declarative information is "explicit" in that it is directly encoded. Procedural information is "implicit" in that the procedure has to be executed in order to get the information.

In this chapter we have argued that what is declarative and what is procedural information is context dependent. That is, any realistic information processing system has several levels of processing and interpretations, and what is procedural at one level of interpretations is most likely declarative at a different level—indeed, at the level where some interpretive process operates upon the procedure in order to execute it. The system is eventually grounded in the primitives of the system and in actual physical actions. And at this level, all the actions of the system are "procedural."

Data Structure and Process

Representational systems consist of at least two parts:

The data structures, which are stored according to some representational format;

The processes that operate upon the data structures.

Much confusion has arisen in the comparison of representational systems because of a lack of recognition that both data and process are essential; one cannot be understood without reference to and understanding of the other. Note that the distinction between data structures and interpretive processes varies with different modes of representation. Thus, one difference between declarative and procedural representations has to do with the relative tradeoff between the division of the knowledge between the data structures and the interpretive system. [...] In all cases, both need to be considered in order to understand the representational system. Data structure and their interpretive processes are intrinsically intertwined; the two must be considered as an inseparable pair in determining the properties and powers of the representation.

Multiple Representations

There is no single answer to the question "how is information represented in the human?"; many different representational formats might be involved within the human representational system. Thus, within the representing world, different aspects of the represented world might be represented through different representational formats. This allows each dimension to be represented by the system that maps best into the sets of operations that one wishes to perform upon them. Different representational systems have different powers, and the choice of which one is used reflects those powers.

Like every other representational decision, the decision to use multiple representations of the same information has its tradeoffs. In this case, the extra powers must be traded off against the problem of coordinating the information in the separate representations, so that when a change is made, all structures are properly synchronized so as to reflect the same represented world.

[...]

ICM – C*

One of the problems in attempting to assess a person's knowledge structure is that some of that knowledge may be directly represented, and some may be indirectly coded, inferred or otherwise generated at the time of test. Modern representational theory—as represented by the discussions in this chapter—provides a rich set of possibilities for the possessor of knowledge. The research recognizes that people have the capability of making new inferences even as they answer a query, that much of what is reported may be generated, on-line, in real-time, at the time of answering the questions put to them, using the representational properties of inheritance and logical inference, and using prototypical schemas to structure the organization of what is being generated, complete with default values. The possessor of the knowledge itself cannot distinguish between memory retrievals that are regenerated on the spot according to some generic properties and memory retrievals that are accurate reflections of the actual events. Finally, the problem of determining a person's memory structures are amplified by the fact that much knowledge may be represented procedurally, and procedural knowledge—by definition—is inaccessible to its possessor.

REFERENCES

Abelson, R. (1975) Concepts for representing mundane reality in plans. In D. G. Bobrow & A. M. Collins (Eds.), *Representation and understanding: Studies in cognitive science.* New York: Academic Press.

Anderson, J. R. (1976) *Language, memory, and thought.* Hillsdale, N.J.: Lawrence Erlbaum Associates.

Bartlett, F. C. (1932) *Remembering.* Cambridge: Cambridge University Press.

Bobrow, D. G., & Norman, D. A. (1975) Some principles of memory schemata. In D. G. Bobrow & A. M. Collins (Eds.), *Representation and understanding: Studies in cognitive science.* New York: Academic Press.

Bower, G. H., Black, J. B., & Turner, T. J. (1979) Scripts in memory for text. *Cognitive Psychology, 11,* 177–220.

Collins, A. M., & Loftus, E. F. (1975) A spreading activation theory of semantic processing. *Psychological Review, 82,* 407–428.

Collins, A. M., & Quillian, M. R. (1969) Retrieval time from semantic memory. *Journal of Verbal Learning and Verbal Behavior, 8,* 240–247.

Collins, A. M., & Quillian, M. R. (1970) Facilitating retrieval from semantic memory: The effect of repeating part of an inference. In A. F. Sanders (Ed.), *Attention and performance III.* Amsterdam: North Holland. (Also published in *Acta Psychologica,* 1970, *33,* 304–314.)

Cooper, L. A., & Podgorny, P. (1976) Mental transformations and visual comparison processes. *Journal of Experimental Psychology: Human Perception and Performance, 2,* 503–514.

Fahlman, S. E. (1981) Representing implicit knowledge. In G. E. Hinton & J. A. Anderson (Eds.), *Parallel models of associative memory.* Hillsdale, N.J.: Lawrence Erlbaum Associates.

Hewitt, C. (1975) How to use what you know. *Proceedings of the Fourth International Joint Conference on Artificial Intelligence*, 189–198.

Kosslyn, S. M. (1980) *Image and mind*. Cambridge, Mass.: Harvard University Press.

Kosslyn, S. M., & Schwartz, S. P. (1978) Visual images as spatial representations in active memory. In E. M. Riseman & A. R. Hanson (Eds.), *Computer vision systems*. [New York: Academic Press].

Maclean, J., & Schulman, G. (1978) The construction and maintenance of expectancies. *Quarterly Journal of Experimental Psychology, 30*, 441–454.

McClelland, J. L., & Rumelhart, D. E. (1981) An interactive activation model of context effects in letter perception, Part 1: An account of basic findings. *Psychological Review, 88*, 375–407.

Metzler, J., & Shepard, R. N. (1974) Transformational studies of the internal representation of three-dimensional objects. In R. Solso (Ed.), *Theories in cognitive psychology: The Loyola Symposium*, Hillsdale, N.J.: Lawrence Erlbaum Associates.

Meyer, D. E. (1970) On the representation and retrieval of stored semantic information. *Cognitive Psychology, 1*, 242–299.

Meyer, D. E., & Schvaneveldt, R. W. (1971) Facilitation in recognizing pairs of words: Evidence of a dependance between retrieval operations. *Journal of Experimental Psychology, 90*, 227–234.

Minsky, M. (1975) A framework for representing knowledge. In P. Winston (Ed.), *The psychology of computer vision*. New York: McGraw-Hill.

Neeley, J. H. (1976) Semantic priming and retrieval from lexical memory: Evidence for facilitory and inhibitory processes. *Memory and Cognition, 4*, 648–654.

Newell, A. (1973) Production systems: Models of control structure. In W. Chase (Ed.), *Visual information processing*. New York: Academic Press.

Norman, D. A, & Bobrow, D. G. (1976) On the role of active memory processes in perception and cognition. In C. N. Cofer (Ed.), *The structure of human memory*. San Francisco: Freeman.

Norman, D. A., & Rumelhart, D. E. (1975) *Explorations in cognition*. San Francisco: Freeman.

Palmer, S. E. (1978) Fundamental aspects of cognitive representation. In E. Rosch & B. B. Lloyd (Eds.), *Cognition and categorization*. Hillsdale, N.J.: Lawrence Erlbaum Associates.

Piaget, J. (1952) [*The origins of intelligence in children*] (M. Cook, trans.). New York: International Universities Press.

Quillian, M. R. (1968) Semantic memory. In M. Minsky (Ed.), *Semantic information processing*. Cambridge, Mass: MIT Press.

Rips, L. J., Shoben, E. J., & Smith, E. E. (1973) Semantic distance and the verification of semantic relations. *Journal of Verbal Learning and Verbal Behavior. 12*, 1–20.

Rumelhart, D. E. (1975) Notes on a schema for stories. In D. G. Bobrow & A. M. Collins (Eds.), *Representation and understanding: Studies in cognitive science*. New York: Academic Press.

Rumelhart, D. E. (1977) Toward an interactive model of reading. In S. Dornic (Ed.), *Attention and performance VI*. Hillsdale, N.J.: Lawrence Erlbaum Associates.

Rumelhart, D. E. (1981) *Understanding understanding* (Tech. Rep. CHIP 100). La Jolla, CA: University of California, San Diego, Center for Human Information Processing (January).

Rumelhart, D. E., & McClelland, J. L. (1982) An interactive activation model of context effects in letter perception, Part 2: The contextual enhancement effect and some tests and extensions of the model. *Psychological Review, 89*, 60–94.

Rumelhart, D. E., & Norman, D. A. (1978) Accretion, tuning, and restructuring: Three modes of learning. In J. W. Cotton & R. L. Klatzky (Eds.), *Semantic factors in cognition*. Hillsdale, N.J.: Lawrence Erlbaum Associates.

Rumelhart, D. E., & Ortony, A. (1977) The representation of knowledge in memory. In R. C. Anderon, R. J. Spiro, & W. E. Montague (Eds.), *Schooling and the acquisition of knowledge*. Hillsdale, N.J.: Lawrence Erlbaum Associates.

Schank, R. C. (1975) *Conceptual information processing*. New York: North-Holland.

Schank, R. C. (1980) Language and memory. *Cognitive Science, 4*, 243–284.

Schank, R. C. (1981) Language and memory. In D. A. Norman (Ed.), *Perspectives on cognitive science*. Norwood, N.J.: Ablex. Hillsdale, N.J.: Lawrence Erlbaum Associates.

Schank, R., & Abelson, R. (1977) *Scripts, plans, goals, and understanding*. Hillsdale, N.J.: Lawrence Erlbaum Associates.

Shepard, R. N., & Cooper, L. A. (1982) *Mental images and their transformations*. Cambridge Mass.: MIT Press.

Smith, E. E., & Medin, D. L. (1981) *Categories and concepts*. Cambridge, Mass.: Harvard University Press.

Smith, E. E., Shoben, E. J., & Rips, L. J. (1974) Structure and process in semantic memory: A feature model for semantic decisions. *Psychological Review, 81*, 214–241.

Tulving, E., & Donaldson, W. (Eds.) (1972) *Organization and memory*. New York: Academic Press.

Wilensky, R. (1978) *Understanding goal-based stories*. PhD. Thesis. Yale University, Computer Science Dept., Research Report 140.

Winograd, T. (1972) *Understanding natural language*. New York: Academic Press.

Winograd, T. (1975) Frame representations and the declarative/procedural controversy. In D. G. Bobrow & A. M. Collins (Eds.), *Representation and understanding: Studies in cognitive science*. New York: Academic Press.

3 The Medium and the Message in Mental Imagery: A Theory

Stephen Michael Kosslyn

In the *Theaetetus* Plato likened memory representations to impressions on a wax tablet, perhaps thereby becoming the first theorist to distinguish between representations (the different possible impressions) and the medium in which they occur (the wax tablet). The distinction between a representation and a medium has proven important in the study of visual mental imagery. Although no serious researcher today maintains that images are actual pictures in the head, some still find it reasonable to posit quasi-pictorial representations that are supported by a medium that mimics a coordinate space. On this view, images are not languagelike "symbolic" representations but bear a nonarbitrary correspondence to the thing being represented. Partly because of the primitive origins of this idea, many people seem wary of it. But the idea that images are a special kind of representation that depicts information and occurs in a spacial medium is not patently ridiculous, and in fact can be developed in a very coherent way that violates neither philosophical nor empirical considerations. [...]

BACKGROUND ASSUMPTIONS

Before one begins to theorize one should have a reasonably clear conception of both the domain of the theory and the form the theory should take. [...]

The Domain of the Theory

The goal of this article is to describe a theory of how information is represented in, and accessed from, visual mental images. For example, when asked to count the number of windows in their living room, most people report mentally picturing the walls, scanning over them, and "looking" for windows. The present theory is intended to provide accounts of this "mental picturing" process, of "looking" at images, and of transforming images in various ways. In addition, the theory also specifies when images will be used spontaneously in the retrieval of information from memory (as in the foregoing example).

The Form of a Cognitive Theory of Imagery

A cognitive account of imagery is a theory about the *functional capacities* of the brain—the things it can do—that are invoked during imagery. There are numerous ways to describe the range and kinds of functional capacities involved in any given domain of processing, but most theorists have found it useful to describe these capacities in terms of structures and processes. Let us distinguish between two kinds of structures, *data structures* and *media*, and two general kinds of processes, *comparisons* and *transformations*.

Data Structures.   Data structures are the information-bearing representations in any processing system. They can be specified by reference to three properties, their *format*, *content*, and *organization*. The format is determined by (a) the nature of the "marks" used in the representation (such as ink, magnetic fluxes, or sound waves) and (b) the way these marks are interpreted (the mark *A* could be taken as a token of a letter of the alphabet or a picture of a particular pattern). The format specifies whether a representation is composed of primitive elements and relations and, if so, specifies their nature. The content is the information stored in a given data structure. Any given content can be represented using any number of formats. For example, the information in the previous sentence could be stored on a magnetic tape, on a page, as a series of dots and dashes etched on metal, and so on. The organization is the way elementary representations can be combined. The format of a representation constrains the possible organizations but does not determine them. For example, propositional representations can be ordered into various kinds of lists and networks.

Media.   A medium does not carry information in its own right. Rather, a medium is a structure that supports particular kinds of data structures.

This page, a TV screen, and even the air are media—supporting ink, glowing phosphor, and sound patterns, respectively. Media can be specified by reference to their *formatting* and *accessibility*. The formatting places restrictions on what sorts of data structures can be supported by a medium. A short-term store, for example, might have five "slots" that take "verbal chunks"—but not visual images or abstract propositions. The accessibility characteristics dictate how processes can access data structures within a medium. The slots of a short-term store, for example, might be accessible only in a given sequence.

Note that all of the properties of the media and the data structures are by necessity defined in the context of a particular processing system. Even though structures have an independent existence, and their nature imposes constraints on the kinds of processes that can be used (Hayes-Roth, 1979; Keenan & Moore, 1979; Pylyshyn, 1979), structures attain their functional properties only vis-à-vis the operation of particular processes. For example, if items on a list can be retrieved only in one order on one day and another order on the next day, the functional order of the list has changed—even though the data structure has not.

Comparison Processes.   These procedures compare two data structures or parts thereof and return a match/mismatch decision or a measure of the degree of similarity (defined over a specific metric) between the representations.

Transformation Processes.   There are two very general classes of transformation processes, *alterations* and *productions*. Alteration transformations operate to alter a given data structure by changing its contents (e.g., by adding or deleting an item on a list) or reorganizing it (e.g., by reordering items on a list). Production transformations, in contrast, leave the initial data structure intact but use it as an impetus either to replace or to supplement it with a new data structure. This new data structure may differ from the initial one in its format (as when a pattern is described), in content (as when an initial image is replaced by one with more details), and/or in organization (as when a list is replaced by a new one with the same items but in a different order). It is difficult for me to conceive of how an alteration transformation can itself change the format of a data structure, and this may prove to be a critical distinction between the two classes. . . . I make no commitment as to the form of [the] ultimate abstract expression [of the theory] but only claim that it will express lawful relations among the kinds of cognitive entities described above. The job for empirical research programs at this time, as I see it, is to isolate and develop the clearest possible characterization of the individual functional capacities and their interrelations.

[...]

The general model of image representation and processing we have developed takes the form of a computer simulation (see Kosslyn, 1980; Kosslyn & Shwartz, 1977, 1978). Each process is represented as a subroutine or set of subroutines, and each structure has been implemented as well (as described below). There are numerous virtues in building a general model of the sort we have been developing, but two stand out: First, if one tries to motivate the decisions necessary to model an entire domain in a consistent, precise way, one will be inspired to collect new and interesting data to select among plausible alternative ways of building the model. Second, the model allows one to formulate precise accounts for performance in numerous specific tasks, and these accounts are self-consistent. Thus, one can test the theory as a whole by generating predictions about what should happen in particular tasks, as we in fact have done (see Kosslyn, 1980). On our view, then, the main reason to formulate a model for a particular task is to test the underlying assumptions of the theory that dictated that specific model. It is simply too easy to explain performance in any given task in isolation for this exercise to be very useful ...; it is only when one is trying to provide accounts for all the tasks in a domain that one seems to learn very much.

OVERVIEW OF THE THEORY

The following review outlines the most central claims of the Kosslyn and Shwartz (1977, 1978; Kosslyn, 1980) theory of mental image representation and processing, which will be described in terms of the kinds of structures and processes discussed in the previous section. Properties of the general model embodying the theory will also be described occasionally to clarify the theoretical claims; unless otherwise noted, only the theory-relevant properties of our simulation will be mentioned. . . .

Structures

On our view, images have two major components. The "surface representation" is a quasi-pictorial representation that occurs in a spatial medium; this representation depicts an object or scene and underlies the experience of imagery. The "deep representation" is the information in long-term memory that is used to generate a surface representation.

The Surface Representation

The properties of the surface image are in part a consequence of the properties of the medium in which it occurs, which we call the *visual buffer*. The visual buffer is implemented as an array in our computer simulation (the *surface matrix*); a surface image is represented by a configuration of points in this array that depicts an object or objects.

1. The Medium

Formatting. (a) The visual buffer functions as if it were a coordinate space. This "space" is not an actual physical one but is rather a functional space defined by the way processes access the structure. The functional relations of the loci in the visual buffer need not be determined by actual physical relations any more than the functional relations of cells in an array in a computer need be determined by the physical relations among the parts of core memory. That is, the processes that operate on an image access the medium in such a way that local regions are separated from each other by different numbers of locations (i.e., differences in the number of just-noticeable differences in position in the coordinate space). We posit that the organization of the visual buffer is innately determined and fixed. Information is represented by selectively activating local regions of the space. (b) The visual buffer has a limited extent and specific shape, as measured empirically (see Finke & Kosslyn, 1980; Kosslyn, 1978), and hence can support only representations depicting a limited visual arc. This makes sense if this medium is also used in perceptual processing; if so, then it presumably only needed to evolve to represent input from the limited arc subtended by the eyes.

Accessibility. (a) The visual buffer has a grain, resulting in a limited resolution. Thus, portions of subjectively smaller images (i.e., those which seem to subtend a smaller angle) are more difficult to classify because subtle variations in contour are obscured (Kosslyn, 1975, 1976a) ... (b) The resolution is highest at the center of the visual buffer and decreases toward the periphery (see Finke & Kosslyn, 1980; Kosslyn, 1978). Importantly, although grain is not homogeneous throughout the medium, at any given location is it presumed to be fixed. (c) Representations within the visual buffer are transient and begin to decay as soon as they are activated. This property results in the medium's having a capacity defined by the speed with which parts can be generated and the speed with which they fade; if too many parts are imaged, the ones activated initially will no longer be available by the time the later ones have been imaged. This property was posited in order to explain my finding (Kosslyn, 1975) that images of objects in complex scenes were more degraded than images of objects in simple contexts.

2. The Data Structure

Format.   The surface image *depicts* an object or scene. The primary characteristic of representations in this format is that every portion of the representation must correspond to a portion of the object such that the relative interportion distances on the object are preserved by the distances among the corresponding portions of the representation (cf. Shepard, 1975). Three implications of this characterization are that (a) size, shape, orientation, and location information are not independent in this format—in order to depict one, values on the other dimensions must be specified; (b) any part of a depictive representation is a representation of a part of the represented object; and (c) the symbols used in a depiction (such as points in an array) cannot be arbitrarily assigned their roles in the representation (i.e., a given point must represent a given portion of the object or scene once the mapping function from image to object is established; on our view this function is innately determined and fixed by the human visual system). None of these properties are shared by discursive propositional (or "symbolic") representations. . . .

Thus, surface images consist of regions of activation in the visual buffer that correspond to regions of depicted objects, with distances among the regions on an object (as seen from a particular point of view) being preserved by distances among the regions used to represent it in the medium. Importantly, *distance* in the medium can be defined without reference to actual physical distance but merely in terms of the number of locations intervening between any two locations.

It is important to note that when terms such as *distance* and *orientation* are used to refer to surface images, they are being used in a technical way, referring to functional relations among regions in the visual buffer. Increased distance, for example, will be represented by increased numbers of locations in the visual buffer. Thus, although there is no physical distance or orientation in a depictive representation in the visual buffer, the corresponding states can sensibly be interpreted by using these terms. Contrary to what Pylyshyn (1981) asserts, we have not committed an erroneous "slip of scope" by talking about properties of the image rather than properties of the imaged object. In perception one can talk about properties of the "optical array" (such as those noticed by painters who use perspective) and of the objects themselves; whereas the size of an object does not change with distance, its "size" in the optical array (angle subtended) does. Similarly, in imagery we can speak of properties of the image itself by reference to the position, location, area occluded, and so on in the visual buffer (the analogue spatial medium). In this case it makes no difference what the image is an image of; the "subjective size" is independent of the actual size of the object. And in point of fact, a number of processes—such as scanning (Kosslyn, Ball, & Reiser, 1978)—depend on the subjective size, not on the actual size of objects.

Content. Images depict appearances of objects seen from a particular point of view (and hence are *viewer-centered*). . . . Images may represent the actual objects depicted, or images of objects may be used to represent other information (as occurs, for example, if one represents the relative intelligences of three people by imaging a line with three dots on it, a dot for each person). Note that the content is determined not just by the image itself but also by how the interpretive processes "read" the image. We are specifying the way a system of representations and processes operates in which the properties of the components are to some degree mutually interdependent.

Organization. Individual images may be organized into a single composite representing a detailed rendition of a single object or a scene. Because parts of images are theorized to be generated sequentially, and parts begin to fade as soon as they are imaged, different parts of the image will be at different levels of activation. Level of activation ("fade phase") will dictate an organization of the surface image because points at the same level will be grouped together according to the Gestalt Law of Common Fate.

The Underlying Deep Representations

Our findings suggest that there are two types of representations in long-term memory that can be used to generate images, which we call *literal* and *propositional*. Literal information consists of encodings of how something looked, not what it looked like; an image can be generated merely by activating an underlying literal encoding. Propositional information describes an object, scene, or aspect thereof and can be used to juxtapose depictive representations in different spatial relations in the visual buffer.

The Literal Encoding

1. The Medium

Formatting. The long-term memory medium does not function as if it were a co-ordinate space. Rather, it stores information in nonspatial units analogous to the files stored on a computer. In our computer simulation model, files store lists of coordinates specifying where points should be placed in the surface matrix to depict the represented object or objects (but we do not theorize that images are sets of dots or that underlying literal encodings are sets of coordinate pairs; these implementation details are not meant to be theory-relevant). The units are identified by name.

Accessibility.   The units are accessed by name; the extent of the represented object along a given dimension can be computed without first generating a surface image; and the representation can be sampled a portion at a time. [...]

2. The Data Structure

Format.   We have not as yet made any strong claims about the precise format of the underlying literal encodings.

Content.   The underlying literal encodings have the same content as the surface images they can produce.

Organization.   Every object is represented by a "skeletal encoding," which represents the global shape or central part. In addition to the skeletal encodings, objects may be represented by additional encodings of local regions or parts. [...] Multiple encodings are linked by propositional relations that specify where a part belongs relative to another part of the skeleton. (This property seemed necessary to explain the flexibility with which images may be reorganized and combined in accordance with a new description). ...

The Propositional Encodings

1. The Medium

Formatting.   The medium is structured to contain ordered lists of propositions, and the lists are named.

Accessibility.   Lists are accessed by name, and are searched serially, starting from the "top." (This assumption allowed us to explain the effects of association strength on property-verification times and led to some interesting predictions about image generation). ...

2. The Data Structure

Format.   The entries in these lists are in a propositional format. Propositions are abstract languagelike discursive representations, corresponding roughly to simple active declarative statements. [...]

Content.   Lists contain information about (a) parts an object has (included in order to explain how detailed images can be generated and in order to model question-answering processes); (b) the location of a part on an object (necessary in order to integrate separate encodings into a single image); (c) the size category of a part or object (necessary in order to adjust the size scale so that a part or object will be optimally resolved); (d) an abstract description of a part or object's appearance (required for the interpretive processes to identify the pattern of points depicting a part or object); (e) the name of the object's superordinate category (included for inference procedures used during question answering); and (f) the name of literal encodings of the appearance of the object (necessary in order to integrate multiple encodings into a single image).

Organization. Pointers in lists indicate which other list or lists to look up in sequence, resulting in lists being organized hierarchically or in any graph structure.

Processes

The imagery theory at present provides accounts for four classes of imagery processing: those involved in image generation, inspection, or transformation, and those that determine when imagery will be used spontaneously when people retrieve information from long-term memory. We have also begun to extend the theory to answer questions about how images are encoded as mnemonic devices and the role of imagery in reasoning. [. . .] In brief, the major processing components are as follows.

Image Generation

Image generation occurs when a surface image (which is quasi-pictorial) is formed in the visual buffer on the basis of information stored in long-term memory. Image generation is accomplished by four processing components, which we call PICTURE, FIND, PUT, and IMAGE. The PICTURE process converts information encoded in an underlying literal encoding into a surface image (in the model, it prints points in the cells of the surface matrix specified by the coordinate pairs stored in the underlying literal file). The PICTURE process can map the underlying representation into the visual buffer at different sizes and locations, depending on the values of the size and location parameters given it. (This property was motivated by our finding that people can voluntarily form images of objects at different sizes and locations). . . . The FIND process looks up a description of an object or part and searches the visual buffer for a spatial configuration that depicts that object or part. This process is used when multiple literal encodings are amalgamated to form a single image in the visual buffer; in this case the FIND process locates the "foundation part" where a new part should be added to previously imaged material. The PUT process performs a variety of functions necessary to image a part at the correct location on an image, including looking up the location relation in the list of propositions associated with an object and adjusting the size of the to-be-imaged part. The IMAGE process coordinates the other processing components and, in so doing, determines whether an image will be detailed (i.e., include parts stored in separate literal encodings) or undetailed (i.e., be constructed solely on the basis of the skeletal encoding). The IMAGE process is invoked by a command to form an image of a given object, either detailed or not, at some specified size and location (or at a default size and location). All of the processes used in image generation are production transformations except FIND, which is a comparison process.

Image Inspection

Image inspection occurs when one is asked a question such as, "Which is higher off the ground, the tip of a racing horse's tail or its rear knees?" and one "looks at" an image of the horse with the "mind's eye." The process of "looking" is explained by reference to a number of distinct processing components, notably LOOKFOR (a production transformation). The LOOK-FOR process retrieves the description of a sought part or object, looks up its size, employs the RESOLUTION process (a production transformation) to determine if the image is at the correct scale, adjusts the scale if need be by invoking the ZOOM or PAN process (alteration transformations), scans to the correct location, if necessary, by using the SCAN process (also an alteration transformation), and then employs FIND to search for the sought part. If the sought part is not found, the PUT process is used to elaborate the image further by generating images of parts that belong in the relevant region, and then FIND is used to inspect the image again. Note that because the FIND process is used in both image inspection and image generation, we should discover effects of the ease of executing this process in both kinds of tasks. And sure enough, less discriminable parts are not only more difficult to "see" during image inspection but are more difficult to locate as foundation parts (i.e., places where additional parts will be placed) during image construction. . . .

Image Transformation

According to our theory there are two classes of transformations and two modes of performing these transformations.

Classes of transformations: Field general and region bounded. Field-general (FG) transformations alter the entire contents of the medium, of the visual buffer, without respect to what is actually represented. Region-bound (RB) transformations first delineate a region in the visual buffer and then operate only within the confines of that region. Virtually every FG transform has an RB analogue. For example, "zooming in" is FG but "growth" is RB. According to our theory, the number of objects manipulated should affect processing time only for RB transformations, because each object is manipulated separately here (but not in the FG case). Pinker and Kosslyn (1978) present some data that support this distinction. . . .

Modes of transformation: Shifts and blinks. The bulk of the data on image transformations suggest that images are transformed incrementally, passing through intermediate points along a trajectory as the orientation, size, or location is altered. . . . This property is a hallmark of *shift* transformations, which operate by translating the locations of individual portions of the data structure to new locations in the visual buffer (and it remains an empirical question how to define *portion*). Because the system is inherently noisy . . . if portions are moved too far, they become too scrambled to be realigned by "cleanup routines." Thus, the limits of the cleanup routines force the processor to translate points in a series of relatively small increments. This results in greater transformations requiring more operations and hence more time. Note that this account hinges on the amount of distortion increasing as points are translated greater "distances"; if this were not true then portions could be "moved" the entire "distance" in one increment. The idea of increases in distortion with larger step sizes makes sense if the transformation process makes use of an analogue adder and multiplier in which the bigger the value, the larger the range of error. Further, because scanning is treated as another form of image transformation (in which a SCAN process shifts the data structure through the visual buffer, so that different parts fall in the center of the medium and hence are most sharply in focus), the same principles apply to it as to other forms of image transformation (such as rotation). The ZOOM and PAN processes dilate and contract the image, respectively, and the ROTATE process alters the orientation of the image. All "sizes" and "orientations" are, of course, defined relative to the visual buffer. SCAN, ZOOM, and PAN are field general and ROTATE is region bounded.

We did not initially plan on positing a second mode of image transformation. However, we were stuck with the possibility of *blink* transformations, given our prior claims that surface images can be generated (from the underlying deep representations) at optional sizes and locations and that images fade over time. Given these assumptions, we were forced to assume that people can transform images by letting an initial image fade and then generating another image of the object at a new size or location (and hence the contents or organization of an image can be changed via a production transformation as well as via an alteration transformation). In this case the transformation is discontinuous; images do not pass through intermediate states of transformation. The reason shift transformations are the default, we claim, is that they generally are less effortful (i.e., fewer and less complex operations are required to manipulate an existing image than to generate a new one from the underlying representations). But in the case of shift transformations, effort increases with the extent of the transformation (because more iterations are required)—but not so with blink transformations. Thus, there will come a point when it is "cheaper" to abandon the initial image and generate a new one. [...]

But how do people know which mode of transformation will be more efficient before using one? In scanning, for example, it is possible that people can decide which transformation to use on the basis of an initial estimate of the distance to be scanned, which can be computed in any number of ways, for example by using the underlying propositional representations of location (which we needed to posit in order to explain how parts can be placed at the correct location on an image during the generation process). In addition to explaining data, the distinction between a shift and a blink transformation has led us to make a number of predictions, some of which are not intuitively obvious (Kosslyn, 1980).

Spontaneous Use of Imagery in Fact Retrieval

Imagery is likely to be used in fact retrieval if the fact is about a visible property of an object a person has seen and it has not been considered frequently in the past. According to our theory, image encodings are accessed in parallel with propositional ones. Thus, the more overlearned the propositional information is (and hence the higher the entry on an object's propositional list, according to our theory), the more likely it is that a propositional encoding will be looked up or deduced before image processing is complete (i.e., before an image can be generated and inspected). Thus, imagery will often be used in retrieving information about objects learned "incidentally," as occurs when one retrieves from memory the number of windows in a room or considers the shape of a dog's ears. In addition, images—by the very nature of the format—make explicit information about relative shapes, relative positions of objects or parts thereof, and the appearances of objects and parts as seen from a particular point of view. Thus, when these sorts of information are required in order to make a judgment, imagery will often be used. However, because most objects are categorized, at least roughly, along these kinds of dimensions in a presumably propositional format (which may be well learned and hence likely to be accessed prior to image processing), imagery is most likely to be used when relatively subtle comparisons along these dimensions are required (and the to-be-compared objects fall in the same propositionally encoded category, preventing such category information from being used to make a judgment). For example, imagery should be used if one is asked to decide which is larger, a hamster or a mouse (both presumably are categorized as "small"), but should not be used in deciding which is larger, an elephant or a rabbit (which presumably fall in different categories). These principles are derived from results presented in Kosslyn, Murphy, Bemesderfer, and Feinstein (1977) [and] Kosslyn and Jolicoeur (1980).

[. . .]

The Tacit Knowledge Accounts

Pylyshyn (1979a, 1980, 1981) offers alternative accounts of the data from imagery experiments that rest on three major claims: First, the implicit task demands inherent in the instructions and the tasks themselves lead subjects to recreate as accurately as possible the perceptual events that would occur if they were actually observing the analogous situation. Second, subjects draw on their tacit knowledge of physics and the nature of the human perceptual system to decide how to behave in an experiment. Third, the subjects have the psychophysical skills necessary to produce the appropriate responses, for example by timing the interval between the onset of the stimulus and their pressing a key. There is one additional assumption that is critical for Pylyshyn's argument: The means by which tacit knowledge is invoked and used must not involve a spatial medium. That is, the issue at the heart of the differences in the alternative accounts centers on the existence of "depictive" representational structures in human memory, and thus a demonstration of the effects of tacit knowledge is relevant only if it can also be shown that this knowledge is not represented in a depictive form at some stage during the necessary processing. It would not be surprising if task demands and tacit knowledge sometimes affected imagery processing, given the long-standing claim that imagery can serve as a "dry run" simulation of the analogous physical events; if imagery were not able to be influenced by ideas, it would have only limited use in many forms of reasoning. . . .

Task Demands

Pylyshyn's argument depends on the notion that the instructions and the very nature of our [experimental] tasks always led subjects to imagine what would happen in the analogous real event. However, this assumption fails to explain a number of our findings. Consider [two] examples: First, Kosslyn, Jolicoeur, and Fliegel (described in Kosslyn, [Pinker, Smith & Shwartz,] 1979) performed a study in which subjects were asked to image an object and mentally "stare" at one end of it. Shortly thereafter, the name of a property was presented, and subjects were to judge the appropriateness of the property for the object as quickly as possible. It was stressed that the subject need not use the image in making the judgment. Interestingly, the distance from the point of focus to the property affected verification time only for properties that a separate group of subjects had rated to require imagery to verify (e.g., for a honeybee, "dark head"). No effects of distance were found for properties previously rated not to require imagery, even though the two kinds of items were randomly intermixed (and in fact the subjects had no idea that there were two different kinds of items). Pylyshyn's claim that some unspecified features of the task selectively evoke the "imagery habit" is merely an assertion of faith in the truth of his theory. This claim is tantamount to saying the results are explained by task demands because they must be explained by task demands—which is hardly a satisfactory account of the data.

Second, in another experiment, similar effects of the subjective size of parts of an image were obtained with first graders, fourth graders, and adults (Kosslyn, 1976b). Further, in this experiment subjects began by evaluating a set of items without being asked to use imagery. But after this verification task, the subjects were simply asked whether they had spontaneously tended to "look for" the named properties on images. When data from the first graders were analyzed in terms of which strategy was reported, I found effects of the size of properties only for those subjects who claimed to use imagery spontaneously. The result cannot be interpreted in terms of implicit demands in the instructions, since imagery was never mentioned at all.

[. . .]

Tacit Knowledge of Perception

According to the tacit knowledge position, the imagery data are produced when subjects consider (without making use of analogue images) what something would look like if they were actually seeing it as it typically appears. I have three responses to this claim.

First, this position fails to provide accounts for the discoveries that imagery and perception share certain very counterintuitive properties, properties that people have never had the opportunity to discover in perception and that many people do not initially believe and find surprising when convinced. These properties are only manifest in highly novel laboratory settings, which precludes the subject from developing tacit knowledge about them from prior experience. [. . .]

Second, the tacit knowledge view has considerable difficulty when properties of subjects' images differ from what they believe is typical about an object's appearance. For example, I found that the size . . . at which images are spontaneously generated is different from that at which the objects are reportedly commonly seen (Kosslyn, 1978). If subjects simply recall the typical perceived size of objects when asked to image them, this result makes no sense. If different factors constrain imaged size (such as the extent of an analogue spatial medium within which images are formed) and typical viewed size, the result is not surprising.

Third, it is not enough simply to say that we cannot imagine some things because we could never see them (such as a four-dimensional cube). We should try to specify what it is about the perceptual system and the world that limits the range of possible percepts and images. One possibility, not ruled out by any of Pylyshyn's arguments, is that an analogue medium (such as the visual buffer we posit or the medium that supports a "$2\frac{1}{2}$-D sketch" in the Marr & Nishihara, 1978, model of perceptual processing) is used in both perception and imagery, and properties of this medium are one source of constraints on both what we can see and what we can imagine.

Evaluating the Theories

Theories are often evaluated by applying a set of abstract criteria, such as precision, generality, falsifiability, parsimony, and heuristic value. Let us consider the tacit knowledge theory and compare it to the Kosslyn and Shwartz theory on each of these criteria.

Precision. The tacit knowledge position has not been worked out in sufficient detail to evaluate its precision. The only claim is that there is some set of representations and processes that allows one to "simulate" physical or perceptual events without using analogue representations. In fact, Pylyshyn has presented some general metaprinciples for a theory, not a theory itself. . . . it is worth noting that the tacit knowledge accounts may represent the ultimate in unspecified theories. These accounts seem virtually unconstrained and have no clearly specified parameters, free or otherwise.

The Kosslyn and Shwartz theory, in contrast, is precise enough to be implemented in a running computer simulation model. This general model produces specific models for numerous tasks . . . and these models in some cases account for quantitative relations in the data as well as the qualitative trends. Our theory is clearly more precise than Pylyshyn's.

Generality. To the extent that the tacit knowledge view rests on subjects' knowledge of or beliefs about how things typically happen in reality, the view has considerable generality. Our theory covers the domains of image generation, inspection, transformation, and the role of imagery in fact retrieval. Pylyshyn seems to intend his theory to cover almost all known imagery phenomena, and thus Pylyshyn's theory would appear the more general. But not all imagery phenomena simply mirror the analogous perceptual phenomena, and hence the tacit knowledge story can only go so far. That is, to the extent that imagery exhibits properties that differ from the analogous perceptual or physical ones, Pylyshyn's theory loses generality. [. . .]

Falsifiability. Pylyshyn (1981) claims that tacit knowledge "could obviously depend on *anything* the subject might tacitly know or believe concerning what usually happens in the corresponding perceptual situations" (p. 34). Moreover, "the exact domain of knowledge being appealed to can vary from case to case" (p. 34). Thus, one can never be sure one has controlled for the effects of tacit knowledge in an experiment, in Pylyshyn's view. In other words, whereas the demand characteristics account may be disprovable, Pylyshyn's account, resting on implicit task demands, is sheltered from such a rude fate.

Our theory makes numerous predictions, and these predictions are subject to empirical test (. . . Kosslyn, 1980, and Shwartz, 1979). Because we eschew altering the properties of our theory merely to explain data, if predictions are not borne out, the theory can be falsified. In short, our theory is clearly more "vulnerable," more easily falsified, than Pylyshyn's.

Parsimony. Parsimony is not a property that is inherent in a theory in and of itself. . . . Thus, one must compare two theories and decide which is the more parsimonious. Pylyshyn's theory appears more parsimonious than ours, but this is a consequence of his not filling in any details. Only when the tacit knowledge theory provides accounts at least as precise as ours can we then compare the two in terms of relative parsimony.

Heuristic value. The tacit knowledge account seems to have had little value thus far in producing new data. . . . In contrast, the Kosslyn and Shwartz theory has proven to have a high degree of heuristic value. It has led us to collect data on a whole raft of imagery phenomena, data that all parties must now explain. The fact that Pylyshyn's theory has not led to important discoveries could simply reflect its relatively recent vintage, however, and thus it is premature to pass judgment on it with regard to this criterion.

CONCLUSIONS

[...]
What, then, should we make of the apparent widespread dissatisfaction in the field that the so-called imagery–proposition debate has not yet been resolved? Some have even taken the view that the debate is in principle not capable of resolution (Anderson, 1978). Given the complexity of the issues involved, it seems overly optimistic to expect a speedy solution to such a knotty problem. It is a mistake to think that theoretical issues in other fields have typically been resolved much more quickly. [...] At the present juncture the best we can do is to continue to work out the empirical implications of the respective positions and to continue to collect new data that support one view while putting strain on others. . . . From any point of view, real progress has been forthcoming in a relatively short time.

REFERENCES

Anderson, J. R. (1978) Arguments concerning representations for mental imagery. *Psychological Review, 85*, 249–277.

Finke, R. A., & Kosslyn, S. M. (1980) Mental imagery acuity in the peripheral visual field. *Journal of Experimental Psychology: Human Perception and Performance, 6*, 129–139.

Hayes-Roth, F. (1979) Distinguishing theories of representation: A critique of Anderson's "Arguments concerning mental imagery." *Psychological Review, 86*, 376–392.

Keenan, J. M., & Moore, R. E. (1979) Memory for images of concealed objects: A reexamination of Neisser and Kerr. *Journal of Experimental Psychology: Human Learning and Memory, 5*, 374–385.

Kosslyn, S. M. (1975) Information representation in visual images. *Cognitive Psychology, 7*, 341–370.

Kosslyn, S. M. (1976a) Can imagery be distinguished from other forms of internal representation? Evidence from studies of information retrieval time. *Memory and Cognition, 4*, 291–297.

Kosslyn, S. M. (1976b) Using imagery to retrieve semantic information: A developmental study. *Child Development, 47*, 434–444.

Kosslyn, S. M. (1978) Measuring the visual angle of the mind's eye. *Cognitive Psychology, 10*, 356–389.

Kosslyn, S. M. (1980) *Image and Mind*. Cambridge, Mass.: Harvard University Press.

Kosslyn, S. M., Ball, T. M., & Reiser, B. J. (1978) Visual images preserve metric spatial information: Evidence from studies of image scanning. *Journal of Experimental Psychology: Human Perception and Performance, 4*, 47–60.

Kosslyn, S. M., & Jolicoeur, P. (1980) A theory-based approach to the study of individual differences in mental imagery. In R. E. Snow, P. A. Federico, & W. E. Montague (Eds.), *Aptitude, learning, and instruction: Cognitive processes analysis of learning and problem solving* (Vol. 2). Hillsdale, N.J.: Lawrence Erlbaum Associates.

Kosslyn, S. M., Murphy, G. L., Bemesderfer, M. E., & Feinstein, K. J. (1977) Category and continuum in mental comparisons. *Journal of Experimental Psychology: General, 106,* 341–375.

Kosslyn, S. M., Pinker, S., Smith, G. E., & Shwartz, S. P. (1979) On the demystification of mental imagery. *The Behavioral and Brain Sciences, 2,* 535–581.

Kosslyn, S. M., & Shwartz, S. P. (1977) A simulation of visual imagery. *Cognitive Science, 1,* 265–295.

Kosslyn, S. M., & Shwartz, S. P. (1978) Visual images as spatial representations in active memory. In E. M. Riseman & A. R. Hanson (Eds.), *Computer vision systems.* New York: Academic Press.

Marr, D., & Nishihara, H. K. (1978) Visual information processing: Artificial intelligence and the sensorium of sight. *Technological Review, 81,* 2–23.

Pinker, S., & Kosslyn, S. M. (1978) The representation and manipulation of three-dimensional space in mental images. *Journal of Mental Imagery, 2,* 69–84.

Pylyshyn, Z. W. (1979a) Imagery theory: Not mysterious—just wrong. *Behavioral and Brain Sciences, 2,* 561–563.

Pylyshyn, Z. W. (1979b) Validating computational models: A critique of Anderson's indeterminacy of representation claim. *Psychological Review, 86,* 383–394.

Pylyshyn, Z. W. (1980) Computation and cognition: Issues in the foundations of cognitive science. *Behavioral and Brain Sciences, 3,* 111–133.

Pylyshyn, Z. W. (1981) The imagery debate: Analogue media versus tacit knowledge. *Psychological Review, 87,* 16–45.

Shepard, R. N. (1975) Form, formation, and transformation of internal representations. In R. L. Solso (Ed.), *Information processing and cognition: The Loyola Symposium.* Hillsdale, N.J.: Lawrence Erlbaum Associates.

Shwartz, S. P. (1979) *Studies of mental image rotation: Implications for a computer simulation of visual imagery.* Unpublished doctoral dissertation, Johns Hopkins University.

4 Mental Models

P. N. Johnson-Laird

Explanation depends ... on understanding: if you do not understand something, you cannot explain it. It is easier to give criteria for what counts as understanding than to capture its essence—perhaps because it has no essence. Understanding certainly depends on knowledge and belief. If you know what causes a phenomenon, what results from it, how to influence, control, initiate, or prevent it, how it relates to other states of affairs or how it resembles them, how to predict its onset and course, what its internal or underlying 'structure' is, then to some extent you understand it. The psychological core of understanding, I shall assume, consists in your having a 'working model' of the phenomenon in your mind. If you understand inflation, a mathematical proof, the way a computer works, DNA or a divorce, then you have a mental representation that serves as a model of an entity in much the same way as, say, a clock functions as a model of the earth's rotation.

The first modern formulation of this thesis is to be found in Kenneth Craik's remarkably prescient book, *The Nature of Explanation*, published in 1943. In that work, Craik proposed that human beings are processors of information. He wrote that they make use of three distinct processes in reasoning:

1. A 'translation' of some external process into an internal representation in terms of words, numbers, or other symbols.
2. The derivation of other symbols from them by some sort of inferential process.
3. A 'retranslation' of these symbols into actions, or at least a recogni-

tion of the correspondence between these symbols and external events, as in realizing that a prediction is fulfilled.

Although the digital computer had yet to be invented, Craik anticipated the analogy between it and the brain. After describing the three components of reasoning, he wrote:

> One other point is clear; this process of reasoning has produced a final result similar to that which might have been reached by causing the actual physical processes to occur (e.g. building the bridge haphazard and measuring its strength or compounding certain chemicals and seeing what happened); but it is also clear that this is not what has happened; the man's mind does not contain a material bridge or the required chemicals. Surely, however, this process of prediction is not unique to minds, though no doubt it is hard to imitate the flexibility and versatility of mental prediction. A calculating machine, an anti-aircraft 'predictor', and Kelvin's tidal predictor all show the same ability. In all these latter cases, the physical process which it is desired to predict is imitated by some mechanical device or model which is cheaper, or quicker, or more convenient in operation. Here we have a very close parallel to our three stages of reasoning—the 'translation' of the external processes into their representatives (positions of gears, etc.) in the model; the arrival at other positions of gears, etc., by mechanical processes in the instrument; and finally, the retranslation of these into physical processes of the original type.
>
> By a model we thus mean any physical or chemical system which has a similar relation-structure to that of the processes it imitates. By 'relation-structure' I do not mean some obscure non-physical entity which attends the model, but the fact that it is a physical working model which works in the same way as the processes it parallels, in the aspects under consideration at any moment. . . .
>
> My hypothesis then is that thought models, or parallels, reality—that its essential feature is not 'the mind', 'the self', 'sense-data', nor propositions but symbolism, and that this symbolism is largely of the same kind as that which is familiar to us in mechanical devices which aid thought and calculation. . . .
>
> If the organism carries a 'small-scale model' of external reality and of its own possible actions within its head, it is able to try out various alternatives, conclude which is the best of them, react to future situations before they arise, utilize the knowledge of past events in dealing with the present and future, and in every way to react in a much fuller, safer, and more competent manner to the emergencies which face it.

Like clocks, small-scale models of reality need neither be wholly accurate nor correspond completely with what they model in order to be useful. Your model of a television set may contain only the idea of a box that displays moving pictures with accompanying sound. Alternatively, it may embody the notion of a cathode-ray tube firing electrons at a screen, with the beam scanning across the screen in a raster controlled by a varying electro-magnetic field, and so on. You may conceive of an electron as nothing more than a negatively charged particle whose trajectory is influenced by a magnetic field. There may be no need for you to have any deeper understanding, because you can grasp the way the set works without having to reduce everything to its fundamental principles. A person who repairs television sets is likely to have a more comprehensive model of them than someone who can only operate one. A circuit designer is likely to have a still richer model. Yet even the designer may not need to understand the full ramifications of quantum electro-dynamics—which is just as well, because nobody completely understands them.

There are no complete mental models for any empirical phenomena. What must be emphasized, however, is that one does not necessarily increase the usefulness of a model by adding information to it beyond a certain level. If a television set is represented as containing a beam of electrons that are magnetically deflected across the screen, then this component of the representation serves an explanatory function. It accounts, for example, for the distortion of the picture that occurs when a magnet is held near the screen. Other components of the model may serve no such function. One imagines, say, each electron as deflected by a magnetic field much as a ball-bearing is diverted from its course by a magnet, but there is no representation of the nature of magnetism: the 'picture' is just a picture, which simulates reality rather than models its underlying principles. A model has, in Craik's phrase, a similar 'relation-structure' to the process it models, and hence it can be useful explanatorily; a simulation merely mimics the phenomenon without relying on a similar underlying relation-structure. Many of the models in people's minds are little more than high-grade simulations, but they are none the less useful provided that the picture is accurate; all representations of physical phenomena necessarily contain an element of simulation.

Mental Models and Criteria for Explanations

. . . I have made a claim about mental representations that applies at two distinct levels. At the first level, human beings understand the world by constructing working models of it in their minds. Since these models are incomplete, they are simpler than the entities they represent. In conse-quence, models contain elements that are merely imitations of reality— there is no working model of how their counterparts in the world operate, but only procedures that mimic their behaviour. When men invented numbers, they neither grasped, nor needed to grasp, all of their mathema-tical properties. A limited model of arithmetic is useful, which is fortunate because there can be no consistent formal system that captures all of it. Likewise, to take a more mundane example, many mental representations are kinematic or dynamic; they take place in time, yet no one has much of an explanatory model of time itself. Models either make a direct use of time, or else they simulate it. We use or mimic time; we do not have an explanation of it; we merely work with it so well that we think we understand it.

At the second level, since cognitive scientists aim to understand the human mind, they, too, must construct a working model. It happens to be of a device for constructing working models. Like other models, however, its utility is not improved by embodying more than a certain amount of knowledge. The crucial aspect of mental processes is their functional organization, and hence a theoretical model of the mind need concern only such matters. But the mere possession of a model guarantees very little. It may mean no more than that the model mimics mental phenomena, and hence that a psychological theory based on it merely describes those phenomena accurately. [...] A psychological theory of mental models should also be—in Chomsky's (1965) terms—explanatorily adequate. It must lay down explicit constraints on the class of possible mental models: it must list the elements and operations from which mental models can be composed. Hence such a theory would provide a potential, though abstract, account of how children acquire mental models. Some mental models may be highly artificial and acquired only by dint of deliberate cultural training, e.g., models governing domains of pure mathematics. Other models, however, are presumably natural, acquired without explicit instruction, and used by everyone in the course of such universal processes as inference and language comprehension. To say what makes certain models natural and others artificial, one indeed needs an explanatorily adequate theory. [...]

IMAGES, PROPOSITIONS, AND MODELS

In the first decade of this century, there was a long controversy over the existence of 'imageless thoughts'—mental processes that have no sensory or imaginal content. It lasted until psychologists became so disenchanted with mentalistic notions that they abandoned them for forty years in pursuit of Behavior. With the revival of interest in imagery, a new controversy has arisen over whether images have any explanatory value in psychological theorizing. Perhaps it should be dubbed the 'thoughtless imagery' controversy because, like its inglorious predecessor, it threatens to be prolonged and infertile. I shall propose a resolution of the controversy during the course of this chapter, though I suspect that both parties to the dispute may find my arguments unacceptable—an eventuality that will reinforce my conviction that they owe us some account of how the issue between them could be settled in principle. My thesis is that different types of representation are logically distinguishable at some level of analysis, and, moreover, that they exist as different options for encoding information. In particular, I shall argue that there are at least three major kinds of representation—mental models, propositional representations, and images. I shall outline a theory that relates mental models both to propositional representations and to images, which are treated as a special class of models. However, my primary purpose in entering the debate is to draw a clear contrast between mental models and propositional representations interpreted in a more traditional and narrower sense than has become customary among some cognitive scientists. There are empirical methods, as I shall show, for determining which form of representation subjects make use of on a given occasion.

Images and Symbolic Representations

No one doubts the conscious phenomena of imagery. Many people report that they can use their imaginations to form a visual image of an object or scene. Such images can be mentally rotated at a rate of about sixty degrees per second (Shepard, 1978); they can be suppressed by concurrent visual tasks (Brooks, 1967); they can be used to represent spatial information and to solve problems (Kosslyn, 1980); they are a useful aid to memory (Paivio, 1971; Bower, 1972). What is problematical is the ultimate nature of images as mental representations. They cannot be pictures-in-the-mind, because a picture requires a homunculus to perceive it, and this requirement leads to the slippery slope of an infinite regress—big homunculi need little homunculi to perceive their pictures-in-the-mind, and so on *ad infinitum*. What images really are is a matter that divides psychologists into two opposing schools of thought.

First, there are those such as Paivio, Shepard, and Kosslyn, who argue that images are a distinct sort of mental representation. There is a consensus among these 'imagist' psychologists on four points:

1. The mental processes underlying the experience of an image are similar to those underlying the perception of an object or picture.

2. An image is a coherent and integrated representation of a scene or object from a particular viewpoint in which each perceptible element occurs only once with all such elements being simultaneously available and open to a perception-like process of scanning.

3. An image is amenable to apparently continuous mental transformations, such as rotations or expansions, in which intermediate states

correspond to intermediate states (or views) of an actual object undergoing the corresponding physical transformation. Hence, a small change in the image corresponds to a small change (of view) of the object.

4. Images *represent* objects. They are analogical in that structural relations between their parts correspond to the perceptible relations between the parts of the objects represented.

Second, there are those who argue that images are epiphenomenal and that there is only a single underlying form of mental representation, strings of symbols that correspond to propositions (e.g., Baylor, 1971; Pylyshyn, 1973; Palmer, 1975). These 'propositionalist' theorists are also agreed on four points:

1. The mental processes leading to the strings of symbols that correspond to an image are similar to those underlying the perception of an object or picture.

2. The same element or part of an object may be referred to by many of the different propositions that constitute the description of the object. Such a description may be represented as a set of expressions in a logical calculus (with access to a general procedure for making inferences), or it may be represented in a semantic network.

3. A propositional representation is discrete and digital, but it can represent continuous processes by small successive increments of variables, such as the angle of an object's major axis to the frame of reference. Hence, a small change in the representation will correspond to a small change in the appearance of the object.

4. Propositions are true or false of objects. They are abstract in that they do not directly correspond to either words or pictures. Their structure is *not* analogous to the structure of the objects they represent.

In short, the critics of imagery allow that an image can be constructed from its underlying propositional representation, but assert that the image is epiphenomenal—it does not introduce any new information, but merely makes the stored information easier to manipulate.

It is evident that many of the claims about images and propositional representations are very similar. Their underlying processes can be akin to the perception of an object or picture. They can form coherent and integrated representations. A small change in them can correspond to a small change in the appearance of an object. The only major divergence is that images are said to represent objects, whereas propositions are said to be true or false of them. The overall similarity between the two formats has led some commentators to conclude that the controversy is neither fundamental nor resolvable (see Norman and Rumelhart, 1975).

It is, of course, a universal truth in any science that there can always be more than one theory that explains the data: no observations can ever establish definitely that a single unique theory is the correct one. [...]

Anderson's Mimicry Theorem

John Anderson (1978) has argued that it is impossible to evaluate any claim for a particular sort of mental representation unless the *processes* that operate on this representation are specified in the theory. He bases this claim on a theorem that he proves: given any theory of mental representations and processes, it is always possible to construct an alternative theory making use of a different sort of representation that behaves in an entirely equivalent way. For instance, a theory based on the rotation of images can be mimicked by one based on propositional representations. In fact 'mimicry' is not the right word to describe the manoeuvre in Anderson's proof: rather the second theory invades the first and takes it over like a virus taking over an organism's machinery for producing DNA. This embedding of one theory within another can be illustrated by a specific example.

Let us suppose that according to one theory stimuli are encoded as images that can be mentally rotated by certain specified processes, and that according to another, stimuli are encoded as sets of propositions. The imaginal theory is embedded within the propositional theory by postulating that a stimulus is subject to the following sequence of operations:

1. The stimulus is encoded as a set of propositions.
2. The inverse of the function that encodes stimuli as sets of propositions is applied to the propositional representations in order to recover the original stimulus, or, more accurately, a representation of its sensory image.
3. The perceptual encoding function of the imaginal theory is applied to this representation in order to obtain an image of the stimulus.
4. The image is rotated according to the process employed by the imaginal theory.
5. The inverse of the function encoding the stimulus as an image is applied to the rotated image in order to obtain a representation of the corresponding sensory stimulus.
6. The perceptual encoding function of the propositional theory is applied to the rotated sensory stimulus to recover the corresponding set of propositions.

This embedding of an imaginal theory within a propositional theory is summarized in [Fig. 4.1]. A decision about whether the resulting propositions correspond to the comparison stimulus presented by the experi-

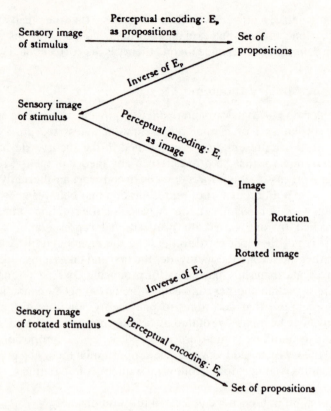

FIG. 4.1   The embedding of an imaginal theory within a propositional
theory according to Anderson's procedure.

menter can be made by using exactly the same sort of stratagem.

The feasibility of embedding one theory within another in this way
requires that the various functions are computable. Because the process of
perception is almost certainly a many-to-one mapping, i.e., a function that
delivers the same representation for many stimuli that are physically
different, there is no guarantee that the inverse of the function will yield
the original sensory image of the stimulus. Hence, the theorem also
requires the existence of a one-to-one mapping between the respective
representations of the two theories. This assumption ensures that the
inverse of the propositional encoding can yield any of the differing stimuli
that might have given rise to the original representation, and it will not
matter which of them is selected, because they will all be treated as
equivalent by the imaginal theory too. If one theory encodes stimuli into
classes that do not correspond one-to-one with the encodings of the other
theory, then of course the whole system of mappings breaks down and the

theorem ceases to hold. Hence, considerable care needs to be taken in drawing conclusions on the basis of the theorem. . . .

The fact that one theory can mimic another by taking it over wholesale is plainly trivial. What is of interest is the possibility of a more direct method of mimicry that does not depend on embedding one theory within another. However, there is no guarantee that such a method can always be found, and Anderson makes only the modest claim: 'it seems we can usually construct [the required operation] more simply than its formally guaranteed specification'. The theorem certainly does not establish that the controversy between imagists and propositionalists is futile. It can be resolved; but not perhaps in the way intended by the controversialists.

How to Distinguish Between Mental Models and Propositional Representations

Suppose you are lost in the maze at Hampton Court Palace. You come to a turning and for a moment you are not sure which way to go. You recognize that you have been at this point before, and, in your imagination, you turn right, proceed down an alley, and are then confronted by a dead end. And so this time around, you decide to turn left. What you did, I assume, was to reconstruct a route through the maze on the basis of a mental model of it. You may hardly have experienced any imagery at all; or you may have had a succession of vivid images like a snippet from an imaginary film that culminates in the leafy cul-de-sac. In either case, there was nothing 'propositional', in the philosophical sense of the word, about your reasoning: there was no process based on the representation of verbal propositions. You navigated your way through your model of the maze much as a rat in a psychological laboratory might have done. However, you might have made your decision in a very different way. You might have recalled that the way to get out of the maze is to keep turning left at every available opportunity, and, since you were faced with such an opportunity, you might accordingly have elected to turn left. This method makes use of a mental representation of verbal propositions.

The two methods illustrate the contrast between exploiting a mental model (perhaps with accompanying imagery) and making use of a propositional representation. [. . .]

To understand a proposition is to know what the world would be like for it to be true. Since a proposition is true or false of the state of affairs to which it refers, a propositional representation is the representation of a function from states of affairs to truth values. And the most general way to represent a function is to express it in a language. This mental language must have a vocabulary, a grammar, and a semantics (cf. Kintsch, 1974; Fodor, 1975). [. . .]

The crucial problem for the mental language is the nature of its semantics. Propositions can refer to the world. [...] Propositions can also refer to imaginary or hypothetical worlds. One proposition may be false of such a world given that others are true of it. Human beings can evidently construct mental models by acts of imagination and can relate propositions to such models. A principal assumption of the theory which I am developing is that the semantics of the mental language maps propositional representations into mental models of real or imaginary worlds: *propositional representations are interpreted with respect to mental models.* In due course, I shall describe how this process of interpretation is carried out, but here I want to pursue the contrast between the different forms of representation, and in particular some potential differences between their structure and content.

The Structure and Content of Mental Representations

Unlike a propositional representation, a mental model does not have an arbitrarily chosen syntactic structure, but one that plays a direct representational role since it is analogous to the structure of the corresponding state of affairs in the world—as we perceive or conceive it. However, the analogical structure of mental models can vary considerably. Models of quantified assertions may introduce only a minimal degree of analogical structure, such as the use of separate elements to stand for individuals. Alternatively, models of spatial layouts such as a maze may be two- or three-dimensional; they may be dynamic and represent a sequence of events; they may take on an even higher number of dimensions in the case of certain gifted individuals. One advantage of their dimensional structure is that they can be constructed, and manipulated, in ways that can be controlled by dimensional variables. But a propositional representation, as Simon (1972) pointed out, can be scanned only in those directions that have been encoded in the representation. Simon also drew attention to the fact that people who know perfectly well how to play noughts-and-crosses [...] are unable to transfer their tactical skill to number scrabble, a game that is isomorphic to noughts-and-crosses. Just as they can scan an external noughts-and-crosses array, so they can scan its internal representation, but that process is irrelevant to the game of number scrabble.

There is plainly a relation between images and mental models, and I shall assume that images correspond to *views* of models: as a result either of perception or imagination, they represent the perceptible features of the corresponding real-world objects. In imagining; say, a rotating object, the underlying mental model of the object is used to recover a representation of its surfaces, reflectances, and so forth—what the late David Marr (1982), in referring to the process of perception, called the '$2\frac{1}{2}$-D sketch'.

Mental rotations in depth appear to be just as easy as those in the picture plane. Hence, as Hinton (1979) argues, when you form an image, you must compute the projective relations from the model to the $2\frac{1}{2}$-D sketch: a model underlies an image.

A characteristic difference in the *contents* of mental models, images, and propositional representations, concerns their specificity. Models, like images, are highly specific—a characteristic which has often drawn comment from philosophers. You cannot form an image of *a triangle in general*, but only of a specific triangle. Hence, if you reason on the basis of a model or image, you must take pains to ensure that your conclusion goes beyond the specific instance you considered. [. . .] Although a model must be specific, it does not follow that it cannot be used to represent a general class of entities. The interpretation of a specific model depends upon a variety of interpretive processes, and they may treat the model as no more than a representative sample from a larger set. Once again, the *function* of the model cannot be ignored: a specification of structure and content must always be supplemented by an account of the processes using the model if one is to formulate what the model represents. However, since language is inherently vague, the content of models invariably embodies some arbitrary assumptions, whereas there is no such need in the construction of propositional representations.

Pylyshyn (1973), echoing many philosophers from Hume onwards, has pointed out a major difference between images and propositional representations:

> It would be quite permissible . . . to have a [propositional] mental representation of two objects with a relation between them such as 'besides'. Such a representation need not contain a more specific spatial relation such as 'to the left of' or 'to the right of'. It would seem an unreasonable use of the word 'image' to speak of an image of two objects side by side, without the relation between them being either 'to the left of' or 'to the right of'.

This distinction is useful because it has empirical consequences: a propositional representation should be able to handle both determinate and indeterminate spatial relations with equal ease, whereas a mental model should handle determinate relations more readily than indeterminate ones. The only way to form a model of one object beside another that is neutral with respect to left and right would be to construct a set of such analogue representations corresponding to the various possibilities. A picture may be worth a thousand words, but a proposition is worth an infinity of pictures.

Since models, images, and propositional representations are functionally and structurally distinguishable from one another, it follows that there is indeed a useful theoretical distinction between different kinds of representations.

Evidence for Propositional Representations and Mental Models

Suppose that you are reading Conan Doyle's (1905) well-known story, 'Charles Augustus Milverton', which recounts how Sherlock Holmes and Dr Watson set out to burgle the house of the eponymous blackmailer, 'the worst man in London', and you come upon the following passage:

> With our black silk face-coverings, which turned us into two of the most truculent figures in London, we stole up to the silent, gloomy house. A sort of tiled veranda extended along one side of it, lined by several windows and two doors.
> 'That's his bedroom,' Holmes whispered. 'This door opens straight into the study. It would suit us best, but it is bolted as well as locked, and we should make too much noise getting in. Come round here. There's a greenhouse which opens into the drawing room.'
> The place was locked, but Holmes removed a circle of glass and turned the key from the inside. An instant afterwards he had closed the door behind us, and we had become felons in the eyes of the law. The thick, warm air of the conservatory and the rich, choking fragrance of exotic plants took us by the throat. He seized my hand in the darkness and led me swiftly past banks of shrubs which brushed against our faces. Holmes had remarkable powers, carefully cultivated, of seeing in the dark. [!] Still holding my hand in one of his, he opened a door, and I was vaguely conscious that we had entered a large room in which a cigar had been smoked not long before. He felt his way among the furniture, opened another door, and closed it behind us. Putting out my hand I felt several coats hanging from the wall, and I understood that I was in a passage. We passed along it, and Holmes very gently opened a door upon the right-hand side. Something rushed out at us and my heart sprang into my mouth, but I could have laughed when I realized that it was the cat. A fire was burning in this new room, and again the air was heavy with tobacco smoke. Holmes entered on tiptoe, waited for me to follow, and then very gently closed the door. We were in Milverton's study, and a portière at the farther side showed the entrance to his bedroom.
> It was a good fire, and the room was illuminated by it. Near the door I saw the gleam of an electric switch, but it was unnecessary, even if it had been safe, to turn it on. At one side of the fireplace was a heavy curtain which covered the bay window we had seen from outside. On the other side was the door which communicated with the veranda. A desk stood in the centre, with a turning-chair of shining red leather. Opposite was a large bookcase, with a marble bust of Athene on the top. In the corner, between the bookcase and the wall, there stood a tall, green safe, the firelight flashing back from the polished brass knobs upon its face.

You may have noticed that some of the details stand out in considerable clarity—the cat that frightened Dr Watson, the cigar smoke, the shining red chair, and the firelight glinting off the knobs of the safe. You may also have observed that Holmes does *not* make one of his celebrated deductions. In fact, the omission is deliberate on my part because I want you to try to make a deduction. Here is a simple plan of the house with the veranda running down one side of it:

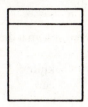

The question is: which way did Holmes and Watson make their way along the veranda—from right to left, or from left to right?

About one out of every hundred people to whom I have read this passage ... can spontaneously give the right answer for the right reason. Most people's representations are too partial to provide the necessary information. Yet, if you read the passage again with the aim of solving this riddle, you will probably be able to construct a sufficiently complete mental model to answer it easily. (The solution. for those who are still perplexed, can be found at the end of the chapter.) There thus appear to be different levels of comprehension. It might be argued that the difference is merely one of detail—the extent to which you furnish your representation of the house with all the paraphernalia mentioned in the story—but the phenomena are also compatible with a difference in kind. What you have to do in order to make the required inference is to build up a mental model of the spatial layout. The fact that you are unlikely to be able to draw the correct conclusion unless you are forewarned lends support to the idea that discourse can be represented either in a propositional form close to the linguistic structure of the discourse, or in a mental model that is closer to a representation of a state of affairs—in this case the plan of a house—than to a set of sentences.

Kannan Mani and I have investigated the hypothesis about levels of representations in a series of experiments, and I shall describe just one of them (see Mani and Johnson-Laird, 1982). Our basic idea was that subjects would tend to form a mental model of a spatially determinate description, but would not do so for an indeterminate description consistent with more than one spatial layout—especially if their task was to check whether the description corresponded to a diagram. They might easily form the 'wrong' model, that is, one that did not match the diagram, though it was equally consistent with the indeterminate description.

The subjects heard a series of spatial descriptions, such as:

The spoon is to the left of the knife.
The plate is to the right of the knife.
The fork is in front of the spoon.
The cup is in front of the knife.

After each description, they were shown a diagram such as:

spoon   knife   plate
fork   cup

and they had to decide whether the diagram was consistent or inconsistent with the description. (If you think of the diagram as depicting the arrangement of the objects on a table top, then obviously this example is consistent with the description.) Half the descriptions that the subjects received were determinate, as in this case, and half were spatially indeterminate. The indeterminate descriptions were constructed merely by changing the last word in the second sentence:

The spoon is to the left of the knife.
The plate is to the right of the spoon.
The fork is in front of the spoon.
The cup is in front of the knife.

This description is consistent with two radically different diagrams:

spoon   knife   plate   spoon   plate   knife
fork   cup   fork   cup

After the subjects had judged the descriptions and diagrams, they were given an unexpected test of their memory for the descriptions. On each trial, they had to rank four alternatives in terms of their resemblance to the original description: the original description, an inferrable description, and two 'foils' with a different meaning. The inferrable description for the example contained the sentence:

The fork is to the left of the cup

in place of the sentence interrelating the spoon and the knife. The description is therefore not a paraphrase of the original, but it can be inferred from the layout corresponding to the original description in the case of both the determinate and the indeterminate descriptions. This inference is only likely to be made if the subjects construct mental models, and, moreover, ones that are symmetrical. If they were to construct an asymmetrical model of, say, the determinate description above:

spoon   knife   plate
fork

cup

then they might well fail to consider that the fork is to the left of the cup.

The subjects remembered the gist of the determinate descriptions very much better than that of the indeterminate descriptions. The percentage of trials on which they ranked the original and the inferrable descriptions prior to the confusion items was 88% for the determinate descriptions, but only 58% for the indeterminate descriptions. All twenty of the subjects conformed to this trend, and there was no effect of whether or not on a particular trial a diagram had been consistent with a description. However, the percentages of trials on which the original description was ranked higher than the inferrable description was 68% for the determinate descriptions, but 88% for the indeterminate descriptions. This predicted difference was also highly reliable.

Evidently, subjects tend to remember the gist of determinate descriptions better than that of indeterminate descriptions, but they tend to remember the verbatim detail of indeterminate descriptions better than that of determinate descriptions. This 'cross-over' effect is impossible to explain without postulating at least two sorts of mental representation. A plausible account of the pattern of results is indeed that subjects construct a mental model of the determinate descriptions, but abandon such a representation in favour of a superficial propositional one as soon as they encounter an indeterminacy in a description. Models are easier to remember than propositions, perhaps because they are more structured and elaborated (cf. Craik and Tulving, 1975) and require a greater amount of processing to construct (cf. Johnson-Laird and Bethell-Fox, 1978). But models encode little or nothing of the linguistic form of the sentences on which they are based, and subjects accordingly confuse inferrable descriptions with the originals. Propositional representations are relatively hard to remember, but they do encode the linguistic form of sentences. Hence, when they are remembered, the subjects are likely to make a better than chance recognition of verbatim content. The controversy is resolved: there is an empirical distinction between mental models and propositional representations.

The Representation of Indeterminate Discourse

Indeterminate descriptions are not necessarily represented in a propositional form on every occasion. Our experiments deliberately employed a task that was likely to favour a propositional representation whenever an indeterminacy occurred. However, there are other potential ways of coping with indeterminate discourse. Consider, for example, the following typical description of a room:

> I have a very small bedroom with a window overlooking the heath. There is a single bed against the wall and opposite it a gas fire with a gas ring for boiling a kettle. The room is so small that I sit on the bed to cook. The only other furniture in the room is a bookcase on one side of the gas fire next to the window—it's got all my books on it and my portable radio—and a wardrobe. It stands against the wall just near to the door, which opens almost directly onto the head of my bed,

The text creates a reasonably clear impression of the room, but is radically indeterminate in that it is consistent with a potentially infinite number of alternative rooms. The problem is not merely a question of the dimensions of the room and furniture: the actual layout itself is not described in a way that permits a unique reconstruction of the spatial relations between the objects. How, then, is such a passage mentally represented? A number of theorists have struggled with this problem, which was first brought home to me on reading Miller's (1979) discussion of it. As he points out, one can analyse the interpretation of discourse by assuming that each successive sentence reduces the number of alternative possibilities that are compatible with the passage. In the present framework of mental models, however, there are at least four different strategies for coping with indeterminacy.

First, you can simply stop constructing a model as soon as you detect an indeterminacy. In fact, you are only likely to detect the indeterminacy if you *are* trying to construct a model. This strategy was evidently adopted by most of the subjects in our experiments. Its likely cost is that memory for the passage will be poor.

Second, you can try to cope with indeterminacy by constructing alternative models representing the different possibilities. Unfortunately, a descriptive passage such as the example above is likely to require a combinatorially explosive number of alternatives, and, as our studies of reasoning showed, people find it difficult to keep in mind even a few alternatives. Hence, this strategy is unlikely to be employed except when the numbers are very small.

Third, you may be able to represent the indeterminacy within a mental model by introducing a propositional-like element of notation. [...]

Kosslyn (1980) has also argued for a similar admixture of image like and propositional-like elements. Unfortunately, it is difficult to represent spatial indeterminacy within a dimensional model. For example, the indeterminate description:

A is on the left of B, which is to the right of C

could receive a mental representation equivalent to:

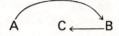

where the arrows represent the relations expressed explicitly in the assertion. But such a format makes no essential use of the analogical properties of the model. That is to say, the representation consists of one particular model of the description supplemented by a propositional representation of the description: the latter renders the former redundant. [. . .] If, then, you were to make use of such a system to represent the description of the room in the example above, there would be so many propositional notations that it would be pointless to embed them within a dimensional framework.

Fourth, you may plump for one specific model of the discourse, perhaps on the basis of an implicit inference. If this interpretation does not conflict with the subsequent discourse, there is clearly no problem. If there is such a conflict, however, you can attempt to reconstruct an appropriate alternative model. This procedure is a demanding one, and obviously depends on access to the previous discourse. You may be forced to abandon the whole enterprise in some confusion. One observes anecdotally both of these outcomes when travellers receive detailed instructions about a route; and Stenning (1981) has found that subjects do tend to make specific assumptions about, say, the direction of a turn when it is not specified explicitly in the description of a route.

There can be little doubt that the radical reconstruction of a mental model is seldom called for in everyday discourse, as Grice (1975) has emphasized, there is a convention that speakers tend to abide by: they do not deliberately mislead their listeners. In other words, if you construct a mental model on the basis of my discourse, then I am likely to order the information in my description so as to prevent you from going astray. I owe you an account that you can represent in a single model without running into a conflict with information that I only subsequently divulge. Of course, no speaker is likely to be able to live up to this principle all the time but nevertheless it is followed on most occasions. A mental model is in essence a representative sample from the set of possible models satisfying the description.

Conclusions

This chapter has presented a case for the existence of at least three types of mental representation: propositional representations which are strings of symbols that correspond to natural language, mental models which are structural analogues of the world, and images which are the perceptual correlates of models from a particular point of view. The distinction is a high-level one; doubtless, everything can be reduced to a uniform code in the language of the brain just as the data structures of a high-level programming language can be reduced to patterns of bits in the machine code of a computer. . . .

Why should the mind make use of these various media? [. . .] Mental models provide a basis for representing premises, and their manipulation makes it possible to reason without logic. The search for alternative interpretations, however, demands an independent representation of the premises, a representation that is propositional in form. [. . .]

In this chapter, I have assumed that descriptions are initially represented propositionally, i.e., by expressions in a mental language, and that the semantics of the mental language maps these propositional representations into mental models.

REFERENCES

Anderson, J. R. (1978) Arguments concerning representations for mental imagery. *Psychological Review, 85*, 249–77.

Baylor, G. W. (1971) Programs and protocol analysis on a mental imagery task. *First International Joint Conference on Artificial Intelligence*, [not published].

Bower, G. H. (1972) Mental imagery and associative learning. In L. Gregg (Ed.), *Cognition in learning and memory*. New York: Wiley.

Brooks, L. (1967) The suppression of visualization by reading. *Quarterly Journal of Experimental Psychology, 19*, 280–99.

Chomsky, N. (1965) *Aspects of the theory of syntax*. Cambridge, Mass.: MIT Press.

Conan Doyle, Sir Arthur (1905) *The return of Sherlock Holmes*. London: Murray.

Craik, F. I. M., & Tulving, E. (1975) Depth of processing and the retention of words in episodic memory, *Journal of Experimental Psychology: General, 104*, 268–94.

Craik, K. (1943) *The nature of explanation*. Cambridge: Cambridge University Press.

Fodor, J. A. (1975) *The language of thought*. Hassocks, Sussex: Harvester Press.

Grice, P. (1975) Logic and conversation. In P. Cole, & J. L. Morgan (Eds.), *Studies in syntax, vol. 3: Speech acts*. New York: Academic Press.

The solution to the riddle about Holmes and Watson is that they must have walked along the veranda from right to left. After they broke into the house round the corner from one end of the veranda, they passed through various rooms and along a corridor, and then they turned *right* into Milverton's study and saw the door that communicated with the veranda.

Hinton, G. (1979) Imagery with arrays. Commentary on S. M. Kosslyn, S. Pinker, G. E. Smith and S. P. Shwartz, "On the demystification of mental imagery". *The Behavioural and Brain Sciences, 2*, 555–6.

Johnson-Laird, P. N., & Bethell-Fox, C. (1978) Memory for questions and amount of processing. *Memory and Cognition, 6*, 496–501.

Kintsch, W. (1974) *The representation of meaning in memory*. Hillsdale, N.J.: Lawrence Erlbaum Associates.

Kosslyn, S. M. (1980) *Images and mind*. Cambridge, Mass: Harvard University Press.

Mani, K., & Johnson-Laird, P. N. (1982) The mental representation of spatial descriptions. *Memory and Cognition, 10*, 181–7.

Marr, D. (1982) *Vision: A computational investigation in the human representation of visual information*. San Francisco: Freeman.

Miller, G. A. (1979) Images and models, similes and metaphors. In A. Ortony (Ed.), *Metaphor and thought*. Cambridge: Cambridge University Press.

Norman, D. A., & Rumelhart, D. E. (1975) Memory and knowledge. In D. A. Norman, D. E. Rumelhart, & the LNR Research Group, *Explorations in cognition*. San Francisco: Freeman.

Paivio, A. (1971) *Images and verbal processes*. New York: Rinehart and Winston.

Palmer, S. E. (1975) Visual perception and world knowledge: Notes on a model of sensory-cognitive interaction. In D. A. Norman, D. E. Rumelhart, & the LNR Research Group, *Explorations in cognition*. San Francisco: Freeman.

Pylyshyn, Z. W. (1973) What the mind's eye tells the mind's brain: A critique of mental imagery, *Psychological Bulletin, 80*, 1–24.

Shepard, R. N. (1978) The mental image. *American Psychologist, 33*, 125–37.

Simon, H. A. (1972) What is visual imagery? An information processing interpretation. In L. W. Gregg (Ed.), *Cognition in learning and memory*, New York: Wiley.

Stenning, K. (1981) On remembering how to get there: How we might want something like a map. In A. M. Lesgold, J. W. Pellegrino, S. D. Fokkema, & J. Glaser (Eds.), *Cognitive psychology and instruction*, New York: Plenum.

PERCEPTION

5 Vision: The Philosophy and The Approach

David Marr

INTRODUCTION

What does it mean, to see? The plain man's answer (and Aristotle's, too) would be, to know what is where by looking. In other words, vision is the *process* of discovering from images what is present in the world, and where it is.

Vision is therefore, first and foremost, an information-processing task, but we cannot think of it just as a process. For if we are capable of knowing what is where in the world, our brains must somehow be capable of *representing* this information—in all its profusion of color and form, beauty, motion, and detail. The study of vision must therefore include not only the study of how to extract from images the various aspects of the world that are useful to us, but also an inquiry into the nature of the internal representations by which we capture this information and thus make it available as a basis for decisions about our thoughts and actions. This duality—the representation and the processing of information—lies at the heart of all information-processing tasks and will profoundly shape our investigation of the particular problems posed by vision.

The need to understand information-processing tasks and machines has arisen only quite recently. Until people began to dream of and then to build such machines, there was no very pressing need to think deeply about them. Once people did begin to speculate about such tasks and machines, however, it soon became clear that many aspects of the world around us ... are primarily phenomena of information processing, and if we are ever to understand them fully, our thinking about them must include this perspective.

The next point . . . is to emphasize that saying that a job is "only" an information-processing task or that an organism is "only" an information-processing machine is not a limiting or pejorative description. Even more importantly, I shall in no way use such a description to try to limit the kind of explanations that are necessary. Quite the contrary, in fact. One of the fascinating features of information-processing machines is that in order to understand them completely, one has to be satisfied with one's explanations at many different levels.

For example, let us look at the range of perspectives that must be satisfied before one can be said, from a human and scientific point of view, to have understood visual perception. First, and I think foremost, there is the perspective of the plain man. He knows what it is like to see, and unless the bones of one's arguments and theories roughly correspond to what this person knows to be true at first hand, one will probably be wrong. . . . Second, there is the perspective of the brain scientists, the physiologists and anatomists who know a great deal about how the nervous system is built and how parts of it behave. The issues that concern them—how the cells are connected, why they respond as they do . . .—must be resolved and addressed in any full account of perception. And the same argument applies to the perspective of the experimental psychologists.

On the other hand, someone who has bought and played with a small home computer may make quite different demands. "If," he might say, "vision really is an information-processing task, then I should be able to make my computer do it, provided that it has sufficient power, memory, and some way of being connected to a home television camera." The explanation he wants is therefore a rather abstract one, telling him what to program and, if possible, a hint about the best algorithms for doing so. He doesn't want to know about rhodopsin, or the lateral geniculate nucleus, or inhibitory interneurons. He wants to know how to program vision.

From a philosophical point of view, the approach that I describe is an extension of what have sometimes been called representational theories of mind. On the whole, it rejects the more recent excursions into the philosophy of perception, with their arguments about sense-data, the molecules of perception, and the validity of what the senses tell us; instead, this approach looks back to an older view, according to which the senses are for the most part concerned with telling one what is there. Modern representational theories conceive of the mind as having access to systems of internal representations; mental states are characterized by asserting what the internal representations currently specify, and mental processes by how such internal representations are obtained and how they interact.

Background

Since the decline of the Gestalt school of psychology, students of the psychology of perception have made no serious attempts at an overall understanding of what perception is, concentrating instead on the analysis of properties and performance. For example, the trichromatism of colour vision has been firmly established (Brindley, 1970). Studies such as those of Wallach and O'Connell (1953) have demonstrated that under suitable conditions, three-dimensional figures can be correctly perceived from two-dimensional monocular images, while, on the other hand Julesz (1960) has shown, using computer-generated random-dot stereograms, that under different conditions the sensation of a three-dimensional image can be caused solely by the stereo disparity between matching elements in the images presented to each eye.

The most recent contribution of psychophysics has been of a different kind but of equal importance. It arose from a combination of adaptation and threshold detection studies and originated from the demonstration by Campbell and Robson (1968) of the existence of independent, spatial-frequency-tuned channels—that is, channels sensitive to intensity variations in the image occurring at a particular scale or spatial interval—in the early stages of our perceptual apparatus. This paper led to an explosion of articles on various aspects of these channels, which culminated ten years later with quite satisfactory quantitative accounts of the characteristics of the first stages of visual perception (Wilson and Bergen, 1979). [. . .]

Recently a rather different approach has attracted considerable attention. In 1971, Roger N. Shepard and Jacqueline Metzler made line drawings of simple objects that differed from one another either by a three-dimensional rotation or by a rotation plus a reflection. They asked how long it took to decide whether two depicted objects differed by a rotation and a reflection or merely a rotation. They found that the time taken depended on the three-dimensional angle of rotation necessary to bring the two objects into correspondence. Indeed, the time varied linearly with this angle. One is led thereby to the notion that a mental rotation of sorts is actually being performed—that a mental description of the first shape in a pair is being adjusted incrementally in orientation until it matches the second, such adjustment requiring greater time when greater angles are involved.

The significance of this approach lies not so much in its results, whose interpretation is controversial, as in the type of questions it raised. For until then, the notion of a representation was not one that visual psychologists took seriously. This type of experiment meant that the notion had to be considered. [. . .]

For a long time, the best hope for an eventual explanation of all these individual phenomena seemed to lie in the field of electrophysiology. The development of increasingly more sophisticated amplification and recording techniques made possible the recording of the firing of individual neurons at successively deeper levels of the visual pathway (Hubel & Wiesel, 1962, 1968).

Barlow (1972) summarized the findings in this field as follows:

> The cumulative effect of all the changes I have tried to outline above has been to make us realise that each *single neuron can perform a much more complex and subtle task than had previously been thought* (emphasis added). Neurons do not loosely and unreliably remap the luminous intensities of the visual image onto our sensorium, but instead they detect pattern elements, discriminate the depth of objects, ignore irrelevant causes of variation and are arranged in an intriguing hierarchy. Furthermore, there is evidence that they give prominence to what is informationally important, can respond with great reliability, and can have their pattern selectivity permanently modified by early visual experience. This amounts to a revolution in our outlook. It is now quite inappropriate to regard unit activity as a noisy indication of more basic and reliable processes involved in mental operations: instead, we must regard single neurons as the prime movers of these mechanisms. Thinking is brought about by neurons and we should not use phrases like "unit activity reflects, reveals, or monitors thought processes," because the activities of neurons, quite simply, are thought processes.
>
> This revolution stemmed from physiological work and makes us realize that the activity of each single neuron may play a significant role in perception.

[...]

I shall return later on to more carefully examine the validity of this point of view, but for now let us just enjoy it. The vigor and excitement of these ideas need no emphasis. At the time the eventual success of a reductionist approach seemed likely. Hubel and Wiesel's (1962, 1968) pioneering studies had shown the way; single-unit studies on stereopsis (Barlow, Blakemore, & Pettigrew, 1967) and on color (DeValois, Abramov, & Mead, 1967; Gouras, 1968) seemed to confirm the close links between perception and single-cell recordings, and the intriguing results of Gross, Rocha-Miranda, and Bender (1972), who found "hand-detectors" in the inferotemporal cortex, seemed to show that the application of the reductionist approach would not be limited just to the early parts of the visual pathway.

[...]

I was myself fully caught up in this excitement. Truth, I also believed, was basically neural, and the central aim of all research was a thorough functional analysis of the structure of the central nervous system. My enthusiasm found expression in a theory of the cerebellar cortex (Marr,

1969). According to this theory, the simple and regular cortical structure is interpreted as a simple but powerful memorizing device for learning motor skills; because of a simple combinatorial trick, each of the 15 million Purkinje cells in the cerebellum is capable of learning over 200 different patterns and discriminating them from unlearned patterns. Evidence is gradually accumulating that the cerebellum is involved in learning motor skills (Ito, 1978), so that something like this theory may in fact be correct.

[...]

But somewhere underneath, something was going wrong. The initial discoveries of the 1950s and 1960s were not being followed by equally dramatic discoveries in the 1970s. No neurophysiologists had recorded new and clear high-level correlates of perception. The leaders of the 1960s had turned away from what they had been doing—Hubel and Wiesel concentrated on anatomy, Barlow turned to psychophysics, and the mainstream of neurophysiology concentrated on development and plasticity (the concept that neural connections are not fixed) or on a more thorough analysis of the cells that had already been discovered. ... [No] new studies succeeded in elucidating the *function* of the visual cortex.

It is difficult to say precisely why this happened, because the reasoning was never made explicit and was probably largely unconscious. However, various factors are identifiable. In my own case, the cerebellar study had two effects. On the one hand, it suggested that one could eventually hope to understand cortical structure in functional terms, and this was exciting. But at the same time the study has disappointed me, because even if the theory was correct, it did not much enlighten one about the motor system—it did not, for example, tell one how to go about programming a mechanical arm. It suggested that if one wishes to program a mechanical arm so that it operates in a versatile way, then at some point a very large and rather simple type of memory will prove indispensable. But it did not say why, nor what that memory should contain.

The discoveries of the visual neurophysiologists left one in a similar situation. Suppose, for example, that one actually found the apocryphal grandmother cell.[1] Would that really tell us anything much at all? It would tell us that it existed—Gross's hand-detectors tell us almost that— but not *why* or even *how* such a thing may be constructed from the outputs of previously discovered cells. Do the single-unit recordings—the simple and complex cells—tell us much about how to detect edges or why one would want to, except in a rather general way through arguments based on

---

[1] A cell that fires only when one's grandmother comes into view.

economy and redundancy? If we really knew the answers, for example, we should be able to program them on a computer. But finding a hand-detector certainly did not allow us to program one.

As one reflected on these sorts of issues in the early 1970s, it gradually became clear that something important was missing that was not present in either of the disciplines of neurophysiology or psychophysics. The key observation is that neurophysiology and psychophysics have as their business to *describe* the behavior of cells or of subjects but not to *explain* such behavior. What are the visual areas of the cerebral cortex actually doing? What are the problems in doing it that need explaining, and at what level of description should such explanations be sought?

The best way of finding out the difficulties of doing something is to try to do it, so at this point I moved to the Artificial Intelligence Laboratory at MIT, where Marvin Minsky had collected a group of people and a powerful computer for the express purpose of addressing these questions.

The first great revelation was that the problems are difficult. Of course, these days this fact is a commonplace. But in the 1960s almost no one realized that machine vision was difficult. The field had to go through the same experience as the machine translation field did in its fiascoes of the 1950s before it was at last realized that here were some problems that had to be taken seriously. The reason for this misperception is that we humans are ourselves so good at vision. The notion of a feature detector was well established by Barlow and by Hubel and Wiesel, and the idea that extracting edges and lines from images might be at all difficult simply did not occur to those who had not tried to do it. It turned out to be an elusive problem: Edges that are of critical importance from a three-dimensional point of view often cannot be found at all by looking at the intensity changes in an image. Any kind of textured image gives a multitude of noisy edge segments; variations in reflectance and illumination cause no end of trouble; and even if an edge has a clear existence at one point, it is as likely as not to fade out quite soon, appearing only in patches along its length in the image. The common and almost despairing feeling of the early investigators . . . was that practically anything could happen in an image and furthermore that practically everything did.

Three types of approach were taken to try to come to grips with these phenomena. The first was unashamedly empirical, associated most with Azriel Rosenfeld. His style was to take some new trick for edge detection, texture discrimination, or something similar, run it on images, and observe the result. Although several interesting ideas emerged in this way, . . . these studies were not as useful as they could have been because they were never accompanied by any serious assessment of how well the different algorithms performed. [. . .]

The second approach was to try for depth of analysis by restricting the scope to a world of single, illuminated, matte white toy blocks set against a black background. The blocks could occur in any shapes provided only that all faces were planar and all edges were straight. This restriction allowed more specialized techniques to be used, but it still did not make the problem easy. [. . .]

These techniques did work reasonably well, however, and they allowed a preliminary analysis of later problems to emerge—roughly, what does one do once a complete line drawing has been extracted from a scene? Studies of this had begun sometime before with Roberts (1965) and Guzman (1968), and they culminated in the works of Waltz (1975) and Mackworth (1973), which essentially solved the interpretation problem for line drawings derived from images of prismatic solids. Waltz's work had a particularly dramatic impact, because it was the first to show explicitly that an exhaustive analysis of all possible local physical arrangements of surfaces, edges, and shadows could lead to an effective and efficient algorithm for interpreting an actual image. [. . .]

The hope that lay behind this work was, of course, that once the toy world of white blocks had been understood, the solutions found there could be generalized, providing the basis for attacking the more complex problems posed by a richer visual environment. Unfortunately, this turned out not to be so. For the roots of the approach that was eventually successful, we have to look at the third kind of development that was taking place then.

Two pieces of work were important here. Neither is probably of very great significance to human perception for what it actually accomplished—in the end, it is likely that neither will particularly reflect human visual processes—but they are both of importance because of the way in which they were formulated. The first was Land and McCann's (1971) work on the retinex theory of color vision. . . . The starting point is the traditional one of regarding color as a perceptual approximation to reflectance. This allows the formulation of a clear computational question, namely, How can the effects of reflectance changes be separated from the vagaries of the prevailing illumination? Land and McCann suggested using the fact that changes in illumination are usually gradual, whereas changes in reflectance of a surface or of an object boundary are often quite sharp. Hence by filtering out slow changes, those changes due to the reflectance alone could be isolated. Horn devised a clever parallel algorithm for this, and I suggested how it might be implemented by neurons in the retina (Marr, 1974).

I do not now believe that this is at all a correct analysis of color vision or of the retina, but it showed the possible style of a correct analysis. Gone are the ad hoc programs of computer vision; gone is the restriction to a special visual miniworld; gone is any explanation *in terms of* neurons—

except as a way of implementing a method. And present is a clear understanding of what is to be computed, how it is to be done, the physical assumptions on which the method is based, and some kind of analysis of algorithms that are capable of carrying it out.

The other piece of work was Horn's (1975) analysis of shape from shading, which was the first in what was to become a distinguished series of articles on the formation of images. By carefully analyzing the way in which the illumination, surface geometry, surface reflectance, and view-point conspired to create the measured intensity values in an image, Horn formulated a differential equation that related the image intensity values to the surface geometry. If the surface reflectance and illumination are known, one can solve for the surface geometry. . . . Thus from shading one can derive shape.

The message was plain. There must exist an additional level of understanding at which the character of the information-processing tasks carried out during perception are analyzed and understood in a way that is independent of the particular mechanisms and structures that implement them in our heads. This was what was missing—the analysis of the problem as an information-processing task. Such analysis does not usurp an understanding at the other levels—of neurons or of computer programs—but it is a necessary complement to them, since without it there can be no real understanding of the function of all those neurons.

[. . .] The important point is that if the notion of different types of understanding is taken very seriously, it allows the study of the infor-mation-processing basis of perception to be made *rigorous*. It becomes possible, by separating explanations into different levels, to make explicit statements about what is being computed and why and to construct theories stating that what is being computed is optimal in some sense or is guaranteed to function correctly. The ad hoc element is removed, and heuristic computer programs are replaced by solid foundations on which a real subject can be built. This realization—the formulation of what was missing, together with a clear idea of how to supply it—formed the basic foundation for a new integrated approach. . . .

UNDERSTANDING COMPLEX INFORMATION-PROCESSING SYSTEMS

[. . .] If one hopes to achieve a full understanding of a system as complicated as a nervous system, a developing embryo, a set of metabolic pathways, a bottle of gas, or even a large computer program, then one must be prepared to contemplate different kinds of explanation at different levels of description that are linked, at least in principle, into a cohesive whole, even if linking the levels in complete detail is impractical. For the specific case of a system that solves an information-processing problem, there are in addition the twin strands of process and representation, and both these ideas need some discussion.

Representation and Description

A *representation* is a formal system for making explicit certain entities or types of information, together with a specification of how the system does this. And I shall call the result of using a representation to describe a given entity a *description* of the entity in that representation (Marr and Nishihara, 1978).

For example, the Arabic, Roman, and binary numeral systems are all formal systems for representing numbers. The Arabic representation consists of a string of symbols drawn from the set $(0, 1, 2, 3, 4, 5, 6, 7, 8, 9)$, and the rule for constructing the description of a particular integer n is that one decomposes n into a sum of multiples of powers of 10 and unites these multiples into a string with the largest powers on the left and the smallest on the right. Thus, thirty-seven equals $3 \times 10^1 + 7 \times 10^0$, which becomes 37, the Arabic numeral system's description of the number. What this description makes explicit is the number's decomposition into powers of 10. The binary numerical system's description of the number thirty-seven is 100101, and this description makes explicit the number's decomposition into powers of 2. In the Roman numeral system, thirty-seven is represented as XXXVII.

This definition of a representation is quite general. For example, a representation for shape would be a formal scheme for describing some aspects of shape, together with rules that specify how the scheme is applied to any particular shape. A musical score provides a way of representing a symphony; the alphabet allows the construction of a written representation of words; and so forth. The phrase "formal scheme" is critical to the definition, but the reader should not be frightened by it. The reason is simply that we are dealing with information-processing machines, and the way such machines work is by using symbols to stand for things—to represent things, in our terminology. To say that something is a formal scheme means only that it is a set of symbols with rules for putting them together—no more and no less.

A representation, therefore, is not a foreign idea at all—we all use representations all the time. However, the notion that one can capture some aspect of reality by making a description of it using a symbol and that to do so can be useful seems to me a fascinating and powerful idea. But even the simple examples we have discussed introduce some rather general and important issues that arise whenever one chooses to use one particular representation. For example, if one chooses the Arabic numeral representation, it is easy to discover whether a number is a power of 10 but difficult to discover whether it is a power of 2. If one chooses the binary representation, the situation is reversed. Thus, there is a trade-off; any particular representation makes certain information explicit at the expense of information that is pushed into the background and may be quite hard to recover.

Process

The term *process* is very broad. For example, addition is a process, and so is taking a Fourier transform. But so is making a cup of tea, or going shopping. For the purposes of this book, I want to restrict our attention to the meanings associated with machines that are carrying out information-processing tasks. So let us examine in depth the notions behind one simple such device, a cash register at the checkout counter of a supermarket.

There are several levels at which one needs to understand such a device, and it is perhaps most useful to think in terms of three of them. The most abstract is the level of *what* the device does and *why*. What it does is arithmetic, so our first task is to master the theory of addition. Addition is a mapping, usually denoted by $+$, from pairs of numbers into single numbers; for example, $+$ maps the pair $(3, 4)$ to 7, and I shall write this in the form $(3 + 4) \rightarrow 7$. Addition has a number of abstract properties, however. It is commutative: both $(3 + 4)$ and $(4 + 3)$ are equal to 7; and associative: the sum of $3 + (4 + 5)$ is the same as the sum of $(3 + 4) + 5$. Then there is the unique distinguished element, zero, the adding of which has no effect: $(4 + 0) \rightarrow 4$. Also, for every number there is a unique "inverse," written (-4) in the case of 4, which when added to the number gives zero: $[4 + (-4)] \rightarrow 0$.

Notice that these properties are part of the fundamental *theory* of addition. They are true no matter how the numbers are written—whether in binary, Arabic, or Roman representation—and no matter how the addition is executed. Thus part of this first level is something that might be characterized as *what* is being computed.

The other half of this level of explanation has to do with the question of *why* the cash register performs addition and not, for instance, multiplication when combining the prices of the purchased items to arrive at a final bill. The reason is that the rules we intuitively feel to be appropriate for combining the individual prices in fact define the mathematical operation of addition. These can be formulated as *constraints* in the following way:

1. If you buy nothing, it should cost you nothing; and buying nothing and something should cost the same as buying just the something. (The rules for zero.)

2. The order in which goods are presented to the cashier should not affect the total. (Commutativity.)

3. Arranging the goods into two piles and paying for each pile separately should not affect the total amount you pay. (Associativity; the basic operation for combining prices.)

4. If you 'buy' an item and then return it for a refund, your total expenditure should be zero. (Inverses.)

It is a mathematical theorem that these conditions define the operation of addition, which is therefore the appropriate computation to use.

This whole argument is what I call the *computational theory* of the cash register. Its important features are (1) that it contains separate arguments about what is computed and why and (2) that the resulting operation is defined uniquely by the constraints it has to satisfy. In the theory of visual processes, the underlying task is to reliably derive properties of the world from images of it; the business of isolating constraints that are both powerful enough to allow a process to be defined and generally true of the world is a central theme of our inquiry.

In order that a process shall actually run, however, one has to realize it in some way and therefore choose a representation for the entities that the process manipulates. The second level of the analysis of a process, therefore, involves choosing two things: (1) a *representation* for the input and for the output of the process and (2) an *algorithm* by which the transformation may actually be accomplished. For addition, of course, the input and output representations can both be the same, because they both consist of numbers. [...] If the first of our levels specifies what and why, this second level specifies *how*. For addition, we might choose Arabic numerals for the representations, and for the algorithm we could follow the usual rules about adding the least significant digits first and "carrying" if the sum exceeds 9. Cash registers, whether mechanical or electronic, usually use this type of representation and algorithm.

There are three important points here. First, there is usually a wide choice of representation. Second, the choice of algorithm often depends rather critically on the particular representation that is employed. And third, even for a given fixed representation, there are often several possible algorithms for carrying out the same process. Which one is chosen will usually depend on any particularly desirable or undesirable characteristics that the algorithms may have; for example, one algorithm may be much more efficient than another, or another may be slightly less efficient but more robust (that is, less sensitive to slight inaccuracies in the data on which it must run). Or again, one algorithm may be parallel, and another, serial. The choice, then, may depend on the type of hardware or machinery in which the algorithm is to be embodied physically.

This brings us to the third level, that of the device in which the process is to be realized physically. The important point here is that, once again, the same algorithm may be implemented in quite different technologies. The child who methodically adds two numbers from right to left, carrying a digit when necessary, may be using the same algorithm that is implemented by the wires and transistors of the cash register in the neighborhood supermarket, but the physical realization of the algorithm is quite different in these two cases. [...]

Some styles of algorithm will suit some physical substrates better than others. For example, in conventional digital computers, the number of connections is comparable to the number of gates, while in a brain, the number of connections is much larger ($\times 10^4$) than the number of nerve cells. The underlying reason is that wires are rather cheap in biological architecture, because they can grow individually and in three dimensions. In conventional technology, wire laying is more or less restricted to two dimensions, which quite severely restricts the scope for using parallel techniques and algorithms; the same operations are often better carried out serially.

The Three Levels

We can summarize our discussion in something like the manner shown in [Fig. 5.1], which illustrates the different levels at which an information-processing device must be understood before one can be said to have understood it completely. At one extreme, the top level, is the abstract computational theory of the device, in which the performance of the device is characterized as a mapping from one kind of information to another, the abstract properties of this mapping are defined precisely, and its appropriateness and adequacy for the task at hand are demonstrated. In the center

Computational Theory	Representation and Algorithm	Hardware Implementation
What is the goal of the computation, why is it appropriate, and what is the logic of the strategy by which it can be carried out?	How can this computational theory be implemented? In particular, what is the representation for the input and output, and what is the algorithm for the transformation?	How can the representation and algorithm be realized physically?

FIG. 5.1 The three levels at which any machine carrying out an information-processing task must be understood.

is the choice of representation for the input and output and the algorithm to be used to transform one into the other. And at the other extreme are the details of how the algorithm and representation are realized physically—the detailed computer architecture, so to speak. These three levels are coupled, but only loosely. The choice of an algorithm is influenced for example, by what it has to do and by the hardware in which it must run. But there is a wide choice available at each level, and the explication of each level involves issues that are rather independent of the other two.

Each of the three levels of description will have its place in the eventual understanding of perceptual information processing, and of course they are logically and causally related. But an important point to note is that since the three levels are only rather loosely related, some phenomena may be explained at only one or two of them. This means, for example, that a correct explanation of some psychophysical observation must be formulated at the appropriate level. In attempts to relate psychophysical problems to physiology, too often there is confusion about the level at which problems should be addressed. For instance, some are related mainly to the physical mechanisms of vision—such as afterimages (for example, the one you see after staring at a light bulb) or such as the fact that any color can be matched by a suitable mixture of the three primaries (a consequence principally of the fact that we humans have three types of cones). On the other hand, the ambiguity of the Necker cube [Fig. 5.2] seems to demand a different kind of explanation. To be sure, part of the explanation of its perceptual reversal must have to do with a bistable neural network (that is, one with two distinct stable states) somewhere inside the brain, but few would feel satisfied by an account that failed to

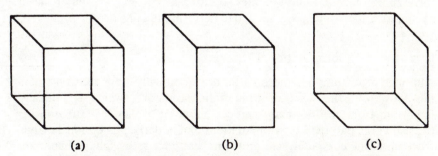

(a)   (b)   (c)

FIG. 5.2.   The so-called Necker illusion, named after L. A. Necker, the Swiss naturalist who developed it in 1832. The essence of the matter is that the two-dimensional representation (a) has collapsed the depth out of a cube and that a certain aspect of human vision is to recover this missing third dimension. The depth of the cube can indeed be perceived, but two interpretations are possible, (b) and (c). A person's perception characteristically flips from one to the other.

mention the existence of two different but perfectly plausible three-dimensional interpretations of this two-dimensional image.

For some phenomena, the type of explanation required is fairly obvious. Neuroanatomy, for example, is clearly tied principally to the third level, the physical realization of the computation. [. . .] Neurophysiology, too, is related mostly to this level, but it can also help us to understand the type of representations being used, particularly if one accepts something along the lines of Barlow's views that I quoted earlier. [. . .]

Psychophysics, on the other hand, is related more directly to the level of algorithm and representation. Different algorithms tend to fail in radically different ways as they are pushed to the limits of their performance or are deprived of critical information. . . . primarily psychophysical evidence proved to Poggio and myself that our first stereo-matching algorithm (Marr and Poggio, 1977) was not the one that is used by the brain, and the best evidence that our second algorithm (Marr and Poggio, 1979) *is* roughly the one that is used also comes from the psychophysics. Of course, the underlying computational theory remained the same in both cases, only the algorithms were different.

More generally, if the idea that different phenomena need to be explained at different levels is kept clearly in mind, it often helps in the assessment of the validity of the different kinds of objections that are raised from time to time. For example, one favorite is that the brain is quite different from a computer because one is parallel and the other serial. The answer to this, of course, is that the distinction between serial and parallel is a distinction at the level of algorithm; it is not fundamental at all—anything programmed in parallel can be rewritten serially (though not necessarily vice versa). The distinction, therefore, provides no grounds for arguing that the brain operates so differently from a computer that a computer could not be programmed to perform the same tasks.

Importance of Computational Theory

Although algorithms and mechanisms are empirically more accessible, it is the top level, the level of computational theory, which is critically important from an information-processing point of view. The reason for this is that the nature of the computations that underlie perception depends more upon the computational problems that have to be solved than upon the particular hardware in which their solutions are implemented. To phrase the matter another way, an algorithm is likely to be understood more readily by understanding the nature of the problem being solved than by examining the mechanism (and the hardware) in which it is embodied.

In a similar vein, trying to understand perception by studying only neurons is like trying to understand bird flight by studying only feathers: it just cannot be done. In order to understand bird flight, we have to understand aerodynamics; only then do the structure of feathers and the different shapes of birds' wings make sense. More to the point, as we shall see, we cannot understand why retinal ganglion cells and lateral geniculate neurons have the receptive fields they do just by studying their anatomy and physiology. We can understand how these cells and neurons behave as they do by studying their wiring and interactions, but in order to understand *why* the receptive fields are as they are—why they are circularly symmetrical and why their excitatory and inhibitory regions have characteristic shapes and distributions—we have to know a little of the theory of differential operators, band-pass channels, and the mathematics of the uncertainty principle. . . .

Perhaps it is not surprising that the very specialized empirical disciplines of the neurosciences failed to appreciate fully the absence of computational theory; but it is surprising that this level of approach did not play a more forceful role in the early development of artificial intelligence. For far too long, a heuristic program for carrying out some task was held to be a theory of that task, and the distinction between what a program did and how it did it was not taken seriously. As a result, (1) a style of explanation evolved that invoked the use of special mechanisms to solve particular problems, (2) particular data structures, such as the lists of attribute value pairs called property lists in the LISP programing language, were held to amount to theories of the representation of knowledge, and (3) there was frequently no way to determine whether a program would deal with a particular case other than by running the program.

The Approach of J. J. Gibson

In perception, perhaps the nearest anyone came to the level of computational theory was Gibson (1966). However, although some aspects of his thinking were on the right lines, he did not understand properly what information processing was, which led him to seriously underestimate the complexity of the information-processing problems involved in vision and the consequent subtlety that is necessary in approaching them.

Gibson's important contribution was to take the debate away from the philosophical considerations of sense-data and the affective qualities of sensation and to note instead that the important thing about the senses is that they are channels for perception of the real world outside or, in the case of vision, of the visible surfaces. He therefore asked the critically important question, How does one obtain constant perceptions in everyday life on the basis of continually changing sensations? This is exactly the right question, showing that Gibson correctly regarded the problem of perception as that of recovering from sensory information "valid" properties of the external world. His problem was that he had a much oversimplified view of how this should be done. His approach led him to consider higher-order variables—stimulus energy, ratios, proportions, and so on—as "invariants" of the movement of an observer and of changes in stimulation intensity.

"These invariants," he wrote, "correspond to permanent properties of the environment. They constitute, therefore, information about the permanent environment." This led him to a view in which the function of the brain was to "detect invariants" despite changes in "sensations" of light, pressure, or loudness of sound. Thus, he says that the "function of the brain, when looped with its perceptual organs, is not to decode signals, nor to interpret messages, nor to accept images, nor to *organize* the sensory input or to *process* the data, in modern terminology. It is to seek and extract information about the environment from the flowing array of ambient energy," and he thought of the nervous system as in some way "resonating" to these invariants. He then embarked on a broad study of animals in their environments, looking for invariants to which they might resonate. This was the basic idea behind the notion of ecological optics (Gibson, 1966, 1979).

Although one can criticize certain shortcomings in the quality of Gibson's analysis, its major and, in my view, fatal shortcoming lies at a deeper level and results from a failure to realize two things. First, the detection of physical invariants, like image surfaces, is exactly and precisely an information-processing problem, in modern terminology. And second, he vastly underrated the sheer difficulty of such detection. In discussing the recovery of three-dimensional information from the movement of an observer, he says that "in motion, perspective information alone can be used" (Gibson, 1966, p. 202). And perhaps the key to Gibson is the following:

> The detection of non-change when an object moves in the world is not as difficult as it might appear. It is only made to seem difficult when we assume that the perception of constant dimensions of the object must depend on the correcting of sensations of inconstant form and size. The information for the constant dimension of an object is normally carried by invariant relations in an optic array. Rigidity is *specified* (emphasis added).

Yes, to be sure, but *how*? Detecting physical invariants is just as difficult as Gibson feared, but nevertheless we can do it. And the only way to understand how is to treat it as an information-processing problem.

The underlying point is that visual information processing is actually very complicated, and Gibson was not the only thinker who was misled by the apparent simplicity of the act of seeing. The whole tradition of philosophical inquiry into the nature of perception seems not to have taken seriously enough the complexity of the information processing involved. For example, Austin's (1962) *Sense and Sensibilia* entertainingly demolishes the argument, apparently favored by earlier philosophers, that since we are sometimes deluded by illusions (for example, a straight stick appears bent if it is partly submerged in water), we see sense-data rather than material things. The answer is simply that usually our perceptual processing does run correctly (it delivers a true description of what is there), but although evolution has seen to it that our processing allows for many changes (like inconstant illumination), the perturbation due to the refraction of light by water is not one of them. And incidentally, although the example of the bent stick has been discussed since Aristotle, I have seen no philosophical inquiry into the nature of the perceptions of, for instance, a heron, which is a bird that feeds by pecking up fish first seen from above the water surface. For such birds the visual correction might be present.

Anyway, my main point here is another one. Austin (1962) spends much time on the idea that perception tells one about real properties of the external world, and one thing he considers is "real shape" (p. 66), a notion which had cropped up earlier in his discussion of a coin that "looked elliptical" from some points of view. Even so,

> it had a real shape which remained unchanged. But coins in fact are rather special cases. For one thing their outlines are well defined and very highly stable, and for another they have a known and a nameable shape. But there are plenty of things of which this is not true. What is the real shape of a cloud? . . . or of a cat? Does its real shape change whenever it moves? If not, in what posture *is* its real shape on display? Furthermore, is its real shape such as to be fairly smooth outlines, or must it be finely enough serrated to take account of each hair? *It is pretty obvious that there is no answer to these questions—no rules according to which, no procedure by which, answers are to be determined.* (emphasis added) (p. 67).

But there *are* answers to these questions. There are ways of describing the shape of a cat to an arbitrary level of precision . . ., and there are rules and procedures for arriving at such descriptions. That is exactly what vision is about, and precisely what makes it complicated.

A REPRESENTATIONAL FRAMEWORK FOR VISION

Vision is a process that produces from images of the external world a description that is useful to the viewer and not cluttered with irrelevant information (Marr, 1976; Marr & Nishihara, 1978). We have already seen that a process may be thought of as a mapping from one representation to another, and in the case of human vision, the initial representation is in no doubt—it consists of arrays of image intensity values as detected by the photoreceptors in the retina.

It is quite proper to think of an image as a representation; the items that are made explicit are the image intensity values at each point in the array, which we can conveniently denote by $I(x,y)$ at coordinate (x,y). In order to simplify our discussion, we shall neglect for the moment the fact that there are several different types of receptor, and imagine instead that there is just one, so that the image is black-and-white. Each value of $I(x,y)$ thus specifies a particular level of gray; we shall refer to each detector as a picture element or *pixel* and to the whole array I as an image.

But what of the output of the process of vision? We have already agreed that it must consist of a useful description of the world, but that requirement is rather nebulous. Can we not do better? Well, it is perfectly true that, unlike the input, the result of vision is much harder to discern, let alone specify precisely, and an important aspect of this new approach is that it makes quite concrete proposals about what the end is. But before we begin that discussion, let us step back a little and spend a little time formulating the more general issues that are raised by these questions.

The Purpose of Vision

The usefulness of a representation depends upon how well suited it is to the purpose for which it is used. A pigeon uses vision to help it navigate, fly, and seek out food. Many types of jumping spider use vision to tell the difference between a potential meal and a potential mate. One type, for example, has a curious retina formed of two diagonal strips arranged in a V. If it detects a red V on the back of an object lying in front of it, the spider has found a mate. Otherwise, maybe a meal. The frog, as we have seen, detects bugs with its retina; and the rabbit retina is full of special gadgets, including what is apparently a hawk detector, since it responds well to the pattern made by a preying hawk hovering overhead. Human vision, on the other hand, seems to be very much more general, although it clearly contains a variety of special-purpose mechanisms that can, for example, direct the eye toward an unexpected movement in the visual field or cause one to blink or otherwise avoid something that approaches one's head too quickly.

Vision, in short, is used in such a bewildering variety of ways that the visual systems of different animals must differ significantly from one another. Can the type of formulation that I have been advocating, in terms of representations and processes, possibly prove adequate for them all? I think so. The general point here is that because vision is used by different animals for such a wide variety of purposes, it is inconceivable that all seeing animals use the same representations; each can confidently be expected to use one or more representations that are nicely tailored to the owner's purposes.

As an example, let us consider briefly a primitive but highly efficient visual system that has the added virtue of being well understood. Werner Reichardt's group in Tübingen has spent the last 14 years patiently unraveling the visual flight-control system of the housefly, and in a famous collaboration, Reichardt and Tomaso Poggio have gone far toward solving the problem (Reichardt and Poggio, 1976, 1979; Poggio and Reichardt, 1976). Roughly speaking, the fly's visual apparatus controls its flight through a collection of about five independent, rigidly inflexible, very fast responding systems (the time from visual stimulus to change of torque is only 21 ms). For example, one of these systems is the landing system; if the visual field "explodes" fast enough (because a surface looms nearby), the fly automatically "lands" towards its center. If this center is above the fly, the fly automatically inverts to land upside down. When the feet touch, power to the wings is cut off. Conversely, to take off, the fly jumps; when the feet no longer touch the ground, power is restored to the wings, and the insect flies again.

In-flight control is achieved by independent systems controlling the fly's vertical velocity (through control of the lift generated by the wings) and horizontal direction (determined by the torque produced by the asymmetry of the horizontal thrust from the left and right wings). [. . .] This system is triggered to track objects of a certain angular dimension in the visual field, and the motor strategy is such that if the visible object was another fly a few inches away, then it would be intercepted success- fully. If the target was an elephant 100 yd away, interception would fail because the fly's built-in parameters are for another fly nearby, not an elephant far away.

Thus, fly vision delivers a representation in which at least these three things are specified: (1) whether the visual field is looming sufficiently fast that the fly should contemplate landing; (2) whether there is a small patch—it could be a black speck or, it turns out, a textured figure in front of a textured ground—having some kind of motion relative to its background; and if there is such a patch, (3) [angular information] for this patch [is] delivered to the motor system. And that is probably about 60% of fly vision. In particular, it is extremely unlikely that the fly has any explicit representation of the visual world around him—no true conception of a surface, for example, but just a few triggers and some specifically fly- centered parameters. . . .

It is clear that human vision is much more complex than this, although it may well incorporate subsystems not unlike the fly's to help with specific and rather low-level tasks like the control of pursuit eye movements. Nevertheless, as Poggio and Reichardt have shown, even these simple systems can be understood in the same sort of way, as information-processing tasks.

Advanced Vision

Visual systems like the fly's serve adequately and with speed and precision the needs of their owners, but they are not very complicated; very little objective information about the world is obtained. The information is all very much subjective—the angular size of the stimulus as the fly sees it rather than the objective size of the object out there, the angle that the object has in the fly's visual field rather than its position relative to the fly or to some external reference, and the object's angular velocity, again in the fly's visual field, rather than any assessment of its true velocity relative to the fly or to some stationary reference point.

One reason for this simplicity must be that these facts provide the fly with sufficient information for it to survive. Of course, the information is not optimal and from time to time the fly will fritter away its energy chasing a falling leaf a medium distance away or an elephant a long way away as a direct consequence of the inadequacies of its perceptual system. But this apparently does not matter very much—the fly has sufficient excess energy for it to be able to absorb these extra costs. Another reason is certainly that translating these rather subjective measurements into more objective qualities involves much more computation. How, then, should one think about more advanced visual systems—human vision, for example. What are the issues? What kind of information is vision really delivering, and what are the representational issues involved?

My approach to these problems was very much influenced by the fascinating accounts of clinical neurology, such as Critchley (1953) and Warrington and Taylor (1973). Particularly important was a lecture that Elizabeth Warrington gave at MIT in October 1973, in which she described the capacities and limitations of patients who had suffered left or right parietal lesions. For me, the most important thing that she did was to draw a distinction between the two classes of patient. . . . For those with lesions on the right side, recognition of a common object was possible *provided* that the patient's view of it was in some sense straightforward. She used the words *conventional* and *unconventional*—a water pail or a clarinet seen from the side gave "conventional" views but seen end-on gave "unconventional" views. If these patients recognized the object at all, they knew its name and its semantics—that is, its use and purpose, how big it was, how much it weighed, what it was made of, and so forth. If their view was unconventional—a pail seen from above, for example—not only would the patients fail to recognize it, but they would vehemently deny that it *could* be a view of a pail. Patients with left parietal lesions behaved completely differently. Often these patients had no language, so they were unable to name the viewed object or state its purpose and semantics. But they could convey that they correctly perceived its geometry—that is, its shape—even from the unconventional view.

Warrington's talk suggested two things. First, the representation of the shape of an object is stored in a different place and is therefore a quite different kind of thing from the representation of its use and purpose. And second, vision alone can deliver an internal description of the shape of a viewed object, even when the object was not recognized in the conventional sense of understanding its use and purpose.

This was an important moment for me for two reasons. The general trend in the computer vision community was to believe that recognition was so difficult that it required every possible kind of information. The results of this point of view duly appeared a few years later in programs like ... Tenenbaum and Barrow's (1976). In [this] program, knowledge about offices—for example, that desks have telephones on them and that telephones are black—was used to help "segment" out a black blob halfway up an image and "recognize" it as a telephone. [. . .] Clearly, we do use such knowledge in real life; I once saw a brown blob quivering amongst the lettuce in my garden and correctly identified it as a rabbit, even though the visual information alone was inadequate. And yet here was this young woman calmly telling us not only that her patients could convey to her that they had grasped the shapes of things that she had shown them, even though they could not name the objects or say how they were used, but also that they could happily continue to do so even if she made the task extremely difficult visually by showing them peculiar views or by illuminating the objects in peculiar ways. It seemed clear that the intuitions of the computer vision people were completely wrong and that even in difficult circumstances shapes could be determined by vision alone.

The second important thing, I thought, was that Elizabeth Warrington had put her finger on what was somehow the quintessential fact of human vision—that it tells about shape and space and spatial arrangement. Here lay a way to formulate its purpose—building a description of the shapes and positions of things from images. Of course, that is by no means all that vision can do; it also tells about the illumination and about the reflectances of the surfaces that make the shapes—their brightnesses and colors and visual textures—and about their motion. But these things seemed secondary; they could be hung off a theory in which the main job of vision was to derive a representation of shape.

TABLE 5.1
Representational Framework for Deriving Shape Information from
Images

Name	Purpose	Primitives
Image(s)	Represents intensity.	Intensity value at each point in the image.
Primal sketch	Makes explicit important information about the two-dimensional image, primarily the intensity changes there and their geometrical distribution and organization.	Zero-crossings Blobs Terminations and discontinuities Edge segments Virtual lines Groups Curvilinear organization Boundaries
2½-D sketch	Makes explicit the orientation and rough depth of the visible surfaces, and contours of discontinuities in these quantities in a viewer-centered coordinate frame.	Local surface orientation (the "needles" primitives) Distance from viewer Discontinuities in depth Discontinuities in surface orientation
3-D model representation	Describes shapes and their spatial organization in an object-centered coordinate frame, using a modular hierarchical representation that includes volumetric primitives (i.e., primitives that represent the volume of space that a shape occupies) as well as surface primitives.	3-D models arranged hierarchically, each one based on a spatial configuration of a few sticks or axes, to which volumetric or surface shape primitives are attached

To the Desirable via the Possible

Finally, one has to come to terms with cold reality. Desirable as it may be to have vision deliver a completely invariant shape description from an image (whatever that may mean in detail), it is almost certainly impossible in only one step. We can only do what is possible and proceed from there toward what is desirable. Thus we arrived at the idea of a sequence of representations, starting with descriptions that could be obtained straight from an image but that are carefully designed to facilitate the subsequent recovery of gradually more objective, physical properties about an object's shape. The main stepping stone toward this goal is describing the geometry of the visible surfaces, since the information encoded in images, for example by stereopsis, shading, texture, contours, or visual motion, is due to a shape's local surface properties. The objective of many eary visual computations is to extract this information.

However, this description of the visible surfaces turns out to be unsuitable for recognition tasks. There are several reasons why, perhaps the most prominent being that like all early visual processes, it depends critically on the vantage point. The final step therefore consists of transforming the viewer-centered surface description into a representation of the three-dimensional shape and spatial arrangement of an object that does not depend upon the direction from which the object is being viewed. This final description is object centered rather than viewer centered.

The overall framework described here therefore divides the derivation of shape information from images into three representational stages: (Table [5.1]): (1) the representation of properties of the two-dimensional image, such as intensity changes and local two-dimensional geometry; (2) the representation of properties of the visible surfaces in a viewer-centered coordinate system, such as surface orientation, distance from the viewer, and discontinuities in these quantities; surface reflectance; and some coarse description of the prevailing illumination; and (3) an object-centered representation of the three-dimensional structure and of the organization of the viewed shape, together with some description of its surface properties.

REFERENCES

Austin, J. L. (1962) *Sense and sensibilia*. Oxford: Clarendon Press.

Barlow, H. B. (1972) Single units and sensation: A neuron doctrine for perceptual psychology? *Perception, 1*, 371–394.

Barlow, H. B., Blakemore, C. & Pettigrew, J. D. (1967) The neural mechanism of binocular depth discrimination. *Journal of Physiology (London), 193*, 327–342.

Brindley, G. S. (1970) *Physiology of the retina and visual pathway*. Physiological Society monograph no. 6. London: Edwin Arnold.

Campbell, F. W. C., & Robson, J. (1968) Application of Fourier analysis to the visibility of gratings. *Journal of Physiology (London), 197*, 551–566.

DeValois, R. L., Abramov, I., & Mead, W. R. (1967) Single cell analysis of wavelength discrimination at the lateral geniculate nucleus in the macaque. *Journal of Neurophysiology, 30*, 415–433.

Gibson, J. J. (1966) *The senses considered as perceptual systems*. Boston: Houghton Mifflin.

Gibson, J. J. (1979) *The ecological approach to visual perception*. Boston: Houghton Mifflin.

Gouras, P. (1968) Identification of cone mechanisms in monkey ganglion cells. *Journal of Physiology (London), 199*, 533–547.

Gross, C. G., Rocha-Miranda, C. E., & Bender, D. B. (1972) Visual properties of neurons in inferotemporal cortex of the macaque. *Journal of Neurophysiology, 35*, 96–111.

Guzman, A. (1968) Decomposition of a visual scene into three-dimensional bodies. In *AFIPS Conference proceedings, 33*, 291–304. Washington, D.C.: Thompson.

Horn, B. K. P. (1975) Obtaining shape from shading information. In P. H. Winston (Ed.),

The psychology of computer vision, 115–155. New York: McGraw-Hill.

Hubel, D. H., & Wiesel, T. N. (1962) Receptive fields, binocular interaction and functional architecture in the cat's visual cortex. *Journal of Physiology (London), 166*, 106–154.

Hubel, D. H., & Wiesel, T. N. (1968) Receptive fields and functional architecture of monkey striate cortex. *Journal of Physiology (London), 195*, 215–243.

Ito, M. (1978) Recent advances in cerebellar physiology and pathology. In R. A. P. Kark, R. N. Rosenberg, & L. J. Shut (Eds.), *Advances in neurology*, 59–84. New York: Raven Press.

Julesz, B. (1960) Binocular depth perception of computer generated patterns. *Bell Syst. Tech. J., 39*, 1125–1162.

Land, E. H., & McCann, J. J. (1971) Lightness and retinex theory. *Journal of the Optical Society of America, 61*, 1–11.

Mackworth, A. K. (1973) Interpreting pictures of polyhedral scenes. *Artificial Intelligence, 4*, 121–137.

Marr, D. (1969) A theory of cerebellar cortex. *Journal of Physiology (London), 202*, 437–470.

Marr, D. (1974) The computation of lightness by the primate retina. *Vision research, 14*, 1377–1388.

Marr, D. (1976) Early processing of visual information. *Philosophical Transactions of the Royal Society of London (B), 275*, 483–524.

Marr, D., & Nishihara, H. K. (1978) Representation and recognition of the spatial organization of three-dimensional shapes. *Proceedings of the Royal Society of London (B), 200*, 269–294.

Marr, D., & Poggio, T. (1977) From understanding computation to understanding neural circuitry. *Neurosciences Research Program Bulletin, 15*, 470–488.

Marr, D., & Poggio, T. (1979) A computational theory of human stereo vision. *Proceedings of the Royal Society of London (B), 204*, 301–328.

Poggio, T., & Reichardt, W. (1976) Visual control of orientation behavior in the fly. Part II. Towards the underlying neural interactions. *Quarterly Review of Biophysics, 9*, 377–438.

Reichardt, W., & Poggio, T. (1976) Visual control of orientation behavior in the fly. Part I. A quantitative analysis. *Quarterly Review of Biophysics, 9*, 311–375.

Reichardt, W., & Poggio, T. (1979) Visual control of flight in flies. In W. E. Reichardt, V. B. Mountcastle, and T. Poggio (Eds.), *Recent Theoretical Developments in Neurobiology*.

Roberts, L. G. (1965) Machine perception of three-dimensional solids. In J. T. Tippett et al. (Eds.), *Optical and electro optical information processing*. 159–197. Cambridge, Mass.: MIT Press.

Shepard, R. N., & Metzler, J. (1971) Mental rotation of three-dimensional objects. *Science, 171*, 701–703.

Tenenbaum, J. M., & Barrow, H. G. (1976) *Experiments in interpretation-guided segmentation*. Stanford: Stanford Research Institute Technical Note 123.

Wallach, H., & O'Connell, D. N. (1953) The kinetic depth effect. *Journal of Experimental Psychology, 45*, 205–217.

Waltz, D. (1975) Understanding line drawings of scenes with shadows. In P. H. Winston (Ed.), *The psychology of computer vision*, 19–91. New York: McGraw-Hill.

Warrington, E. K., & Taylor, A. M. (1973) The contribution of the right parietal lobe to object recognition. *Cortex, 9*, 152–164.

Wilson, H. R., & Bergen, J. R. (1979) A four mechanism model for spatial vision. *Vision Research, 19*, 19–32.

6 Perceptual Organization in Information Processing

James R. Pomerantz

The task of organizing sensory input appears, at first glance, to be awesome. Given the ambiguities of the signals reaching our receptors, given the noise in our sensory channels, and given the apparent capacity limitations of our information-processing network, it is not surprising that some have concluded (privately, if not in public) that perception must be impossible. But like the physicists who some time ago showed that in theory, it was impossible for a bumblebee to fly, we are confronted by the obvious fact that perception is not only possible—it is overwhelmingly successful. Human perception works quite well even under the worst of circumstances. I know of no better illustration of this fact than the work of Johansson (1975), who has shown that when we view movies that show only moving spots that have been filmed by attaching light sources to the actors' joints and limbs, we have little trouble perceiving the actors and their actions correctly. Demonstrations such as these remind us that in the normal environment, the perceptual system is given an embarrassment of riches, much more information than it needs. Perception is not only possible, it seems also to be overdetermined by the stimulus.

An initial goal of the perceptual system is to achieve, at a coarse level, a general outline or map of the environment, including the major objects and surfaces with their respective positions and patterns of motion. Concurrently, at a finer level, the system works toward the identity of and more detailed information about these initially segregated objects and events. At both levels, the system is working toward a representation of things more global than the local, punctate information it must start with at the receptor level. How should a perceptual system begin

127

the task of synthesizing global representations from local information?

The Gestalt psychologists attacked this problem with their well-known laws of grouping and of figure-ground segregation. The distinction between these two sets of laws, which is often ignored, is important for present purposes, because my immediate concern is where visual processing begins. As grouping is the perceptual linking of regions into unified objects and surfaces, it would seem to be logically prior to figure-ground segregation, which is essentially a matter of choosing which of the already unified objects will hold the focus of attention and which will be relegated to the background. If we look at perceptual organization from the perspective of sequential stages of information processing, grouping would seem to be localized in a stage earlier than figure-ground segregation. So let me turn first to the question of grouping.

A DEFINITION OF GROUPING

The purpose of grouping is to divide the perceptual field into units, but what exactly is a *unit*? [...]

Any natural unit is defined by its indivisibility. [...] When a complex structure is broken down into parts, some breakpoints are more likely than others, and these serve to demarcate natural units. [...]

Selective Attention Measures

When it comes to analyzing percepts, it would be convenient if we could drop them on the floor and watch them shatter into natural pieces. [...] In the absence of such a direct technique, more indirect alternatives must suffice. When Garner and I (Pomerantz & Garner, 1973) first approached the problem of grouping and configuration in vision, the dissecting tool we chose was the selective attention task, ... [in which] the subject is presented with stimuli that vary in two of their component parts or dimensions. The task is to classify those objects according to one part while ignoring the other part. The logic of this procedure is that if the two parts in question are dissected into separate perceptual units, then selective attention to just one part should be possible. But if the two parts are parsed into the same perceptual unit or group, then the two should not split, and so selective attention to just one part should be difficult or impossible. In this manner, the success or failure of selective attention becomes an operational measure of perceptual grouping. [...]

The particular stimuli we first used to test this idea are shown in [Fig. 6.1]. Set A shows four stimuli, each composed of two curved line segments (actually, parentheses). Phenomenologically, the two parentheses of each

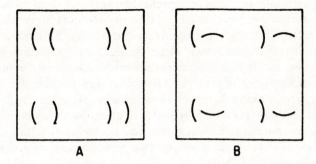

FIG. 6.1. (A) Four stimuli created by combining two possible curved elements on the left with two on the right. These stimuli show perceptual grouping, as defined by the inability to attend selectively to individual elements. (B) The same four stimuli as in Panel A but with the right-hand element rotated 90 degrees. These stimuli do not show perceptual grouping. (From Pomerantz & Garner, 1973.)

stimulus appear to group so that each stimulus has its own definite shape. The stimuli in Set B are the same as those in Set A except that one of the two parentheses in each pair has been rotated 90 degrees. Here, phenomenologically speaking, the stimuli as wholes lack any unified shape or configuration that distinguishes among them.

The specific task the subject was given was to classify stimuli, using a card-sorting procedure, on the basis of one of the two elements—say, the left one. The dependent variable was the time needed to perform 32 such classifications. The irrelevant parenthesis either remained the same for all 32 stimuli or varied randomly from stimulus to stimulus. In the first case (the control condition), the subject might, for example, have to discriminate between the top left and the top right stimulus. Note that here, it is the left parenthesis that is relevant because the right-hand one is the same for both stimuli. In the second case (the filtering or selective attention condition), the subject might have to discriminate the two stimuli in the left-hand column from the two in the right. Again it is the left-hand element of each stimulus that is relevant, but note that the right element is now variable. If the two parentheses of each pattern did not group and so could be attended to selectively, then the two conditions should produce equal performance. The reason for this is that the two differ only with respect to the irrelevant parenthesis, and that parenthesis would not be attended to. But if selective attention were not possible and the stimuli had to be processed as wholes, then the selective attention condition should be harder than the control, if only because there are four alternative stimuli to be classified in the former and only two in the latter.

The RTs [reaction times] for Set A showed that this irrelevant variation interfered substantially with performance. Our interpretation of this outcome was that the pairs of parentheses in Set A could not be broken apart perceptually but had to be processed as wholes. Subjects could not *avoid* attending to the irrelevant element, and so performance suffered. With the stimuli in Set B, however, variation in the irrelevant element had no effect, indicating that selective attention was possible here. Thus, subjects seem to perceive these stimuli as two separate entities.

[...] It is an open question *why* selective attention fails when grouping occurs. For the moment, however, it is enough to note that a processing difference exists between Sets A and B that would not exist if selective attention were at work in both sets.

Divided Attention Measures

The notion that perceptual grouping of parts implies a failure of (or at least the absence of) selective attention to those parts suggests an immediate corollary. This corollary states that if two parts belong to the same perceptual unit, then divided attention between the two parts should be easy, whereas if they do not, then divided attention should be difficult. Although this corollary might seem straightforward, it is nonetheless important to test. [...]

This corollary has been tested in two separate laboratories. Working with integral and separable stimulus dimensions, Gottwald and Garner (1975) showed that attention is more easily divided over integral than over separable dimensions. Working with configural dimensions, Schwaitzberg and I (Pomerantz & Schwaitzberg, 1975) have shown similarly that attention is more readily divided over elements that group than over elements that do not. Moreover, we have shown that for elements that group, divided attention is easier than selective attention.

The divided attention task we used is called a condensation task (Posner, 1964). Look again at the four stimuli of Set A; the subject's task is to classify the upper left and lower right stimuli into one response category and the two remaining stimuli—those on the upper right and the lower left—into the other. To perform this task properly, one must look at both parts of each stimulus. Therefore, the processing requirements of this task are opposite those in the selective attention task, where only one part need be attended.

The results of this experiment are shown in Fig. [6.2]. When the parentheses were spaced closely so that there was a failure of selective attention (more on this later), divided attention proved quite easy. In fact, the condensation task was easier than the selective attention task, which (stated in other terms) means that it was easier to pay attention to two things simultaneously than to just one! On the other hand, when the parentheses were spaced farther apart, selective attention became quite easy, whereas divided attention became enormously difficult. So this is one piece of evidence supporting the corollary.

The second piece of evidence comes from an experiment I have never reported; in fact, I have never performed the formal experiment because the effect it demonstrates is so obvious that it needs no experiment. It concerns the possibility of divided attention with the stimuli of Set B in Fig. [6.1]. Consider the ease with which you could perform the condensation task with these stimuli. Here the upper left and lower right stimuli require one response, whereas the upper right and the lower left require the other response. I have tried this task with a number of subjects, and their performance reminds me of subjects attempting to do the Stroop test. By my estimate, RTs with Set B average more than three times longer than

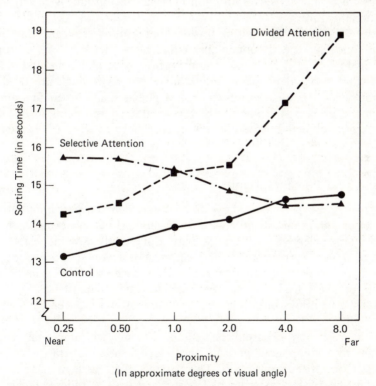

FIG. 6.2.   Reaction-time data showing how—when the elements of Fig. 6.1 A are moved apart—grouping weakens, as indexed by improved selective attention and worsened divided attention. (Adapted from Pomerantz & Schwaitzberg, 1975.)

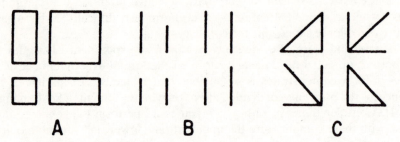

A   B   C

FIG. 6.3. Three sets of stimuli constructed in a manner similar to those in Fig. 6.1, all showing configural effects.

when the stimuli in Set A of Fig. [6.1] are used. In short, it is a frustrating and difficult task, despite its overt simplicity. So again we find that parts that group by the selective attention measure also group by the divided attention measure.

Before I create the misimpression that parentheses are the only stimuli one can use to obtain grouping effects, let me present some more in Fig. [6.3] [...] What is noteworthy about all of these stimulus sets is that two independent dimensions (or parts), which are used to generate each stimulus, group to form a global shape or configuration; and in the process, the identity of the separate parts seems to become lost. Again, objective experimentation corroborates what is obvious to the eye.

Divisibility of Perceptual Units

The preceding experiments show that we may define a perceptual group as a set of parts that are processed as an all-or-none unit even when we try to attend selectively to a single part. But exactly how indivisible are perceptual units? It seems clear that most perceptual groups can be broken up into parts, given a conscious effort to do so. For example, the stimuli of Fig. [6.1] can be seen as individual parentheses, just as pointillistic paintings or newspaper photographs can be seen as isolated dots. [...]

In the case of the parenthesis stimuli ... subjects may analyze the stimulus into component parts in the selective attention task, but this process requires time and effort. The evidence that this is the case comes from an unpublished experiment I performed with a student, Lawrence Sager. The stimuli used in this experiment appear in Fig. [6.4]. These stimuli each have 4 parts, instead of only 2 with the parentheses patterns; so a total of 16 different patterns are possible instead of only 4. In our

```
 ( (        ( (        ( (        ( (
 ( (        ) (        ( )        ) )


 ) (        ) (        ) (        ) (
 ( (        ) (        ( )        ) )


 ( )        ( )        ( )        ( )
 ( (        ) (        ( )        ) )


 ) )        ) )        ) )        ) )
 ( (        ) (        ( )        ) )
```

FIG. 6.4. A set of 16 stimuli created from all possible combinations of four elements, each having two alternative orientations. These stimuli show strong configural effects.

control condition, subjects had to discriminate between 2 patterns that differed in only 1 part (e.g., the upper left element); the other 3 parts remained constant. In the first of three selective attention conditions, 1 of the irrelevant parts also varied, resulting in a total of 4 different stimuli to be classified. In a second selective attention condition, 2 of the 3 irrelevant parts varied, resulting in 8 stimuli. In the final selective attention condition, all 3 irrelevant parts varied, resulting in 16 stimuli. Note that if subjects did not attend only to the relevant part of the stimulus, these tasks would become progressively harder, because there would be more stimulus alternatives to process or, put another way, because there would be progressively more irrelevant information to filter. The results from our experiment were as follows: In the control condition, reaction time averaged 433 msec. In the selective attention conditions, RTs averaged 497, 509, and 511 msec with 4, 8, and 16 alternative stimuli, respectively. The small differences among these three conditions were neither systematic nor significant. So although performance was worse in the selective attention conditions than in the control conditions, it did not continue to deteriorate significantly with more irrelevant information, as would be predicted if these stimulus patterns were perceived wholistically and could not be processed as separate parts.

On the basis of this evidence and also on phenomenological grounds, it appears that it is indeed possible to break up perceptual units into smaller parts. This is an important inference, for it shows that grouping is not the result of an automatic, nonstrategic, and innate process. . . . But before we can claim that perceptual grouping comes under conscious control, we must rule out the possibility that the control is mediated by peripheral sensory adjustments. . . . it is possible to destroy the global organization of a pointillistic painting simply by standing too close to it. Similarly, changes in visual fixation can influence perceptual reversal of a Necker cube. The important issue here is whether grouping or other aspects of perceptual organization can be brought under *central* cognitive control.

Preattentive Processing. Cognitive psychology has not invested much time in analyzing perceptual organization in information-processing terms. Models of pattern recognition, for example, usually bypass the problem. They assume that the input to the pattern recognizer has been cleaned up, as it were, and that there is no ambiguity in the signal as to where the stimulus is located in the field. Grouping and figure-ground segregation are assumed to have been taken care of already by some early, "preattentive" stage of processing, to use Neisser's term (1967). The characteristics of preattention are that it works at high speed, spatially in parallel, and that it is automatic. The term *automatic* is intended to mean that the preattentive processes are invoked by the stimulus without a conscious decision being made to do so, and that these processes are carried out without guidance from later, so-called "attentive" or "focal attentive" processes, which by contrast are slow, serial, conscious, and have a limited capacity for processing information. According to Neisser's analysis, the purpose of the preattentive stage is to parse the perceptual field into units upon which attention may operate, and to direct attention toward certain units in the perceptual input that seem particularly salient to the preattentive system, based on its crude analysis of the signal.

This sort of two-stage system has a great appeal on a priori grounds. Because conscious processing is slow and limited, and given that our sensory receptors are constantly bombarded by incoming information, one can hardly imagine a more useful device than a gatekeeper that sorts the input into crude categories, that filters out low-level redundancies, and that sets priorities. This would be especially true if the gatekeeper could be left on its own, without any monitoring or supervision.

One trouble with such a gatekeeper, upon further analysis, is that it might use inappropriate or obsolete rules. If the virtue of the gatekeeper is its simplicity, this same simplicity could prove an enormous liability in a changing environment. Therefore, it would be most advantageous if the gatekeeper could be sent new instructions from time to time telling it how to change its procedures.

[. . .] Examples [of this] are not difficult to find in skilled motor behavior. For instance, when an easy task (such as driving down a straight road) becomes difficult (when an unexpected turn in the road is encountered), we switch off our "automatic pilot" and turn to "manual control." Another and perhaps better example is breathing; normally, we breathe without any conscious awareness or effort, but when we wish to, we may inhibit or induce breathing freely (within certain limits, of course).

The gatekeeper analogy and the breathing analogy imply different processing mechanisms. In the breathing analogy, conscious, attentive processes override preattentive processes, whereas in the gatekeeper analogy, consciousness merely instructs preattention how to behave. In terms of stage models for information processing, the issue is whether information bypasses the preattentive stages of processing when conscious control is exerted or whether it does not.

I do not believe we can make a firm choice between these two models on the present evidence, but my own thinking leans toward the gatekeeper analogy. [. . .] [However] it seems [that although] the gatekeeper is on duty at all times . . . it has some very firmly rooted habits that it is unwilling to change at a moment's notice. In any event, regardless of which analogy is more appropriate, it is not sufficient merely to ask whether perceptual organization is automatic or is strategic, for it clearly has properties of both.

SOME CAUSES OF GROUPING

Given a satisfactory working definition of grouping, it becomes possible to isolate those factors that produce it. The classical Gestalt work on grouping identified two kinds of factors at work. The first kind was associated with certain laws of grouping, including similarity, proximity, and common fate. What these have in common is that they are all at least potentially measurable aspects of the stimulus. The second kind of factor is associated with the concepts of good figure, good continuation, and, in general, Prägnanz. The upshot of this second set of grouping principles is that the visual field will group so as to yield the "best," most stable organization.

Is the distinction between these two kinds of factors equivalent to the distinction between "bottom-up" and "top-down" processing? Essentially, bottom-up or "data-driven" processing begins with the raw stimulus and works its way toward some conceptual structure; top-down or "conceptually driven" processing works oppositely, beginning with some conceptual structure and working toward some particular stimulus. [. . .] In recognizing patterns, for example, one may sample enough aspects of the stimulus to infer the identity of the object; or one may begin with a hypothesis about the stimulus and proceed by checking this hypothesis against sensory data. [. . .]

Grouping by proximity, similarity, and common fate could readily be accomplished by bottom-up processing (given that these three concepts were tightly defined within the processing system). However, grouping based on good figure, good continuation or Prägnanz could be based on top-down processing. If grouping proceeds so as to yield the "best" figure, then processing begins with the goal of grouping, and the task is to find some organization most consistent with that goal. Thus, this type of grouping would seem to be conceptually driven. A processing strategy consistent with Prägnanz would have the perceptual system begin processing an unknown input by making parsimonious hypotheses about how it might be structured. In other words, it would begin with a bias toward simple, or good, figures.

Local Factors

Proximity. Grouping by proximity [has already been demonstrated by the results reported in Fig. 6.2] [...]

Another information-processing demonstration of grouping by proximity comes from an ingenious experiment by Banks and Prinzmetal (1976). ... They presented subjects with arrays of letterlike stimuli, all of which were the same except one. This discrepant stimulus was either a *T* or an *F*, and the task was to decide which one of these two was present as quickly as possible. The number of background stimuli—which were drawn to resemble a combination of a *T* and an *F*—was varied, as was the spatial arrangement of these background stimuli. Figure [6.5] shows some of the arrays they tested. Because the target letter could appear in any of the four corner positions of these arrays, the task was basically one of search.

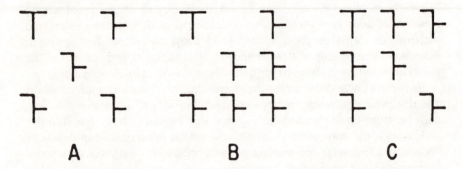

FIG. 6.5. The *T* is detected fastest in Panel B and slowest in Panel C. (Adapted from Banks & Prinzmetal, 1976.) This contradicts the usual finding from detection tasks wherein reaction time is shortest for the display with the fewest elements (Panel A).

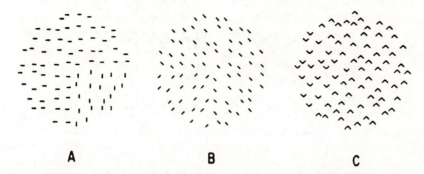

A   B   C

FIG. 6.6.   The task is to locate the region of the field containing the
disparate elements. These panels show how elements group on the basis of
similar line slope to make the task easy in Panels A and B but difficult in
Panel C. (Adapted from Olson & Attneave, 1970.)

Normally in search tasks, increasing the number of background stimuli
to be searched through increases reaction time. This is what makes Banks
and Prinzmetal's result so striking: They found that reaction times to detect
the target were consistently shorter with arrays like the one in Panel B
(which contains six background elements) than in Panel A (which contains
only four). In other arrays, like the one shown in Panel C, reaction times
were longer than in Panel A. The point is that if background (or "noise")
elements are added in the proper way, they can actually improve
performance.

The best explanation of Banks and Prinzmetal's finding may be that in
Panel B, the background elements all group together because of their
proximity (and, of course, their physical identity). This leaves the target
item perceptually isolated, because it is no farther removed from the rest of
the stimuli in the array than any other corner element. Finally, in Panel C,
the item that stands out as figure is not the target; but because, as figure, it
captures attention, this delays the process of detecting the real target.

Similarity. [...] The most systematic look at grouping by similarity using
performance measures comes from the studies of Beck (1966, 1967) and his
associates and from the work of Olson and Attneave (1970). An example
of this work is shown in Fig. [6.6]. The subject is presented with a circular
field containing many elements. One sector of the circle contains elements
different from those comprising the remainder of the array. The task is to
locate this disparate sector. Reaction-time measures and phenomenological impressions tell the same story here: The task is much easier with some
arrays than with others. In particular, differences in line slope between the
disparate sector and the rest of the array make for easy discrimination. Of

FIG. 6.7.   The task is again to locate the region of the field containing the disparate elements. (A) Line-slope differences are present, and the task is easy. (B) Line-slope differences are absent, and the task is easy. (C) Line-slope differences are present, and the task is easy but no easier than in Panel B. (D) Line-slope differences are present, but the task is hard. Taken together, these panels show that differences in line slope are neither necessary nor sufficient for grouping.

course, other kinds of disparities are helpful, too, such as color or brightness differences . . . but with respect to dimensions of shape or form, slope differences are critical. Thus, slope similarity seems to be a critical factor in perceptual grouping. [. . .]

What makes these kinds of procedures different from ordinary, garden-variety measures of stimulus discriminability is that they tap special features of the perceptual grouping process that are not shared by other processes. In other words, these results do much more than just demonstrate that elements that differ in line slope are more dissimilar than those that do not. In fact, Beck's later work has shown that grouping by similarity has little in common with "ordinary" similarity. To illustrate, Beck and Ambler (1972) showed that in a field of several upright Ts, a tilted T is much easier to detect than is an L. The tilted T differs in line slope from an upright T, whereas an L does not. Thus, this result corroborates the preceding ones. Interestingly, however, by conventional measures such as similarity ratings (Beck, 1967), T and tilted *T* are no more dissimilar than are T and L. Moreover, the superiority of tilted *T* over L in the detection tasks above only held up when there were two or more upright Ts present as background elements in the array; otherwise, the superiority vanished.

These results show that the pairwise similarity of two elements taken in isolation does not predict whether they will group in a structured or cluttered visual field. Different stages of the perceptual system apparently use different criteria for similarity. [...]

The work of Beck, [and] of Olson and Attneave ... has contributed much to our understanding of grouping by similarity. Still, there remain a number of unresolved questions. [...] Figure [6.7] demonstrates some problems with the line-slope hypothesis. Panel A shows an array like the one shown in Fig. [6.6B], where a difference in line slope presumably makes discrimination of the disparate sector easy. Panel B shows a case where despite the absence of line-slope differences, the disparate sector is still quite readily perceptible or is at least as easy to spot as in Panel C, where line-slope differences *do* exist. Panel D shows a case where despite the *presence* of line-slope differences, discrimination is difficult, so in this case, the prediction fails in a different way than in Panel B. Thus, line-slope differences are neither necessary nor sufficient for discrimination, but just what the missing factor might be is far from clear. ...

A second difficulty for the line-slope hypothesis is illustrated in Fig. [6.8]. Panel A shows a blowup of the center four elements of Panel A in Fig. [6.7]. Here there are only four diagonal line segments, with one segment having a slope opposite that of the other three. Sager and I have

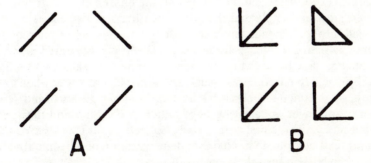

FIG. 6.8.   (A) A blowup of the four centermost elements of Fig. 6.7A, but in contrast to Fig. 6.7A, the task of locating the disparate element here is difficult. (B) A blowup of the four centermost elements of Fig. 6.7C, but the task remains easy. It is argued that in Fig. 6.8A, the four elements group to form a unitary configuration, whereas in Fig. 6.8B, the elements remain as four separate stimuli.

found that it is extremely difficult to identify the disparate element in this array, even though Fig. [6.7A] suggests that it should be easy. The problem is that subjects consistently select the wrong element as the disparate one. In this particular stimulus, they see the lower left element as odd, although a little scrutiny shows that in reality, the odd one is hiding in the upper right. The likely basis of this illusion is (once again) perceptual grouping but not grouping by similarity. Rather, the four diagonals in Panel A appear to group into a unitary shape, looking like an open box with a stick popping out. The three lines forming the box are perceptually grouped into a single unit, and subjects perceive the solitary stick as the disparate element. (I return to this phenomenon later.) Panel B of Fig. [6.8] shows a set of elements where the odd element is easy to detect. Here there is no tendency for the entire array to be perceived as a global unit, as was the case in Panel A. A problem for theory is to explain why grouping works so differently in these two cases.

[. . .]

Global Factors

Although some of the factors influencing grouping can be identified with stimulus properties such as proximity, similarity, and good continuation, other factors are more closely tied to global or conceptual properties. Gestalt demonstrations have shown that the role played by any one part of a configuration may be dictated by the configuration as a whole. A simple curved line, for instance, can be processed as the letter C when embedded in text but can be coded as a nose when embedded in a cartoon face. Thus, some local and perhaps minor perturbation in the perceptual field can have consequences for organization throughout the entire field. . . . If this claim is correct, it would imply that the probability that any two elements in the field will group depends on what other elements are simultaneously present. Pomerantz and Schwaitzberg (1975) demonstrated this in a performance task by showing that the grouping that exists between two normally oriented parentheses—such as)(—can be destroyed when a third parenthesis is added—such as)(). In this example, the first and second elements no longer appear to group; rather, the second and third group together and leave the first perceptually isolated. . . . It is reassuring that a standard textbook phenomenological demonstration of perceptual reorganization can be demonstrated objectively as well.

Prägnanz. The law of Prägnanz (or the minimum principle) states that the visual field will be organized in the simplest or best way possible. Phenomenological demonstrations of Prägnanz abound (Hochberg, 1974). If we accept Prägnanz as a fact, the question becomes: *How* does the perceptual field come to be organized in the best possible way? (Let us ignore for the moment the longstanding problem of defining what is "best" without circularity.) Three alternatives suggest themselves.

The first is that organization is achieved in a purely top-down fashion. That is, the perceptual system begins with a simple organizational scheme and sees if it will work. If the elements of the field will fit this best organization, the organization is accepted, and no further schemes are tried. . . . If not, the next best organization is attempted, and so forth. This is a pure top-down approach, because the starting point is an organizational scheme, to which one tries to fit the sensory data.

A second logical possibility is that the perceptual system rapidly attempts a large number of organizations in no particular order, and after a critical number of organizations have been attempted, or after a critical amount of time has elapsed, the best organization is accepted. This inelegant, brute-force approach is also top-down in spirit.

The third alternative, and the one that I believe comes closest to the original Gestalt theory, holds that Prägnanz works from the bottom up. Recall that according to Gestalt theory, organization worked automatically without influence from learned or strategic processing. Just as a soap bubble achieves the simplest possible configuration (e.g., the most symmetrical) without the need for goals or purposes, so does perception work automatically toward the good figure. For some, it may seem odd to link Gestalt phenomena—which are so global in nature—with bottom-up processing—with its frequent emphasis on local constraints; but this is, I believe, the correct way to classify original Gestalt theorizing in terms of current information-processing concepts.

Let me illustrate how local processing can lead to the best figure by describing a study Joseph Psotka and I performed in 1974. Subjects were presented with dot patterns of the type Garner has used in his studies of pattern goodness. Their job was to indicate how they saw each pattern to be organized by drawing lines between the elements, as in the children's game of connect-the-dots. The idea was that people organize these collections of dots as they organize clusters of stars into constellations resembling simple or familiar figures. Figure [6.9] shows some of these organizations.

For certain stimuli, subjects were in virtually unanimous agreement about how the pattern should be organized. Not surprisingly, these were, for the most part, Garner's "good" patterns. For the "poor" patterns, however, there were almost as many different perceived organizations as there were subjects in the experiment. Thus, we have another way of demonstrating Garner's rule that good patterns have few alternatives (Garner, 1970), one that can be applied to individual stimuli (and not just to reflection and rotation subsets).

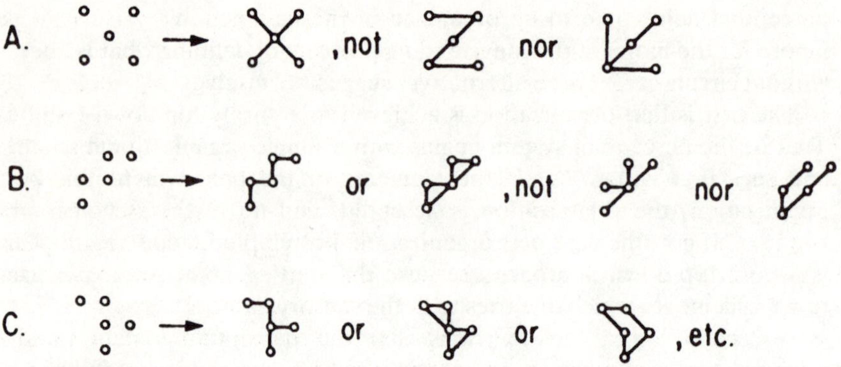

FIG. 6.9.   The task is to connect the dots of each pattern with lines so as to reflect its perceived organizations. The better the dot pattern, the more agreement there is across subjects as to how it is seen to be organized. Some sample organizations that were given, and some that were not, are shown.

Both the particular organizations with which these stimuli were perceived as well as the generally greater intersubject agreement for good patterns may be explained by bottom-up principles alone. Consider first, Pattern A in Fig. [6.9]. This pattern is most often organized as an X-shaped configuration. Of all the possible ways in which this pattern could have been organized, this particular organization minimizes both the total length of the path connecting the dots and the total number of straight lines used in the path. No other organization would connect the dots so efficiently with respect to path length (i.e., proximity) or number of lines used (good continuation). Note that it also preserves the symmetry inherent in the original dot pattern; of the other logically possible connecting schemes, many would violate this symmetry. Next, look at Pattern B. This pattern is of intermediate goodness according to both Garner's objective measure (size of the rotation-reflection equivalence set) and goodness ratings. The most popular organization selected by our subjects is the "staircase" shown. This organization is optimal as it is the only one that minimizes total path length; also, it preserves fully the symmetry inherent in the unconnected dot pattern (although there are other organizations that do this equally well). But the most popular organization does not minimize the number of straight lines used in the connecting path; it employs four line segments, although only three are required. So in this case, the rules of proximity and of symmetry point toward one set of organizations, and the role of good continuation points toward a different set. Two organizations that minimize the number of straight line segments used are also shown in the figure. Note that one of these two (the third from the left) preserves the symmetry of the dot pattern, but it requires a greater path length. This organization was never selected by our subjects. So for this particular pattern, two rules of organization—proximity and good continuation—are in conflict, and proximity seems to have dominated.

Psotka and I collected perceived organizations on large numbers of dot patterns from dozens of subjects, and two general principles seem to hold. First, one can predict perceived organizations with remarkable success on the basis of a few objective, measurable properties of the stimulus. For example, for 14 of the 17 dot patterns tested in one experiment, the most popular organization was also one with the shortest path length. Second, the "good" patterns are the ones for which the *various rules of grouping all point to a single, unique organization.* These are the patterns that the subjects rate as good and for which different subjects tend to select identical organizational schemes. For the poor patterns, the story is quite different. First, the different organization rules come into conflict with one another; and second, each rule does not point toward a single solution but rather to several equally good solutions.

In conclusion, one need not appeal to hypothesis testing or similar top-down processing strategies to account for perceived organization of simple dot patterns. The best possible organization of a dot pattern can be achieved from the bottom up through the application of low-level rules. The most appropriate model would be one in which separate subsystems of preattention struggle independently to achieve a stable organization of a figure based on one grouping rule or another. If enough of these subsystems "vote" for the same organization, then the pattern will be organized quickly and predictably, and it will be seen as a good configuration. If the voting is split, then compromises will be necessary, the final organization will be slow in coming, it will be unpredictable, and the result will be seen as a poor configuration [. . .]

Pattern Recognition Models. The distinction between top-down and bottom-up processing is most often raised in the context of models for pattern recognition and object recognition. A widely held belief . . . is that bottom-up models of recognition are inadequate. These models state that the identity of an object, say, is inferred from the set of features detected. The biggest stumbling block for bottom-up theories has proved to be certain Gestalt phenomena—particularly those that demonstrate that by rearranging the same features, different objects may be perceived. The whole is more than the sum of its parts, because the parts do not uniquely determine the whole.

Top-down models are relatively immune from such criticism, because they do not claim that stimuli are recognized from their features alone. In these models, the perceptual system starts with a hypothesis and then samples sensory data to see if they fit the hypothesis. Where does the original hypothesis come from? Many sources are possible, but the most important one is context. A secondary source of hypotheses is a crude (preattentive) bottom-up analysis of the input signal (which would imply a mixture of top-down and bottom-up processing). Given an unknown object, a rough estimate of its size, color, shape, and the like can go a long way toward eliminating alternative hypotheses. When a hypothesis is matched by the sensory data, recognition takes place regardless of whether other hypotheses would fit the data as well or even better.

SOME CONSEQUENCES OF GROUPING

Wholistic Processing

[If the] function of grouping is to create the segmented and coherent units upon which later stages may operate, [then] there should be detectable consequences of grouping on these later processes. The major consequence of unit formation is that the units so formed should be relatively indivisible. Independent processing of the components forming a unit should be difficult, whereas processing of the unit as a whole should be easy. I have already summarized a good deal of evidence from selective and divided attention tasks suggesting that this notion is correct. Let me now present corroborating evidence from two other paradigms. The first is a matching task used in an experiment by Sekuler and Abrams (1968). Subjects were presented with two dot patterns, which were created by filling in cells in a four-by-four matrix. Subjects had to decide, under time pressure, whether the two patterns were the same or different. One group of subjects was told to respond "same" if and only if the two dot patterns were identical in every respect; if any cell did not correspond between the two patterns, they should respond "different." A second group was told to respond "same" so long as at least one cell corresponded between the two matrices; only if the two patterns were different in *every* respect were they to respond "different."

If dot patterns are organized preattentively into unitary configurations, then we should not expect that subjects could process them dot by dot; rather, wholistic processing should be mandatory or at least primary. This is just what Sekuler and Abrams found. Subjects were much faster in responding under the first set of instructions (which called for total identity of the two patterns) than under the second (which did not). In fact, when two patterns were identical, subjects were faster to respond that they matched in all their cells than to respond that they matched in at least one cell! This is a remarkably powerful demonstration of wholistic processing. [...]

A second piece of evidence comes from a study of Clement and Weiman (1970). They asked subjects to classify tachistoscopically presented dot patterns. Patterns were presented one at a time, but only two alternative patterns were possible in any block of trials. As in the Sekuler and Abrams study, the dot patterns were constructed by filling in cells of an imaginary matrix. In some of the conditions, the stimuli were "good" dot patterns, ... whereas in others, they were "poor." In order to classify two of these dot patterns, it is necessary only to find a single cell of the matrix that differentiates between the two and to decide, on each trial, whether a dot is present or absent in that cell. Clement and Weiman reasoned that if subjects employed this simple strategy, they would not be processing entire patterns, and so there should be no effect on performance of the goodness of the whole patterns.

The results showed that subjects processed the good patterns much faster than the poor ones. Clement and Weiman next wondered whether subjects simply did not realize that they could use the strategy of attending to a single cell, and so the experimenters pointed out this possibility to them; but the superiority of good over poor patterns still held. In subsequent experiments, progressively more pressure was placed on subjects to process dots rather than patterns, but it was not until whole-pattern processing was made virtually impossible that the difference between good and poor patterns vanished. Thus, if wholistic processing is not absolutely mandatory, it surely is the natural or primary mode of processing, and experimenters must go to pains to induce subjects to process part by part.

So in two more types of task—"same"–"different" and two-alternative discrimination—wholistic processing of dot patterns appears to be the norm. What is more, as far as the "same"–"different" task is concerned, wholistic processing may be the norm regardless of what kinds of stimuli are used. It is a common finding that when subjects must match complex, multidimensional stimuli, the "same" response is faster than the "different" response. ... This finding poses a problem for feature analytic models of processing. In order to respond "same," it must be determined that the two stimuli match with respect to every feature or component part; but to respond "different," only one featural difference need be detected. Accordingly, "different" should be at least as fast as "same" and usually faster. Despite this straightforward logic, "same" is often faster than "different," even when the features or dimensions of the stimuli are separable in Garner's sense of the word. ...

Global Superiority

In discussing the consequences of grouping, my emphasis so far has been on the indivisibility of perceptual units in processing. I hope to have established that wholes are not perceived by independent processing of parts. But how *are* they perceived? In approaching this question, a useful starting point is the fact that organized wholes can be recognized faster and better than can the parts from which the wholes are constructed. This is perhaps a counterintuitive assertion; so let me review the evidence that substantiates it.

Configural Superiority Effects.   Pomerantz, Sager, and Stoever (1977) examined a large number of discriminations between simple visual elements, such as a positive versus a negative diagonal line; a horizontal versus a vertical line; a left- versus a right-curving line; and a short versus a long line. Take as an illustration the curved-line discrimination, which uses as stimuli ordinary parentheses. We know from the selective attention studies described earlier ... that [there is a grouping effect with parentheses]. The immediate question is whether such a group can be processed faster than a single parenthesis presented by itself.

Figure [6.10] shows the paradigm used to answer this question. Subjects were presented with four stimuli arranged in a square. Three of these stimuli were always identical to one another, whereas the fourth—located at random at one of the four corners—was always different. The task was to locate this odd stimulus, and the measure was reaction time.

Figure [6.10] shows the results when the parentheses were used as stimuli. When the stimulus in each corner of the array was a single parenthesis, reaction time to locate the odd one was about 2.4 sec. When a second parenthesis was added to each corner so as to create groups, reaction time dropped to 1.5 sec, which represents a 40% reduction. Note that the parenthesis added to each corner was the same, so the context *by itself* contained no useful cues to aid discrimination. This result demonstrates that perceptual wholes can be processed faster than the component parts that differentiate them. The bottom row of the figure shows the effects of adding a horizontally oriented parenthesis. Recall that the resulting stimuli do not group by selective attention measures and so do not form perceptual wholes. Reaction time to locate the odd stimulus in this case jumped to 3.0 sec, which represents a 23% increase. Thus the context elements acted like noise and interfered with processing.

Figure [6.11] shows two more examples of context either facilitating or impeding performance. Here the basic discrimination is between a positively and a negatively sloped diagonal line. Reaction time to detect the oppositely sloped line averaged 1.9 sec. When we added a context that

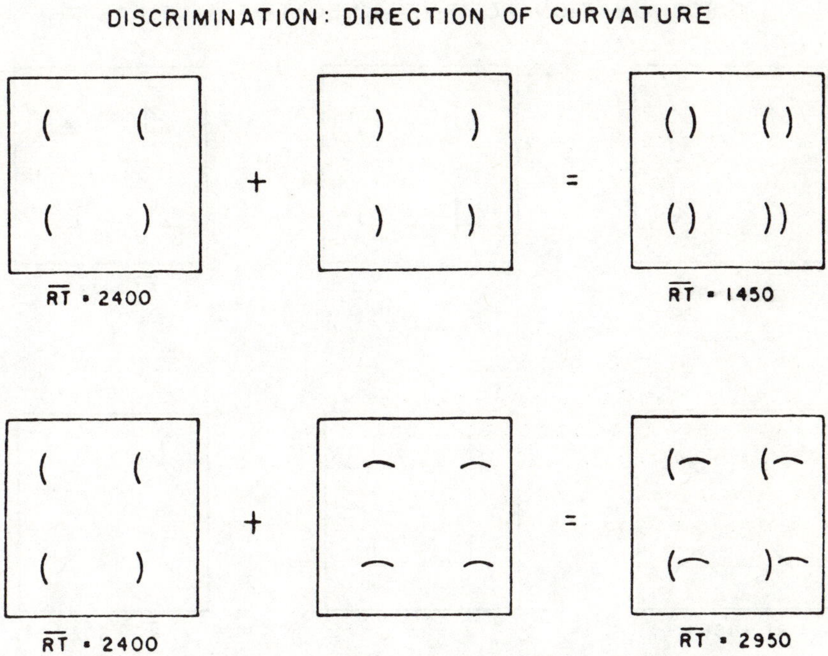

DISCRIMINATION: DIRECTION OF CURVATURE

$\overline{RT} \bullet 2400$ + $\overline{RT} \bullet 1450$ =

$\overline{RT} \bullet 2400$ + $\overline{RT} \bullet 2950$ =

FIG. 6.10. Reaction times to locate the disparate stimulus with no context elements averaged 2400 msec. In the context of elements that create perceptual groups (top row), reaction time drops to 1450 msec. In the context of elements that do not group, reaction time rises to 2950 msec. Note that the context elements do not differ from one another in either the top center or bottom center panels.

converted the stimuli into triangles and arrows, reaction time dropped to .75 sec, for a 60% reduction. When a slightly different context was added, which created stimuli appearing less wholistic, reaction time increased by 7% to about 2 sec. Finally, Fig. [6.12] shows two more cases where adding a context that appears to create good figures improves perception. The first case involves discriminating the position of a line relative to a fixed point, whereas the second involves discriminating horizontal from vertical lines. In both cases, contexts are added that create triangle versus arrow discriminations. Reaction times to locate the odd stimulus are reduced by 65% and 34%, respectively, by the addition of context.

The point of these examples is to show that context can either *improve* or *impede* performance, depending on what kind of configuration results when context is added. The improvement, which I have called a "configural superiority effect," is the more interesting phenomenon, because it implies that wholes are not recognized by way of their component parts or

DISCRIMINATION: POSITIVE vs NEGATIVE DIAGONAL

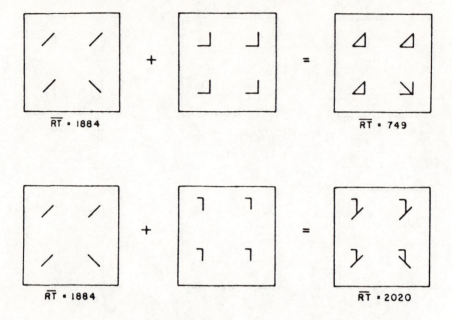

FIG. 6.11.   The task is to discriminate the line whose slope is different from the rest. The top context helps, whereas the bottom context impedes performance compared to having no explicit context present.

at least not by way of those parts the experimenter identifies. Here context does not aid perception by way of a redundancy gain (a "horse race"), because the context by itself contained no clues or information useful to the task. Instead, context aids perception by creating *emergent features*— that is, features that are possessed by perceptual wholes but not by the parts of which these wholes are constructed. . . .

Emergent Features.   As an example, consider the arrow-versus-triangle discrimination in Fig. [6.12]. These figures possess features not shared by the line segments that comprise them. One *local* emergent feature distinguishing a triangle from an arrow is the fork-shaped intersection possessed by the arrow but not by the triangle. One *global* feature is the property of closedness possessed by the triangle but not by the arrow. I would contend that the arrow and triangle are more discriminable than are the lines comprising them because these emergent features are more salient to the perceptual system than are those features that the line segments alone may have. [. . .]

Emergent features are not simply defined on simpler features; they are

DISCRIMINATION : RELATIVE POSITION OF A LINE

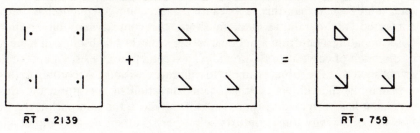

RT • 2139   RT • 759

DISCRIMINATION: HORIZONTAL vs VERTICAL

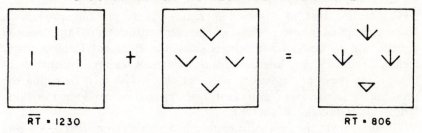

RT • 1230   RT • 806

FIG. 6.12. Two more discriminations that are markedly improved by the addition of context.

more than the sum of their parts. Certain theories of shape recognition . . . claim that angles are derived from lines in the visual system. The support for this claim comes not only from a priori plausibility but also from the arguments of the neurophysiologists Hubel and Wiesel (1962, 1965) that simple, complex, and hypercomplex cells in the visual cortex are interconnected in a serial, hierarchical fashion. If figures such as triangles and arrows were recognized by their component angles and intersections, and if these angles and intersections were in turn recognized from their constituent line segments, then one would not predict the configural superiority effects I have been describing. If the sloped line segment were the "natural" unit of shape perception, then these line segments should be processed faster than, or at least as fast as, more complex features constructed from line segments. [. . .]

Accordingly, the most plausible interpretation of configural superiority is that the emergent features possessed by perceptual wholes are detected directly by the visual system and are not derived from the output of line detectors. [. . .]

[. . .]

Return for a moment to Fig. [6.10], which shows the parenthesis discrimination task. When performance is improved by adding context, one could claim that this is because an absolute judgment has been converted into a relative one; in short, the context *adds* an anchor. Discriminating a left from a right parenthesis may be an absolute judgment of direction of curvature. By providing a second parenthesis, an anchor is established that the subject can use to calibrate decisions. According to this explanation, the subject is still judging direction of curvature, but this judgment has been made easier. The difficulty with this approach is that it fails to explain why some contexts help whereas others do not help at all. Why does adding a vertically oriented parenthesis help whereas adding a horizontal one hurts?

According to the emergent feature hypothesis, context does not serve to add an anchor. Instead, it serves to create—via the grouping process—a novel perceptual whole possessing emergent features that are detected directly. In the case of parenthesis pairs, the emergent features might include symmetry ... closedness, and others less readily describable. In recognizing these perceptual wholes, the visual system is detecting the presence or absence of emergent features and is no longer making judgments of direction of curvature.

To summarize, the emergent feature hypothesis claims that processing stimuli like ( ) and)(is *qualitatively* different from processing) and (. Context does not speed up a fixed process but instead induces a different process.

During the course of our research, Sager and I noticed that when processing individual parentheses, subjects showed strong stimulus-response compatibility effects. When classifying these stimuli by means of button presses or by sorting cards into piles, subjects had strong preferences about whether they should classify the stimulus (to the left and) to the right or vice versa. This kind of directional preference makes sense given that the discrimination is of direction of curvature. But with parenthesis pairs such as () and)), directional preference declined or disappeared. This supports my claim that the basis for discrimination shifts qualitatively to detection of emergent features with these two-element stimuli.

Forests Before, After, During, or Instead of Trees?

In the preceding section, I contrasted the processing of wholes with processing of component parts presented *in isolation*. The data reviewed there suggest that the processing of wholes cannot be predicted well from the processing of isolated parts. But how are parts processed when they are presented within a context? We can usually recognize parts when they are contained within larger configurations; we can perceive both the forest and the trees. How does this processing of local and global (part and whole) information proceed? I have already argued that wholes are not recognized by way of recognizing component parts, but I have not addressed any differences that may exist between part and whole processing. Let us consider the relative *speeds* of local and global perception. Which do we see first—the forest or the trees?

This question is a complex one, which must be asked correctly to get a sensible answer. Let me review some of the evidence on the matter and show where problems of interpretation may arise. This evidence comes from three sources: first, from research on configural superiority effects; second, from studies on the speed of processing of global configurations versus local details; and third, from experiments on embedded figures.

Superiority Effects.   First of all, we have the ... configural superiority effects I have already elaborated upon. If a complex stimulus can be perceived faster than any of its component parts presented in isolation, this might be taken as compelling evidence that we see the forest before the trees. But there are at least three reasons to question this conclusion. First, this experimental outcome does not occur much more often than does its opposite; recall the several configural *inferiority* effects I presented earlier. Given this state of affairs, it is impossible to generalize about the relative speed of perceiving forests versus trees. Second, superiority effects do not speak directly to the question as it has been phrased. The issue is whether, when presented with a forest, one sees the forest first or the trees first. Because the superiority effect experiments compare perception of a forest with perception of a solitary tree, the comparison misses the mark. Third, as I have argued earlier, when we are presented with a forest, often we may not process the trees at all, either before or after the forest. We may process emergent features of the forest (such as its density, texture, and so forth) instead. Under these circumstances, the question of before versus after is inappropriate.

Global Configurations Versus Local Details.   A second line of evidence on this question comes from experiments that use stimuli where part and whole information can be manipulated independently. Figure [6.13] gives some concrete examples from an experiment I did with Sager (Pomerantz & Sager, 1975). The idea is to construct large configurations from small ones. ... The question is whether the larger configuration or its component elements are recognized first following the onset of the entire array.

Sager and I attacked this problem by using the familiar integrality paradigm. Subjects were presented with arrays that varied in two dimensions—the global configuration portrayed and the local elements used to construct them. They had to classify the patterns using one of these

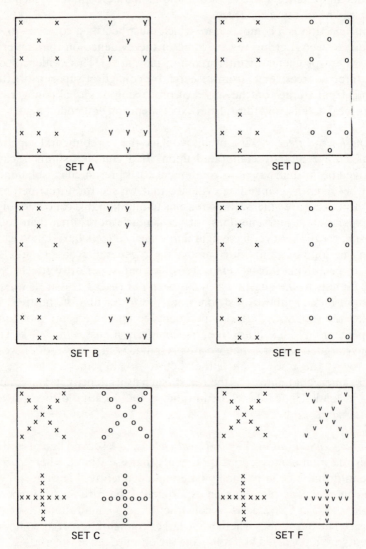

FIG. 6.13. Large (global) configurations made up from small (local) ones. The data indicate that neither the local nor the global configurations enjoy an inherent advantage in perception: which is processed faster depends on sensory factors such as visual angle and masking effects. (From Pomerantz & Sager, 1975.)

dimensions and ignore the other dimension. We wished to find whether it is easier to ignore the elements or the global configuration. We reasoned that if part information became available before whole information, as a structuralist theory might hold, then it should be easier to attend to the local elements and ignore the global configuration than vice versa. But if wholistic processing was primary, as a Gestaltist theory might hold, then the opposite outcome would be predicted.

Before the proper experiment could be conducted, it was necessary to find stimuli for which the global dimension and the local dimension possess equal discriminability, because all other things being equal, the dimension having the greater discriminability will clearly be the harder one to ignore. . . . Although this might be an interesting effect, it was not the one we were looking for. The results from our experiment, in which the baseline discriminability of the two dimensions *was* matched, showed that neither dimension could be ignored completely. Thus, the dimensions appear to be integral. But the global dimension proved to be consistently easier to ignore than the local one, even in conditions where the global dimension was more descriminable than the local one. This outcome is therefore closer to a structuralist prediction than to a Gestalt one.

Two Types of Configurations   Part of the apparent confusion that arises from experiments on global versus local processing may be due to the existence of two distinct types of stimulus configurations that may be constructed from local elements. Figure [6.14] illustrates this distinction. Panel A of this figure shows stimuli similar to the ones used in the

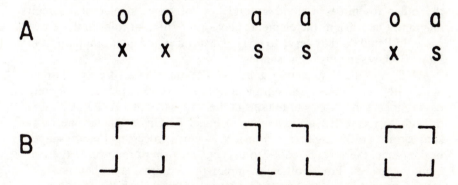

FIG. 6.14.   Two types of configurations. In Panel A, identity of the local elements does not affect the identity of the global configuration. As in Fig. 6.13, the elements serve only as placeholders. In Panel B, where a different set of local elements is used, each set of elements creates a different global configuration. Note that in other respects, the sets in Panel A and in Panel B are equivalent.

experiments just described. Four elements are arranged into a square configuration, and this configuration remains the same regardless of what elements are employed. Panel B shows a structurally equivalent set of stimuli that produces a greatly different perceptual effect, because changing any single element here changes the global configuration. That is, the whole is *not* independent of the identity of the parts, as it was in Panel A.

These two types of configurations may have little to do with one another, and if we do not distinguish between the two in our experiments and our theorizing, we will end up attempting to make generalizations over unrelated phenomena. With the stimuli in Panel A, the elements serve mainly as "placeholders" for the global configurations. The identity of the elements is of no consequence for the larger configuration (save for indicating texturelike information), and there is no reason why information about these elements would have to precede information about the wholes in the processing stream. In Panel B, however, the elements delineate the contours that define the configuration; so extracting the identity of the elements could, at least in principle, be of great value in recognizing the global stimulus.

Figure [6.15] shows another example of this distinction. The two arrays in Panel A are similar to the ones I presented earlier in describing Olson and Attneave's (1970) research. In these arrays, the elements serve to define different textures. The two arrays in Panel B show the four centermost elements of the arrays in Panel A. Here the elements do not serve to define different textures but rather to define shapes. For example, one of the stimuli looks like a box with a stick protruding from it, whereas the other resembles a tilted ground symbol from an electrical circuit diagram. Once again, the elements play vastly different roles in these two cases. In Panel A, they serve to mark out surfaces and their boundaries; in Panel B, they serve to define shapes.

What does this distinction gain us? For one thing, it helps resolve apparently anomalous results in the literature. For example, . . . it is quite easy to locate the disparate regions in the arrays in panel A, but it is quite difficult to locate the odd element in Panel B. Given that in one case, subjects are processing textured surfaces but are processing unitary shapes in the other, there is no reason to expect similar performance on the two kinds of arrays. For another example, this contrast may help resolve inconsistencies in the "forest-before-trees" studies. With the stimuli used . . . by Pomerantz, Sager, and Stoever (1977), the elements serve to define the overall configuration, and global stimuli are perceived better than component parts. But with the multielement stimuli used by Pomerantz and Sager (1975) . . . the global configurations are independent of the elements, and the evidence for superior global processing is quite weak.

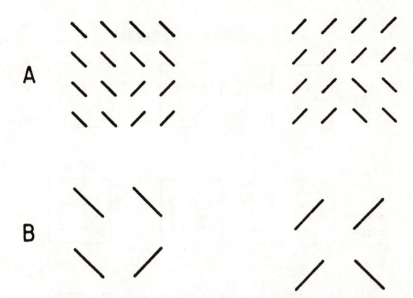

FIG. 6.15.   In Panel A, the local elements define textures (or surfaces) rather than configurations, as happened also in Figs. 6.6 and 6.7. In Panel B, only the four centermost elements of the stimuli in Panel A are shown. Here the elements group to form shapes, and the identity of the shape is determined by which elements it includes.

Embedded Figures.   The final line of evidence bearing on the forest-before-trees question comes from studies on embedded figures. ... The impression one gets from viewing certain configurations is that the whole masks the parts, or that the forest hides the trees. For example, one does not normally perceive the numeral 3 embedded in the shape of the numeral 8 or the numeral 4 in the capital letter *H*. It is not difficult to "see" embedded figures, because their contours are clearly visible. The problem is that the embedded figure does not stand out as a discrete unit. In theoretical terms, the embedded figure—or target—groups perceptually with the context, and this grouping prevents selective attention to the target. Typically, figures are hidden by capitalizing on the laws of good continuation and symmetry, as in the case of the 3 embedded within the 8. One might argue that in cases like this, the context does not merely hide the target but actually eliminates it by eliminating its component features. For instance, if one feature of the numeral 3 were the *termination* of a line segment, then context would have destroyed the target, not hidden it. If so, such stimuli would tell us little about the relative speed of processing parts and wholes.

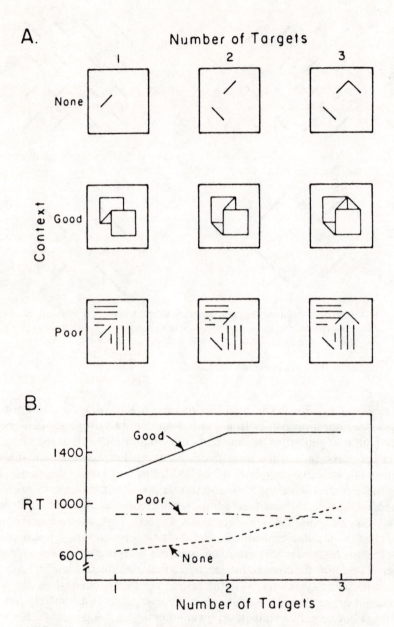

FIG. 6.16. (A) The task is to count the number of diagonal lines contained in the array (1, 2, or 3). The horizontal and vertical context lines are not to be counted. (B) Reaction times for counting. The "good", cubelike context impeded performance the most; the "poor", sticks context interfered little if at all.

There are cases, however, where the target figure remains virtually intact despite the addition of context. Consider, for example, the stimuli used by Weisstein and Harris (1974), some of which are shown in Fig. [6.16]. In their paradigm, the targets are the diagonal line segments, whereas the context is provided by the horizontal and vertical lines. Even in the case where the targets group with the context to form cubelike figures, the target lines are still quite apparent to the eye. Nevertheless, their appearance is altered by the context: in particular, the target lines may not appear diagonal. Instead, the stimulus is seen as a cubelike structure, drawn in perspective, containing only 90-degree angles. If the target the subjects are searching for is a diagonal line, the cube context could impede performance by hiding the target.

In an unpublished study, Lawrence Sager and I tested this possibility. To do this, it was necessary to devise a task that forced subjects to process the target lines individually, instead of processing unitary wholes. The task we chose was *counting* . . ., where the subject had to indicate the number of target lines present in an array. The stimuli we used are shown in Panel A of Fig. [6.16]. Target lines were presented either by themselves or in one of two different contexts, which consisted of horizontal or vertical lines. Each stimulus contained one, or two, or three (diagonal) target lines, and the subject indicated how many targets were present by pressing one of three response keys.

Panel B of Fig. [6.16] shows the results. For the three types of stimulus arrays, counting was by far the slowest with the cubelike configurations. So it appears, in this case, that the forest actually does hide the trees. Recall that the cubelike context *improves* performance relative to the flat "sticks" context in the superiority effects experiments, but it *hinders* performance here. This result provides an insight into the mechanism behind the object superiority effect of Weisstein and Harris (1974): Context does not improve the perceptibility *of component parts*. That is, the cubelike surround does not improve the detectability of the diagonal target lines, which is one possible interpretation of this particular superiority effect. Instead, the context makes the targets *harder* to perceive. The explanation for the superior perception of the cube stimuli in comparison to the sticks stimuli . . . is that with the cubes, subjects are processing salient emergent features that the other stimulus configurations lack. One task of future research will be to determine what those emergent features may be.

REFERENCES

Banks, W. P., & Prinzmetal, W. (1976) Configurational effects in visual information processing. *Perception and Psychophysics, 19*, 361–367.

Beck, J. (1966) Perceptual grouping produced by changes in orientation and shape. *Science*, *154*, 538–540.

Beck, J. (1967) Perceptual grouping produced by line figures. *Perception and Psychophysics*, *2*, 491–495.

Beck, J., & Ambler, B. (1972) Discriminability of differences in line slope and in line arrangement as a function of mask delay. *Perception and Psychophysics*, *12*, 33–38.

Clement, D. E., & Weiman, C. F. R. (1970) Instructions, strategies, and pattern uncertainty in a visual discrimination task. *Perception and Psychophysics*, *7*, 333–336.

Garner, W. R. (1970) The stimulus in information processing. *American Psychologist*, *25*, 350–358.

Gottwald, R. L., & Garner, W. R. (1975) Filtering and condensation tasks with integral and separable dimensions. *Perception and Psychophysics*, *18*, 26–28.

Hochberg, J. (1974) Higher order stimuli and interresponse coupling in the perception of the visual world. In R. B. MacLeod, & H. L. Pick (Eds.), *Perception: Essays in honor of James J. Gibson*. Ithaca, N.Y.: Cornell University Press.

Hubel, D. H., & Wiesel, T. N. (1962) Receptive fields, binocular interaction and functional architecture in the cat's visual context. *Journal of Physiology*, *160*, 106–154.

Hubel, D. H., & Wiesel, T. N. (1965) Receptive fields and functional architecture in two nonstriate visual areas (18 and 19) of the cat. *Journal of Neurophysiology*, *28*, 229–289.

Johansson, G. (1975) Visual motion perception. *Scientific American*, *232*, 76–88.

Neisser, U. (1967) *Cognitive psychology*. New York: Appleton-Century-Crofts.

Olson, R. K., & Attneave, F. (1970) What variables produce similarity grouping? *American Journal of Psychology*, *83*, 1–21.

Pomerantz, J. R., & Garner, W. R. (1973) Stimulus configuration in selective attention tasks. *Perception and Psychophysics*, *14*, 565–569.

Pomerantz, J. R., & Sager, L. C. (1975) Asymmetric integrality with dimensions of visual pattern. *Perception and Psychophysics*, *18*, 460–466.

Pomerantz, J. R., Sager, L. C., & Stoever, R. J. (1977) Perception of wholes and of their component parts: Some configural superiority effects. *Journal of Experimental Psychology: Human Perception and Performance*, *3*, 422–435.

Pomerantz, J. R., & Schwaitzberg, S. D. (1975) Grouping by proximity: Selective attention measures. *Perception and Psychophysics*, *18*, 355–361.

Posner, M. I. (1964) Information reduction in the analysis of sequential tasks: *Psychological Review*, *71*, 491–504.

Sekuler, R., & Abrams, M. (1968) Visual sameness: A choice time analysis of pattern recognition processes. *Journal of Experimental Psychology*, *77*, 232–238.

Weisstein, N., & Harris, C. S. (1974) Visual detection of line segments: An object superiority effect. *Science*, *186*, 752–755.

IV LANGUAGE

7 General Constraints on Process Models of Language Comprehension

Robert de Beaugrande

THE SENTENCE COMPREHENSION PARADIGM

[...]

For many years, the major concern of "psycholinguistics" was defined as: to test the psychological reality of current linguistic theories or models. This outlook encouraged researchers to construe structural analysis (as performed by professional linguists) as the model of language comprehension (as performed by human language users). This tactic was adopted variously for immediate constituent analysis (e.g. Johnson, 1965) and transformational grammar (e.g. Mehler, 1963), while some researchers (e.g. Clark & Clark, 1977) experimented with eclectic combinations of many kinds of approaches. The usual assumption was that people comprehend language by sorting words and phrases according to much the same criteria as those used by linguistics itself.

Given the priorities of linguistics and psycholinguistics, this assumption was only to be expected. But I shall argue that the assumption is at best unproven, and at worst, incoherent. In the first place, the structural analysis performed by linguistic scholars is a specialized activity based on training that normal language users do not receive. In the second place, the taxonomies developed for language, as Sapir (1921) already pointed out, will never be totally complete or formalized, even for the specialist. How, for example, is the normal language user to decide if 'bright' is an adjective or an adverb in:

(1)   The moon shone bright.

when even linguists do not all agree? Research shows that people are not uniformly able to decide what does or does not constitute a permissible sentence of their language (Greenbaum, 1977); yet in all linguistic approaches so far, the sentence is the basic category from which all other analysis proceeds.

Consequently, structural analysis of linguists inspires a highly implausible picture of language comprehension. *Quantitatively*, it suggests an unduly lengthy treatment of surface structure, whereas normal language users may well be doing only a partial, approximative analysis (cf. Burton, 1976; Schank, Liebowitz, & Birnbaum, 1978; Masson, 1979). *Qualitatively*, it incorporates distinctions and formalities normal language users could scarcely meet. People obviously do not delay all comprehension processes until they have been given a complete sentence; they start as soon as they have a few words (Schank et al., 1975). Moreover, the boundaries of sentences are often indistinct in speech, as in this recorded sample (a "/" indicates a pause):

(2)   this time everyone was really paranoid because everyone was pretty wasted / and / luckily / we all made it through without getting checked / got on the bus and started partying and just kept mixing drinks and drinking / and some people were taking drugs and things / um

Even if the listeners waited for a sentence boundary, they often would be unable to identify it. There is a substantial literature ... showing that pauses do not necessarily indicate the boundaries of constituents or sentences. Yet linguistic analysis, whether based on immediate constituents or on transformational structures, always *begins* with the complete sentence. Though transformational grammar at least has detailed rules, it still *analyzes* a sentence only by running through all the ways it could *generate* (structurally describe) the sentence, a method that is enormously explosive and inefficient (Woods, 1978).

Further qualitative problems arise in regard to *integrating* the structural analysis into the total activity of language comprehension. Most approaches foresee a relatively independent syntactic stage that is internally well-ordered, but externally poorly integrated with meaning and purpose in real communicative situations. The general trend had been to try forcing semantics and pragmatics into the same categories of analysis as those for syntax. But the limited success of those trends suggests that the categories of different levels are probably not of the same character. For example, there is no good evidence that a proposition or a speech act must [have the same] boundaries [as] a sentence.

In recent years, psycholinguistics has moved away from a literal transposition of linguistics into comprehension. But the sentence continues to be viewed as the basic unit. The following quotations are symptomatic:

The problem of when and how a sentence is understood is, in my view, the central problem of experimental psycholinguistics. (Gough, 1971, p. 109)

The fundamental problem in psycholinguistics is simple to formulate: What happens when we understand sentences? (Johnson-Laird, 1974, p. 143)

How do we understand the relevant meaning of sentences used in ordinary contexts? This is a central problem in psychology and a primary pre-occupation of the psycholinguist. (Tanenhaus, Carroll, & Bever, 1976, p. 244)

The agreement here is all the more striking because these researchers represent totally different approaches to language research. It is also rather ominous, because normal language users do not have a well-defined notion of the sentence or of its constituent word classes. ... *What is in fact comprehended is not sentences, but conceptual content*; at most, the sentence is one surface unit among many that can be used as an aid for that task (O'Connell, 1977). But to presuppose the centrality of the sentence in everyday comprehension is to construe a special case as the general one.

In a neutral perspective, the sentence might be viewed as follows. It is a *format* which is imposed on *stretches of written discourse* to suggest several sorts of processing instructions. First, the inner organization of the sentence signals the *conceptual relatedness* of the content underlying its bounded constituents (cf. Miller & Kintsch, 1980). In one common sentence type, the subject is mapped onto an agent, and the verb onto an action; it is then expected that all parts of the subject are conceptually related to the agent, and all parts of the predicate to the action. But this kind of expectation is only a preferred hypothesis that will be modified in many contexts.

Second, the inner organization of the sentence signals the *perceptual character of a scene, object, event,* etc. being mentioned or described (Osgood & Bock, 1977). Charles E. Osgood and his associates have consistently argued that the order in which things are perceived influences the order in which words are arranged in syntactic formats. One reason that the agent is a common candidate for the subject slot in English sentences is that agents are perceived readily as the "figure" before the "ground," i.e. as the most active element in an environment; thus the subject slot, being toward the start of English sentences, is a "natural" position.

Third, the inner organization of the sentence signals the *informational hierarchy* of the underlying content. For the famous examples:

    (3)   I smeared paint on the wall.
    (4)   I smeared the wall with paint.

Fillmore (1977) showed that the item placed in the direct object slot is taken as more important to the event; only in (4) do people assume that the entire wall was covered. For the sequence:

(5)   Witness A: Before the accused emptied the safe, he shot the watchman.
       Witness B: That's not true!

Posner (1980) points out that the denial of Witness B only attacks the content underlying the main clause (the "shooting"), while that underlying the subordinate clause ("emptying the safe") remains uncontested, because it is assumed to be outside the main focus.

Fourth, the boundaries of sentences help to control the *rate* at which *chunks* of discourse content get constructed, and also the *size* of those chunks. The end of a sentence is a usual, though not obligatory, point to consolidate building blocks. Of course, conceptual relatedness extends beyond sentence boundaries, if the discourse is to be coherent. But normally, a reader can afford to pause briefly at the end of the sentence in order to integrate the current chunk with the content that has accrued so far. This procedure is sometimes described in terms of "clearing a buffer" that has been filled by the current sentence (cf. Miller & Kintsch, 1980).

These four functions of the sentence in discourse seem reasonably secure. [. . .] The point here is that in each function, the sentence is never the *only* entity capable of being so used. Thus, it hardly seems justified to uphold the sentence (or a taxonomy or sentence structures) as a theoretical framework for comprehension research. For example, though numerous experiments have been designed to contrast active sentence against passives (cf. surveys in Osgood & Bock, 1977, pp. 99–102; Levelt, 1978, pp. 24–25), the human decision to use an active or a passive depends on non-syntactic factors such as salience, imagery, vividness, activeness, etc. in the conceptual content. A purely syntactic definition of "passive sentence" thus describes no empirically unified phenomenon.

[. . .]

LANGUAGE WITHIN COGNITION AND ACTION

Abandoning the traditional contention of linguists that language is an isolated faculty, let us define language processes as *specializations* of more general process types. Syntax would then be a special case of *linear intelligence* (cf. Beaugrande, 1981a, 1981b, 1982a); semantics a special case of the *acquisition and utilization of knowledge* (Hörmann, 1976; Kintsch, 1977; Beaugrande, 1980a); and pragmatics a special case of the *construction and implementation of plans and goals* (Schank & Abelson, 1977; Cohen, 1978; McCalla, 1978; Allen, 1979; Beaugrande, 1979, 1980b). We can easily see that these three domains are themselves highly interdependent. For example, linearity applies to sequences of events in stored knowledge, and to the arrangement of steps in a plan. Thus, domains like syntax, semantics, and pragmatics are themselves distinctive only as *specializations of otherwise analogous processing capacities*. In this sense, we could envision a particular process being assigned to a *specialist*, e.g., a "semantic specialist" that keeps track of referents in the world of a discourse (cf. Winograd, 1972). The processor would be an agglomerate of *routines plus specialist communities*: these two components interact for the performance of a given task.

It follows that theories of language comprehension should be stated within those constraints which are known to apply to human processes in general. A theory that deliberately excludes limitations upon resources and memory (e.g. Chomsky, 1965) merits no further consideration, because it is humanly unreasonable. Of course, general processing constraints will not uniquely determine one theory as "correct" above all others—they will only narrow down the class of theories that are worth pursuing, and will indicate how language is situated within larger human contexts.

To begin with, the *surface text* is by necessity *linearly ordered*, either as a stream of sound or as a succession of printed images. *Linear intelligence* would be the capacity to process language, or any other task depending upon a linear mode. [. . .]

Linear processing is further defined by the nature of cognitive resources like attention and memory. Language is sufficiently complex that a processor can't hope to attend to all levels or features at once. Older models assumed that processing was done in *sequential* stages, like a relay from one black box to the next (e.g., Fromkin, 1971; Gibson, 1971). The current trend is to favor *parallel* stages that run in concurrent or overlapping ways, consulting each other freely as needed (e.g. Marslen-Wilson, 1975; Rumelhart, 1977; Woods, 1978), e.g. using semantics to eliminate syntactic ambiguities. However, the notion of "specialist communities" allows for flexible scheduling to meet varying contingencies, and thereby suspends the opposition between serial vs. parallel models.

Resource limitations suggest that parallel processing involves a shifting of *dominance* from level to level. Dominance would entail an assignment of resources above a *threshold* that is set according to the overall resources available for the occasion. If processing must be done at great speed, these thresholds would be lowered throughout the system's operations, producing what Norman and Bobrow (1975) call a "graceful degradation" of performance. The same would apply to the thresholds of *initiation* (the criteria where a process is selected and run) and of *termination* (the criteria where results are considered satisfactory and processing stops). The lower the available resources, the more inclined the processor would be to accept fuzzy, provisional criteria for these thresholds. Even so, processing does reasonably well, as shown for instance in studies of skim-reading (Masson, 1979).

One important factor in ongoing processing is of course *memory*. The principles of look-back and look-ahead require both a *retrospective* and a *predictive* representation of the text. The scheme I have worked out (Beaugrande, 1981b, 1982a) is given in [Fig. 7.1]. The various levels of processing are shown with the "shallower" levels on the top and the "deeper" ones on the bottom. The levels are factored according to the materials they process, either from the text or the processor's memory: sounds/letters, words, syntactic phrasing, concepts/relations, ideas, and goals. The text is factored (left to right) into: retrospective representation of prior text, perception of current text, and predictive representation of subsequent text. The direct contact with the surface text, according to this scheme, is only a very brief interval of perception; everything else depends upon mental representations that differ from the surface text . . . in being a complex, multi-dimensional array, not a simple word-sequence. . . .

The exact time point of perception is indicated by the zero on the time continuum. The various *memory stores* can be distinguished along this continuum by reference to their *span* (time of perseverence): *short-term sensory storage* (one or two seconds), *short-term memory* (some twenty seconds), and *long-term memory* (unlimited). . . . In early work, it was implied that each store was exclusively devoted to one sort of materials, e.g. short-term memory to syntax and long-term memory to conceptual meaning, because these materials decay at different rates. . . . However, in the approach I am outlining, these tendencies are viewed as a further instance of *specialization*. Short-term sensory storage is specialized for sounds and letters; short-term memory for syntactic phrasings and local chunks of concepts and relations; and long-term memory for ideas and goals. However, sensory perception can have at least some access to deeper levels such as conceptual meaning (Raser, 1972; Shulman, 1972). And long-term memory can retain some traces of the surface, e.g. the recollection of whether an item was presented visually or acoustically (Bray & Batchelder, 1972; Hintzman, Block, & Inskeep, 1972). Intriguingly, the latter two papers indicate that the trace of visual vs. acoustic mode has no profound effect on long-term retention of content.

Finally, there is a store of working memory defined not according to its rate of decay, but according to its capacity of about seven chunks (cf. Miller, 1956; Kintsch & Polson, 1979). Often, working memory has been simply equated with short term memory, perhaps due to the tendency to think of memory stores as distinct "locations" where materials were "sent." This static, spatial viewpoint now seems inappropriate (Kintsch, 1977). If the stores are instead differential modes of activation and specialization, then working memory can take its materials from any of the

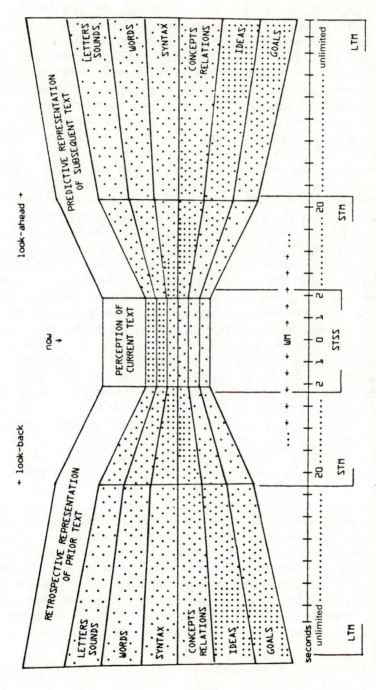

FIG. 7.1.   LTM: long-term memory; STM: short-term memory; STSS: short-term sensory storage; WM: working memory.

three stores defined by their spans.

The specializations of the memory stores are suggested by dot shadings in [Fig. 7.1]. The different spans of the stores are indicated by squeezing the graph toward its middle. So far, there is little experimental support for the right-hand side of predictive memory. I am provisionally assuming that predictive memory should be more or less symmetrical to retrospective memory, though probably shorter in spans. Intuitively, this assumption seems reasonable. A language processor can look ahead to main ideas or goals much further than to detailed concepts or syntactic phrasings; anticipation of exact words or letters is possible only over very slight distances.

The nature of the mental representation that serves in place of the text in retrospective and predictive operations is as yet hardly explored. It should have a format suitable for the tasks performed upon it. It could scarcely be a linear string of words, simply because that format is not efficient: it would unrealistically demand traces of every word . . .; it would give undue prominence to the surface and thereby neglect the underlying meaning and purpose of discourse; it would mediate against those processes that require a hierarchical arrangement to organize text content on a large scale. . . . On the other hand, the representation must be highly compatible with the surface text, because it evidently guides the impressive ability of understanders to anticipate future events. For example, eye movement studies reveal high skills in fixating those words that will contribute best to the gist, especially during skim-reading (Just, 1981). It would seem reasonable to envision the mental representation as a multi-directional network constructed and annotated to serve all the levels of processing, including words and phrases (Beaugrande, 1981b). This format would be economical in enabling operations of same or similar patterning to be consolidated in operation (Woods, 1978). One illustration could be a general look-back that searches for materials required by the various levels (e.g. a co-referent for a pronoun, a subject for a predicate, a concept for a relation, etc.) at the same time, rather like a bus whose passengers are watching for their personal destinations. . . .

The factors outlined so far—linearity, processing level, memory store specialization, distribution of resources—cannot stipulate exactly what must happen at a given instant of processing. The interaction between *routines* and *specialists* allows flexible, adaptive processing for specific contexts, occasions and human beings. For example, the amount of processing expended on an unfamiliar word is lower if the word appears in a familiar story (Wittrock, Marks, & Doctorow, 1975). Therefore, there cannot be one uniform procedure that treats all words in all settings.

QUESTIONS, QUESTIONS

Theories and models of language processing have had a long and diffuse history, ranging from "associative chaining" . . . to "behavioral conditioning" . . . to "grammatical transformations". . . . At present, new directions are emerging, but there is little agreement about what research should be done for what motives. At most, there is a consensus that the analysis of strings of words, the favorite approach of past decades, is no longer very rewarding.

The notion of *schema* had surfaced as a framework for organizing memory (Bartlett, 1932), word order (Lashley, 1951), and actions (e.g. Oldfield, 1954; Evans, 1967). It remained on the periphery of experimental psychology, however, because it complicates the design and interpretation of experiments. Recent research has returned to the schema with new emphasis, especially as a memory pattern (Kintsch, 1977; Rumelhart, 1980). Language processing is seen as the application of interactive schemas on the various levels (e.g. Rumelhart & Ortony, 1977; Adams & Collins, 1979).

As yet, the notion of schema is still too vague (Thorndyke & Yekovich, 1980) to be much more than a *label* for organized patterns of action or knowledge, rather than an *explanation*. We need to know more about how schemas are formed; how they evolve during use; how strictly they control processing; what conditions trigger their selection; and how they can interact or compete with each other. Their *structure* is less crucial than their *active use*.

The issues raised in [the last] section constitute a challenge to schema theories. No doubt schemas are vital for linear activities, as Lashley (1951) proposed. But they must also serve in a multitude of operations such as search, pattern-matching, scheduling, classifying, and so forth. If the distinction between routines and specialists is valid . . ., then schemas may be created on the spot, not just summoned from storage as fixed frames. . . . Also, a schema might itself be quite flexible about the materials that would trigger it and fill its variables. . . . All these possibilities need exploration if we are to overcome the limitations imposed by a literal adherence to structural analysis.

I would accordingly like to conclude not with a set of data, but with a set of questions. Until there are at least some provisional answers, it will be hard to know how our data should be interpreted in the larger picture of language within cognition and action.

How and when are actual operations scheduled? Given the large numbers of mathematically possible combinations of steps, how and when does a processor decide which ones to use in real life? Can provisional selections be revised at the last minute? Is there a distinct group of "scheduling specialists" called in when routines fail to apply? Or does scheduling result as a consequence of the specialists that watch over resource allotment among the concurrently operative processing levels?

How are limited resources actually allotted? Does a processor have routines for allotting resources? Can they be overridden by context, and when? How are decisions about text, type, audience, purpose, etc., translated into resource allotments?

How is overload created, noticed, or reduced? If there is a rise along several parameters [such as] complexity, informativity, etc., overload would be expected. Is the processor able to anticipate such cases and react before degradation becomes obvious? What indicators could be consulted, and what counter-measures taken? Options might include: slowing processing down; increasing redundancy: rescheduling simultaneous operations into successive ones; and so forth (Beaugrande, 1982a, 1982b).

To what extent can parallel processing combine the tasks of different levels? It would be economical if redundant or similarly patterned operations could be done in a single run-through . . ., but such may not be the case. Perhaps this economy would overtax the specialists needed to enact it. Possibly, too, the system is too diffuse for optimal co-ordination among all its subsystems.

To what extent is each act of comprehension unique, and to what extent is it comparable to others? Uniqueness of processing events is a troubling prospect when researchers set out in search of general findings. However, the essential commonalities among classes of processing events may be on a much higher plane of operational power than that of "noun phrases," "relative clauses," and the other popular entities of early psycholinguistics. High-powered processes could easily deal with a unique event as a complex intersection of the subprocesses it controls within a stipulated context.

Are there weak spots and bottlenecks in text processing? If increased limitations or overloading should arise, are there typical points in the overall system where degradation should be expected? Can increased resources or conscious training offset such cases?

How are criteria tightened or relaxed? If so many processes depend upon defining the conditions for an action (e.g., those for initiation, termination, or goodness of fit), how can such definitions be adjusted? Can search procedures be instructed to take less thorough samples, or to be satisfied with approximate candidates? Would such instructions be specific, or generally distributed throughout the whole system?

How are automatic processes consolidated? Automatic sub-routine packages would be an efficient way to operate. They might intersect one another and thereby create large complexes of activity without controls from the central feedback mechanism. These packages might make no demands on attention unless they had to be changed or suppressed. But if attention is a time-sharing mechanism, the packages would eventually interfere when enough of them were running at once to overload the system. Can attention be injected at trouble spots without degrading operations?

How rigid are the contingencies among processes? At least some processes should require the results of others in order to function. But is it absolutely necessary to obtain those results, or is it sufficient to estimate or predict them? Are the contingencies themselves routine, or do they arise sporadically? Is there some delicate timing of contingencies that might become disrupted, for example, if people had to drastically alter their rate of action?

How does a processing system arise in a child, and how does it evolve as the child matures and develops? The human processing system must traverse stages in order to deal with increased complexity. Steady accrual of experience should allow for refinement of both routines and specialists, and for generalizing across larger classes of events. But a non-strategic organization might prevent the evolution of the system and create learning blocks. . . .

Can properly designed training help to optimize processing? More elaborated processing models might make it apparent how schooling could promote comprehension skills in a more detailed, circumspect, and effective fashion than hitherto. Much language training is currently based upon very simplified or implausible models, encouraging such wasteful techniques as rote learning—a brute force attempt to build surface traces without regard for cognitive organization. In consequence, children are usually left alone to devise their own methods of comprehending or learning texts. It would be a striking coincidence if many of them did not develop less than optimal systems. . . .

How should measurable time differences in experimental data be interpreted? The classical experimental paradigm is to devise conditions, one of which includes some postulated process, and one that excludes it; if the inclusive task consumes more time, then the existence of that process appears supported or confirmed. Recent overviews (e.g. Clark & Clark, 1977; Levelt, 1978) indicate that this method has been extensively employed in the study of language comprehension as well. But if comprehension is composed of complex interactions of levels in parallel, and of detailed schedulings and contingencies, there is no clear reason to assume that all processes should be detected via increases in processing times. Automatized packages of sub-routines . . . would not show up if they run simultaneously with other operations. Time would be linearly additive only for those processes demanding attention above a certain threshold. Moreover, time increments might indicate any of a great number of processes that participate in comprehension.

How can research deal with the multiple interpretability of data? The time question . . . is just one illustration of a more general difficulty: the lack of a univocal causality between a processing event and an observable, measurable action. The traditional method has been to design and test simplistic theories based upon such single causalities: if the variance was accounted for, all was well. Such a method is not sufficient for pursuing complex process models. Instead, we need to incorporate all plausible causes into a single model. We can then try to manipulate each factor independently and watch for variances in observed data. We can show that the several causes *potentially* affect processing; but we will not normally be able to prove which cause *actually* affected an event occurring spontaneously in a natural setting. . . .

The questions raised . . . cannot be easily answered, yet they cannot be ignored either. They call for a fundamental reorganization both in theory design and in scientific methodology. We will have to learn to live with complexity not by factoring it out, but by enriching our theoretical models. In this paper, I have argued that progress will be more decisive if we concentrate less upon the structural analysis of brief artifacts, and more upon the exigencies of maintaining operations within complex, interactive systems.

REFERENCES

Adams, M., & Collins, A. (1979) A schema-theoretic view of reading. In R. Freedle (Ed.), *New directions in discourse processing*. Norwood, N.J.: Ablex, 1–22.

Allen, J. (1979) *A plan-based approach to speech act recognition*. Toronto: University of Toronto Dissertation.

Bartlett, F. (1932) Remembering. Cambridge, England: CUP.

Beaugrande, R. de. (1979) Text and sentence in discourse planning. In J. S. Petofi (Ed.), *Text vs. sentence*. Hamburg: Buske, 467–494.

Beaugrande, R. de. (1980a) *Text, discourse, and process*. Norwood, N.J.: Ablex.

Beaugrande, R. de. (1980b) The pragmatics of discourse planning. *Journal of Pragmatics, 4,* 15–42.

Beaugrande, R. de. (1981a) The linearity of reading: Fact, fiction, frontier? In J. Flood (Ed.), *Issues in reading comprehension*. Newark: IRA.

Beaugrande, R. de. (1981b) Text, attention, and memory in reading research. In R. J. Tierney, J. Mitchell, & P. Anders (Eds.), *Understanding reader's understanding*. Hillsdale, N.J.: Lawrence Erlbaum Associates.

Beaugrande, R. de. (1982a) *Text production*. Norwood, N.J.: Ablex.

Beaugrande, R. de. (1982b) Learning to read and reading to learn in the cognitive science approach. In H. Mandl, N. Stein, & T. Trabasso (Eds.), *Learning from text*. Hillsdale, N.J.: Lawrence Erlbaum Associates.

Bray, N., & Batchelder, W. (1972) Effects of instructions and retention interval on memory of presentation mode. *Journal of Verbal Learning and Verbal Behavior, 11,* 367–374.

Burton, R. (1976) *Semantic grammar*. Cambridge: BBN.

Chomsky, N. (1965) *Aspects of the theory of syntax.* Cambridge: MIT.
Clark, H., & Clark, E. (1977) *Psychology and language.* New York: Harcourt, Brace and Jovanovich.
Cohen, P. (1978) *On knowing what to say: Planning speech acts.* Toronto: University of Toronto Dissertation.
Evans, S. (1967) A brief statement of schema theory. *Psychonomic Science, 8,* 87–88.
Fillmore, C. (1977) The case for case reopened. In P. Cole, & J. Sadock (Eds.), *Grammatical relations.* New York: Academic Press.
Fromkin, V. (1971) The non-anomalous nature of anomalous utterances. *Language, 47,* 27–52.
Gibson, E. (1971) Perceptual learning and the theory of word perception. *Cognitive Psychology, 2,* 351–368.
Gough, P. (1971) Experimental psycholinguistics. In W. Dingwall (Ed.), *A survey of linguistic science.* College Park: University of Maryland.
Greenbaum, S. (Ed.), (1977) *Language and acceptability.* The Hague: Mouton.
Hintzman, D., Block, R., & Inskeep N. (1972) Memory for mode of input. *Journal of Verbal Learning and Verbal Behavior, 11,* 741–749.
Hörmann, H. (1976) *Meinen und Verstehen.* Frankfurt: Suhrkamp.
Johnson, N. (1965) The psychological reality of phrase structure rules. *Journal of Verbal Learning and Verbal Behavior, 4,* 469–475.
Johnson-Laird, P. N. (1974) Experimental psycholinguistics. *Annual Review of Psychology, 5,* 135–160.
Just, M. (1981) *What your mind does when your eyes are reading.* Paper at the AERA, Los Angeles.
Kintsch, W. (1977) *Memory and cognition.* New York: Wiley.
Kintsch, W., & Polson, P. (1979) On nominal and functional serial position: Implications for short-term memory models? *Psychological Review, 4,* 407–413.
Lashley, K. S. (1951) The problem of serial order in behavior. In L. Jeffress (Ed.), *Cerebral mechanisms of behavior.* New York: Wiley, 112–146.
Levelt, W. (1978) A survey of studies in sentence perception: 1970–1976. In W. Levelt & G. Flores d'Arcais (Eds.), *Studies in the perception of language.* New York: Wiley.
Marslen-Wilson, W. (1975) Sentence perception as an interactive parallel process. *Science, 189,* 226–228.
Masson, M. (1979) *Cognitive processes in skimming stories.* Boulder: University of Colorado Dissertation.
McCalla, G. (1978) *An approach to the organization of knowledge for the modelling of conversation.* Vancouver: University of British Columbia TR 78–4.
Mehler, J. (1963) Some effects of grammatical transformations on the recall of English sentences. *Journal of Verbal Learning and Verbal Behavior, 2,* 250–262.
Miller, G. A. (1956) The magic number seven, plus or minus two. *Psychological Review, 63,* 81–97.
Miller, J., & Kintsch, W. (1980) Readability and recall of short prose passages. *Journal of Experimental Psychology: Human Learning and Memory, 6,* 335–354.
Norman, D., & Bobrow, D. (1975) On data-limited and resource-limited processes. *Cognitive Psychology, 7,* 44–64.
O'Connell, D. (1977) One of many units: The sentence. In S. Rosenberg (Ed.), *Sentence production: Developments in research and theory.* Hillsdale, N.J.: Lawrence Erlbaum Associates, 307–313.
Oldfield, R. (1954) Memory mechanisms and the theory of schemata. *British Journal of Psychology, 45,* 14–23.
Osgood, C, & Bock, K. (1977) Salience and sentencing: Some production principles. In S.

Rosenberg (Ed.), *Sentence production: Developments in research and theory*. Hillsdale, N.J.: Lawrence Erlbaum Associates, 89–140.

Posner, R. (1980) Types of dialogue: The functions of commenting. *Discourse Processes, 3*, 381–398.

Raser, G. A. (1972) Recoding of semantic and acoustic information in memory. *Journal of Verbal Learning and Verbal Behavior, 11*, 692–697.

Rumelhart, D. (1977) Toward an interactive model of reading. In S. Dornic (Ed.), *Attention and performance VI*. Hillsdale, N.J.: Lawrence Erlbaum Associates.

Rumelhart, D. (1980) Schemata: The building blocks of cognition. In R. Spiro, B. Bruce, & W. Brewer, (Eds.), *Theoretical issues in reading comprehension*. Hillsdale, N.J.: Lawrence Erlbaum Associates, 33–58.

Rumelhart, D. & Ortony, A. (1977) The representation of knowledge in memory. In R. Anderson, R. Spiro, & W. Montague (Eds.), *Schooling and the acquisition of knowledge*. Hillsdale, N.J.: Lawrence Erlbaum Associates, 99–135.

Sapir, E. (1921) *Language*. New York: Harcourt, Brace, and Co.

Schank, R., & Abelson, R. (1977) *Scripts, plans, goals, and understanding*. Hillsdale, N.J.: Lawrence Erlbaum Associates.

Schank, R., Goldman, N., Rieger, C., & Riesbeck, C. (1975) *Conceptual information processing*. Amsterdam: North Holland.

Schank, R., Liebowitz, M., & Birnbaum, L. (1978) *Integrated partial parsing*. New Haven: Yale CS-TR 143.

Shulman, H. (1972) Semantic comparison errors in short-term memory. *Journal of Verbal Learning and Verbal Behavior. 11*, 221–227.

Tanenhaus, M., Carroll, J., & Bever, T. (1976) Sentence-picture verification models as theories of sentence comprehension. *Psychological Review, 8*, 310–317.

Thorndyke, P., & Yekovich, F. (1980) Critique of schemata as a theory of human story memory. *Poetics, 9*, 23–49.

Winograd, T. (1972) *Understanding natural language*. New York: Academic Press.

Wittrock, M., Marks, C., & Doctorow., M. (1975) Reading as a generative process. *Journal of Educational Psychology, 67*, 484–489.

Woods, W. (1978) Generalizations of ATN grammars. In W. Woods, & R. Brachman, (Eds.), *Research in natural language understanding*. Cambridge: BBN Technical Report 3963. Pp. 21–77.

8 What Does It Mean to Understand Language?

Terry Winograd

INTRODUCTION

[...]

My interests have centered around natural language. I have been engaged in the design of computer programs that in some sense could be said to "understand language," and this has led to looking at many aspects of the problems, including theories of meaning, representation formalisms, and the design and construction of complex computer systems. There has been a continuous evolution in my understanding of just what it means to say that a person or computer "understands," and this story can be read as recounting that evolution. It is long, because it is still too early to look back and say "What I was *really* getting at for all those years was the one basic idea that . . ." I am too close and too involved in its continuation to see beyond the twists and turns. The last sections of the paper describe a viewpoint that differs in significant ways from most current approaches, and that offers new possibilities for a deeper understanding of language and a grasp on some previously intractable or unrecognized problems. I hope that it will give some sense of where the path is headed.

[...]

In the mid 1960s, natural language research with computers proceeded in the wake of widespread disillusionment caused by the failure of the highly touted and heavily funded machine translation projects. There was a feeling that researchers had failed to make good on their early confident claims, and that computers might not be able to deal with the complexities of human language at all. In AI research laboratories there were attempts

175

to develop a new approach, going beyond the syntactic word-shuffling that dominated machine translation and other approaches based on key word search or statistical analysis. It was clear that for effective machine processing of language—whether for translation, question answering, or sophisticated information retrieval—an analysis of the syntactic structures and identification of the lexical items was not sufficient. Programs had to deal somehow with what the words and sentences meant.

There were a number of programs in this new vein described in the early collections of AI papers. Each program worked in some very limited domain (baseball scores, family trees, algebra word problems, etc.) within which it was possible to set up a formal representational structure corresponding to the underlying meaning of sentences. This structure could be used in a systematic reasoning process as part of the overall language comprehension system. The model of language understanding that was implicit in those programs and in many AI programs since then is illustrated in [Fig. 8.1].

This model rests on some basic assumptions about language and representation:

1. Sentences in a natural language correspond to facts about the world.
2. It is possible to create a formal representation system such that:
   (a) For any relevant fact about the world there is a corresponding structure in the representation system;
   (b) There is a systematic way of correlating sentences in natural language with the structure in the representation system that correspond to the same facts about the world; and
   (c) Systematic formal operations can be specified that operate on the

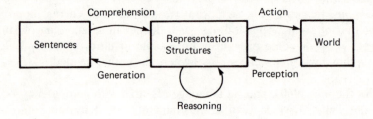

FIG. 8.1.   Basic AI model of language understanding.

representation structures to do "reasoning." Given structures corresponding to facts about the world, these operations will generate structures corresponding to other facts, without introducing falsehoods.

[...]

The critical element in this model that distinguishes it from the pre-AI programs for language is the explicit manipulation of a formal representation. Operations carried out on the representation structures are justified not by facts about language, but by the correspondence between the representation and the world being described. This is the sense in which such programs were said to "understand" the words and sentences they dealt with where the earlier machine translation programs had "manipulated them without understanding."

[...]

In fact, AI programs dealing with language do not really fit the model of [Fig. 8.1], since they have no modes of perception or action in a real world. Although they converse about families, baseball or whatever, their interaction is based only on the sentences they interpret and generate. A more accurate model for the programs (as opposed to the human language comprehension they attempt to model) would show that all connection to the world is mediated through the programmer who builds the representation. The reason that "dog" refers to dog (as opposed to referring to eggplant parmesan or being a "meaningless symbol") lies in the intention of the person who put it in the program, who in turn has knowledge of dogs and of the way that the symbols he or she writes will be used by the interpreter. [...]

SHRDLU

SHRDLU (Winograd, 1972) was a computer program for natural language conversation that I developed at MIT between 1968 and 1970. The program carried on a dialog (via teletype) with a person concerning the activity of a simulated "robot" arm in a tabletop world of toy objects. It could answer questions, carry out commands, and incorporate new facts about its world. It displayed the simulated world on a CRT screen, showing the activities it carried out as it moved the objects around.

SHRDLU had a large impact, both inside and outside the field, and ten years later it is still one of the most frequently mentioned AI programs, especially in introductory texts and in the popular media. There are several reasons why so many people (including critics of AI, such as Lighthill (1973)) found the program appealing. One major factor was its comprehensiveness. In writing the program I attempted to deal seriously with all of the aspects of language comprehension illustrated in the model. Earlier programs had focussed on one or another aspect, ignoring or shortcutting others. Programs that analyzed complex syntax did not attempt reasoning. Programs that could do logical deduction used simple patterns for analyzing natural language inputs. SHRDLU combined a sophisticated syntax analysis with a fairly general deductive system, operating in a "world" with visible analogs of perception and action. It provided a framework in which to study the interactions between different aspects of language and emphasized the relevance of nonlinguistic knowledge to the understanding process.

Another factor was its relatively natural use of language. The fact that person and machine were engaged in a visible activity in a (pseudo-)physical world gave the dialog a kind of vitality that was absent in the question-answer or problem-solution interactions of earlier systems. Further naturalness came from the substantial body of programs dealing with linguistic phenomena of conversation and context, such as pronouns ("it," "that," "then," etc.), substitute nouns ("a green *one*"), and ellipsis (e.g., answering the one-word question "Why?"). Dialog can be carried on without these devices, but it is stilted. SHRDLU incorporated mechanisms to deal with these phenomena in enough cases (both in comprehension and generation) to make the sample dialogs feel different from the stereotype of mechanical computer conversations.

In the technical dimension, it incorporated a number of ideas. Among them were:

1. Use of a reasoning formalism . . . based on the "procedural embedding of knowledge." Specific facts about the world were encoded directly as procedures that operate on the representation structures, instead of as structures to be used by a more general deductive process. The idea of "procedural embedding of knowledge" grew out of early AI work. . . . The difference between "procedural" and "declarative" knowledge has subsequently been the source of much debate (and confusion) in AI. [. . .]

2. An emphasis on how language triggers action. The meaning of a sentence was represented not as a fact about the world, but as a command for the program to do something. A question was a command to generate an answer, and even a statement like "I own the biggest red pyramid" was represented as a program for adding information to a data base. This view that meaning is based on "imperative" rather than "declarative" force is related to some of the speech act theories discussed below.

3. A representation of lexical meaning (the meaning of individual words and idioms) based on procedures that operate in the building of representation structures. This contrasted with earlier approaches in which the lexical items simply provided (through a dictionary lookup) chunks

to be incorporated into the representation structures by a general "semantic analysis" program. This was one of the things that made it possible to deal with conversational phenomena such as pronominalization. [. . .]

4. An explicit representation of the cognitive context. In order to decide what a phrase like "the red block" refers to, it is not sufficient to consider facts about the world being described. There may be several red blocks, one of which is more in focus than the others because of having been mentioned or acted on recently. In order to translate this phrase into the appropriate representation structure, reasoning must be done using representation structures corresponding to facts about the text preceding the phrase, and structures corresponding to facts about which objects are "in focus."

The attempt to deal with conversational phenomena called for an extension to the model of language understanding, as illustrated in [Fig. 8.2]. It includes additional structures (as part of the overall representation in the language understander) labelled "model of the text" and "model of the speaker/hearer." The label "model of the speaker" was chosen to reflect the particular approach taken to the problem. It is assumed that inferences about which objects are in focus (and other related properties) can be made on the basis of facts about the knowledge and current internal state (presumably corresponding to representation structures) of the other participant in the conversation. The question "could I use this phrase to refer to object X?" is treated as equivalent to "if I used this phrase would the hearer be able to identify it as naming object X?" On the other side, "what does he mean by this phrase?" is treated as "what object in his mind would he be most likely to choose the phrase for?"

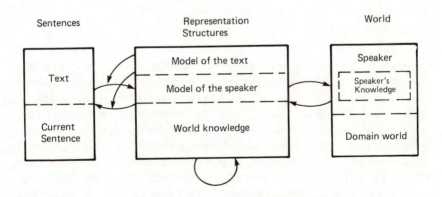

FIG. 8.2   Extended AI model of language understanding.

In addition to reasoning about the domain world (the world of toy blocks), the system reasons about the structure of the conversation and about the hypothesized internal structure and state of the other participant. In SHRDLU, this aspect of reasoning was not done using the same representation formalism as for the domain world, but in an *ad hoc* style within the programs. Nevertheless, in essence it was no different from any other reasoning process carried out on representation structures.

SEEING SOME SHORTCOMINGS

SHRDLU demonstrated that for a carefully constrained dialog in a limited domain it was possible to deal with meaning in a fairly comprehensive way, and to achieve apparently natural communication. However, there were some obvious problems with the approach, summarized here and discussed below:

1. The explicit representation of speaker/hearer internal structure was *ad hoc*, and there was no principled way to evaluate extensions.
2. The notion of word definition by program, even though it opened up possibilities beyond more traditional logical forms of definition, was still inadequate.
3. It took rather strained reasoning to maintain that the meaning of every utterance could be structured as a command to carry out some procedure.
4. The representation and reasoning operations seemed inadequate for dealing with common-sense knowledge and thought reflected in language.

The Internal Structure

In building a simpler system as illustrated in [Fig. 8.1], the programmer is creating a model of the language comprehension process. In creating the representation structures corresponding to facts about the domain, he or she is guided by an idea of what is true in the domain world—in representing facts about blocks, one can draw on common-sense knowledge about physical objects. On the other hand, in trying to create structures constituting the model of the speaker/hearer as in [Fig. 8.2], there is no such practical guide. In essence, this model is a psychological theory, purporting to describe structures that exist in the mind. This model is then used in a reasoning process, as part of a program whose overall structure itself can be thought of as a hypothesis about the psychological

structure of a language understander.
[...]
The problem is hard to delimit, since it touches on broad issues of understanding. In SHRDLU, for example, the program for determining the referent of a definite noun phrase such as "the block" made use of a list of previously mentioned objects. The most recently mentioned thing fitting the description was assumed to be the referent. Although this approach covers a large number of cases, and there are extensions in the same spirit which cover even more, there is a more general phenomenon that must be dealt with. Winograd (1974) discusses the text "Tommy had just been given a new set of blocks. He was opening the box when he saw Jimmy coming in."

> There is no mention of what is in the box—no clue as to what box it is at all. But a person reading the text makes the immediate assumption that it is the box which contains the set of blocks. We can do this because we know that new items often come in boxes, and that opening the box is a usual thing to do. Most important, we assume that we are receiving a connected message. There is no reason why the box has to be connected with the blocks, but if it weren't, it couldn't be mentioned without further introduction. (Winograd, 1974)

Important differences in meaning can hinge on subtle aspects of the speaker/hearer model. For example, in the first sentence below, it is appropriate to assume that the refrigerator has only one door, while in the second it can be concluded that it has more than one. On the other hand, we cannot conclude from the third sentence that the house has only one door.

> When our new refrigerator arrived, the door was broken.
> When our new refrigerator arrived, a door was broken.
> When we got home from our vacation, we discovered that the door had been broken open.

The problem, then, is to model the ways in which these connections are made. In general this has led to an introspective/pragmatic approach. Things get added to the representation of the speaker/hearer because the programmer feels they will be relevant. They are kept because with them the system is perceived as performing better in some way than it does without them. There have been some interesting ideas for what should be included in the model of the speaker/hearer, and how some of it might be organized but the overall feeling is of undirected and untested speculation, rather than of persuasive evidence or of convergence towards a model that would give a satisfactory account of a broad range of language phenomena.

Word Definition

The difficulty of formulating appropriate word definitions was apparent
even in the simple vocabulary of the blocks world and becomes more
serious as the domain expands. In SHRDLU, for example, the word "big"
was translated into a representation structure corresponding to "having X,
Y, and Z coordinates summing to more than 600 units (in the dimensions
used for display on the screen)." This was clearly an *ad hoc* stopgap, which
avoided dealing with the fact that the meaning of words like "big" is always
relative to an expected set. The statement "They were expecting a big
crowd" could refer to twenty or twenty thousand, depending on the
context. By having word definitions as programs, it was theoretically
possible to take an arbitrary number of contextual factors into account,
and this constituted a major departure from more standard "compositional" semantics in which the meaning of any unit can depend only on
the independent meanings of its parts. However, the mere possibility did
not provide a guide for just what it meant to consider context, and what
kind of formal structures were needed.

On looking more closely, it became apparent that this problem was not
a special issue for comparative adjectives like "big," but was a fundamental part of the meaning of most words. [. . .] In classical discussions of
semantics, "bachelor" has been used as an example of a word with a clear
paraphrase in more elementary terms—"unmarried adult human male."
But if someone refers to a person as a "bachelor" in normal conversation,
much more is meant. It is inaccurate if used in describing the Pope or a
member of a monogamous homosexual couple, and might well be used in
describing an independent career woman.

[. . .] When we move to a larger vocabulary, the problem becomes
even more obvious. Each of the nouns in the sentence "The administ-
ration's dishonesty provoked a crisis of confidence in government" raises
a significant problem of definition, and it is clear that purpose and
context play a major role in determining what will be called a "crisis,"
"dishonesty," or even in deciding just what constitutes an "administ-
ration."
[. . .]

Meaning as Command

SHRDLU was based on a formalism in which the meaning of a sentence
was represented as a command to carry out some action. A question is a
command to generate a sentence satisfying a set of constraints, and a
statement is a command to add a formula to the data base. This shift of
viewpoint from meaning-as-statement to meaning-as-command provided

some interesting ways of talking about sentences, but in its naive form it is clearly unworkable.

The good part of the idea was the view of an utterance as triggering some kind of activity in the hearer. The bad part of the idea was the analogy with computer programming languages, in which there is a direct correspondence between the linguistic form and the sequence of activities to be carried out. In the case of natural language, much more is going on. Both speaker and hearer are engaged in ongoing processes of trying to make sense of their conversations and the world they inhabit. The interpretation of utterances is only one of many activities, and interacts with perception, reasoning, memory, and all the other aspects of cognition. ... When I utter a sentence, I have no way of anticipating in any detail the processing it will invoke in the hearer. It clearly includes much more than simply obeying or storing away a fact. The following simple examples illustrate some of what goes on.

1. Tom has never failed a student in Linguistics 265.
2. I'm sorry I missed the meeting yesterday. My car had a flat tire.
3. There's an animal over there in the bushes.

Sentence 1 is true in many circumstances, including the one in which Tom has never taught Linguistics 265. However, in ordinary conversation, the hearer makes the additional implication that Tom has taught the course, and is justified in accusing the speaker of bad faith if the implication is not warranted. Similarly in sentence 2, the hearer assumes that there is a coherence to the events being described. If the second sentence were "There are fifteen million people in Mexico City" the hearer would be puzzled, and if the flat tire had nothing to do with missing the meeting (even though it actually did happen), the speaker is practicing deception.

Sentence 3 is a more subtle case. If the hearer looks over and sees a dog in the bushes, and finds out that the speaker knew it was a dog, he or she will feel that the statement was inappropriate, and might say "If you knew it was a dog, why didn't you say so?". On the other hand, the statement 'There's a dog over there in the bushes" is perfectly appropriate even if both speaker and hearer know that it is a beagle, and sentence 3 would be fine for a dog if it were a response to something like "There are no animals anywhere around here."

The common element in all of these is that the "meaning" for a hearer is the result of a complex process of trying to understand what the speaker is saying and why. In effect, every statement is the answer to a question, which may be implicit in the context. Its meaning depends as much on the question as on the form of the answer. There is an important germ of truth in saying that the meaning of a sentence "is" the process it invokes, but this view is not compatible with a formal compositional semantics of the kind that has generally interested linguists and philosophers. What is needed is an understanding of meaning-as-triggering, which deals with the interaction between the utterance and the full range of cognitive processes going on in the language user.

Natural Reasoning

In looking at any significant sample of natural language, it becomes quickly apparent that only a small fraction of human "reasoning" fits the mold of deductive logic. One is often presented with a fragmentary description of some object or situation, and on the basis of knowledge about what is "typical", jumps to a number of conclusions that are not justifiable as logical deductions, and may at times be false. Most AI systems have been based (either explicitly or unwittingly) on a notion of deduction that does not account for this style of reasoning. In the "opening the box" example quoted above, it was assumed that "the box" was the one in which the blocks arrived even though this is not rigorously deducible from the text, or even from knowledge of the world. This kind of inference is a predominant aspect of reasoning and one which calls for formal systems having very different properties from deductive logic.

[...]

Subjective Relativism

[This] issue can be described in simplistic terms as a dispute about two different starting points for understanding language:

> *Objectivity:* an utterance has meaning by virtue of corresponding to a state of affairs. We approach the study of language by analyzing how the structures of utterances correspond systematically to the states of affairs they describe.

> *Subjectivity:* an utterance has meaning by virtue of triggering processes within a hearer whose cognitive structure depends on prior history and current processing activity. We approach the study of language by analyzing the nature of those cognitive structures and activities.

The examples given above suggest that a subject-dependent view must be taken even in such seemingly objective issues as the appropriate use of "John is a bachelor." If we are seriously interested in understanding the regularities in the use of real language in real situations we will be misled by persisting with idealizations of objective truth. [...]

But there is a problem with unbridled relativism. If the "meaning" of an utterance can only be described in terms of its effects on a particular understander with a particular history, how do we talk about inter-

subjective meaning at all? Since no two people have identical histories, and since any aspect of cognitive structure can potentially have an effect on the processing triggered by a particular utterance, there is a different meaning for every hearer. There is no objective "right meaning"—only a meaning for a particular person at a particular moment in a particular situation. Carried to an extreme, if you interpret my use of the word "dog" as referring to eggplant parmesan, what allows me to argue that you are wrong? We want to understand meaning in a way that makes sense of the fact that you and I may not have identical (or even mutually consistent) understandings of "democracy" or "system," but we cannot ignore the common sense intuition that there are broad areas of obvious agreement.
[. . .]

UNDERSTANDING IN A DOMAIN OF ACTION

In getting to this point we have described language in three different phenomenic domains. [. . .] In focussing on one domain as central we are led to ask certain questions and pay attention to certain phenomena. For any choice, there are some phenomena that become more easily describable, and others that become more obscure. The three domains we have discussed so far are:

> *The domain of linguistic structure.* This is the domain of traditional linguistics. One looks for regularities in the patterning of structural elements (phonemes, words, phrases, sentences, etc.) in utterances and text . . . most of the work on the larger-scale structure of discourse is in this domain, even when it is reformulated in terms of "schemas."

> *The domain of correspondence between linguistic structures and the world.* In this domain, one is concerned with regularities in the correspondence between the structures of linguistic objects and the states of affairs in the world that those objects describe. Much of the current work in the philosophy of language is an attempt to formalize this correspondence. Much of the AI work on natural language has had this orientation as well.

> *The domain of cognitive processes.* In this domain the relevant regularities are not in the linguistic structures themselves, or their correspondence to a world, but in the cognitive structures and processes of a person (or machine) that generates or interprets them. This is the domain explored in much of cognitive psychology and artificial intelligence.

My current work is moving in the direction of a fourth domain for understanding language:

> *The domain of human action and interaction.* In this domain the relevant regularities are in the network of actions and interactions within a human

society. An utterance is a linguistic *act* that has consequences for the participants, leading to other immediate actions and to commitments for future action.

This domain has been explored under the rubric of *speech acts*. The work of Austin (1962) and Searle (1970, 1975) has shown that utterances can be understood as acts rather than as representations. In giving a command or making a promise, a person is not uttering a sentence whose meaning lies in whether it does or does not correspond truthfully to the world. The speaker is entering into an interaction pattern, playing a certain role, committing both speaker and hearer to future actions, some linguistic and others not. In this domain the relevant question about an utterance is "What is the speaker doing?" Understanding is connected with the ability to recognize what the speaker is doing and to participate in the appropriate pattern of actions.

[. . .]

Statements as Speech Acts Initiating Commitment

In the basic works on speech acts, there is a separation between the propositional content of an utterance and its illocutionary force. The fact that my utterance is a promise is its illocutionary force. The fact that it involves my attendance at a particular meeting at a particular time is its propositional content. In further pursuing the connection between meaning and speech acts, it is possible to view more of meaning (including what has been seen as propositional content) in the domain of action, rather than the domain of correspondence with the world.

Consider the following dialog:

A: I'm thirsty.
B: There's some water in the refrigerator.
A: Where? I don't see it.
B: In the cells of the eggplant.

A claims that B's first response was a lie (or "misleading"), whereas B contends that everything he said was literally true. Most work in semantics (including artificial intelligence) can be seen as providing formal grounds to support B. But there is an important sense in which a theory of "meaning" needs to deal with the grounds for A's complaint. In making the statement "There's some water in the refrigerator" B is doing something more than stating an abstract objective fact.

At first, it seems like it might be possible to expand on the definition of "water." Perhaps there is a "sense" of the word that means "water in its liquid phase in a sufficient quantity to act as a fluid," and the statement about water is ambiguous in whether it refers to this sense or to a sense dealing purely with chemical composition. But this doesn't help us in dealing with some other possible responses of B to the initial request:

B: There's no water in the refrigerator, but there's some lemonade.
B: There's a bottle of water in the refrigerator, with a little lemon in it to cover up the taste of the rust from the pipes.

In the first case, the presence of lemon in the water is taken as making it not "water." In the second, the lemon (perhaps the same quantity) is considered irrelevant. The difference lies in a background of assumptions the speaker has about the hearer's purposes and experience. After any amount of fiddling with the definition, one can always come up with a new context (e.g., what if the person were doing a science experiment or checking for sources of humidity), in which the acceptability of the statement "There is water" would not be accounted for by the definition. Every speech act occurs in a context, with a background understood by speaker and hearer. There are "felicity conditions" that depend on mutual knowledge and intentions. The speaker is responsible for things he can anticipate that the hearer will infer from what he says, not just its abstract correspondence with the state of affairs.

What happens, then, if we try to understand the problem of "truth" in the terms of social action and commitment? In making a statement I am doing something like making a promise—committing myself to acting in appropriate ways in the future. In this case, there is a different kind of satisfaction condition. There is no specific action that I am bound to, but there is a structure of potential dialog that we could enter into in the face of a "breakdown." If I say "There is water in the refrigerator" and you can't find any, I am committed to give you an account. Either we agree that I was wrong, or we discuss the assumed background ("I assumed we were talking about something to drink." "I assumed we were talking about chemical composition").

There are several reasons why this shift of viewpoint is potentially advantageous:

It lets us deal with what happens when we actually make statements. Formal approaches to meaning often take as their model the language of mathematics, in which it is generally assumed that the truth of a statement can be determined without reference to outside context or situation. But in real language, we rarely if ever make a statement that could not be construed as having a literal meaning we don't intend. If I say "snow is white" you can point to the murky grey polluted stuff at our feet. I reply "I meant pure snow," and you respond "You didn't say so, and anyway no snow is absolutely pure." It is an edifying exercise to look at the statements we make both in our writing and our everyday conversation and see how few of them can even apparently be judged true or false without an appeal to an unstated background.

ICM - G*

It shifts us out of the objective/subjective dichotomy. In the previous section we saw a dilemma arising from trying to identify the "meaning" of a word or utterance. By assuming it had an objective meaning independent of a particular speaker/hearer situation, we banished many aspects of meaning that play a central role in language. But in assuming that meaning is defined in terms of effect on a particular individual in a situation, we lose the sense that meaning can be the same across individuals and situations. In moving to the domain of interactions (rather than that of objective truth correspondence or cognitive process), we are directing attention to the interactional situation in which something is uttered. We draw generalizations across these situations (and their potential for continued conversation) rather than across objective correspondence or mental states.

It places central emphasis on the potential for further articulation of unstated background. By looking at statements as language acts analogous to promises, we bring into prominence the fact that human action always occurs in an unarticulated background. When I promise to do something, it goes without saying that the commitment is relative to a large number of assumptions about the rest of our world continuing as expected. The same properties carry over to language acts. [. . .] We can never make the background fully explicit, but we can study the nature of the dialog by which people come to a consensus about things that were previously in the background.

DEVELOPING THEORIES AND FORMALISMS

[. . .]We need an appropriate "calculus of language acts" if we want to develop detailed theories of language interaction. There will be several parts of such a theory:

1. *Illocutionary logic.* The basic groundwork of speech act theory includes an analysis of the different kinds of illocutionary points and the structure of the felicity conditions associated with them. Searle (1975) proposes a universal taxonomy of five basic illocutionary points. . . . This analysis can serve as a starting point for understanding the structure of larger composite patterns made up of the basic acts. For example an "offer-negotiation-acceptance" sequence is a standardly observed pattern made up of individual "commissives" and "requests." The formal tools for describing the "syntax" of such patterns may be quite different from those used in traditional linguistics, since they must take into account the passage of time (e.g., not overtly responding to an invitation constitutes a kind of response).

2. *Taxonomy of linguistic grounding.* In order to carry out the suggested program of viewing the truthfulness of statements in the domain of interaction, we need a "logic of argument," where "argument" stands for the kind of elucidation of background assumptions discussed above. When

I make a statement, I am making a commitment to provide some kind of "grounding" in case of a "breakdown." This grounding is in the form of another speech act (also in a situational context) that will satisfy the hearer that the objection is met. There appear to be three basic kinds of grounding: experiential, formal, and social.

> *Experiential:* If asked to justify the statement "Snow is white" I may give a set of instructions ("Go outside and look!") such that a person who follows them will be led to concur on the basis of experience. The methodology of science is designed to provide this kind of grounding for all empirical statements. . . . the "objectivity" of science derives from the assumption that for any observation, one can provide instructions that if followed by a "standard observer" will lead him or her to the same conclusion. This does not necessarily mean that the result is observer free, simply that it is anticipated to be uniform for all potential observers.

> *Formal:* Deductive logic is based on the playing of a kind of "language game" in which a set of basic rules are taken for granted, and argument proceeds as a series of moves constrained by those rules. For example, if I expect you to believe that all Swedes are blonde and that Sven is a redhead, then I can use a particular series of moves to provide grounding for the statement that Sven is not Swedish. Of course, this depends on the grounding of the statements used in the process—one can recursively demand grounding for each of them. Under this category fall most of the issues that have been discussed in formal semantics, but with a different emphasis. The focus is not on their coherence as a mathematical abstraction, but on the way they play a role in the logic of conversation.

> *Social:* Much of what we say in conversation is based neither on experience nor logic, but on other conversations. We believe that water is H_2O and that Napoleon was the Emperor of France not because we have relevant experience but because someone told us. One possible form of grounding is to "pass the buck"—to argue that whoever made the statement could have provided grounding. This is also recursive, but we assume that the buck stops somewhere. [. . .]

Just as one can develop taxonomies and structural analyses of illocutionary points, it is important to develop a precise analysis of these structures of argumentation. There are many ways in which such a logic will parallel standard formal logic, and others in which it will not. In particular, it seems that the role of analogy and metaphor will be much more central when the focus is on patterns of argumentation between individuals with a shared background rather than on deductive inference from axioms.

[. . .]

Computer Systems.

Much of cognitive science has been both stimulated by and directed towards the construction of computer programs that behave "intelligently." Hundreds of books and articles have been written on how computer systems will soon become prevalent in every arena of life. The question asked of the cognitive scientist is: "What kind of theories do we need in order to build intelligent systems we can use?"

The prevalent view is that in AI we design "expert systems" that can stand as surrogates for a person doing some job. From a viewpoint of human interaction we see the computer's role differently. It is not a surrogate expert, but an intermediary—a sophisticated medium of communication. A group of people (typically including both computer specialists and experts in the subject domain) build a program incorporating a formal representation of their beliefs. The computer communicates their statements to users of the system, typically doing some combinations and rearrangements along the way. The fact that these combinations may involve complex deductive logic, heuristic rule application or statistical analysis does not alter the basic structure of communicative acts.

A person writing a program (or contributing to its "knowledge base") does so within a background of assumptions about how the program will be used and who will be interpreting its responses. Part of this can be made explicit in documentation, but part is an implicit background of what can be "normally understood." Except for systems operating within strongly constrained domains there inevitably comes a time when the system "breaks down" because it is being used in a way that does not fit the assumptions. This is true not only of "expert systems," but of computer programs in all areas. Many of the biggest failures of mundane computer systems (management systems, inventory systems, etc.) have come not because the system failed to do what the designers specified, but because the assumptions underlying that specification were not appropriate for the situation in which the program was used. This will become even more the case as we build systems that are more flexible—that allow the user to develop new modes of interaction in the course of using the program, rather than staying within a fixed set of alternatives.

[. . .]

CONCLUSION

Those who are familiar with the philosophical discussion about artificial intelligence will have noticed that many of the ideas and sources discussed here . . . are among those cited by critics like Dreyfus (1979), who deny the possibility of developing any formalization of human thought and know-ledge. A conclusion one might draw is that having brought these questions to light, we can only proceed by abandoning formal cognitive science and our attempts to program computers to do things we consider "intelligent."

It should be clear from the previous section that this is not my conclusion. I am not advocating (or planning) the abandonment of the scientific study of cognition, but trying to better understand what we are doing, and refocusing my efforts in the light of that understanding. However, it could be argued that the path described in this paper is one leading away from the paradigm of cognitive science. Even granting that an orientation towards language as social action is interesting and useful, it is arguable that it is not "cognitive science"—that it represents a turning away from the domain of "cognitive processing" (or, as it is often called, "information processing"). In some ways this observation is valid, but in others it is misleading.

It is important to recognize what we are doing [when] we apply words like "cognitive" or "science" to a particular enterprise or approach. In our writing, teaching, and interactions with people (both in the field and outside), we are performing speech acts that give those words meaning. Different orientations lead to different practical suggestions, to different ways of interpreting and acting. As has been pointed out in the philosophy of science, the importance of a paradigm may not lie so much in the answers it provides as in the questions it leads one to consider, and a paradigm (like a crisis) is created by a web of interlinked speech acts.

[. . .]

REFERENCES

Austin, J. L. (1962) *How to do things with words*, Cambridge, Mass.: Harvard University Press.

Dreyfus, H. (1979) *What computers can't do: A critique of artificial reason.* (2nd Ed.) San Francisco: Freeman.

Lighthill, Sir J. (1973) *Artificial intelligence: A general survey.* London: Science Research Council.

Searle, J. (1970) *Speech acts.* Cambridge: Cambridge University Press.

Searle, J. (1975) A taxonomy of illocutionary acts. In K. Gunderson (Ed.), *Language, mind and knowledge: Minnesota studies in the philosophy of science,* Vol. XI. Minneapolis, Minn.: University of Minnesota Press.

Winograd, T. (1972) *Understanding natural language.* New York: Academic Press.

Winograd, T. (1974) When will computers understand people? *Psychology Today,* pp. 73–79.

9 Realistic Language Comprehension

Christopher K. Riesbeck

INTRODUCTION

[...]

... I would like to look at what constitutes reasonable input material for building and testing language-understanding models. It is becoming increasingly obvious in the field that we have to deal with real texts, texts that were originally generated to communicate, not to test parsers. The days when we can compare programs by how well they handle "Max went to the store" have passed. In fact, the days of dealing with single sentences have pretty much disappeared.

This change has come about for several reasons. First, despite many false starts, there has been real progress in natural-language understanding. We are now writing programs to deal with multisentential connected texts, rather than just talking about writing them. Second, we are tackling tasks demanding far greater ranges in input than ever before.

At Yale, many of these tasks require programs that can deal, in a serious way, with everyday newspaper articles. But the informal, sometimes incoherent, nature of newspaper texts requires significant advances for language-comprehension models. Here are some examples of the kinds of sentences that appear in newspaper articles:

> Several dozen injuries were reported in the clashes in Teheran today between supporters and opponents of the Shah Mohammed Riza Pahlevi.

> A small earthquake shook several Southern Illinois counties Monday night, the National Earthquake Information Service in Golden, Colo., reported.

A gunman who diverted a Vermont bound bus with more than 25 passengers from the Bronx to Kennedy International Airport and killed two hostages surrendered on a runway late last night ending a day long siege of terror and gunfire.

With sentences like these, who needs paragraphs? The sentences are full of idioms and clichéd phrases. The last example, a classic run-on sentence, seems to delight in squeezing a series of events (which may have taken days) into one sentence. Prepositional and adverbial phrases abound, and finding what they connect to is nontrivial.

Furthermore, newspaper articles are but one of a myriad number of sources of texts that do not fit into the neat templates we use when we talk about "normal" English sentences. For example, the MARGIE conceptual analyzer was developed to handle sentences like "John gave Mary a kiss." and "Bill prevented Rita from taking the bike by giving it to John." Needless to say, when the MARGIE analyzer had to be extended to handle sentences like the previous examples, its more complex control structures were, if not wrong, certainly irrelevant to the problems at hand.

But things are not quite as hopeless as the preceding examples might suggest. In fact, each of the three sentences has already been handled by some computer program. The first example was treated by a program called ELI (Gershman, 1979), the second by one called FRUMP (DeJong, 1979), and the third by one called IPP (Schank, Lebowitz, & Birnbaum, 1978).

I would like to call programs and systems that are designed to deal with large numbers of long natural-language texts, produced not by the programmers but by the outside world, Realistic Language Comprehension (or RLC) systems. These systems need a great deal of robustness and flexibility to be able to deal both with malformed input and with their own internal inadequacies. How can we build such systems?

SCRIPT-DRIVEN PARSING

FRUMP (DeJong, 1979) was our first conceptual analyzer that worked quickly and with unedited real input texts. It took newspaper stories straight from the UPI newswire and, for several dozen different domains, skimmed and summarized each story in less than a minute. [. . .]

FRUMP . . . generated its summaries on the basis of an internal description of the story, not from the words of the input text. This internal description, called a *sketchy script*, was a template of basic elements that normally occurred in events of the type being reported. For example, the template for earthquake stories had slots for the time and place of the earthquake, its severity (on the Richter scale), the amount of damage caused, and the number of people killed or hurt. Any particular story about an earthquake was treated as an instance of this template, with the slots filled with specific values. The summaries were generated from the filled-in script. Because this internal description was language independent, the generation of summaries in other languages, such as Spanish or Chinese, was simple and no different in kind than the generation of the English summaries (DeJong, 1979).

The most important aspect of FRUMP as an RLC system was its use of the sketchy scripts to direct the analysis process. The principle is simple, though there are, of course, many complex details. FRUMP scanned the first sentence of each newspaper story, looking for words or phrases whose meaning (as given in its dictionary) referred to one of the known sketchy scripts. Once a script was picked, processing became totally top-down. The script had slots that needed to be filled and each slot had rules that specified where to look in the input text for the words and phrases whose meanings might fill the slot. A specification of where to look might say that the item was to the left or right of the verb, after a certain preposition, or next to some keyword (as in "5.2 on the Richter scale").

Because FRUMP's processing was driven by the sketchy script, it knew what it was looking for in conceptual terms. It automatically ignored those things that did not fit into the script because it never even asked about them. Once FRUMP had a script, it never asked "Which meaning of this word is right?" Instead it asked, "Can this word mean what I want it to?"

The fact that FRUMP ignored things that it was not looking for was one of its strengths and also one of its weaknesses. Once FRUMP had picked a script, it worked very hard to see the story in terms of that script. Unfortunately, there were often few external clues that a script was inappropriate in a story, because many of the things that any script looked for—such as names and places—appeared in every story. A classic mistake that FRUMP made was caused by the following headline to a story:

POPE'S DEATH SHAKES THE WESTERN HEMISPHERE.

SUMMARY: THERE WAS AN EARTHQUAKE IN THE WESTERN HEMISPHERE. THE POPE DIED.

FRUMP recognized an earthquake from the conceptual structure "land moves" and from that point on it was doomed. Notice, though, that this mistake in some ways shows just how smart FRUMP was. It found a possible mention of earthquake without relying on the word 'earthquake,' and its summary was clearly not built from piecing together text fragments. To be this dumb, FRUMP actually had to be fairly smart.

FRUMP's mistakes came from two major sources: inadequate syntactic and semantic constraints, and the fundamental principle of ignoring what you are not looking for. The inadequate constraints can be fixed, although care must be taken not to destroy the speed of processing that made FRUMP so useful. Further, it must be noted that FRUMP's goal was to skim for summarization, rather than read for pleasure. It was supposed to throw away what the average reader might consider the most interesting part of a news story—namely, those things that did not fit the normal pattern. The Integrated Partial Parsing (IPP) system attacks the issue of finding interesting items head on.

INTEREST-DRIVEN PARSING

Integrated Partial Parsing is our second attempt at an RLC system (Schank, Lebowitz, & Birnbaum, 1978). The script-driven aspect of FRUMP is maintained, but in IPP the frames are brought into play much more often (frequently several times in one sentence), adding a bottom-up flavor to the top-down system. The frames are called MOPs, which stands for Memory Organization Packets (Schank, 1979). A MOP is like a script but smaller, more modular, more integrated with other MOPs, and tied directly to episodic memory. Furthermore, each MOP is given an intrinsic interest value. The idea behind IPP is that the more interesting MOPs, when referred to in a sentence, become the driving force in understanding the rest of that sentence.

For example, if a sentence begins with "An Arabic speaking gunman . . .," the word 'gunman' causes several things to happen. First, the meaning of 'gunman' is looked up. Its definition says that a gunman is a person who is the main actor in the MOP for terrorism. The terrorism MOP describes not only shootings, but also the goals and results of terrorist activities in general.

The terrorism MOP is rated as very interesting. Hence, it takes control of the analysis, looking for pieces to fill slots in the MOP. Both future inputs and previous ones that were ignored because they were uninteresting are now picked up and attached to the MOP, if relevant. Hence, "Arabic speaking" is picked up to fill in the nationality of the actor of the terrorist event.

Furthermore, the terrorism MOP (with the gunman as actor) makes conceptual predictions about the sentence. For example, "sprayed" in "An Arabic-speaking gunman sprayed . . ." is disambiguated to mean "shot" because of predictions about what gunmen do. An example of a full sentence handled by IPP is:

An Arabic speaking gunman shot his way into the Iraqi Embassy here (Paris) yesterday morning, held hostages through most of the day before surrendering to French policemen, and then was shot by Iraqui security officials as he was led away by the French officers.

The output for this sentence, in English, was:

TERRORISM
    ACTOR—Arab gunman
    PLACE—Paris, Iraqi Embassy
    SCENES
        HOSTAGES—some
        CAPTURE
            ACTOR—French policemen
            OBJECT—Arab gunman
            PLACE—Paris, Iraqi Embassy
  UNEXPECTED RESULT: ACTOR—Iraqi officers
                ACTION—SHOOT
                OBJECT—Arab gunman
                RESULT
                    ACTOR—Arab gunman
                    STATE—dead

As IPP goes through a sentence, other MOPs may be invoked because an input word or phrase will refer to an interesting MOP that is not picked up by the ones currently active. These new MOPs take over the analysis. Newspaper stories commonly have very long sentences that string together several events and descriptions, such as:

> One unconfirmed report said that up to 100 armed men, believed to be members of the Shiite Moslem sect, took a number of persons hostage and occupied Mecca's Great Mosque, killing a Saudi clergyman in the process.

One thing that both FRUMP and IPP have in common is that they go directly from the input text to the higher-level knowledge structures (scripts in FRUMP, MOPs in IPP). That is, "gunman" goes straight to the terrorism MOP and therefore allows everything that IPP knows about terrorism to be used in understanding the rest of the sentence.

IPP, like FRUMP, tends to ignore much of the sentence because much of the sentence just is not that interesting. The advantage of this is that many of the most troublesome words in English (or in any natural language, most likely), such as 'be,' 'have,' 'give,' and so on, are ignored because they do not refer to interesting MOPs. IPP is an experiment to see if understanding can still occur even when these words are ignored. For an interesting domain such as terrorism, they apparently can be. Note, for example, that 'take' in a template for the form "(terrorists) take (people) hostage" really says nothing that is not already clear from the terrorism MOP and the word "hostage."

The major problem with IPP is that it models how we read interesting things, but does not say how we read dull things. That is, how do we read a text that contains no interesting parts, but that is, as a whole, important for us to understand?

GOAL-DRIVEN PARSING

McMAP is a preliminary attempt at modeling understanding that is driven by a domain-specific task. It is a throwback to our earlier analyzers (Birnbaum & Selfridge, 1979; Gershman, 1979; and Riesbeck & Schank, 1976). It is based on McELI (Riesbeck & Charniak, 1978), a pedagogical word-by-word analyzer that attempts to understand how each word fits together in the sentence, with very little of the flexibility that seems essential for an RLC system. Despite this, McMAP handles several different real multisentence texts, including the following set of directions telling someone how to get to a post office in San Diego.

I-5 south

Rosecrans exit—get over to the far left—and it will be about the third stoplight that's the Midway Drive intersection

To the left a steakhouse or wooden looking building that's some kind of restaurant. Catty-corner is an automobile dealership. On the western corner is another restaurant. I can't remember what's on the direct right.

Be in the left-hand only lane. And turn left on Midway Drive.

About two to three long blocks down on the right is the main post office. You can't miss it. It looks rather like San Quentin.

This text has incomplete sentences, missing punctuation, and even a missing verb (there should be an "is" after "to the left")! Yet McMAP can understand each sentence well enough to produce representations such as:

(MOTION TYPE (GO)
    VIA (ROADWAY TYPE (HIGHWAY) LABEL (I-5) DIRECTION (SOUTH)))
for "I-5 south,"

(MOTION TYPE (GO)
    TO (LANDMARK TYPE (STOPLIGHT) TIMES (FUZZY CENTER (3.))))
for "and it will be about the third stoplight,"

(DESCRIPTION TYPE (SUBPART) OF (PLACE DIRECTION (LEFT))
        HAS (BUILDING MATERIAL (WOOD)
                FILLER (BUILDING TYPE (RESTAURANT)
                        SUBTYPE (STEAKHOUSE))))
for "To the left a steakhouse or wooden looking building," and

(DESCRIPTION TYPE (SUBPART) OF (PLACE DIRECTION (RIGHT))
    HAS (SOMETHING))
    for "I can't remember what's on the direct right."

The first example requires a fragment to be expanded, the second example requires turning what appeared to be a description into an action, the third example requires overcoming a missing "is," and the last example requires removing the irrelevant "I can't remember . . ."

Furthermore, the preceding representations are not the only thing produced by McMAP. It also says that the directions appear to be clear as a whole, although several sentences are clear only in context. For example, "and it will be about the third stoplight" is unclear by itself, but the next sentence, "that's the Midway Drive intersection," removes the unclarity.

Finally, the entire processing of this text, including the inferences just mentioned and others, requires less than 8 seconds of CPU time, on a DEC-20, using an interpreted LISP version of the program. How was this accomplished?

McMAP is a goal-driven program. The actual analysis is, compared to FRUMP and IPP, fairly bottom-up, using expectations found by looking up the words in the sentence in its lexicon. Only the most recent unsatisfied expectations are considered, so the number of things that must be checked is kept small. Normally this approach is fast but much too fragile for an RLC program, because the failure of one expectation can block other expectations that were dependent on it, and the whole analysis falls apart.

In order to alleviate this problem, caused by things like fragments and ungrammatical sentences, McMAP uses several techniques. First, like CA (Birnbaum & Selfridge, 1979), McMAP does not limit itself to building only one conceptual structure to a sentence. It keeps a list of all the structures built so far that have not been tied together. It does, however, have a set of rules for linking up the meanings of adjoining noun groups, adverbs, and so on. Thus, "a steak-house or wooden looking building" is initially analyzed as two concepts, a steak-house building and a wooden building, and then these are tied into one structure.

If, when the sentence ends, there are still several structures in the list, more inference rules are applied to try to infer a larger structure that will tie them together. These rules handle fragments such as "I-5 south" and "To the left a steakhouse."

These inference rules add a great deal of flexibility to McMAP because when the analysis breaks down due to bad sentences or inadequacies in the analyzer, there is still a chance that a reasonable interpretation will be made. In fact, some complicated words, such as conjunctions, are treated in McMAP entirely by these general inference rules. In this, McMAP is like IPP and FRUMP.

The phrase "a reasonable interpretation" is a key one for McMAP because even after the initial analysis is done, McMAP is not finished. McMAP also has a set of inference rules that say which conceptualizations are reasonable and which are not, given the task of direction understanding. If an analysis is not acceptable, then inference rules are applied to fix it.

For example, one reasonability rule says that descriptions are acceptable only when applied to the location that would be current at the time of travel. This rule rejects "and it will be about the third stoplight." So a conversion inference is invoked that changes it into an instruction to go to about the third stoplight. But another reasonability rule says that motions cannot have fuzzy numbers, such as "two or three" (descriptions can, but not motions). Therefore, "go to about the third stoplight" is judged to be unclear. Because the instruction cannot be made any clearer, an expectation is set up that says that the next sentence will be a clear description of the location to be gone to.

In the directions quoted earlier, the next sentence was "that's the Midway Drive intersection." This is interpreted as a description of the current location, and judged as clear because of a rule that says that labeled roads are clear. Hence, the interpretation of the second sentence satisfies the expectation from the first sentence and the pair of sentences together form a clear unit.

Similar rules convert the initial analysis of "I can't remember what's on the direct right" into the description "something is on the direct right." This is marked as unclear but acceptable because descriptions of locations are allowed to be less clear than instructions about where to go. However, McMAP would not accept "I can't remember when you turn," because this would be analyzed into the unclear instruction "You turn at some unknown place."

McMAP's contribution to the realm of RLC systems is its explicit set of rules for judging the reasonability of the interpretations it produces and for reformulating or expanding those analyses that are inadequate. Its weaknesses are that it is much too passive and lazy in the application of this knowledge. It waits until a whole clause is processed before checking to see if it makes sense. The only top-down control it has comes from individual words predicting the senses of other words that are likely to follow. Also, McMAP, like IPP, uses parsing rules based on domain-specific knowledge, but does not show how the domain-specific knowledge could be used to generate these rules in the first place.

DISCUSSION

We have surveyed three recent attempts to create natural-language comprehension programs with enough robustness to handle real texts and enough speed to make them practical:

1. FRUMP: A script, referenced by concepts in the lead sentence of an article, controls the analysis of the remainder of the story. The script looks for the concepts it needs and ignores everything else.
2. IPP: MOPs of high intrinsic interest value, referenced by concepts in a sentence, collect together the remaining pieces of the sentence.
3. McMAP: Word-indexed expectations produce a conceptual analysis for the sentence, and additional inference rules check the reasonability of the analysis, modifying it if necessary.

The input for these three programs is natural text generated for the purposes of communication, not to test some linguistic theory. Both FRUMP and IPP have dealt with hundreds of input texts, all without any preediting. McMAP has dealt with half a dozen, but is still a prototype program only.

How far along the road to a real RLC system are we? At the beginning of this chapter, I presented some texts, taken from newspapers, that had been handled by existing computer programs. Let me present some more:

Grasso poised to stump in region for president   [Headline]

President Carter has won round two of the 1980 Democratic presidential race, beating a strong challenge by Sen. Edward Kennedy in caucuses in Maine, a New England state that was on Kennedy's "must win" list.
[Lead sentence]

TONIGHT: Cloudy, flurries
TOMORROW: Clearing   [Weather box]

1 Distant
5 Do a crewman's job
9 Potato chip   [Crossword puzzle]

Center Cut Pork Chops $1.29 lb.   [Advertisement]

13   [Page number]

The first two examples are the kinds of things that FRUMP and IPP have been developed to handle. There are short headlines with pieces that have to be put together using a lot of world knowledge, and there are very long sentences with complex noun phrases and only tenuous connections between different phrases and clauses.

But the examples show that even a newspaper does more with language than just tell stories. Some of the just-listed items, such as the advertisement, the crossword puzzle clues, and the page number, would be out of place in a sentence. But put them in the right position on a page, next to certain other pieces of text, and the average reader has no trouble at all recognizing their function. Furthermore, there are many other places beside newspapers where language is used in a special manner: poetry, kit instructions, chess books, mathematical theorems, and so on.

[...]

Realistic language comprehension must involve an ability to deal flexibly and rapidly with language in a variety of contexts and forms. When I see a push button in an elevator that says "DOOR," I am not fooled into thinking that the button IS a door; I know from the context that the button controls the door. When I see words on the spine of a book, I know from the physical context that the words are the title and author of the book.

If an RLC system is to be this flexible, then it must be able to rapidly index contextual frames. Sentences, such as "John told Mary that Bill gave a kiss to Sarah." do not give a proper idea of the importance of contextual recognition. But as soon as we move into a broader view of language use, there is no escaping it. Furthermore, this recognition must be capable of intimately affecting the language analysis, so that a string like "1 Distant" should, in the context of a crossword puzzle, be as natural as "John went home" in another context.

Another essential part of RLC is the ability to deal with stereotypical phrasings rapidly, and, to some extent, sloppily. That is, canned phrases are used freely but often carelessly. An RLC system must not get lost in what the phrase exactly means, but must be able to infer what it probably means in the given context. And, by phrases I am dealing here with the kinds of open-ended templates, not necessarily idiomatic, that Becker has discussed (Becker, 1974). For example, the sentence . . .:

> The impact of transformational grammar on modern linguistics cannot be underestimated.

was obviously intended by the original author to say that transformational grammar did indeed have a great impact on modern linguistics. Most people reading this sentence interpret it that way. In fact, however, the accurate reading of the sentence is just the opposite. It says that no estimate, no matter how small, is an underestimate of transformational grammar's effect. It should be pointed out that this example was first noticed because of a similar sentence in an earlier chapter that said that the importance of something else would not be *overestimated*. One of the sentences had to be wrong. But neither sentence looks wrong at first glance. And it is this first-glance interpretation that an RLC system should be able to get. The phrasal forms "*X* cannot be overestimated," and "*X* should not be underestimated," are both used to say "*X* is important." The appearance of either "underestimated" or "overestimated" preceded by "not" seems enough to index the interpretation "*X* is important."

A phrasal component should be an important addition to an RLC system. For IPP and FRUMP, a major source of mistakes comes from the fact that they only see the contentful, interesting words, such as 'earthquake' or 'gunman.' If the intent of the sentence depends strongly on some combination of words that FRUMP and IPP do not care about, then serious misunderstandings can arise.

A phrasal component would also help a program such as McMAP. McMAP tries to handle all the words in a sentence with equal care, and hence becomes bogged down in the complexities and ambiguities of common words. Not only does the analysis take time, but often nothing is gained by it. Many sentences turn out to be more ambiguous the more you look at them, and the only way to resolve the ambiguities is to use the kinds of the content-driven expectations found in FRUMP and IPP. Even though greater care in processing can reduce mistakes, it increases the problem of ambiguity.

A good phrasal component would handle many of the uses of dull words with an advanced kind of dictionary look-up. We would be gaining speed by using more storage space. We would also, by the set of phrases stored, be saying in advance what certain combinations of words are most likely to mean.

However, there does not exist a good system for dealing with phrases at this time. To be practical, the phrases have to have generalized components, as in "(terrorists) held (victims) hostage," and must be able to deal with simple variations in syntax. But how to do this without making phrases as complex to process as the kinds of rules in a program like McMAP is unknown. Furthermore, we do not know any efficient way to index a large library of phrases, except by having words point to all the phrases they appear in. This is not practical if we have thousands of phrases, and also raises questions of psychological validity. Can you name all the phrases that the word "break" appears in? Although no good phrasally based analyzer exists, some people are currently working on the problem (e.g., Wilensky & Arens, 1980).

CONCLUSION

Realistic language comprehension was defined as the ability to deal with a wide variety of naturally produced texts, from fragments to entire articles. Three approaches to doing this were FRUMP, IPP, and McMAP. FRUMP approached the problem by looking only for those things in the text that it needed to fill out its sketchy scripts. IPP looked only at those things in the text that were interesting and that provided frames for putting the other pieces together. McMAP looked at everything in the text, and modified its analyses using domain-specific rules of reasonability. FRUMP attacked the problem of tying a long text together, IPP attacked the problem of focusing on the interesting parts of the text, and McMAP attacked the problem of making sure things made sense. A phrasally based component could be of value in attacking the problem of dealing with the lower-interest, lower-content combinations of words that organize the syntactic structure of many sentences, which FRUMP and IPP ignore and which McMAP deals with very poorly. A merger of the ideas in these programs would look something like Fig. [9.1].

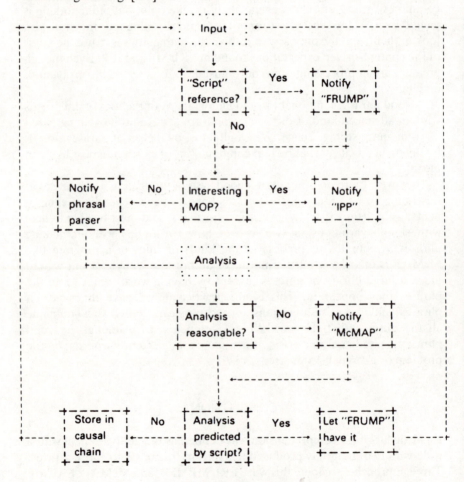

FIG. 9.1.   FRUMP-IPP-McMAP.

The quotation marks around script, FRUMP, IPP, and McMAP are to indicate that a real merger would not really be of the systems described, but of ones that have the same general principle. We certainly would not want to limit an RLC system to script-based stories, particularly when our notion of what scripts are has been replaced with MOPs since FRUMP was created. Furthermore, the separate boxes in Fig. [9.1] are not meant to suggest that there is not a lot of interaction going on. For example, the judgments about interest and reasonability are based on what MOPs "FRUMP" and "IPP" have activated.

Still Fig. [9.1] does show how the basic ideas interrelate in an RLC system. Knowledge structures are used to drive the analysis in an error-tolerant way, judge the reasonability of what is produced, and organize the results in coherent form. There is a very strong top-down component to this system. Things that are predicted are used to fill out the structure that predicted them. Things that are not predicted either generate new structures that drive the analysis, or are part of phrasal frames that tie the text together.

Any new structure built is tested for reasonability in the domain and modified if something is wrong and there is a known way to reinterpret it. This check-and-correct facility must be part of any near-term RLC program, I think, although its function in human understanding is more controversial. In an RLC program, things have to be reformed because of mistakes in the text, indirect and metaphoric constructions, and mistakes and inadequacies in the program. In my research, I assume that people almost always find the best interpretation first, and look for ways they might do this. But any practical RLC program built now will have to take a longer way round, I fear.

REFERENCES

Becker, J. (1974) The phrasal lexicon. In R. C. Schank & B. L. Nash-Webber (Eds.), *Theoretical issues in natural language processing*. Cambridge, Mass.: Bolt Beranek and Newman.

Birnbaum, L., & Selfridge, M. (1979) *Problems in conceptual analysis of natural language* (Research Rep. #168). Computer Science Department, Yale University, New Haven.

DeJong, G. (1979) *Skimming stories in real time: An experiment in integrated understanding.* Doctoral dissertation, (Research Rep. #158), Computer Science Department, Yale University, New Haven.

Gershman, A. (1979) *Knowledge-based parsing.* Doctoral dissertation, (Research Rep. #156), Computer Science Department, Yale University, New Haven.

Riesbeck, C., & Charniak, E. (1978) *Micro-SAM and Micro-ELI: Exercises in popular cognitive mechanics* (Research Rep. #139). Computer Science Department, Yale University, New Haven.

Riesbeck, C. & Schank, R. C. (1976) *Comprehension by computer: Expectation-based analysis of sentences in context* (Research Rep. #78). Computer Science Department, Yale University, New Haven. Also, in W. J. M. Levelt & G. B. Flores d'Arcais (Eds.) (1979), *Studies in the perception of language*. Chichester, Eng.: Wiley.

Schank, R. C. (1979) *Reminding and memory organization: An introduction to MOPs* (Research Rep. #170). Computer Science Department, Yale University, New Haven.

Schank, R., Lebowitz, M., & Birnbaum, L. (1978) *Integrated partial parsing* (Research Rep. #143). Computer Science Department, Yale University, New Haven.

Wilensky, R., & Arens, Y. (1980) *PHRAN: A knowledge-based approach to natural language analysis* (Memorandum No. UCB/ERL M80/34). Electronics Research Laboratory, University of California, Berkeley.

V MEMORY

10 Domains of Recollection

Alan D. Baddeley

Although cognitive psychology developed primarily within the experimental laboratory, it is showing an increasing tendency to extend its influence into the outside world. There are two major reasons for this development.

The first of these stems from the search for ecological validity, driven by the conviction that cognitive psychology should be concerned with understanding human behavior in general. This is often coupled with the suspicion that some of the laboratory studies of the 1960s may be telling us a great deal about the way college students play the particular cognitive games presented by our conventional laboratory tasks, but little else. Fortunately, many of the theoretical concepts of cognitive psychology appear sufficiently robust to be applicable outside the laboratory, and although the results one obtains in the outside world are not always predictable from laboratory studies, nonetheless the relation does seem to be sufficiently close to be encouraging (Baddeley, 1981).

The second reason for an extension of cognitive psychology beyond laboratory-based theoretical studies stems from a growing concern with applied problems, influenced in part no doubt by the changed economic and political climate. Research funds are tighter, and the need to offer justification for research to the nonscientist has become considerably more pressing. [...]

In the past, applied and academic research have often proceeded in parallel with little or no interaction. If cognitive psychology is to continue to flourish, however, it is important that cross-fertilization occur between pure and applied research. The present paper argues that such links are both possible and healthy and supports this claim by describing three concepts developed from applied problems that are applicable to central issues in the theoretical study of human memory. The way these developed from applied problems will be outlined, and their relation to concurrent developments in more laboratory-based studies of memory will be discussed.

A major aim of this article is to argue that applied problems can give rise to potentially important theoretical insights. Hence, I suggest that applied research can provide a fruitful avenue to the discovery of new basic phenomena and novel concepts with which to explain them. The relation between pure and applied research in this view then is one of partnership between two methods, both converging on a similar set of theoretical concepts. In order to make this case, I propose first to present the novel concepts, then to demonstrate their usefulness in tackling a range of applied questions, and finally to relate them to current theoretical work in human memory.

THE CONCEPTS

The Starting Point

The two theoretical approaches I attempt to apply are Craik and Lockhart's levels-of-processing and Tulving's encoding-specificity hypothesis. In their levels-of-processing approach to memory, Craik and Lockhart (1972) suggest that a great deal of evidence can be explained on the assumption that the amount of information recalled is a function of the type of processing required during learning. More specifically, they assume that information processing is hierarchical, with an incoming stimulus such as a written word being processed first in terms of its visual and orthographic characteristics, then in terms of its phonological characteristics, and subsequently in terms of its meaning. Orthographic processing is assumed to be shallow and to give rise to poor subsequent retention; the slightly deeper phonological code is more durable, whereas the even deeper semantic code is the most durable.

The encoding-specificity hypothesis, which was subsequently elevated by its proposers to the level of a principle, states that "specific encoding operations performed on what is perceived determine what is stored, and what is stored determines what retrieval cues are effective in providing access to what is stored" (Tulving & Thomson, 1973, p. 369). The principle was devised to account for the role of retrieval cues in memory, a retrieval cue being a stimulus, in most experiments presented during learning, which proves to enhance retrieval when re-presented at recall. [...]

Both levels and encoding specificity have subsequently been extended and modified into a richer and more complex framework. The three concepts that follow can perhaps best be conceptualized as part of this process of conceptual elaboration and enrichment.

Processing Domains

It is suggested that the concept of levels of processing be replaced by the more general concept of processing domains. A domain is an area of memory within which there are extensive associative links and connections. Such areas of memory will often be associated with particular cognitive processes that may well be separable functionally and possibly, indeed, anatomically. Hence, the orthographic processing of a word may be carried out in a separate cognitive system from its semantic processing. Bearing this in mind, it is tempting to identify domains with the codes employed by clearly separable processing systems. However, although this may be the case for relatively peripheral domains such as those involved in reading, this definition would be far too constricting when applied to long-term memory, where it seems reasonable to identify a wide range of domains and subdomains, without necessarily implying that these utilize uniquely different codes. Indeed, even such a clear distinction as that between the domains involved in visual and verbal processing cannot be attributed with any degree of confidence to differential codes. The available evidence clearly indicates differences between visual and verbal memory but is quite compatible with the conceptualization of a common abstract long-term code. Differences between visual and verbal memory could be reflected in such a system by the type of material stored in this abstract code, and also by the preferred means of manipulating such material during storage and output (Baddeley & Lieberman, 1980; Kosslyn, 1980).

A processing domain, then, is essentially an area of memory containing a rich network of links and connections; such domains will often be associated with separable cognitive processing systems, but this need not be the case. Finally, although the rich interconnections are referred to as associations, it is not intended to tie the concept to any particular associationist assumptions. [. . .] Domains are connected to other domains and may be divided into subdomains, so the distinction is not absolute although it is, however, a useful one.

The concept of domains differs from the concept of levels in a number of ways. Unlike levels, it does not assume a linear sequence or a hierarchy of processes, because information may be processed within a number of domains simultaneously, in a parallel heterarchical manner. In the absence of a hierarchy, it does not have necessary implications for the durability of memory traces within any given domain, although it is likely that processing within different domains will have different mnemonic consequences. Similarly, the concept of a domain does not have any necessary implications for whether maintenance rehearsal will lead to learning. In short, the concept of a domain is a very much more general theoretical structure than that assumed by levels of processing. I should point out, however, that most of the stronger assumptions made by levels of processing have proved to be either unjustified or else explicable in terms of other more general principles, such as elaboration or cue overload, both of which are applicable within the more general concept of a domain (Baddeley, 1978).

To what extent is it worth retaining such a pale shadow of the levels-of-processing concept? As I hope to demonstrate later, it is extremely useful to have a concept that allows one to express the fact that certain types of information are closely related and interact strongly, whereas other types are relatively separate. An obvious case in point is that of visual and verbal memory. It is clear that words can evoke visual images, and visual stimuli suggest words, but nonetheless, the abundant evidence for separate visual and verbal coding indicates that visual and verbal memory can usefully be conceptualized as distinct but related domains (. . . Paivio, 1971; Woodhead & Baddeley, 1981).

[. . .]

A concept such as domains of processing is not in any simple sense testable, nor is there any one experiment one can carry out that will tell us whether the concept is useful or useless. There is little doubt, however, that we do need to explore the interrelation among lexical, semantic, and episodic representations in memory, and the test of a concept such as domains of processing lies in whether it proves useful in guiding and encouraging the exploration of such relations without allowing strong prior assumptions to constrain investigation unduly.

Interactive and Independent Context

It is suggested that context may influence learning and subsequent memory in two separate ways. The most dramatic effect of context will occur when the context determines the way an item is encoded. In the classic verbal-memory studies by Tulving and his collaborators (e.g., Tulving & Thomson, 1973), the word to be remembered (TBR) is accompanied by a low-frequency associate; for example, the TBR word *cold* might be accompanied by the word *ground*. Under such conditions, subjects may be more likely to recall the TBR word given the retrieval cue *ground* than they would be to recognize the word *cold* when they have generated it in another context, for example, as an associate of the word *hot* (Tulving & Thomson, 1973). It is suggested that this is because the word *ground* actively modifies the way in which subjects interpret the TBR word *cold* so that what they store is an experience created by the interaction of the two, for instance, the thought of a grave or perhaps a field under a frost. Interactive context therefore operates by changing what is stored. One consequence of this is that interactively coded context will influence both recall and recognition.

Context need not, however, always be interactive. The subject may encode both the TBR word and the cue quite separately, particularly if they come from very different domains. Environmental context generally appears to operate in this way; subjects encode the word at the same time as they encode its environmental surroundings. Reinstating the environment will enhance recall, but in contrast to interactive context, which also influences recognition, independent context appears to leave recognition memory unaffected.

As we shall see later, the distinction between interactive and independent context applies not only to the role of environmental context but also to results in the role of semantic context in face recognition (Baddeley & Woodhead, 1982), and under certain conditions to verbal memory (Gardiner & Tulving, 1980).

[...]

As in the case of the concept of processing domains, the concept of interactive versus independent context cannot be tested by means of a single experiment. It should be evaluated first on the basis of whether it is useful in giving a convincing account of existing data and, second, on the question of whether it generates research leading to a better understanding of the role of context in memory.

Recollection

The term *recollection* is used to refer to the active problem-solving aspect of retrieval that subjectively appears to play an important part in remembering. Although such factors have sometimes been discussed ... they have largely been ignored in laboratory studies of retrieval during the 1970s. In some ways this is surprising because the active role of the subject in organizing and learning formed an important tenet of cognitive psychology during this period. It is interesting to note that Tulving (..., 1966), one of the strongest advocates of the view that learning depends on active organization by the subject, has emphasized an essentially passive interpretation of retrieval. Underpinning the concept of encoding specificity (Tulving & Thomson, 1973) is the concept of a set of retrieval cues that automatically evokes the appropriate response. The concept of recollection does not deny that such automatic processes form an important component of retrieval. It suggests, however, that they offer only a partial account of the complex process of retrieval. We are able to "search" our memory probably by actively setting up plausible retrieval cues. More importantly, when trying to remember something, we do not blindly accept every candidate memory as veridical. We have ways of evaluating memories and subsequently using these to refine our recall of an event or situation. The term recollection is used to refer to this active process of setting up prospective retrieval cues, evaluating the outcome, and systematically working toward a representation of a past experience that we find acceptable. Labeling this set of processes "recollection" does not of course constitute an explanation; it is, however, a reminder of an important aspect of human memory that has been sadly neglected.

[...]

SOME APPLIED PROBLEMS

Context-Dependent Memory in Divers

It has been known for many years that material learned in one environment may often be recalled better in that environment than in an alternative setting. Although it is sometimes difficult to produce a reliable effect in the laboratory ..., my colleagues and I incidentally observed what appeared to be a massive effect of context dependency when divers were asked to recall passages of prose or lists of unrelated words learned under water (Baddeley, Cuccaro, Egstrom, Weltman, & Willis, 1975; Davis, Baddeley, & Hancock, 1975), though neither gave any indication of context dependency when memory was tested by recognition. In an experiment designed specifically to investigate context dependency, Godden and I (Godden & Baddeley, 1975) had divers learn lists of words either on the beach or under about 15 feet (4.55 m) of water. When the recall environment differed from that in which learning took place, there was a decrement of over 30% in number of words remembered.

Such a result has obvious practical implications; it suggests that diver training should not rely too heavily on teaching on dry land and, furthermore, indicates that if divers are being used as inspectors, then they should record their observations as they make them and not rely on memory. From a theoretical point of view, this result seems to fit very neatly into the framework suggested by the encoding-specificity hypothesis: Words that are originally encoded in the context of the underwater environment will be most easily recalled when that context is revived.

In a subsequent experiment (Godden & Baddeley, 1980), we extended our study to look at the influence of environmental context on recognition memory. Once again we used divers who were required to learn lists of words either on land or under water. This time, however, they were tested by recognition instead of recall. We obtained a small decrement when learning took place under water but no suggestion of a context-dependency effect, with subjects recognizing 72.0% of the words when the environment was reinstated and 72.5% when it was changed.

[. . .]

The encoding-specificity principle has of course no difficulty in explaining why context influences recall; if the environmental cues were encoded during list learning, then there is every reason for them to serve subsequently as retrieval cues, enhancing recall. It is, however, far from obvious how one can account for the failure of environmental context to influence recognition. It is clear from our first study that divers do encode context, but equally clear from our second that this does not influence their recognition performance. Because recognition involves retrieval (Tulving & Thomson, 1973), why does the environment not provide a retrieval cue? A contextual-tagging theory (e.g., Anderson & Bower, 1973) is no more successful in resolving this paradox. If the environment makes the contextual tags more accessible or discriminable in the recall condition, then it should be equally helpful in recognition.

Our results seem to demand two modifications to the view of retrieval suggested by the early version of encoding specificity. First, Tulving and Thomson (1973) state clearly that they "make no theoretical distinction between recall and recognition" (p. 354). Our results imply a clear distinction. Second, our results suggest that Tulving and Thomson's rejection of two-stage generate-and-recognize models of retrieval may have been premature. Although they were no doubt justified in arguing against certain specific two-stage tagging models, our data indicate that environmental context will influence the accessibility of the memory trace (generation) but will not influence the subject's ability to evaluate the trace as that of a "new" or "old" item (recognition). Our diving data are particularly cogent here because the dramatic environmental change induced by diving produces an extremely large contextual effect, making it quite clear that the absence of such an effect under conditions of recognition is not simply due to the insensitivity of the experiment. Our data then argue for a distinction between recall and recognition and favor a two-stage model.

A problem raised by our result stems from the contrast between environmental context, which we found did not influence recognition, and verbal context, which has been shown by Tulving and Thomson (1973) and many others to be a potent factor in recognition. The proposed distinction between interactive and independent context offers a plausible explanation for this apparent discrepancy. When a verbal stimulus word is accompanied by a low-frequency associate, the two are likely to interact, hence influencing the subject's encoding and interpretation of the TBR item. In the case of environmental context, however, there is no reason why the interpretation of a randomly selected set of words should depend on whether they are experienced on land or under water. The environmental context will therefore be encoded independently and in parallel. Such an encoding may enhance the accessibility of the memory trace laid down during learning. Under conditions of recognition, however, access to the trace is not a major problem; the difficulty comes in deciding whether the word represented was in fact previously presented. This evaluation is clearly not influenced by independent context.

Face Recognition

During the 1970s there was a considerable growth of interest in memory for faces. This stemmed very largely from a concern with the role of the eyewitness in legal cases, and much of the work has been concerned with demonstrating the unreliability of witnesses and the ease with which eyewitness testimony may be manipulated (Clifford & Bull, 1978; Loftus, 1979). Our own interest was slightly different in that we were concerned with the problem of whether one could improve a person's ability to remember and recognize faces.

We first studied a training course that was designed on the basis of the view that performance could be improved by teaching the trainee to analyze a face into its constituent features and then categorize these. . . . Unfortunately, the only effects of this course were to make the trainees perform more poorly under certain recognition conditions (Woodhead, Baddeley, & Simmonds, 1979).

A more promising approach to the problem seemed to be offered by levels of processing, which suggests that faces might be remembered better if they are processed more deeply. A study by Bower and Karlin (1974) claimed to have demonstrated this. Subjects were given either the "shallow" task of deciding whether each of a sequence of faces was male or female or the "deeper" task of assessing the intelligence or honesty of the people represented. The deeper encoding led to better subsequent recognition. However, it is quite possible that judgments of sex might be made much more rapidly than judgments of honesty or intelligence so that subjects in the shallow condition simply spent less time observing and processing the faces. If so, this result could simply be another demonstration of the total-time hypothesis, whereby the greater the amount of time spent on learning, the better the subsequent recall or recognition (Cooper & Pantle, 1967). We therefore decided to conduct a stricter test of the levels-of-processing interpretation of face recognition.

In our study (Patterson & Baddeley, 1977), subjects categorized faces on the basis of either physical dimensions, such as nose size or thickness of lips, or personality dimensions, such as nice–nasty and intelligent–dull.

Our subjects were subsequently required to recognize the faces among a range of distractors. We observed a significant but disappointingly small effect of encoding instructions. At the same time, we observed massive effects of disguise and substantial effects of pose, but neither of these interacted with encoding strategy. Our failure to find a major effect of encoding is consistent with other studies that suggest that, provided the subject is required to treat the face as a whole rather than as a set of independent features, the manner of encoding is of little significance. [...] Such findings suggest that the important factor is not depth of processing but rather whether the subject processes the face as a set of isolated features or as a single gestalt in which the whole range of physical features participate and interact.

By this stage in the project, however, the concept of levels of processing had been modified by Craik and Tulving (1975) to include the concept of elaboration. It seemed possible, therefore, that if a genuine depth-of-processing effect was occurring, then it might be possible to enhance it by inducing a greater degree of semantic elaboration. We attempted to achieve this in a series of studies in which faces were presented either together with simply a name and age under control conditions or accompanied by a semantic context, describing the person's occupation, background, and habits (Baddeley & Woodhead, 1982). We conducted two such experiments, [but neither] provided any evidence for the suggestion that semantic elaboration of faces would enhance subsequent recognition.

By this time we were becoming a little disenchanted with a levels-of-processing approach to face recognition. Not only had we failed to amplify our previous small effect but we had lost it altogether. Why should that be? A possible interpretation is suggested by Fisher and Craik (1980), whose study using verbal material indicated that although elaboration may enhance recall, it will only influence recognition when the elaborating material is highly compatible with the material to be remembered. It seems likely that our random assignment of contexts to faces would not produce a particularly compatible mapping. Our results are therefore consistent with those of Fisher and Craik, who themselves suggest that their results should generalize to faces. Our views concur with those of Fisher and Craik in suggesting that these results argue against the original Craik and Tulving (1975) position that elaboration has its effect by producing an enriched and hence more discriminable trace of the target item. Such a view predicts a clear effect of elaboration on both recall and recognition. Our data suggest that this will occur only if the item and its context are encoded interactively, a type of coding that is likely to be difficult unless target and context are reasonably compatible.

[...]

Overall, then, our results appear to suggest that the attempt to apply the concept of levels of processing to recognition of faces was premature. At a practical level, at least, it seems unlikely that inducing the subject to encode a face deeply or elaborately will necessarily enhance subsequent recognition. However, although the concept of levels of processing has not proved helpful in studying face recognition, I would like to suggest that the concept of a domain, and subdomain, does remain a useful one.

Although the concept of a domain does not of itself generate testable predictions, it does provide a framework for discussing face recognition. Consider first the learning and recognition of unfamiliar faces. It is likely that the face is processed as a gestalt rather than being processed as a set of independent additive features. The combination of these features gives rise to the perception of a person who often will be seen as having certain characteristics, for example, ugly or handsome, intelligent or stupid, shifty or reliable, Nordic or Arabic. One might therefore distinguish two subdomains, one concerned with features and the topography of faces and the other concerned with their semantic associates, real or imagined. The existence of stereotypes indicates reasonably strongly the connections between these two subdomains.

Consider now the face of someone who is familiar, for example, ex-president Nixon. This conception will not only include topographic characteristics together with one's assessment of such characteristics as whether he looks trustworthy but will also be associated with a great deal of semantic information peculiar to this particular face: the fact that he was president, the association with Watergate, McCarthyism, and so forth. In this case we have a very clear link with a much broader domain of our memory system than is the case with an unfamiliar face. Similarly, the face of a member of one's family clearly conjures up enormously rich associations that go well beyond the domain of physiognomy.

[. . .]

Retrieval and Aphasia

The final area of practical importance discussed is one that has not traditionally concerned memory researchers, namely, the understanding of word finding in aphasic patients. It is commonly the case that damage to the left side of the brain produces substantial problems in the normal utilization of speech, often associated with a particular difficulty in retrieving the names of objects. One of the roles of a speech therapist is to try to help such patients recover their ability to retrieve words efficiently and appropriately. There is, however, relatively little understanding of this retrieval process. The section that follows represents an attempt to take the concepts of retrieval developed in the study of episodic memory and attempt to use these to throw light on the question of word finding both in aphasic patients and in normal subjects.

Once again, the concepts of levels of processing and encoding specificity will be used. It is, however, important to emphasize that neither of these concepts was explicitly designed for application to semantic memory. Although that does not prevent them from being used as a source of ideas, any failure of the two concepts to explain problems of word finding in aphasia does not of course reflect on the usefulness of the two concepts in the area of episodic memory for which they were originally devised. Whether they are successful, the attempt to apply such concepts to word finding should have interesting implications for similarities and differences between semantic and episodic memory.

It has often been suggested . . . that aphasic patients function basically like normal subjects except that their processes of word retrieval are slowed down. If this is the case, it implies both that normal concepts of word retrieval may help one understand aphasia and that studies of aphasia may help our understanding of normal word retrieval. With this in mind, Hatfield, Howard, Barber, Jones, and Morton (1977) studied the influence of context on object naming in aphasic patients.

An appropriate context has been shown to facilitate the perception of both words (Morton, 1969) and objects (Palmer, 1975). Furthermore, speech therapists have claimed that aphasic patients find it easier to access the name of an object in the context of its use, for then "the patient will be led into the mental attitude in which the words occur. This makes it much easier for him to retrieve the appropriate word" (Hatfield, 1971, p. 24). [. . .] Such a view would, of course, be quite compatible with an encoding-specificity interpretation; the name of an object is likely to be acquired in the context of that object and its utilization, and hence, a realistic representation of the object in an appropriate context should maximize the probability of recalling its name.

However, although it was generally believed that an appropriate context and a realistic representation helped aphasics in word retrieval, the available evidence was far from convincing. [. . .]

In a direct test of the effect of realism, Rochford and Williams (1965) required their patients to name either eight pictures of objects or eight parts of the experimenter's body that were pointed to. There was no difference in probability of naming between the pictorial representation and the real body parts. Although there are clearly problems in interpreting this last result due to the nonequivalence of the two types of items, it does cast doubt, nevertheless, on the view that greater realism enhances object naming.

[In particular] the observation that a rhyming word is a better cue to the name of an object than a functional description [Rochford & Williams, 1962] would appear to be at odds with any suggested interpretation in terms of either levels of processing or encoding specificity. It creates problems for a simple levels-of-processing interpretation because it seems to suggest that phonemic rather than semantic encoding is more useful, whereas a simple encoding-specificity hypothesis would be faced with the problem of explaining why a rhyming word (e.g., *candle*) should serve as a good retrieval cue for *handle* when the two must rarely, if ever, have been presented to the subject together. In view of the importance of this point and the comparative lack of evidence to support it, Hatfield et al. (1977) decided to investigate in more detail the role of realism and context in word finding by aphasic patients.

Hatfield et al. performed three experiments. In the first, drawings of objects in different situations were used. One condition consisted of the object in a highly plausible context: For example, the object might be a brush with a drawing of a girl looking under a bed for the brush. This was accompanied by the sentence "Ann is looking under the bed for the _____." A second condition involved a somewhat less plausible scenario, "Albert hits the nail with a _____," whereas the third represented the least plausible condition, "The snake is hiding in the _____"; all were illustrated by appropriate drawings. Although the probability of naming an object did increase over three successive presentations, there was no evidence that appropriateness of the context enhanced naming.

In their second study, Hatfield et al. (1977) manipulated visual rather than semantic context, drawing a series of objects either alone or in an appropriate context. An example might be that of a snail, pictured together with a drawing of flowers, leaves, grass, and so forth. In this study the probability of recalling the items when presented free of context was .56, whereas in a context it was .55, once again indicating no facilitation of naming by context.

The final experiment by Hatfield et al. was a direct test of the role of realism in naming. They presented their aphasic patients with objects, photographs of such objects, or line drawings and compared the probability of the subject producing the correct name. There was no significant difference between conditions, with naming probabilities for the objects, photographs, and drawings being .84, .76, and .77, respectively.

In accounting for their results, Hatfield et al. distinguished three stages in their naming task: recognition of the objects, leading to recovery of knowledge about the object that is then used to find the name. They suggest that the role of context in tachistoscopic recognition of words and objects by normal subjects (Morton, 1969; Palmer, 1975) occurs because under such degraded stimulus conditions the first stage, namely, that of object recognition, is the limiting factor on performance. In the case of aphasic patients, they have no difficulty in perceiving the object and knowing what its purpose is; they simply cannot access its name. That being so, improving the realism of the stimulus is unlikely to be helpful because it merely enhances a stage that is already functioning perfectly adequately. What is required is assistance in accessing the name. This can be facilitated in the short term, at least, by priming within the lexical domain; hence, a patient is able to repeat a word he or she has just heard. Hatfield et al. (1977) found evidence of priming in all three studies because the probability of retrieving an item increased over successive tests; it appears that having retrieved the name once, the patient has for a short time a higher probability of retrieving it, even though the retrieval context is dramatically changed (e.g., from a brush with a snake in it to a girl looking for a brush under her bed).

A second way of enhancing lexical retrieval is by spelling the word out or using a rhyme (Rochford & Williams, 1962). This presumably works because associations within the lexicon avoid the need to access the name code directly from the semantic representation. The use of cliché, for example, cueing the word *butter* with the cliché "bread and ____," is another powerful retrieval cue in this context (Rochford & Williams, 1962), once again because the associations presumably operate within the lexical domain and do not rely on a lexical–semantic link.

What then are the theoretical implications of these studies? It might seem reasonable to suppose that the name of an object such as a snail will have been initially learned primarily in the context of real snails, or at least pictures of snails. That being so, these might be expected to form more appropriate retrieval cues for the response *snail* than would a rhyming word such as *pale*. This clearly is not so. Such results are more compatible with a view that separates the various processing domains involved in picture naming. Hence, the lexical-access component of naming—the availability of the name itself—is distinguished from the visual and semantic characteristics of the task. An aphasic patient can see and know what a snail is without being able to "remember" that it is called a snail. Although such a basic distinction may seem trivially obvious, it does imply a complex relation between objects, words, and their meaning.

One might reasonably argue that these results may not apply outside the rather constrained area of aphasic speech. How plausible is it that evidence from aphasics might extend to normal word retrieval? The most obvious link is via the tip-of-the-tongue phenomenon first studied by R. Brown and McNeil (1966). They read out definitions of low-frequency words to their subjects and studied instances where subjects were certain they knew the word in question but could not produce the relevant name. Under these circumstances subjects frequently knew the number of syllables in the missing word and when urged to recall the initial letter were correct on 57% of the occasions, well above chance level. They were also able to reject plausible alternatives and subsequently respond with great confidence once the appropriate word had become available. Gruneberg (1978) required geography students to recall the names of capitals of various countries. When students could not recall a capital, they were asked to rate their strength of conviction that they did actually know it. They were then cued by being given the first letter of the name. There was a clear tendency for the first-letter cue to enhance recall, an effect that was particularly clear in the case of those capitals that were widely known by the group. In short, the first-letter cue appears to be effective but only when the information is there to be cued. [. . .]

The importance of the first letter of a word is also demonstrated in episodic memory tested by free, paired-associate, or serial recall in a series of experiments by D. L. Nelson and his associates (Nelson, 1979). Nelson and Rowe (1969) required their subjects to learn paired-associate lists comprising three-letter words as stimuli and digits as responses. They varied the intralist stimulus similarity, having words share either initial, middle, or terminal letters. They found a clear tendency for intralist similarity to impair performance, with impairment being greatest when initial letters were shared by several stimuli.

[. . .] Nelson's work clearly demonstrates the importance of such shallow cues as initial letter in verbal long-term memory. Such results do not fit easily into a levels-of-processing framework but are entirely consistent with a view that distinguishes between lexical and semantic domains and accepts that both are involved in verbal long-term memory.

One characteristic of the tip-of-the-tongue phenomenon is a tendency for retrieval to be dominated by a plausible but incorrect response. A little while ago I was attempting to generate the term that an optician would use for being short-sighted; the word that kept popping up was *astigmatic*, which I knew perfectly well was incorrect; yet try as I may, whenever I searched, *astigmatic* was the word that popped up, completely blocking out *myopic*, a word that I would normally not have any difficulty in producing.

A more systematic exploration of this phenomenon was carried out by A. Brown (1979), who gave his subjects definitions of relatively low-frequency objects accompanied by either a rhyming word, an unrelated word, or a semantically closely related word. He found that presenting a semantically related item actively inhibited recall relative to a totally unrelated word. Why should this occur? Presumably, if we are to talk, then it is necessary to produce a fluent string of lexically appropriate items. At many points there may be several potentially appropriate words. For the process of speech to operate smoothly, it is necessary to choose one word and inhibit the rest, and typically, it is more important to do this than to choose the exactly perfect word at any given moment [. . .] The smooth operation of the lexicon therefore seems to require that all items synonymous with the word being produced be inhibited. Because the process of speech is fluent, the inhibition must not extend to all words.

Analogous inhibition effects have been shown in category generation by J. Brown (1968) and in free recall by Tulving and Hastie (1972) and Slamecka (1968). The simple assumption of a separate lexical domain therefore offers a framework for explaining a wide range of phenomena from naming in aphasic patients through the tip-of-the-tongue effect and initial letter cueing to the inhibitory effects of items that are semantically associated with the inaccessible name in both semantic and episodic tasks.

The nature of the semantic domain in verbal memory is a particularly crucial one. It is also an area in which there are many conflicting views and little firm agreement. I would like to suggest, however, that any concept of meaning must allow some form of mapping from words—individual discrete verbal units—onto experience of the world that must be multi-dimensional, continuous, and capable of registering without difficulty new experiences that have never previously occurred. As Watkins and Gardiner (1979, p. 700) point out, this means that the end result of any adequate representation of meaning cannot simply be excitation of a single node. This creates problems for an interpretation of memory that assumes tagging of specific nodes.

The problem is avoided, however, if one assumes the distinction drawn by Tulving (1972) between semantic and episodic memory. Semantic memory represents knowledge, general information that is not confined to a single experience. The meaning of words, geographical information, and facts about people or objects are all examples of information stored in semantic memory. Episodic memory by contrast is concerned with the representation of specific individual experiences. The knowledge that Borg [was] the men's champion at Wimbledon for five successive years is information in my semantic memory, as is the fact that he won the 1980 championship. My recall of the particular circumstances in which I myself watched the match reflect my episodic memory. The two aspects of memory clearly often interact; my specific experience of the match was influenced by knowing Borg had won on four previous occasions, whereas my semantic memory itself was obviously modified, if only to the extent of updating the number of successive titles won by Borg.

In the case of learning word lists, the lexical representation of each word will access one or more semantic nodes that form an intermediate stage in creating episodic experiences from words. Take, for example, the experiment by Tulving and Osler (1968) in which subjects were presented with a target word (e.g., CITY) accompanied by a cue word that is an associate of the target (e.g., *dirty* or *village*). It is suggested that what is experienced and stored by the subject in the case of CITY *dirty* is a representation of that aspect of the city that is associated with dirt, perhaps an image of litter or smoke, possibly based on a particular remembered episode. In the case of

CITY village, the experience is likely to be very different, possibly representing a quiet, secluded villagelike neighborhood within a city.

What will be remembered, then, is probably not primarily the lexical representation of *city*, *village*, and *dirty*, nor some simple semantic representation of each of these, but rather an episode that is created from these constituent units. A simple analogy is with that of color printing, where a small number of "pure" colors may be combined to produce a continuous color range; hence, yellow combined with blue will give green, whereas combined with red it will give orange. The color printer uses a limited and discontinuous set of components to produce a continuous range of color simply by combining the component in different proportions. I suggest, therefore, that the crucial aspect of semantic encoding of words in an episodic-memory task is analogous to the continuously variable picture that results from the printing and that this should not be confused with the discrete and discontinuous meanings of the individual words presented, on which the episode experienced is based.

PRECEDENTS AND CONSEQUENCES

In discussing these views with colleagues who have been more directly involved in current theoretical controversies regarding the processes of retrieval, two questions tend to crop up: first, whether my views are inconsistent with some form of encoding specificity and, second, whether they are testable. I will discuss these questions in turn.

First, the concept of encoding specificity, as with most fruitful concepts, has not remained static over the years. I believe that my views, and the results I cite, are inconsistent with a simple view of encoding specificity that states that cues will enhance recall or recognition only if they are both encoded at the time of learning and reinstated by the experimenter at the time of test. Such a rigid view is not, however, necessitated by more recent versions of encoding specificity (... Tulving, 1982). I assume, therefore, that the encoding-specificity theorist does allow some form of mediation via semantic memory between the retrieval cue presented at the test and that presented during learning. There is no reason why such a process cannot be extended to cover the concept of recollection.

[...]

The second question that may be raised with regard to the proposed framework is that it is not directly testable. Having been brought up on the writings of Popper (1959), I must confess that I have raised this objection, for example, in connection with the concept of levels of processing. I suggest, however, that as a blanket criterion for evaluating all kinds of theory, it is misguided. Theoretical concepts can operate at a whole series of levels ranging from the detailed and precise to the very general. The criteria for evaluating an explanatory concept will depend on the level and purpose for which it is devised. In the present instance the purpose of the theoretical concepts in question is to provide a coherent framework to assist in the understanding of a wide range of phenomena. In this view, a theoretical concept should be evaluated not by whether it approximates some absolute truth but by the extent to which it performs the useful function of interpreting what we already know while facilitating further discovery.

In what was no doubt an attempt to stimulate counter proposals, Tulving and Thomson (1973) claimed, "The formulation of the encoding specificity principle is so general that it covers all known phenomena of episodic memory and retrieval and in a weak sense provides an understanding of them" (p. 370). Unfortunately, the many studies that followed this claim have been concerned not with the adequacy of encoding specificity as a general theory of retrieval but with the specific ingenious but somewhat complex experimental procedure used by Tulving and Thomson in their case against the simple generate–recognize hypothesis. [. . .] How can we avoid becoming the prisoners of our methods? I would suggest that one effective antidote is to move out of the laboratory from time to time and attempt to apply our theories and techniques to practical problems. The more bracing air of the outside world may prove too much for some of our laboratory-raised concepts, but I am enough of an optimist to believe that many will survive and flourish.

REFERENCES

Anderson, J. R., & Bower, G. H. (1973) *Human associative memory*. London: Wiley.

Baddeley, A. D. (1978) The trouble with levels: A reexaminatin of Craik and Lockhart's framework for memory research. *Psychological Review, 85*, 139–152.

Baddeley, A. D. (1981) The cognitive psychology of everyday life. *British Journal of Psychology, 72*, 257–269.

Baddeley, A. D., Cuccaro, W. J., Egstrom, G., Weltman, G., & Willis, M. A. (1975) Cognitive efficiency of divers working in cold water. *Human Factors, 17*, 446–454.

Baddeley, A. D., & Lieberman, K. (1980) Spatial working memory. In R. S. Nickerson (Ed.), *Attention and performance VIII*. Hillsdale, N.J.: Lawrence Erlbaum Associates.

Baddeley, A. D., & Woodhead, M. M. (1982) Depth of processing, context, and face recognition. *Canadian Journal of Psychology, 36*, 148–164.

Bower, G. H., & Karlin, M. B. (1974) Depth of processing pictures of faces and recognition memory. *Journal of Experimental Psychology, 103*, 751–757.

Brown, A. S. (1979) Priming effects in semantic memory retrieval processes. *Journal of Experimental Psychology: Human Learning and Memory, 5*, 65–77.

Brown, J. (1968) Reciprocal facilitation and impairment of free recall. *Psychonomic Science, 10*, 2.

Brown, R., & McNeil, D. (1966) The "tip of the tongue" phenomenon. *Journal of Verbal Learning and Verbal Behavior, 5*, 325–337.

Clifford, B. R., & Bull, R. (1978) *The psychology of person identification.* London Routledge & Kegan Paul.

Cooper, E. C., & Pantle, A. J. (1967) The total-time hypothesis in verbal learning. *Psychological Bulletin, 68*, 221–234.

Craik, F. I. M., & Lockhart, R. S. (1972) Levels of processing: A framework for memory research. *Journal of Verbal Learning and Verbal Behavior, 11*, 671–684.

Craik, F, I. M., & Tulving, E. (1975) Depth of processing and the retention of words in episodic memory. *Journal of Experimental Psychology: General, 104*, 268–294.

Davis, F. M., Baddeley, A. D., & Hancock, T. R. (1975) Diver performance: The effect of cold. *Undersea Biomedical Research, 2*, 195–213.

Fisher, R. P., & Craik, F, I, M. (1980) The effects of elaboration on recognition memory. *Memory and Cognition, 8*, 400–404.

Gardiner, J. M., & Tulving, E. (1980) Exceptions to recognition failure of recallable words. *Journal of Verbal Learning and Verbal Behavior, 19*, 194–209.

Godden, D. R., & Baddeley, A. D. (1975) Context-dependent memory in two natural environments: On land and underwater. *British Journal of Psychology, 66*, 325–331.

Godden, D. R., & Baddeley, A. D. (1980) When does context influence recognition memory? *British Journal of psychology, 71*, 99–104.

Gruneberg, M. M. (1978) Memory blocks and memory aids. In M. M. Gruneberg & P. Morris (Eds.), *Aspects of memory.* London: Methuen.

Hatfield, F. M. (1971) Some uses of videotape recordings in language after brain damage. *Medical and Biological Illustration, 21*, 166–177.

Hatfield, F. M., Howard, D., Barber, J., Jones, C., & Morton, J. (1977) Object naming in aphasics: The lack of effect of context or realism. *Neuropsychologia, 15*, 717–727.

Kosslyn, S. M. (1980) *Image and mind.* Cambridge, Mass.: Harvard University Press.

Loftus, E. F. (1979) *Eyewitness testimony.* Cambridge, Mass.: Harvard University Press.

Morton, J. (1969) Interaction of information in word recognition. *Psychological Review, 76*, 165–178.

Nelson, D. L. (1979) Remembering pictures and words: Appearance, significance, and name. In L. Cermak & F. I. M. Craik (Eds.), *Levels of processing in human memory.* Hillsdale, N.J.: Lawrence Erlbaum Associates.

Nelson, D. L., & Rowe, F. A. (1969) Information theory and stimulus encoding in paired-associate acquisition: Ordinal position of formal similarity. *Journal of Experimental Psychology, 79*, 342–346.

Paivio, A. (1971) *Imagery and verbal processes.* New York: Holt, Rinehart & Winston.

Palmer, S. E. (1975) The effects of contextual scenes on the identification of objects. *Memory and Cognition, 3*, 519–526.

Patterson, K. E., & Baddeley, A. D. (1977) When face recognition fails. *Journal of Experimental Psychology: Human Learning and Memory, 3*, 406–417.

Popper, K. (1959) *The logic of scientific discovery.* London: Hutchinson.

Rochford, G., & Williams, M. (1962) Studies in the development and breakdown of the use of names: Experimental production of naming disorders in normal people. *Journal of Neurology, Neurosurgery and Psychiatry, 25*, 228–233.

Rochford, G., & Williams, M. (1965) Studies in the development of breakdown in the use of names. Part IV: The effects of word frequency. *Journal of Neurology, Neurosurgery and Psychiatry, 28*, 407–413.

Slamecka, N. J. (1968) An examination of trace storage in free recall. *Journal of Experimental Psychology, 76*, 504–513.

Tulving, E. (1966) Subjective organization and effects of repetition in multi-trial free-recall learning. *Journal of Verbal Learning and Verbal Behavior, 5*, 193–197.

Tulving, E. (1972) Episodic and semantic memory. In E. Tulving & W. Donaldson (Eds.), *Organization of memory*. New York: Academic Press.

Tulving, E. (1982) Synergistic ecphory in recall and recognition. *Canadian Journal of Psychology, 36*, 130–147.

Tulving, E., & Hastie, R. (1972) Inhibition effects of intralist repetition in free recall. *Journal of Experimental Psychology, 92*, 297–304.

Tulving, E., & Osler, S. (1968) Effectiveness of retrieval cues in memory for words. *Journal of Experimental Psychology, 77*, 593–601.

Tulving, E., & Thomson, D. M. (1973) Encoding specificity and retrieval processes in episodic memory. *Psychological Review, 80*, 352–373.

Watkins, M. J., & Gardiner, J. M. (1979) An appreciation of generate–recognize theory of recall. *Journal of Verbal Learning and Verbal Behavior, 18*, 687–704.

Woodhead, M. M., & Baddeley, A. D. (1981) Individual differences and memory for faces, pictures and words. *Memory & Cognition, 9*, 368–370.

Woodhead, M. M., Baddeley, A. D., & Simmonds, D. C. V. (1979) On training to recognize faces. *Ergonomics, 22*, 333–343.

11 Reminding and Memory Organization

Roger C. Schank

A key question for researchers in cognitive science is the problem of how human memory is organized. The solution to this problem is fundamental to cognitive scientists regardless of whether their basic orientation is towards Artificial Intelligence or cognitive psychology. The theories that we test by means of psychological experiments ought to have some ramifications on how we build computer models of the processes tested by those experiments, and the computer models that we build ought to supply testable hypotheses for psychologists. [. . .]

[. . .] In particular, our work on scripts, as embodied in the SAM (Cullingford, 1978; Schank & Yale Group, 1975) and FRUMP (DeJong, 1979) programs has caused various researchers outside of our group to attempt to test such notions experimentally (Bower, Black, & Turner, 1979; Graesser, Gordon, & Sawyer, 1979; Owens, Bower, & Black, 1979; Smith, Adams, & Schorr, 1978). Some of those experiments have begun to have an effect upon our theories and upon our subsequent programs, . . . [and the] solutions we are proposing are at least partially a result of this interplay of psychological and computational concerns.

In addition to showing that script-like considerations are relevant in story understanding, one of the most valuable things to come out of empirical research on scripts was the problem it presented for us. Recognition confusions were found by Bower et al. to occur between stories about visits to the dentist and visits to the doctor. Intuitively, this result is not surprising, because most people have experienced such confusions. But what accounts for it? Should we posit a "visit to a health-care professional" script to explain it? Clearly, such a script would be beyond our initial conception of what a script was.

[...]

Another question for AI researchers is, why have we not run headlong into this problem before? The answer is, I think, that although psychologists worry about recognition confusions in due course, as a part of their natural interest in memory (see Crowder, 1976; Kintsch, 1977), AI has not really concerned itself with memory at all. We have not been constructing our programs with memory in mind, so the issue has not come up. However, it seems obvious that what we posit as a processing structure is likely to be a memory structure as well, and this has profound implications for an understanding theory.

LEVELS OF MEMORY

The problem that we must deal with, then, is the question of what kinds of knowledge are available to an understander. In answering this question, we must realize that every theory of processing must also be a theory of memory. To put this another way, if psychologists were to prove that recognition confusions occur between two entities in memory, it would have to be taken as a disproof of a theory that claimed those two entities should be processed by entirely different means.

Thus, in order to address the question of what kinds of processing structures people have, we should investigate the kinds of things people are capable of remembering and confusing. It seems obvious that people have processed whatever they have in memory at some time prior to its presence there, so this seems a natural place to begin.

One type of thing that people can remember in some detail are particular experiences that they have had. So, we postulate a level of memory that contains specific remembrances of particular situations. We call this EVENT MEMORY. Examples of what might be found in EVENT MEMORY include all the details of "going to Dr. Smith's dental office last Tuesday and getting your tooth pulled" and "forgetting your dental appointment and having them call you up and yell at you and charge you for it last month." EVENTS are remembered as they happen, but not for long. After a while, the less salient aspects of an EVENT fade away. Such details would include, for instance, where you got the phone call, or why you forgot your appointment. [...] What is left are GENERALIZED EVENTS plus the unusual or interesting parts of the original event from EVENT MEMORY (EM).

A GENERALIZED EVENT is a collocation of EVENTS whose common features have been abstracted. This is where general information about situations that have been experienced numerous times is held. Particular experiences are initially a part of EVENT MEMORY. However, when such particular experiences refer to a common generalized event, *that generalized event is brought in to help in the processing of the new input.* Once the connection between an event and the generalized event that it references is established, the event itself is liable to gradually fade away, leaving only the pointer to the generalized event and the salient features of the event not dominated by the generalized event.

Memory for generalized events relies in a similar way upon what we call SITUATIONAL MEMORY. *Situational memory contains information about situations in general.* For example, information about "going to a health professional's office" or "getting a health problem taken care of" are instances of the kind of knowledge that resides in *SITUATIONAL MEMORY* (SM).

In the understanding process, information found in Situational Memory is used to provide the overall context for a situation. When we go to a dentist's office and something happens there, e.g., you are overcharged, or you meet a pretty girl, the specifics of the dental part of the experience are unimportant in the same way that what telephone you were using is unimportant in the example given for Event Memory above. Situational Memory serves as a repository of relevant contextual knowledge as well as the final storage place for relevant parts of new events in memory. Thus it contains relevant contexts and the rules and standard experiences associated with a given situation in general. For example, the fact that health-care assistants wear white uniforms is information from Situational Memory. This comes from what we previously called the "visit to health-care professional" script, but it should be clear that it is by no means a script. The form that it takes will be discussed later.

The next level of memory experience is INTENTIONAL MEMORY. Information encoded in Intentional Memory includes such things as "going to any organization's office" or "getting any problem taken care of by a societal organization". What resides here are the rules for getting people to do things for you and other plan-like information. But the distribution of memories among various levels could lead, once again, to memory lapses or confusions. Thus, specific events would lose the particulars that were best encoded at other levels on their way up to the Intentional level, leaving things like: "once I had a problem that I was getting some guy in an office to handle, I don't remember where or why I was there, when I got so mad. . . ."

People often cannot recall the full details of a situation they are trying to remember (Bartlett, 1932). Often they can recall just the intentions and not the specifics or alternatively just the specifics and not the intentions. What such experiences suggest is that events can be decomposed into the pieces having to do with their intentional basis and these intentions can then serve as the organizational focus where the relevant parts of such experiences can be found (Black & Bower, 1979).

THE PLACE OF SCRIPTS

What, then, has happened to scripts? . . . [For example], what is the dentist script and where can it be found in memory? The answer is that there is no dentist script in memory at all, at least not in the form of a list of events of the kind we have previously postulated.

What is particular to a dentist's office is, perhaps, the X-ray machine, or the dental chair, or the kind of light that is present, and so on. These items are not scriptal in nature. Rather, they are just pieces of information about dental offices that are stored as part of what we know about them. For example, one might expect to find a giant toothbrush in a dentist's office. Such information is stored at the GEM level. However, it is also available from the EM level in terms of those particular experiences that can be remembered at that level of detail. (Such memories fade fast, however.) That is, to answer questions about dental offices, there is nothing to prevent us from consulting our knowledge of dental offices in general (GEM) or of particular prior experiences (EM) to the extent that they still exist.

So, where is the dentist script? So far it has not surfaced. In fact, it will not appear directly in memory at all. The next two levels complete the framework for allowing *dynamic creation of the pieces of the dental script that are applicable in a given situation for use on demand.* The dentist script itself does not actually exist in memory in one precompiled chunk. Rather, it, or more likely its needed subparts, can be constructed to be used as needed.

According to this view of the information in memory, then, scripts do not exist as permanent memory structures. Script-like structures are constructed from higher-level general structures *as needed* by consulting the rules about the particular situation from the three other levels.

The words "as needed" are very important. Why bring an entire script in while processing if only a small piece of it will be used? If scripts are being constructed rather than being pulled in whole from memory, only the parts that there is reason to believe will be used (based upon the input) would be brought in. The economy of such a scheme is very important. Its implementation would require the kind of modularity in memory structures advocated, for different reasons, by Charniak (1978).

The next key question is: What is the organization of the knowledge store? There are two other relevant questions to ask of memory, which are related. First, how does any given experience get stored so that it will provide a capability for understanding new experiences in terms of it? And, second, why do recognition confusions occur at all?

One answer to the second question depends on the notion of memory as a constructive process, one that abstracts general information from a class of particulars to build concepts made up of episodically generated facts. Because each new piece of information is stored in terms of the higher-level structure that was needed to interpret it, two kinds of confusions occur. Connections between items in the same episode that are interpreted by different high-level structures will tend to break down. A waiting-room scene will tend to disconnect from the dentist script of which it was a part because it was interpreted by a different high-level structure than other parts of the story.

The second kind of confusion will occur within a script. When a high-level structure is deemed relevant, all inputs are interpreted in terms of the norm. This causes small details not normally part of a script to get lost and normalized. Normalization does not occur for very interesting or weird deviations from a script. The reason for this has to do with the answer to the first question previously discussed.

Suppose you had an experience where you wanted to donate blood, stood on a long line in a school gym to do so, and were rejected. Then imagine an experience a year later of standing on a long line at an eye bank to sign up to donate an eye and also being rejected. It seems obvious that the second experience would remind you of the first. How can we explain this? We could hypothesize a "rejection after waiting to donate body part" category, but how would this category be found? To further focus this question, we can ask whether we would normally expect to find a list of all rejection experiences or of all mass health-care donation visits? Somehow neither of these seems quite right. When asked to remember rejections, people tend to first imagine situations in which such a rejection might have occurred.

On the other hand, someone who regularly gives blood might very reasonably be expected to have compiled these experiences in a script with discriminations as we have described. So which organization of memory is right?

The answer, I think, is that all of these are right. Memory is highly idiosyncratic. One person's organization is not another's. How people categorize experiences initially is how they remember them later. If Burger King is seen as an instance of MacDonald's, it will be stored in terms of whatever features the understander noticed as relevant at that time. However, it is possible for a person to make multiple categorizations. Thus, a person can see Burger King as "something tasteless that kids love," a "place where red and yellow uniforms are worn," and a "place where you can have it your way." Each of these could then be used as a path by which Burger King can be accessed. A fight with one's child in a Burger King might be stored solely as an instance of a fight with a child, or as a fight in a restaurant, or as a fight in a Burger King. If the latter categorization were used, fights with a child in MacDonald's might not be noticed. Thus, an intelligent understater stores experiences as high up and as generally as possible so as to be able to learn from them—that is, so as to make them available for use as often as possible or in as many situations as possible.

It is important, then, to have Burger King (and every other item in memory) accessible by a large number of very complicated discriminations:

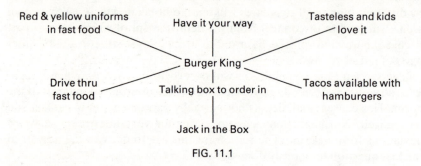

FIG. 11.1

One problem in understanding, then, is to make initial categorizations of new input that correspond to old categorizations in terms of which items have been stored in memory. The total number of discriminations that point to a concept indicates how well that concept has been initially categorized and thus understood. Undergoing an experience and not making lots of discriminations that lead to it is an instance of not really paying attention or understanding. An intelligent person, paying lots of attention to what is going on, will create a large number of discriminations (sometimes ones that are quite unique) for what he or she has seen.

The first problem is making the initial categorizations, the second to be able to find them again. For example, a categorization in terms of the results of an experience seems likely. Thus, if all fast-foods places are seen as "tasteless and kids love it," then we can expect an understander to classify them all together. Then, at the bottom of the same node, unless discriminations are made, distinctions will get lost:

FIG. 11.2

The solution to problem one, then, is not having Burger King or any other memory item accessible by only one possible path in memory. That is, different aspects of Burger King are stored in different memory classifications of various aspects of Burger King. Thus, it is possible to have inconsistent beliefs about Burger King such that it would be very difficult to retrieve all that we know about Burger King on command.

If small distinctions such as "tasteless food" or "having it your way" are relegated to being all the way at the end of a complicated discrimination tree, then there will be little possibility for understanding by analogy experiences that cross gross initial characterizations. We might expect that we would be reminded of Burger King by a fried chicken fast-food place (say, Texas Fried Chicken) that allowed a choice of herbs and spices. But how are we to be reminded of Burger King by Texas Fried Chicken if the only way to find the Burger King experience is by first entering a tree whose top node is "hamburger place"?

This problem can be solved by having all the small, particular characterizations at the very top of the available discrimination trees. Doing this implies having a very large number of initial categorizations at the bottom of which can be found Burger King. Thus, if Burger King is available in many different places and *there are many different ways to get to aspects of what is essentially the same node*, then understanding by analogy can take place:

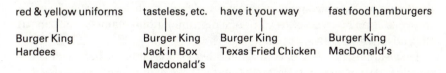

red & yellow uniforms	tasteless, etc.	have it your way	fast food hamburgers
Burger King	Burger King	Burger King	Burger King
Hardees	Jack in Box	Texas Fried Chicken	MacDonald's
	Macdonald's		

FIG. 11.3

But doing it this way indicates that the same unique token for Burger King is what is to be found at the bottom of each tree. In the normal form of the type-token distinction, that is what happens. But this is not necessarily the case here. There is no reason to believe that all memories of Burger King are available simply by reference to any one of them. It is not necessarily the case that these links are traversable both ways.

What is even more likely is that all memories of Burger King experiences are not stored in the same place at all. The only time we would expect a Burger King experience to be stored with another one is when those experiences were not distinguishable in any significant way. Interesting aspects of Burger King (or any other experience) are stored in a multitude of places depending on the aspects of the experience deemed significant at the time of initial processing. Again, we see that the key question is exactly what kinds of initial categorizations are likely to be made at processing time. In attempting to answer this question, we must keep in mind that a good answer would have any one of these initial categorizations dependent on some processing issue. That is, there should have been a reason at the time of processing, because of processing considerations, to make the initial categorization in that way.

One processing argument might be that the "have it your way" path to Burger King must have gotten there by once noticing that in a Burger King, there was a choice of ingredients within the normal functioning of the fast-food script. Now, this could be represented in a number of ways within memory. First, it could be part of the script in schematic form, such that whenever a similar script break occurs, normal processing would find the Burger King event stored at that breakpoint. Another way of dealing with it might be to pop up a level, storing it as something like "breaks from the normal in fast-food restaurants," or "script-failure problems," or "choices while eating." Probably all of these are used as discriminations in a myriad number of trees all of which point at the bottom to Burger King.

Two consequences of this proposal appear immediately. First, the initial processing that takes place will now have the burden of having to categorize each input in terms that begin the discrimination process. Second, we can see that the trees that result from these categorizations will be very sparse with next to no depth. For example, Burger King can be dealt with as "establishment where more choices than usual occur." Such a categorization gives us a "tree" of one discrimination—namely, that one at the end of which is Burger King.

Now suppose that we encounter another establishment where a choice is possible. We will not necessarily characterize it that way—that is, that might not be a salient feature to an understander at processing time. If that were the case, no "reminding" of Burger King would take place. But, if that were noticed, then such a "reminding" would occur. The consequence and use of the reminding would be to bring to bear other possible expectations from scripts associated with Burger King or particular experiences associated with Burger King. These expectations are what makes processing go and enables understanding.

[...]

In summary, memory can be conceived of as being organized around processing considerations. Particular experiences in memory are likely to be found at the structures that were used to process them, with fine discriminations being used to create an essentially infinite set of such structures. The use of such structures is for prediction and explanation of future events based upon prior experience. The initial discriminations or categorizations in memory include those related to the tracking of goals in general. Memory is thus organized by both goal issues and processing considerations. Reminding may be at times simply an artifact, but it is, at other times, an important part of the basic understanding mechanism.

[...]

MEMORY ORGANIZATION PACKETS

If the chunks we have been calling scripts are not solely processing devices, the demands on them change. Just as we would not expect that a sensibly organized memory would have the fact that George Washington was the first President stored in 15 different places, we would not expect that "you eat when you are hungry," or "you order after reading a menu," or "if you don't pay your dentist bill you can be sued" would be stored in 15 different places either. This does not mean that there is no redundancy at all in memory. Indeed, particular experiences can always be used to retrieve generalizations drawn from them if need be.

Once the requirement that you have to find one and only one place to store such *general* information comes into play, the question of where that information is stored becomes extremely important. To decide that question, notions such as scripts must be tightened up considerably so that information shared by any two scripts becomes a significant generalization made from them, and is stored outside them in memory. To do this requires ascertaining what it might mean for two scripts to share the same information, and finding out when such sharing is "realized" in memory and when it is not.

Whereas we require that general information be stored in only one place in memory, specific episodes are treated differently. Specific episodes can be multiply categorized—that is, remembered as instances of many different phenomena at once. Thus, experiences can be recalled through many different aspects of them. Often, pointing to an episode by virtue of having used a particular characterization of that episode can cause other parts of that episode to be recalled. In those instances the different aspects are being used as pointers to the one place in memory where the entire episode resides. [...]

Experiences are constantly being organized and reorganized on the basis of similar experiences and cultural norms. The abstraction and generalization process for experientially acquired knowledge is thus a fundamental part of adult understanding. When you go to the dentist for the first time, everything in that experience is stored as one chunk. Repeated experiences with the same dentist, other dentists, and vicarious experiences of others, serve to reorganize the original information in terms of what is peculiar to your dentist, yourself in dental offices, dentists in general, and so on. The important point is that this reorganization process never stops. When similarities between doctors and dentists are seen, a further reorganization can be made in terms of health-care professionals. When doctors' and lawyers' similarities are extracted, yet another organization storage point emerges. An important part of understanding, then, is the classification of new experiences in terms of old ones that are deemed most appropriate or most relevant to that new experience. Information in memory is thus collocated in what we call memory organization packets, or MOPs, which serve to organize our experiences that have been gathered from different episodes into sensible units organized around essential similarities.

The purpose of a MOP is to provide expectations that enable the prediction of future events on the basis of previously encountered, structurally similar events. These predictions can be at any level of generality or specificity. Thus, such predictions can come from nearly identical or quite different contexts or domains because a context or domain can be described at many different levels of generality. The creation of a suitable MOP provides a class of predictions organized around the common theme of that MOP. The more MOPs that are relevant to a given input, the more predictions will be available to help in understanding that input and the better the understanding will be. The ability of MOPs to make useful predictions in somewhat novel situations for which there are no specific expectations but for which there are relevant experiences from which generalized information is available is crucial to our ability to understand.

Seen this way, a MOP is a kind of high-level script. The restaurant script is itself a kind of MOP but it is also related to many different and more general MOPs. There is a MOP about social situations, a MOP about requesting service from people whose profession is that service, and a MOP about business contracts, to name three that are relevant to restaurants.

Actually, a great many MOPs relate to the restaurant script. The function of most of these MOPs in the actual use of the restaurant script in processing is minimal. A MOP serves as a storage point for general information abstracted from particular experiences for use by other experiences. Thus, restaurants serve as a source of information from which various MOPs were created because the restaurant experience is likely to have been temporally prior to the creation of the relevant MOPs. When we eat in a restaurant, we need not think about the job MOP or the professional service MOP that motivates the waitress. Indeed, we are likely never to have thought about such things much at all and certainly not in our early childhood experience with restaurants.

But such information can be of use in dealing with problems that might occur in a restaurant (for example, a waitress who refuses to serve you) or in explaining the behavior of other people in similar situations ("she's just like a waitress"). Those situations are understood in terms of MOPs about jobs and waitresses rather than in terms of the restaurant script. Similarly, calling the police when one cannot pay one's restaurant bill is information about contracts and is thus not part of the restaurant script itself.

To see how MOPs function in processing, we consider the information relevant to a visit to a doctor's office. The primary job of a MOP in processing new inputs is the creation of processing structures (i.e., sets of expectations) necessary to understand what is being received. Thus, MOPs are responsible for constructing script-like entities that can recognize the proper place of a new input by filling in implicit information about what events must have happened but were unstated. At least five MOPs are relevant to the construction of the processing structures necessary for understanding a doctor's office visit. They are: PROFESSIONAL OFFICE VISIT; CONTRACT; FIND SERVICE PROFESSIONAL; USE SERVICE; and FIX PROBLEM.

These five MOPs overlap quite a bit. There is nothing wrong with that; indeed, it should be expected that any memory theory would propose overlapping structures because they are the source of both memory confusions and the making of useful generalizations across domains.

When a script is available, it can be used without really looking at a MOP. However, because storage of information needs to be economical, we would not expect what is best stored at a MOP to be found in a script as well. Thus, the doctor script would not have the doctor suing the patient for nonpayment of the bill directly in it. Neither would the bill itself be in the domain of the doctor script. Each of those is best stored as part of a MOP about CONTRACTs that becomes active whenever the doctor script is activated. A doctor visit need not be actively thought about as a contract most of the time. Nonetheless, the fact that it is one is highly relevant to processing some episodes in doctor visits. In order to be ready to make use of this information, then, the CONTRACT MOP must help to construct what we can sloppily call the DOCTOR "script" that might actually be useful in processing.

It is important to mention that $DOCTOR is connected to the CONTRACT MOP by a strand of the MOP, but that $DOCTOR does not contain that strand—that is, does not contain information about payment other than the presence of that MOP strand. Thus, $DOCTOR is smaller than is obvious at first glance, because we have essentially taken the paying scene out of the script. The actual DOCTOR script that exists in memory contains only the doctor-specific parts of the doctor experience.

Thus waiting-room information is not part of $DOCTOR. Waiting rooms are part of PROF OFFICE VISIT, which is also a MOP. And PROF OFFICE

VISIT is different from MAKE CONTRACT, which is different from PROF SERVICE. Each of these MOPs helps in the construction of what we call the doctor *superscript*. This superscript is what we have previously called a script. The difference here is that superscripts are not extant memory structures. Rather, they are constructed for use as necessary to help in processing.

Because MOPs serve a great many purposes in memory and processing, it is necessary that they contain many different kinds of information. Further, it is necessary that that information be structured in such a way as to be available for use in different ways to suit the current purpose. To begin our discussion, then, we must first delimit the kinds of uses to which a MOP can be put:

1. MOPs help to build superscripts for processing.
2. MOPs direct question answering.
3. MOPs enable reminding.
4. MOPs help one to draw conclusions and notice patterns.
5. MOPs enable recognition of old situations in new guises.

To illustrate how these functions involve MOPs, we can consider the MOP PROF OFFICE VISIT. The primary function of PROF OFFICE VISIT (henceforth POV) is to provide the correct sequencing of the appropriate scenes that contribute to the construction of superscripts that make references to POV. In order to build the doctor superscript, we must recognize that the various MOPs that contribute to the construction of the superscript are applicable. How do we do this? Consider the following story:

> I went to the doctor's yesterday. While I was reading a magazine I noticed that a patient who arrived after me was being taken ahead of me. I am going to get even by not paying my bill for 6 months!

Previously, in our script-based theory we would have said that the first line of this story called in the doctor script. But the doctor script that we meant there was what we are now calling the doctor superscript. We are currently maintaining that no such entity should exist in memory as a prestored chunk. The reason for this is that recognition confusions about whether things that occurred in waiting rooms took place in doctors' waiting rooms or lawyers' waiting rooms would not happen if the requirement that every structure used in processing also be an episodic memory organizer were maintained and the doctor superscript existed as a permanent memory structure. That is, it must be possible to disassociate events that occur in waiting rooms from the superscript in which they are found in order to account for Bower, Black, and Turner's results about recognition confusions. As another example of this, it might be convenient to imagine that Cyrus Vance has a negotiation script that he uses to organize all the events that comprise a trip to a foreign country to negotiate a peace treaty. But a plane trip is still a plane trip and we might expect Vance to confuse a trip that was part of a negotiation with one that took him to a state funeral.

The point is that there are natural collocations of memories. No matter how convenient it might seem to organize things under negotiation trip or doctor visit for processing any given story, a memory that had such high-level structures would not behave the way human memories behave. Furthermore, we would not be able to take advantage of similarities across experiences. That is, a system organized in that way would not be able to make significant generalizations and it could never learn. Thus, it is imperative that memory be reconstructive in nature, building up super-scripts as necessary.

Therefore, in processing the first sentence of this story, what we must do is call in the relevant MOPs insofar as we can determine them, and begin to construct the doctor superscript to help in processing the rest of the story. This is done as follows: The phrase "went to the doctor" refers to $DOCTOR, which is the script part of the doctor superscript that handles the actual doctor-specific parts of the entire episode. To begin to construct the superscript, we search the DOCTOR MOP. To see what the requirements of this search must be, we should first examine the contents of the DOCTOR MOP.

What is likely to be in a DOCTOR MOP? The answer here is simple: Everything we know about doctors should be accessible through the DOCTOR MOP. Either the information we seek is stored directly in the DOCTOR MOP, or else the DOCTOR MOP contains a pointer to some other MOP or some specific episode that is relevant to the reconstruction of that information.

Fig. 11.4 is a sketchy view of the MOPs that contribute to providing all the expectations necessary to understand what is going on in a visit to a doctor's office. The function of each of the MOPs used here is to provide information relevant to the part of the overall situation for which the MOP is relevant. What is finally produced in the end is a superscript that looks very much like any given selected path through a script of the kind we discussed in Schank and Abelson (1977). . . . A superscript functions in the same way as what we used to call scripts did, except that it has been constructed from memory rather than having been retrieved from memory. One consequence of this is that there is no limit to what can and cannot be a superscript because there are such a large number of possible combinations of the various pieces of the various MOPs. [. . .] Neither is there a memory structure that corresponds to the superscript. The superscript is merely the output of the process of combining MOPs in order to build a

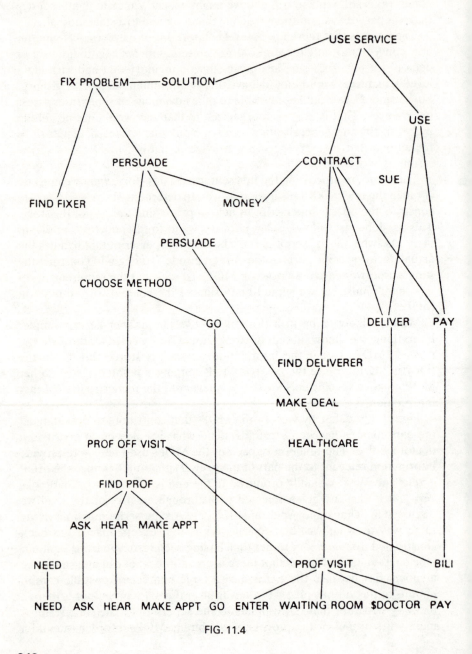

FIG. 11.4

242

processing structure that will aid in understanding a situation. It in no sense exists in memory except for an instant as it is being constructed. Memories are absorbed by the MOPs that were connected to their appropriate pieces.

Reliance on a MOP can also often tell us what information is irrelevant. Thus, PERSUADE has a strand for CONVINCING that connects to CONTRACT that connects to HEALTHCARE. Thus, when we understand a doctor visit, we need not wonder how the doctor got convinced to help out. We find that an implicit contract has been made . . . and that no actual convincing strategy had to be used. The replacement of a MOP strand by an entire other MOP serves as a stylized way of accomplishing the filling of a strand. That is, we need not plan when a standard method is available for a solution.

PROCESSING WITH MOPs

Memory Organization Packets serve not only as the basis of memory, but as the basis of processing. As we have said earlier, processing and memory must employ the same structures. In order to understand an input, it is necessary to find an episode in memory that is most like the new input. (As we noted, reminding is one way of noticing that such things are happening.)

Processing an input means finding a relevant memory piece. When such a piece is found, expectations are created that come from all the pieces to which the initial memory piece is connected. Thus, when we receive an input we look for a relevant MOP. Upon finding this MOP, we create expectations at every level to which that MOP is naturally connected. Thus, expectations from scripts that have been activated create demands for certain conceptualizations. Expectations are simultaneously generated from all the MOPs that the relevant script fills slots in, as well as from the "meta-MOPs" that those MOPs filled the slots of, and so on. (A meta-MOP is a MOP whose strands are exclusively filled by MOPs.)

Some of these expectations are extremely high level. For example, upon noticing that someone was trying to fix a drain, we might begin to expect to receive inputs or have to make inferences relevant to: payment for plumbers, asking for help in general, the consequences of failing to fix the drain properly, the consequences of success, and so on. But we also would expect tools, and water, and turning actions, and we would make other low-level predictions. These come from the various levels of MOPs that are applicable. Such predictions are useful in processing because they help to make sense of what is going on. They also bring to bear many particular episodes in memory that have been stored at each of the activated MOPs. In addition, these MOPs soak up the new inputs that are relevant to them, altering the MOP that has soaked it up, as well as breaking up the remembrances of the episode being understood into its MOP-related pieces.

To illustrate how some of this works, consider a story beginning: "My drain pipe was overflowing." For our purposes, the point is not whether this is the first line of the story or not. Rather, it is important that this simply be an input to a cognitive system. The fact that you might hear such a thing in everyday conversation is important also. The questions we need to address are:

1.   What comes to mind upon hearing such a sentence?
2.   What structures are being activated in memory that cause such things to come to mind?
3.   What state is the mind in after having received this input?

We have so far taken the position that to have precompiled chunks of memory such as a plumber script does not explain the facts of memory with regard to recognition confusions, memory searches, and forgetting based upon the breaking up of an experience into chunks. A great deal of information can be retrieved about plumbers (what a plumber is likely to wear, the estimated size of the bill, etc.) that is in no sense a part of the script. So it seems safe to say that some reconstruction is going on; various pieces of memory are being searched when an input is being processed. In our discussion we assume that there is no plumber script in anything but the simplest of all forms, and that the main problem in responding to an input such as the preceding one is the accessing of the memory structures relevant to the creation of the plumber superscript.

What kind of high-level structures might be relevant to "My drainpipe is overflowing"? Clearly it is relevant that drains are part of sinks or houses. This fixes the general location of the item in question. Such information is part of the meaning of "drain." It is unlikely that there would be a "drain MOP" available with that information in it. The existence of such a MOP implies that memories about drains are organized together in one place. This seems unlikely. However, there is nothing immutable about what can be a MOP. Different individuals with different levels of expertise are likely to have different needs in memory organization.

"Drain" points to information about bathrooms and kitchens, and so on. Such information is stored by using "room frames." Such frames contain primarily visual information rather than episodic information (although again this is possible). The visual information attached to the room frame here is helpful for understanding future inputs such as: "To fix it I sat on the toilet," or "The overflow ruined $20 worth of cleanser stored underneath." Such statements would be quite impossible to understand without these frames being active and ready. But such frames are not MOPs; they are just, on occasion, used by MOPs.

One way they are used by MOPs here is that, because these rooms are parts of houses, the combination of the implicit house and the possessive "my" causes information about HOMEOWNERSHIP to be activated. HOME-OWNERSHIP has information in it derived from preservation goals (P-GOALS; see Schank & Abelson, 1977) and, among other things, points to the FIX PROBLEM MOP.

Of course, people have drains in places they rent as well. This possibility is activated in the absence of knowledge to the contrary by activating D-AGENCY (Schank & Abelson, 1977). D-AGENCY points to knowledge about AGENCY relationships (which is what "landlords" are) so that HOMEOWNER-SHIP can still be used although it would be mediated by D-AGENCY.

Until we see "overflowing" we do not really know what is being told to us. But, after we have seen it, a great many structures must become active. First, the conceptualization that is to be constructed here contains empty slots for what object is being PROPELLED (which comes from "overflow") and to where. The OBJECT defaults to "water" by consulting the "normal contents" part of the conceptual dictionary item for "drain." The "TO" slot is filled by consulting the relevant frames; in this case, some candidates are "in house," "on floor," and "on carpet."

The activation of FIX PROBLEM causes the attempt at the creation of a solution.... FIX PROBLEM has as its strands FIND FIXER, PERSUADE, and SOLUTION. Each of these, as it turns out, is a possible topic of conversation for which the first input is our aforementioned sentence. Thus we might hear:

1. I know a good plumber.
2. My, that's going to cost a lot of money.
3. Have you tried Drain-Fixing Drano?

The fact that all of these are quite possible as responses here is an important indication that all of these structures are active in the mind of the understander of these sentences. To further test the validity of the active high-level structures in this way, consider other possible responses based on the other structures given earlier:

4. That sink of yours has been rotten for ages.
5. I told you not to get such an old house.
6. Boy, isn't it a pain to own a house?

Each of these is perfectly plausible as a response. We attribute this to the fact that some high-level memory structure would have had to have been activated by the input. What other kinds of statements might be acceptable here? Some possibilities are:

7. Oh, isn't that awful?
8. Did you have to stay home from work?
9. Water can be awfully damaging.
10. Do you know how to fix it?
11. Would you like to borrow my Stilson wrench?
12. And with your mother coming to visit, too!
13. This has certainly been a bad month for you, hasn't it?

Assuming that these too are all legitimate, what structures do they come from?

The ultimate question here then is what kinds of MOPs are there and how many of them are likely to be active at any given time? It seems plausible that the following high-level structures are likely to be active during the processing of our input sentence:

JOB; FAMILY RELATIONS

HOMEOWNERSHIP

FIX PROBLEM; PERSUADE

USE SERVICE

PROF HOME VISIT

FAMILY VISIT TO HOME

FIND PROF

MAKE CONTRACT

$PLUMBER

Are all these structures MOPs? Some of them clearly are and some of them fall into a rather grey area. Recall that a MOP is an organizer of information and can be used . . . to create a superscript. Recall further that MOPs serve to organize terminal scenes that have within them a backbone of a sequence of events that are episodes from memory organized in terms of that backbone. These terminal scenes are either script-like (in which case they contain deviations from the normal flow of the script encoded as actual memories) or else they are locative in nature (in which case they contain actual episodes that are organized in a nonevent based manner, possibly visually). Thus, a MOP is an organizer of terminal scenes or actual memory episodes. By this analysis, PROF HOME VISIT, FAMILY VISIT TO HOME, FIND PROF, and MAKE CONTACT are all MOPs. They each organize terminal scenes such as PAY, PHONING FOR AN APOINTMENT, FAMILY DINNER, and so on. As we have said, these terminal scenes are where actual memories are to be found.

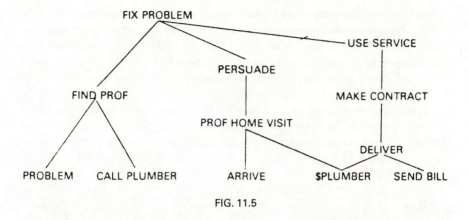

FIG. 11.5

We also know that FIX PROBLEM, PERSUADE, and USE SERVICE are meta-MOPs—that is, they organize MOPs [but] contain no memories themselves. . . .

This leaves us with JOB, FAMILY RELATIONS, and HOMEOWNERSHIP as active knowledge structures that do not fit in with our previously established definition of MOPs and the structures that both organize and are organized by MOPs. What are these structures and how do they differ from MOPs?

The first thing to notice about these labels is that we have a great deal of information about them in our memories. In fact, we have so much information and it is of such great importance to us (i.e., it concerns our high-level goals) that to begin to think that we can break such structures down into MOPs that organize terminal scenes . . . is absurd. There is, for example, a JOB MOP that contains scenes about applying for jobs, getting paid, terminating employment, and so on. But there is a great deal more information about one's job or knowledge of jobs in general that could not be neatly contained in the JOB MOP. The point here is that such information is at a higher level than that of MOPs. [. . .]

The MOPs that we have specified and the other high-level structures that we have not specified relate as [in Fig. 11.5] for this story.

CONCLUSION

The theory I have been trying to build here is an attempt to account for the facts of memory to the extent that they are available. In order to do natural-language understanding effectively (whether by humans or machine), it is necessary to have as part of the working apparatus of such a system an episodic memory. Scripts and other higher-level knowledge structures are not simply static data structures in such a memory. Rather they are both active processors and organizers of memory. Processing and storage devices must be the same in order to account for the phenomenon of reminding. In order to account for the fact that reminding and recognition confusions in memory both can be disembodied from large notions of a script to much smaller pieces, it was necessary to restructure our notion of a script to be much more particular. Full-blown scripts of the kind SAM used would have to be reconstructed by memory. This reconstruction implies a subsequent decomposition. Thus, we can expect pieces of stories or experiences to be stored in different parts of memory, commonly with no link between them. The advantage of this set up is to understand more effectively the world around us. This more-effective understanding manifests itself in better predictions about what will happen in particular well-constructed experiences that have been built up over time. But, these predictions are only as good as the initial categorizations of the world that we make. Thus, an effective categorization of new experience is the major problem for an under-stander as well as the major research problem facing those of us who work on understanding.

The negative effect of this breaking up of experience in order to make more effective predictions about the world is imperfect memory. People have imperfect memories because they are looking to make generalizations about experience that will serve as a source of useful predictions in understanding. That imperfect memory is a byproduct of predictive understanding capabilities is a very important point for those of us working in computer modeling. I do not believe that there is any alternative available to us in building intelligent machines other than modeling people. People's supposed imperfections are there for a reason. It may be possible that in the distant future we will build machines that improve upon what people can do. But, they shall have to equal them first, and I mean equal very literally.

ACKNOWLEDGMENTS

I would like to thank the following people for their help both in the writing of and the formation of ideas in this chapter: Wendy Lehnert, Christopher Riesbeck, Robert Abelson, Michael Lebowitz, Janet Kolodner, Mark Burstein, and Lawrence Birnbaum.

REFERENCES

Bartlett, F. C. (1932) *Remembering*. Cambridge, Eng.: Cambridge University Press.

Black, J. B., & Bower, G. H. (1979) Episodes as chunks in narrative memory. *Journal of Verbal Learning and Verbal Behavior, 18*, 309–318.

Black, J. B., & Bower, G. H. (in press) Story understanding as problem-solving. *Poetics*.

Bower, G. H., Black, J. B., & Turner, T. J. (1979) Scripts in text comprehension and memory. *Cognitive Psychology, 11*, 177–220.

Charniak, E. (1978) On the use of framed knowledge in language comprehension. *Artificial Intelligence, 11*, 225–265.

Crowder, R. G. (1976) *Principles of learning and memory*. Hillsdale, N.J.: Lawrence Erlbaum Associates.

Cullingford, R. E. (1978) *Script application: Computer understanding of newspaper stories* (Research Rep. #116). Yale University, New Haven.

DeJong, G. F. (1979) *Skimming stories in real time: An experiment in integrated understanding* (Research Rep. #158). Yale University, New Haven.

Graesser, A. C., Gordon, S. E., & Sawyer, J. D. (1979) Recognition memory for typical and atypical actions in scripted activities: Tests of a script pointer and tag hypothesis. *Journal of Verbal Learning and Verbal Behavior, 18*, 319–332.

Kintsch, W. (1977) *Memory and Cognition*. New York: Wiley.

Owens, J., Bower, G. H., & Black, J. B. (1979) The "soap opera" effect in story recall. *Memory and Cognition, 7*, 185–191.

Schank, R. C., & Abelson, R. P. (1977) *Scripts plans goals and understanding*. Hillsdale, N.J.: Lawrence Erlbaum Associates.

Schank, R. C., & Yale, A. I. Group (1975) *SAM—A story understander* (Research Rep. #55). Yale University, New Haven.

Smith, E. E., Adams, N., & Schorr, D. (1978) Fact retrieval and the paradox of interference. *Cognitive Psychology, 10*, 438–464.

VI PROBLEM SOLVING

12 Information-Processing Theory of Human Problem Solving

Herbert A. Simon

... The first part of [this] chapter sets forth the general theory of human problem solving that has emerged from research in the past two decades, especially research that has employed the methods of computer simulation and analysis of thinking-aloud protocols. The second part examines recent and ongoing research aimed at giving an account of the role of perceptual processes in problem solving and a description of the processes for generating problem representations, and research aimed at extending the theory to problem solving in domains that are rich in semantic information and less well structured than those that have been examined in the past. The third part of the chapter discusses some of the methodological issues that must be faced in using the methodologies of simulation and protocol analysis and, in general, to test detailed processing models of human cognitive performance.

... The theory discussed in this chapter applies both to Greeno's category of problems of transformation and his category of problems of arrangement. The relation of the theory to problems of inducing structure is discussed in Simon and Lea (1974). For the purposes of the present chapter, problems will be classified according to the definiteness of their structure and the amount of semantic information that must be supplied in order to solve them.

A GENERAL THEORY

A human being is confronted with a problem when he has accepted a task but does not know how to carry it out. "Accepting a task" implies having some criterion he can apply to determine when the task has been successfully completed. Problem solving is a nearly ubiquitous human activity; it is doubtful whether anyone spends an hour of his life without doing at least a little of it. The domain of problems ranges from highly structured, puzzle-like tasks often presented to subjects in the psychological laboratory to fuzzy, ill-structured tasks of large magnitude encountered in real life. Solving some problems requires only the information contained in the problem statement—a common characteristic of puzzles. Solving other problems may require drawing upon large stores of information in long-term memory or in external reference sources. Problems presented in the laboratory may take only 15 minutes or less to solve. Some problems presented in real life (for example, certain problems of scientific discovery) may occupy a substantial part of the problem solver's waking time for years.

Information-processing theories have made especially good progress in providing explanations of the processes for solving relatively well-structured, puzzle-like problems of the sorts that have been most commonly studied in the psychological laboratory. The theories describe the behavior as an interaction between an *information-processing system*, the problem solver, and a *task environment*, the latter representing the task as described by the experimenter. In approaching the task, the problem solver represents the situation in terms of a *problem space*, which is his way of viewing the task environment. These three components—information-processing system, task environment, and problem space—establish the framework for the problem-solving behavior (Newell & Simon, 1972, Chapter 14). Specifically:

1.   A few, and only a few, gross characteristics of the human information-processing system are invariant over task and problem solver. The information-processing system is an adaptive system, capable of molding its behavior, within wide limits, to the requirements of the task and capable of modifying its behavior substantially over time by learning. Therefore, the basic psychological characteristics of the human information-processing system set broad bounds on possible behaviour but do not determine the behaviour in detail.

2.   These invariant characteristics of the information-processing system are sufficient, however, to determine that it will represent the task environment as a problem space and that the problem solving will take place in a problem space.

3.   The structure of the task environment determines the possible structures of the problem space.

4.   The structure of the problem space determines the possible programs (strategies) that can be used for problem solving.

These four propositions are *laws of qualitative structure* for human problem solving. We are so accustomed to taking Newton's Laws of Motion as a model of what a theory should look like—or Maxwell's equations, or quantum mechanics—that it is worth reminding ourselves that a large number of important scientific theories do not resemble those in form. Instead, they consist of qualitative statements about the fundamental structure of some set of phenomena (Newell & Simon, 1976). An excellent example is the germ theory of disease, which, as announced by Pasteur, amounted to the following. If you encounter a disease, especially one that spreads rapidly, look for a microorganism. Darwinian evolution is another example, as are the tectonic plate theory of continental drift, the atomic theory of matter, and the cell theory. Sometimes, laws of qualitative structure are later expanded into quantitative theories, sometimes they are not. But at any given moment, they constitute a substantial part of our basic scientific knowledge. The predictions they support are, of course, weaker than the predictions that can be made from more highly quantitative theories, when these are available.

Thus, from a knowledge of the task environment, we can make predictions, but only incomplete ones, about the characteristics of the problem space and from a knowledge of the problem space, incomplete predictions about the problem-solving strategy. In addition, problem space and program must be compatible with the known characteristics of the information-processing system.

A. The Information-Processing System

A few basic characteristics of the human information-processing system shape its problem-solving efforts. Apart from its sensory organs, the system operates almost entirely serially, one process at a time, rather than in parallel fashion. This seriality is reflected in the narrowness of its momentary focus of attention. The elementary processes of the information-processing system are executed in tens or hundreds of milliseconds. The inputs and outputs of these processes are held in a small short-term memory with a capacity of only a few (between, say, four and seven) familiar symbols, or *chunks*. The system has access to an essentially unlimited long-term memory, but the time required to store a new chunk in that memory is of the order of seconds or tens of seconds.

Although many of the details of the system are still in doubt, this general picture of the information-processing system has emerged from psychological experiments of the past 30 years (Norman, 1969). Problem solvers exhibit no behavior that requires simultaneous rapid search of disjoint parts of the problem space. Instead, the behavior takes the form of sequential search, making small successive accretions to the store of information about the problem.

Data for estimating some of the system parameters come from simple laboratory tasks. Rote memory experiments provide evidence that 5 to 10 sec is required to store a chunk in long-term memory. Immediate-recall experiments indicate a short-term memory capacity of perhaps four chunks. Experiments requiring searches down lists or simple arithmetic computations indicate that some 200 msec is needed to transfer symbols into and out of short-term memory. (Some of this evidence is reviewed in Newell & Simon, 1972; Simon, 1974, 1976).

Notice that the limits these parameters place on the behavior of the system are very general. Moreover, except for the capacity limit of short-term memory, they are mostly limits on speed of processing rather than on what processing can be done.

To these processing parameters must be added the organizational characteristics of long-term memory. The classical notion that the human memory is an associative net has been modified into the notion that it may be represented as an organization of list structures (alternatively referred to as node-link structures and by mathematicians as colored directed graphs). How memory can be modeled with such structures is discussed by Newell and Simon (1972) and Anderson and Bower (1973). The distinction between a classical associative memory and a list structure memory is that the former consists of simple undifferentiated associations between pairs of nodes, while the latter consists of specific, and distinguishable, relations between such pairs. Thus, a memory of the former kind can represent a node only as being associated to another, whereas a list structure memory can represent a node as denoting the color of the object denoted by another, its size, its opposite, a subclass, and so on. List structure memories were anticipated in the *directed associations* of the Würzburg psychologists.

B.   Structure of the Task Environment

A puzzle-like problem that has been frequently studied is the missionaries and cannibals problem (Greeno, 1974; Reed, Ernst, & Banerji, 1974; Simon & Reed, 1976; Thomas, 1974). Three missionaries and three cannibals stand on one side of a stream, with a boat capable of carrying just two persons. All six persons are to be transported across the stream, with the condition that at no time, on either side of the stream, may missionaries be outnumbered, even momentarily, by cannibals. Human subjects generally find this a fairly difficult problem, although there are very few alternative legal moves, and it would be easy with paper and pencil to map out the entire problem space and solve the problem directly. As long as subjects confine themselves to legal moves (they usually make only a small percentage of illegal ones), their behavior is highly restricted by the structure of the problem space. Moreover, taking account of the goal—to move people from one bank of the river to the other—we might also predict that most moves would consist in taking a full boatload (two persons) across and a single person back. The difficulty of the problem is connected with the fact that at one point along the solution path *two* persons must return to the starting side. This move appears inconsistent with the perceived task requirements.

The structure of the problem space constrains behavior in a variety of ways. First, it defines the legal moves. Second, it defines the goal and usually, though implicitly, the direction of movement toward or away from the goal. Third, it interacts with the limits on short-term memory to make some solution paths easier to find than others. If an information-processing system follows a sequence of moves down a blind alley, it must back up to a previous position and search from there in a new direction. But to do this requires some memory of previous positions, which is difficult or imposs-ible to retain for searches of any great size. Hence, when available, methods of search that avoid the necessity of backup will be adopted. If the problem can be factored, for example, and each factor dealt with separately, trying out all combinations of the individual factors may be avoided.

In the well-known cryptarithmetic problem, DONALD + GERALD = ROBERT (Bartlett, 1958; Newell & Simon, 1972), ten distinct digits must be substituted for the ten distinct letters in such a way that the resulting expression is a correct arithmetic sum (526485 + 197485 = 723970). As the problem is usually posed, the hint is given that D = 5. Almost all subjects who solve the problem find the values for the individual letters in a particular sequence: T = 0, E = 9, R = 7, A = 4, L = 8, G = 1, N = 6, B = 3, O = 2. The reason is that only if this order is followed can each value be found definitely without considering possible combinations with the values of the other letters. With this order, the solver does not have to remember what alternative values he has assigned to other variables, or to back up if he finds that a combination of assignments leads to a contradiction.

This characteristic of the problem can be determined by examining the structure of the problem itself (not all cryptarithmetic problems have this property); and its strong influence on the search behavior of the information-processing system derives directly from the system's small short-term memory capacity. The empirical fact that solvers do make the assignments in roughly this same order provides us with one import-ant piece of evidence (others can be obtained by analyzing thinking-aloud protocols and eye movements) that the human information-pro-cessing system operates as a serial system with limited short-term memory.

C. Problem Spaces

To carry on his problem-solving efforts, the problem solver must represent the task environment in memory in some manner. This representation is his problem space. The problem space—the way a particular subject represents a task in order to work on it—must be distinguished from the task environment—the omniscient observer's way of describing the actual problem. Nevertheless, since the information-processing system is an adaptive system, problem space and task environment will not be unrelated. The simplest problem space for a task, usually called the *basic problem space*, consists of the set of nodes generated by all legal moves.

The relative ease of solving a problem will depend on how successful the solver has been in representing critical features of the task environment in his problem space. Although the problem space and the solver's program are not task-invariant, they constitute the adaptive interface between the invariant features of the information-processing system and the shape of the environment and can be understood by considering the functional requirements that such an interface must satisfy.

Each node in a problem space may be thought of as a possible state of knowledge that the problem solver may attain. A state of knowledge is simply what the problem solver knows about the problem at a particular moment of time, knows in the sense that the information is available to him and can be retrieved in a fraction of a second. After the first few moves in the missionaries and cannibals problem, the subject knows only the current locations of missionaries, cannibals, and boats; the starting situation; and the goal situation. He probably remembers little about the exact situations he has reached before, although after he has worked on the problem for a time, he may begin to store such information in long-term memory. The search for a solution is an odyssey through the problem space, from one knowledge state to another, until the current knowledge state includes the problem solution.

Problem spaces, even those associated with relatively simple task environments, may be enormous. Since there are 9! possible assignments of nine digits to nine letters, the basic DONALD + GERALD space contains a third of a million nodes. The sizes of problem spaces for games like chess or checkers are measured by very large powers of ten. As we have seen, however, the space for a fairly difficult problem like missionaries and cannibals may be very small (only 16 legal positions). Water jug problems (Atwood & Polson, 1976; Luchins, 1942) have problem spaces of about this same size.

Another difficult problem that has a relatively small space of legal moves is the Tower of Hanoi puzzle (Egan, 1973; Gagné & Smith, 1962; Horman, 1965; Klix, 1971; Simon, 1975). In this problem, there are three pegs, on one of which is a pyramid of wooden disks. The disks are to be moved, one by one, from this peg, and all placed, in the end, on one of the other pegs, with the constraint that a disk may never be placed atop a smaller one. If there are four disks, the problem space comprised of possible arrangements of disks on pegs contains only $3^4 = 81$ nodes, yet the problem is nontrivial for human adults. The five-disk problems, though it admits only 243 arrangements, is very difficult for most people; and the problems with more than five disks are almost unsolvable, until the right problem representation is discovered!

Problems like the Tower of Hanoi and missionaries and cannibals, where the basic problem space is not immense, tell us that the human information-processing system is capable of, or willing to endure, very little trial-and-error search. Problems with immense spaces inform us that the amount of search required to find solutions, making use of representations that capture the structure of the task environment, bears little or no relation to the size of the entire space. An information-processing system need not be concerned with the size of a haystack, if a small part can be identified in which there is sure to be a needle. Effective problem solving involves extracting information about the structure of the task environment and using that information for highly selective heuristic searches for solutions.

D. Information Embedded in Problem Spaces

Problem spaces differ not only in size—a difference we have seen to be usually irrelevant to problem difficulty—but also in the kinds of structure they possess. Structure is simply the antithesis of randomness, providing redundancy and information that can be used to predict the properties of parts of the space not yet visited from the properties of those already searched. This predictability becomes the basis for searching selectively rather than randomly.

The simplest example of information that can be used to solve problems without exhaustive search is the progress test, the test that shows that one is "getting warmer." Most of the principles of selection that problem solvers have been observed to use are based on the "getting warmer" idea. In the cryptarithmetic problem, for example, the number of letters for which definite substitutions have been found is a measure of progress. In the Tower of Hanoi task, the number of disks on the goal peg is a measure of progress. In missionaries and cannibals, the number of persons on the far bank of the river is such a measure. Observations of subjects working on these kinds of problems show that they are generally aware of, and make use of, such criteria of progress. How are the criteria used?

Each knowledge state is a node in the problem space. Having reached a particular node, the problem solver can choose an *operator* from among a set of operators available to him and can apply it to reach a new node. Alternatively, the problem solver can abandon the node he has just reached, select another node from among those previously visited, and proceed from that node. Thus, he must make two kinds of choices: choice of a node from which to proceed and choice of an operator to apply at that node.

We have already noted that because of limits of short-term memory, problem solvers do not, in fact, often backtrack from the current node, for this would require them to keep in mind nodes previously visited. Instead, they tend to focus almost exclusively on proceeding from the current situation, whatever that may be. However, when suitable external memory is provided, as when successive moves are written down on paper, problem solvers may be more willing to back up from an unpromising current situation to a more promising one that was reached earlier. Such branching search is frequently observed, for example, with subjects who are seeking to construct proofs for theorems.

We can think of information as consisting of one or more evaluations (not necessarily numerical, of course) that can be assigned to a node or an operator. The most important kind of evaluation for human problem solvers ranks the operators at each node with respect to their promise as a means of continuing from that node. When we examine what information problem solvers' draw on for their evaluations, we discover several varieties. In the simplest of these, an evaluation may depend only on properties of a single node. Thus, in theorem-proving tasks we find frequent statements in subjects' protocols to the effect that "it looks like Rule 7 would apply here."

In most problem spaces, however, the choice of an efficient next step cannot be made by absolute evaluation of the sort just mentioned. Instead, it is a function of the problem that is being solved. In theorem proving, for example, what to do next depends on what theorem is to be proved. Hence, an important technique for extracting information to be used in evaluators is to compare the current node with characteristics of the desired state of affairs and to extract *differences* from the comparison. These differences serve as criteria for selecting a relevant operator. Reaching a node that differs less from the goal state than nodes visited previously is progress, and selecting an operator that is relevant to reducing a particular difference between current node and goal is a technique for (possibly) approaching closer to that goal.

The particular heuristic search system that finds differences between current and desired situations, then finds an operator relevant to each difference, and applies the operator to reduce the difference is usually called *means–ends analysis*. Its common occurrence in human problem-solving behaviour has been observed and discussed frequently since Dunker (1945; see also Atwood & Polson, 1976; Simon & Reed, 1976; Sydow, 1970). The procedure is captured in concrete information-processing terms by the General Problem Solver (GPS) program, which has now been described several times in the psychological literature.[1] The GPS find-and-reduce-difference heuristic played a central role in the theory of problem solving for a decade beginning with its formulation in 1957, but more extensive data from a wider range of tasks have now shown it to be a special case of the more general information-extracting processes being described here.

E. Summary

This, in sum, is a first-order approximation to an account of human problem solving in information-processing terms. A serial information-processing system with limited short-term memory uses the information extractable from the structure of a problem space to evaluate the nodes it reaches and the operators that might be applied at those nodes. Most often, the evaluation involves finding differences between characteristics of the current node and those of the desired node (the goal). The evaluations are used to select a node and an operator for the next step of the search. Operators are usually applied to the current node, but if progress is not being made, the solver may return to a prior node that has been retained in memory, the choice of prior node being determined mostly by short-term memory limits.

This theory of the qualitative structure of problem-solving processes has been shown to account for a substantial part of the human behaviors observed in the half dozen task environments that have been studied intensively. In addition to conventional tests based on experiments and observations, the theory has been supported by strong tests of a novel kind. The theory postulates that problem-solving behavior is produced by a small set of elementary information processes, organized into strategies or programs. It asserts that a system capable of performing these processes can solve problems and produce behavior that closely resembles human behavior in the same problem-solving situations. The sufficiency of these elementary information processes for problem solving has been demonstrated by constructing computer programs that simulate human behavior in considerable detail.

---

[1] Brief descriptions of GPS can be found in Hilgard and Bower (1974) and Hilgard, Atkinson and Atkinson (1975). For an extensive analysis of GPS, see Ernst and Newell (1969). The relation of GPS to human behavior is discussed in Newell and Simon (1972, Chapter 9).

EXTENSIONS OF THE THEORY

The theory described in the previous section needs to be altered in several respects to fit the data better and is incomplete in other respects. First, varieties of search that use somewhat different forms of means–ends analysis than have been described thus far must be accommodated. Second, a role must be provided for perceptual processes, and especially recognition processes, in problem solving. Third, no account has been given of how the problem solver generates the problem space from the description of task environment or from other information that he has available. Fourth, little has been said about tasks that are less well structured than the puzzle-like problems that have been studied in the laboratory. The present section will discuss empirical evidence bearing upon these four topics.

A. Information-Gathering Strategies

Consider a student trying to prove the geometry theorem (new to him) that the base angles of an isoceles triangle are equal. This can be accomplished by proving that the two base angles are corresponding angles of congruent triangles. Appropriate congruent triangles can be constructed by dropping a line from the vertex of the isoceles triangle to its base. This line can be drawn (*a*) perpendicular to the base of the triangle, (*b*) cutting the base at its midpoint, or (*c*) bisecting the vertex angle. (It is the same line in all three cases, but this must be proved and is not assumed in the constructions.) In case *a* the two triangles are congruent because they are right triangles with equal hypotenuses and an equal pair of legs. In case *b* they are congruent because they have three sides equal. In case *c* they are congruent because they have two sides and the included angle equal.

Greeno (1976) has observed that students confronted with this prob-lem established the goal of proving two triangles congruent and carried out one of the constructions. But they did not plan in advance which of the theorems on congruent triangles they would use or which parts of the corresponding triangles they would prove equal. They simply made the construction (one of them), determined what parts were consequently equal, then *recognized* that these equalities matched the hypotheses for one of the theorems on congruent triangles.

The process used by the students might be outlined as follows: to reach G, reach G1, G2, or G3, any one of which leads directly to G. Proceed from the givens of the problem to attain P1, P2, P3 . . . until one of these is recognized as leading directly to G1 or G2 or G3. This process can be described as a form of means-ends analysis, but it has some interesting features. First, some of the problem-solving is done at an abstract planning level, rather than in the concrete problem space of geometry theorems. The subject develops the plan of proving two angles equal by proving they are corresponding angles of congruent triangles. The two triangles are to be proved congruent by proving various (but unspecified) sides and angles to be equal. This plan is readily stated in the language of means and ends: in order to prove two angles equal, prove two triangles congruent; in order to prove two triangles congruent, prove that various parts are equal. Each step in the plan establishes subsidiary problem-solving goals.

Second, while the planning step involves working backward from the final theorem, proving that the two triangles are congruent involves working forward from known premises toward a rather ill-defined goal: the goal of applying *some* theorem about congruent triangles. As Greeno (1976) points out, the subject does not deliberately aim at proving a particular congruence theorem, but *recognizes* when he has established enough premises about equal parts so that one of the available theorems is applicable. The recognition process retrieves the theorem "automatically," just when that stage is reached.

The same aspect of taking action on the basis of local criteria, and without specific reference to the precise problem goal, shows up in many other problem-solving performances. The simplest behavior of this kind represents working forward from the current situation in the general direction of the goal, making use of some kind of criterion of directionality. Simon and Reed (1976), for example, have shown that subjects' behavior in the missionaries and cannibals problem can be modeled quite well by assuming that they choose moves on the criterion of taking as many persons across the river as possible on each trip, and as few back as possible and that they have a modest capability to avoid repeating moves by holding in short-term memory some recollection of the immediately preceding situation. Ericsson (1975) has observed slightly more elaborate behavior, involving the establishment of subgoals, in the 8's puzzle; but once subgoals were established, his subjects used a similar crude test of directionality to aim their moves at the subgoals.

The relation of these simple procedures to the behavior described by Greeno (1976) becomes clearer if we observe that in theorem-proving and equation-solving tasks (including the cryptarithmetic task) any step that assigns a definite value to a previously unknown variable can be regarded as progress toward the goal (Simon, 1972). In the cryptarithmetic problems, for example, a means for progressing toward an assignment for all the letters is to find a correct assignment for any one of them. In many algebra problems involving more than one variable, if the equations are processed in the right order, they can be solved successively for individual variables, and these values substituted in the remaining equations. Such behavior has been observed, for example, in students solving problems in chemical-engineering thermodynamics (Bhaskar & Simon, 1977). In all of these cases, as in Greeno's case, the problem-solving activity can be described as a search for information—replacing unknowns by known values—rather than a search to reach a particular goal. In such activity, recognition processes play a crucial role (*a*) in determining when enough information is available to establish the value of another variable, and (*b*) when enough values have been established to reach the problem goal.

B. Perception in Problem Solving

The importance of perceptual processes in problem solving was demonstrated early by de Groot (1966) in his studies of the choice of moves in chess. He showed that a grandmaster might discover the correct move in a complex position within 5 sec or less of looking at the position for the first time (but might then spend 15 min verifying the correctness of the move). Continuing research on perception in chess (see, for example, Chase & Simon, 1973, and a discussion by Greeno, [Estes, W. (ed.) (1979). Handbook of Learning and Cognitive Processes, Vol 5. Hillsdale, N.J.: Lawrence Erlbaum Associates.] has built a substantial body of evidence that an important component of the grandmaster's skill is his ability to recognize a great variety of configurations of pieces in chess positions and to associate with the recognized patterns information about possibly appropriate actions. The chess master's vocabulary of familiar patterns has been estimated to be in the order of 50,000, a number comparable to the natural language vocabulary of a college-educated person.

The organization of a problem solver based on perceptual recognition can be described with the help of the concept of *production* (Newell, 1973; Newell & Simon, 1972). A production is a process with two components: a condition component and an action component. The condition component consists of a set of tests to be applied, for example, to a sensory stimulus. If the stimulus is, for example, a picture of a simple colored geometric shape, as in standard concept-attainment experiments, the condition component of a production might apply the test "red and round." The output of the condition is "true" or "false," as the tests are, or are not, satisfied by the stimulus.

If the condition of a production is satisfied, then the action of the production is executed; if the condition is not satisfied, nothing is done. Thus, the general paradigm for a production is:

If stimulus is X, then do Y; else exit.

An information-processing system can be constructed wholly of productions, the device being a perfectly general one. Such a system takes on psychological interest when we impose on it some conditions about the nature of the conditions and actions that will be admitted. We consider two classes of productions:

In Class P, the perceptual productions, the conditions are tests on sensory stimuli; the actions transfer symbols from long-term memory to short-term memory.

In Class G, the general productions, the conditions are tests on the contents of short-term memory; the actions are motor acts, changes in short-term memory, or changes (storage or retrieval) in long-term memory.

The perceptual productions, which are the ones of main interest for the present discussion, perform acts of recognition: the condition of each such production is satisfied by some class of stimuli. Recognition of a stimulus as belonging to that class accesses the node in long-term memory where associated information is stored and brings a symbol designating that node into short-term memory.

The Elementary Perceiver and Memorizer (EPAM) (Feigenbaum, 1961; Simon & Feigenbaum, 1964; Gregg & Simon, 1967a) is a system that performs recognitions in this way and also learns to discriminate new stimuli, gradually acquiring an appropriate set of productions in the process. Since the EPAM program has had considerable success in explaining a whole range of empirical phenomena from rote-learning experiments, it provides support for postulating this sort of mechanism in the human recognition process.

To return to the case of chess perception, Simon and Gilmartin (1973) constructed a system, MAPP (Memory And Perceptual Processor), that simulates the chessplayer's perceptual capabilities, growing, in EPAM fashion, a set of patterns it is capable of discriminating and recognizing as a result of exposure to those patterns. The conditions of the productions in this case identify a configuration of pieces on a chessboard. When such a configuration is recognized, a symbol designating it is retrieved from long-term memory and placed in short-term memory. Short-term memory capacity is interpreted as the number of such symbols that can be held simultaneously.

Along with the long-term memory symbol designating a pattern, other information can be stored, for example, a move that would be plausible to consider when that pattern is present on the board. Upon recognition of the pattern by execution of a P production, a G production, detecting the symbol in short-term memory, could retrieve the associated chess move and place *it* in short-term memory. Then a second G production could cause the move to be made on the board. This system could, in fact, play entire games of chess, simply recognizing plausible moves in each position and making them. It would not play good chess, for the first potential move recognized in a position might not be the correct one and, in any event, would not usually be accepted by a player without additional analysis. However, the system would probably be a good representation of the processes used in playing rapid-transit chess, when only a few seconds are allowed for a move. It is well known that grandmasters can play strong games (at expert level) but not grandmaster games under these conditions.

Greeno (1976) has shown how the geometry theorem-proving processes can be simulated by a production system very like the one just described. The conjunction of the premises of a theorem constitutes the condition for a production that retrieves the theorem. When a theorem is retrieved, the instance of it that applies to the specific problem being solved is generated and held in memory.

Simon (1975) has constructed for the Tower of Hanoi problem a whole family of alternative production systems that are capable of solving that problem. This collection of systems demonstrates that quite different information-processing strategies may produce functionally equivalent behaviors. One system that solves a problem may be primarily goal driven: it uses goal and subgoal structures to determine what to do next. Another system may be primarily stimulus driven: it uses visual cues from the current state of the problem apparatus to determine what to do next. A third system may be primarily pattern driven: it uses a stored pattern or rule to calculate each successive move in the solution path. A fourth system may solve the problem simply by rote memory of the sequence of correct moves.

Little empirical research has yet been done to determine, in situations like these where numerous alternative solution strategies are available, which strategies human subjects will use or within what limits their strategies can be determined by problem instructions, past experience, or other experimental manipulations. The potential significance of this line of investigation is demonstrated by the experiments of Katona (1940), who taught subjects alternative strategies for solving the same problem. Subjects taught a rote strategy for solving the problem were less successful in retaining the solution and in transfering the strategy to similar problems than subjects who were taught a strategy based upon perception or analysis of the problem structure.

C. Generation of the Problem Representation

When a subject is presented with a novel problem in the laboratory, he cannot begin to try to solve it until he understands it. As psychological experiments are usually conducted, the subject is introduced to the task through instructions and explanations from the experimenter, followed by an opportunity to practice on some examples. Only then does the gathering of data on his behavior ordinarily begin. Under these circumstances, by the time the actual experiment begins, the subject already understands the task and has generated for himself a problem space within which he can represent it. Within this paradigm, there is no opportunity to discover the process he uses to generate his representation of the problem.

Hayes and Simon (1974, 1976a) have used isomorphs of the Tower of Hanoi problem to study how subjects generate problem representations. Two problems are isomorphic if there is a one-to-one mapping of legal moves of the first problem onto legal moves of the second, such that the starting and goal situations of the first are mapped onto the starting and goal situations of the second. Unlike the original Tower of Hanoi problem, the isomorphs employed by Hayes and Simon do not use an external display, but are described in words. Thinking-aloud protocols covering the entire interval from the time when the subject reads the problem instructions to the time when he is ready to begin work on solving the problem reveal the main features of the subject's behavior while he is generating a representation for a new problem.

This process has been simulated by a computer program called UNDER-STAND. As hypothesized by the program, the understanding process contains two subprocesses: one for interpreting the language of the instructions, the other for constructing the problem space. The process for interpreting language reads the sentences of the problem text and extracts information from them, guided by a set of information-extraction rules. These rules identify the moods of the text sentences, identify noun groups that refer to physical objects and activities, and assign such relations to them as "agent," "instrument," "property," "location," and so on, much in the manner of a case grammar (Fillmore, 1968).

The construction process accepts information, sentence-by-sentence, from the language-interpreting process and builds a representation of the problem space in two parts: a situation description and a set of operators. The description of the situation, based on information extracted from sentences in the indicative mood, represents the problem elements (for example, the pegs and disks in the Tower of Hanoi problem), relations among problem elements (for example, the relation of a disk being on a peg), and the initial and goal states of the problem.

The set of operators, identified from information extracted from conditional statements and sentences in the subjunctive mood, constitutes a production system in which the conditions are represented as states (or aspects of states) of the situation, and the actions are represented as processes for making changes in the situation. A major responsibility of the construction process is to make certain that the representation of the situation is compatible with the representation of the operators, so that the operator processes will perform correctly in changing the situation.

Thus, the model views problem solving by the naive subject as employing two complex processes: an understanding process that generates a problem space from the text of the problem and a solving process that explores the problem space to try to solve the problem. The understanding process is also assumed to proceed in two steps: a language interpretation process followed by a construction process. In the human protocols from which this model was induced, these steps do not occur in invariable sequence. Instead, there is frequent alternation between the understanding process and the solving process and, within the understanding process, between the language interpretation process and the construction process. The solving process appears to exercise overall control in the sense that it begins to run as soon as enough information has been generated about the problem space to permit it to do anything. When it runs out of things to do, it calls the understanding process back to generate more specifications for the problem space. The text of the instructions appears to be interpreted only to the extent that is necessary in order for the solving process to arrive at a problem solution.

The protocols show that the problem representation the subject constructs is determined sensitively by the precise way in which the problem is stated. As the Tower of Hanoi problem is usually described, disks are associated with pegs, and a legal move consists of moving a disk from one peg to another. An isomorphic problem can be constructed in which pegs are associated with disks, and a legal move consists of changing the peg that is associated with a particular disk. Experiments show (Hayes & Simon, 1976b) that if the problem is described in the instructions in one of these ways, it will almost invariably be represented by the subject in memory in that same way. The experiments also show that the difficulty of solving such problems varies greatly, depending on which of the two representations is used. (In particular, the second representation described above makes the problem about twice as difficult, measured by time required for solution, as the first representation. From these data we conclude that subjects do not ordinarily search for the most efficient representation for a problem—the representation that will make solving it easiest—but adopt the representation that derives in the most direct and straightforward way from the language of the problem instructions.

The research on the Tower of Hanoi isomorphs treats of problems that are novel to the problem solver. In the case of problems of types that he encountered previously, the understanding process may be determined by that previous experience and may be different for different subjects. Paige and Simon (1966), studying performance in solving algebra word problems, found that some subjects interpreted the problem test almost entirely by syntactic translation from natural language to algebraic equations. Other subjects generated a semantic representation of the situation from the problem text, then used that representation to derive the equations.

Bhaskar and Simon (1977), studying the performance of a skilled subject solving thermodynamics problems, found that the subject used standard formats to express the basic problem conditions in equations, instead of constructing the representation for each problem ab initio.

D. Ill-Structured Problems

The great bulk of the research that has been done on problem solving has made use of task environments whose structure is well defined. It is reasonable to ask to what extent the mechanisms that have been discovered to govern problem solving in well-structured domains are also applicable and used in domains that are more loosely structured. Since there is little evidence as yet to answer this question, my comments on this topic are necessarily somewhat speculative.

There is no precise boundary between problems that may be regarded as well structured and those that are ill structured. Rather, there is a continuum from problems like the Tower of Hanoi or cryptarithmetic puzzles to problems like the task of composing a fugue or designing a house. Among the features that distinguish the second group from the first are these:

1. The criterion that determines whether the goal has been attained is both more complex and less definite.
2. The information needed to solve the problem is not entirely contained in the problem instructions, and indeed, the boundaries of the relevant information are themselves very vague.
3. There is no simple "legal move generator" for finding all of the alternative possibilities at each step.

The earlier discussion of geometry theorem proving shows that even in well-structured domains, although the final goal may be quite definite, less definite intermediate goals may be pursued along the way. The same phenomenon shows up clearly in the domain of chess. There is no ambiguity in determining whether a player has won the game (has checkmated his opponent), but in choosing moves, the consequences of these moves cannot always be pursued to this final result. Instead, moves must be evaluated by means of sometimes vague and complex criteria that take into account pieces won or lost, positional advantages, and so on. Since problem-solving mechanisms have been demonstrated that operate in the face of these complexities and ambiguities, it appears that no processes beyond the ones we have already mentioned have to be postulated to take care of the first of the three aspects of ill-structuredness listed above.

Reitman (1965), in a study of the protocol of a professional composer writing a fugue, addressed himself to all three aspects. From the protocol evidence, it appeared that over any short interval of time, the composer was dealing with perfectly well-defined subproblems of the total problem. From his long-term memory he repeatedly evoked new information and new generators of alternatives that gradually and continually transformed the problem space in which he was working. Again, the mechanisms appear to be quite similar to those that have been identified in other, more tightly structured, task environments. In particular, recognition of features in the melodic or harmonic fragments he had already created evoked ideas that were associated with those features in long-term memory, much as chess patterns evoke information from the long-term memory of skilled chess players.

Simon (1973) has proposed that, in general, the processes used to solve ill-structured problems are the same as those used to solve well-structured problems. In working on ill-structured problems, however, only a small part of the potentially relevant information stored in long-term memory and in external reference sources plays an active role in the solution processes at any given moment in time. As recognition of particular features in the situation evokes new elements from long-term memory, the solver's problem space undergoes gradual and steady alteration. A production system, he argues, containing a rich repertory of recognition processes and associated with a large store of information in long-term memory, would produce precisely the kind of continually changing problem space that has been observed in protocols of subjects solving such problems.

Some beginnings have been made in building and testing theories of the organization of long-term memory (Abelson, 1973; Anderson & Bower, 1973; Quillian, 1968; Rumelhard, Lindsay, & Norman, 1972; Schank, 1972). Most of this work has been done outside the context of problem-solving tasks. Recently, however, Bhaskar and Simon (1977) have undertaken an analysis of the structure of long-term memory used by students solving problems in a college-level course in chemical-engineering thermodynamics. Inventories of the information actually available to persons engaged in skilled performance of professional-level tasks and investigations of how this information is evoked during problem solving will clarify whether the mechanisms and processes that have already been identified in well-structured problem solving are sufficient to account for performance in less structured and information-rich domains.

METHODOLOGICAL QUESTIONS

... the development of an information-processing analysis of problem solving has made use of new experimental and observational methodologies. In this section, these new methodologies are discussed, namely, how the temporal density of observations has been increased and how the modern computer has been used to build and test information-processing theories of the observed behavior.

A. Increasing the Density of Observations

In typical psychological experiments, a stimulus is presented to the subject, he makes a response, and the time required for the response and its correctness become the principal data for analysis. But in a problem-solving situation, 15 min or more may intervene between presentation of stimulus (the problem instructions) and the final response (the answer). The interval between stimulus and response is filled by the subject's information-processing activities, which can form a very long sequence, since the elementary information processes may each occupy no more than a few hundred msec of processing time.

The task of problem-solving research is to identify the organization of processes that enables a subject to solve a problem and that determines how long it takes him and the probability that he will make one or more errors along the way. Since taking measurements of behavior only at the start and the finish seems an unpromising way of learning about the intervening processes, much attention has been given to securing additional observations of the subject's behavior during the course of the problem-solving activity. Two techniques that have been used to increase the density of observations of the information-processing stream are recording thinking-aloud protocols of the problem solver's verbalizations during his activity and recording his eye movements.

In whatever way the subject is induced to externalize some of his behavior during problem solving—whether with the help of the eye-movement camera or with the use of tape recorder and verbalization—the interpretation of the evidence requires at least a rudimentary theory that connects these behaviors with the problem-solving processes. (This is not an unusual requirement for observation. In physics, for example, the physical theory of the instruments of observation must be understood, at least in first approximation, in order to interpret the observations.) The theory and practice of interpreting verbal protocol data will be discussed in a later section of this chapter.

B.   Computer Simulation

The revival of problem solving as a topic for research is closely connected with the discovery that the modern digital computer can be used not only to carry out numerical calculations but to do nonnumerical symbolic information processing as well. This discovery opened the way to programming the computer to simulate human behavior in problem-solving and other cognitive tasks.

Formally speaking, a computer program is a set of difference equations that determines, for each possible state of the computer, what process it will execute next. If $S(t)$ defines the state of a computer at time t, $I(t)$ its input, and P its program, then we may describe its behavior by $S(t + 1) = P[S(t), I(t)]$. Difference equations have the same logical structure as differential equations, with the exception that the former treat time as discontinuous, the latter as continuous. Many of the most important theories of physics take the form of systems of differential equations (for example, Newtonian mechanics, Maxwell's equations, wave mechanics). This fact has suggested the idea that computer programs, viewed as difference equations, might provide a powerful language for expressing theories of information-processing systems.

The fundamental hypothesis that motivates the information-processing approach to the study of cognition may be stated thus: The human cognitive system is to be viewed as an information-processing system. The system consists of a set of memories, receptors, and effectors, and processes for acting on them. The memories contain data (information) and programs of information processes. The state of the system at any given moment of time is determined by the data and programs contained in these memories, together with the stimuli that are presented to the receptors.

When a system of differential or difference equations is sufficiently simple—as are some of the equations systems of physics—the equations can be integrated, and invariant properties of the system can be derived that hold generally, not just for special cases. When the system is more complex, the only method that may be available for predicting its behavior is to simulate that behavior for particular circumstances. In general, this is the course that has to be followed when information-processing theories are expressed as computer programs. To explain the behavior of a particular subject, for example, in a specific problem-solving situation, the program is presented with the identical problem.

In those cases where the problem-solving process draws upon semantic information stored in semantic memory, the program that is to simulate the behavior must be provided with that information, or an approximation of it. So, a program that is to simulate the pattern-recognition capabilities of a skilled chess player must be provided with an appropriate vocabulary of familiar patterns, stored in memory in such a way that they will be recognized when presented (Simon & Gilmartin, 1973).

It is sometimes argued that because of the particularistic nature of the programs used for simulation, they cannot be regarded as theories of the cognitive phenomena. But this objection represents a misconception. Simulation programs will vary from one problem-solving environment to another and from one task to another, because different semantic knowledge and processes are used for different problems and by different problem solvers. There can be no invariants in the theory that are not invariants in the behavior to be explained; and the behavior is not invariant, in all particulars, over tasks and over subjects. ... This is a principal reason why the laws of information-processing psychology take the form of laws of qualitative structure. We must seek these qualitative regularities, not in the specific information that a specific subject uses in solving a specific problem, but in the structural invariants that are shared by the programs describing the behavior of the same subject over a range of problem-solving tasks or the behavior of different subjects in a particular task environment.

In spite of this variability in human behavior, it remains the case that computer-programming languages provide a means for stating theories of human information processing with a precision that is not available from ordinary language. The requirement that the programs should, in fact, solve the same problems as the human subjects removes any doubts that a genuine mechanism is being postulated that is adequate to account for the observed behavior and that the real bases for the behavior are not being cloaked in vague nonoperational language. If it is objected that the programs say too much—go beyond the invariants in the behavior—then the theory can be identified with "representative programs," which capture the general mechanisms that have been found, without simulating any particular single person. The "representative program" would play the same role in information-processing psychology as the "representative firm" has played in economic theory, and for the same reason. The programs that have been described in this chapter are mainly representative programs in this sense.

C. Interpretation of Protocol Data

The final methodological question we shall consider is the status of thinking-aloud protocols as a source of data for testing information-processing theories. Three separate issues are involved: (a) whether thinking-aloud instructions change the thought process, (b) how the information contained in the protocols is related to the underlying thought processes, and (c) how thinking-aloud protocols can be compared with the traces of behavior produced by computer-simulation programs.

The first of these questions presents the least difficulty. Even if there are differences between the behavior of a subject solving a problem silently and the same subject solving the equivalent problem while thinking aloud, both performances are examples of human problem solving, and an adequate theory of the one should have as much interest for psychology as a theory of the other. Moreover, the small amount of empirical evidence we possess comparing the two performances suggests that the differences between them are not generally large. The evidence has been reviewed recently by Ericsson (1975). He found that under some circumstances the problem-solving behavior while thinking aloud is somewhat more deliberate and planful, and sometimes a little slower, than the behavior when the subject is not vocalizing. Further, there seems to be some qualitative change in the behavior on tasks where vocalizing leads to recoding of visual stimuli that are not easily describable in words. In tasks where the latter difficulty is not present, however, the weight of evidence indicates a close similarity of the problem-solving processes in the two conditions. There are no reasons to believe that thinking-aloud instructions cause gross changes in the problem-solving behavior.

There is very little explicit evidence on the relation of the information contained in the thinking-aloud protocols to the underlying thought processes. Most experimenters who have analyzed protocols have assumed that the vocalizations corresponded to a subset of the symbol structures that were temporarily present in short-term memory during the course of the problem-solving process (see Newell & Simon, 1972). That is, only items that pass through short-term memory, but not all of these, will be vocalized. Again, Ericsson (1975) has explored this general hypothesis in some detail. The task he studied (the 8's puzzle) had a substantial perceptual component and, hence, may have been less favorable to relatively complete vocalization than some others. Ericsson found that subjects tended not to vocalize goals that could be realized immediately as often as longer range goals that were reachable through intermediate subgoals. Vocalization decreased as subjects became more proficient in the task, and their responses were "automatic." Ericsson found positive evidence that subjects' goal statements were predictive of their subsequent moves.

In summary, problem-solving behavior during vocalization is genuine problem-solving behavior, hence deserving of study. Moreover, under most circumstances, vocalizing does not greatly alter the behavior. The protocol represents only incompletely the stream of symbols that pass through short-term memory, but there are good reasons to believe that the vocalizations are not an epiphenomenon, but follow closely the actual path of the thinking.

If protocols are accepted as a valid, if highly incomplete, record of the path followed by thought, the problem remains of using them as clues for the underlying processes. The first step in comparing the course of thought with the trace produced by a simulation program is to encode the protocol without destroying its semantic content. A set of process categories is selected to represent the processes that the subject is postulated to be using. Items in the protocol are assigned, clause-by-clause, to these categories. In many cases a clause can be assigned reliably on the basis of its explicit content. Sometimes, especially when it is elliptical or contains anaphoric references, it has to be interpreted in context. The information retained includes not only the process class, but also its particular instantiation. That is, a statement like, "I'm going to move two missionaries across now," might be encoded, "Move(2M,across)," designating the statement as denoting a move, but also specifying what move it is.

It is not difficult to achieve an acceptable level of reliability in clause-by-clause coding of protocols, and some progress has been made toward automating the process (Waterman & Newell, 1973). The greatest difficulty with encoding as a procedure for treating protocols is its irksomeness as a task for the coder. Hence, automation, or even semiautomation by means of a prompting procedure (Bhaskar & Simon, 1977) is highly desirable.

The new task is to compare protocol with computer trace in order to test the veridicality of the computer-simulation program as a theory of problem solving. As is well known (Gregg & Simon, 1967b), standard statistical tests of hypotheses provide no help in comparing data with models. In particular, the common practice of taking the model as the null hypothesis for such tests is completely unjustified. On the one hand, this practice leads to the verdict "not rejected" whenever the samples are sufficiently small and the data sufficiently noisy. Hence, the theory embodied in the model is more likely to be accepted with bad data than with good, certainly an undesirable result. On the other hand, this practice leads, when the data are plentiful and good, to rejecting models that explain a large part of the data but are only approximately correct (and it is unreasonable to expect theories to be more than that). Hence, statisticians are unanimous in agreeing that statistical tests are inapplicable to these situations.

The alternative approach is to try to provide some measure of the fraction of the variance in the original data that is accounted for by the model. To this end, the encoded protocol statements may be compared, one by one, with the trace statements. Two kinds of discrepancies between protocol and trace need to be distinguished: errors of omission and errors of commission. For the reasons stated earlier, we must expect that many elements of the program trace, which will always be compulsively complete, will not have corresponding elements in the protocol. Of more consequence are errors of commission, where there is a positive difference between what is predicted by the trace and what actually is found in the protocol.

The extent to which a given degree of fit between protocol and trace should be regarded as supporting the theory will depend also on how parsimoniously the theory is stated. Unfortunately, there is no standard, accepted way to count the number of degrees of freedom in a computer program. Because of the amount of process detail that they make explicit, computer programs appear to have an immense number of degrees of freedom, and it is sometimes thought by the inexperienced that they can be made to fit any behavior path simply by fiddling with them. However, the apparent malleability of programs is largely an illusion. Changing a program to improve the fit to the data in one portion of a protocol will often cause a change in its behavior in other portions, worsening the fit there. But until additional progress has been made toward formally characterizing the parsimony of programs, the evaluation of the goodness of fit between protocol and trace will be a judgmental matter (a not uncommon state of affairs in all of the sciences).

D. Conclusion

A considerable body of tested theory now exists that describes and explains the processes of human problem solving in well-structured task domains having minimal semantic content ("puzzle-like" problems). At the present time, considerable work is going forward that undertakes to extend the theory to broader task domains and, in particular, to explore information-gathering strategies, the interaction between perceptual and cognitive processes in problem solving, and the generation of problem representations. Progress in these directions is bringing various classes of problems, hitherto regarded as ill-structured, within the scope of the theory.

Information-processing approaches to cognition have introduced new methodologies and raised new methodological questions. Computer simulation has been introduced as a major tool for formulating information-processing theories and for testing theories by comparing simulated outputs with longitudinal human data. This has raised novel questions, for which fully satisfactory answers have not yet been found, of how the fit of theory to data should be judged.

Studying human information processes effectively calls for a high temporal density of observations. Several techniques have proved themselves valuable for increasing this density, in particular, recording eye movements, and tape-recording verbal thinking-aloud protocols. Research is beginning to be undertaken on the methodological problems associated with the use of these kinds of empirical data.

REFERENCES

Abelson, R. P. (1973) The structure of belief systems. In R. C. Schank & K. Colby (Eds.), *Computer models of thought and language.* San Francisco: Freeman, pp. 287–339.
Anderson, J. R., & Bower, G. H. (1973) *Human associative memory.* Washington, D.C.:

Winston.

Atwood, M. E., & Polson, P. G. (1976) A process model for water jug problems. *Cognitive Psychology, 8*, 191–216.

Bartlett, F. C. (1958) *Thinking*. New York: Basic Books.

Bhaskar, R., & Simon, H. A. (1977) Problem solving in semantically rich domains: An example from engineering thermodynamics. *Cognitive Science, 1*, 193–215.

Chase, W. G., & Simon, H. A. (1973) Perception in chess. *Cognitive Psychology, 4*, 55–81.

de Groot, A. D. (1965) *Thought and choice in chess*. The Hague: Mouton.

de Groot, A. D. (1966) Perception and memory vs. thought: Some old ideas and recent findings. In B. Kleinmuntz (Ed.), *Problem solving: Research, method and theory*. New York: John Wiley & Sons.

Duncker, K. (1945) On problem solving. *Psychological Monographs, 58*, 5 (Whole No. 270).

Egan, D. E. (1973) *The structure of experience acquired while learning to solve a class of problems*. Unpublished doctoral dissertation, University of Michigan.

Ericsson, K. A. (1975) *Instruction to verbalize as a means to study problem solving processes with the 8-puzzle: A preliminary study* (No. 458). Stockholm: The University of Stockholm.

Ernst, G. W., & Newell, A. (1969) *GPS: A case study in generality and problem solving*. New York: Academic Press.

Feigenbaum, E. (1961) The simulation of verbal learning behavior. *Proceedings of the Western Joint Computer Conference, 19*, 121–132.

Fillmore, C. J. (1968) The case for case. In E. Bach & R. T. Harms (Eds.), *Universals in linguistic theory*. New York: Holt, Rinehart, & Winston, pp. 1–90.

Gagné, R. M., & Smith, E. C., Jr. (1962) A study of the effects of verbalization on problem solving. *Journal of Experimental Psychology, 63*, 12–18.

Greeno, J. G. (1974) Hobbits and orcs: acquisition of a sequential concept. *Cognitive Psychology, 6*, 270–292.

Greeno, J. G. (1976) Cognitive objectives of instruction: Theory of knowledge for solving problems and answering questions. In D. Klahr (Ed.), *Cognition and instruction*. Hillsdale, New Jersey: Lawrence Erlbaum Associates, pp. 123–159.

Gregg, L. W., & Simon, H. A. (1967a) An information-processing explanation of one-trial and incremental learning. *Journal of Verbal Learning and Verbal Behavior, 6*, 780–787.

Gregg, L. W., & Simon, H. A. (1967b) Process models and stochastic theories of simple concept formation. *Journal of Mathematical Psychology, 4*, 246–276.

Hayes, J. R., & Simon, H. A. (1974) Understanding written problem instructions. In L. W. Gregg (Ed.), *Knowledge and cognition*. Potomac, Maryland: Lawrence Erlbaum Associates, pp. 167–199.

Hayes, J. R., & Simon, H. A. (1976a) Understanding complex task instructions. In D. Klahr (Ed.), *Cognition and instruction*. Hillsdale, New Jersey: Lawrence Erlbaum Associates.

Hayes, J. R., & Simon, H. A. (1976b) The understanding process: Problem isomorphs. *Cognitive Psychology, 8*, 165–190.

Hilgard, E. R., & Bower, G. H. (1974) *Theories of learning* (4th ed.) New York: Appleton-Century-Crofts.

Hilgard, E. R., Atkinson, R. C., & Atkinson, R. L. (1975) *Introduction to psychology* (6th ed.). New York: Harcourt, Brace, & World.

Hormann, A. M. (1965) Gaku: An artificial student. *Behavioral Science, 10*, 88–107.

Katona, G. (1940) *Organizing and memorizing*. New York: Columbia University Press.

Klix, F. (1971) *Information und Verhulten*. Berlin: VEB Deutscher Verlag der Wissenschaften.

Luchins, A. S. (1942) Mechanization in problem solving. *Psychological Monographs, 54* (6, Whole No. 248).

Newell, A. (1973) Production systems: Models of control structures. In W. G. Chase (Ed.), *Visual information processing.* New York: Academic Press, pp. 463–526.

Newell, A., & Simon, H. A. (1972) *Human problem solving.* Englewood Cliffs, N.J.: Prentice-Hall.

Newell, A., & Simon, H. A. (1976) Computer science as empirical inquiry: Symbols and search. *Communications of the Association for Computing Machinery, 19,* 113–126.

Norman, D. A. (1969) *Memory and attention: An introduction to human information processing.* New York: John Wiley & Sons.

Paige, J. M., & Simon, H. A. (1966) Cognitive processes in solving algebra word problems. In B. Kleinmuntz (Ed.), *Problem solving.* New York: John Wiley & Sons, pp. 51–119.

Quillian, M. R. (1968) Semantic memory. In M. Minsky (Ed.), *Semantic information processing.* Cambridge, Mass.: M.I.T. Press, pp. 216–270.

Reed, S. K., Ernst, G. W., & Banerji, R. (1974) The role of analogy in transfer between similar problem states. *Cognitive Psychology, 6,* 436–450.

Reitman, W. R. (1965) *Cognition and thought.* New York: John Wiley & Sons.

Rumelhart, D. E., Lindsay, P. H., & Norman, D. A. (1972) A process model for long-term memory. In E. Tulving & W. Donaldson (Eds.), *Organization of memory.* New York: Academic Press, pp. 198–246.

Schank, R. C. (1972) Conceptual dependency: A theory of natural language understanding. *Cognitive Psychology 3,* 552–631.

Simon, H. A. (1972) The theory of problem solving. *Proceedings of the IFIP Congress.* Amsterdam: North-Holland Publishing Co.

Simon, H. A. (1973) The structure of ill-structured problems. *Artificial Intelligence, 4,* 181–202.

Simon, H. A. (1974) How big is a chunk? *Science, 183,* 482–488.

Simon, H. A. (1975) The functional equivalance of problem solving skills. *Cognitive Psychology, 7,* 268–288.

Simon, H. A. (1976) The information-storage system called "human memory." In M. R. Rosenzweig & E. L. Bennett (Eds.), *Neutral mechanisms of learning and memory.* Cambridge, Mass.: M.I.T. Press, pp. 79–96.

Simon, H. A., & Feigenbaum, E. A. (1964) An information-processing theory of some effects of similarity, familiarization, and meaningfulness in verbal learning. *Journal of Verbal Learning and Verbal Behavior, 3,* 385–396.

Simon, H. A., & Gilmartin, K. (1973) A simulation of memory for chess positions. *Cognitive Psychology, 5,* 29–46.

Simon, H. A., & Lea, G. (1974) Problem solving and rule induction: A unified view. In L. W. Gregg (Ed.), *Knowledge and cognition.* Potomac, Maryland: Lawrence Erlbaum Associates, pp. 105–127.

Simon, H. A., & Reed, S. K. (1976) Modeling strategy shifts in a problem-solving task. *Cognitive Psychology, 8,* 86–97.

Sydow, H. (1970) Zur metrischen Erfassung von subjectiven Problemzuständen und zu deren Veränderung im Denkprozess, I and II. *Zeitschrift fur Psychologie, 177*: 145–198, *178*:1–50.

Thomas, J. C., Jr. (1974) An analysis of behavior in the hobbits-orcs problem. *Cognitive Psychology, 6,* 257–269.

Waterman, D. A., & Newell, A. (1973) PAS-II: An interactive task-free version of an automatic protocol analysis system. *Proceedings of the Third International Joint Conference on Artificial Intelligence,* pp. 431–445.

13 Analogical Problem Solving

Mary L. Gick and Keith J. Holyoak

INTRODUCTION

Where do new ideas come from? What psychological mechanisms underlie creative insight? This fundamental issue in the study of thought has received a great deal of informal discussion, but little empirical psychological investigation. The anecdotal reports of creative scientists and mathematicians suggest that the development of a new theory frequently depends on noticing and applying an analogy drawn from a different domain of knowledge. ... The hydraulic model of the blood circulation system, the planetary model of atomic structure, and the "billiard ball" model of gases all represent major scientific theories founded on analogies.

While the process of solving analogy test items of the form A:B::C:D has been studied quite extensively (Sternberg, 1977a, 1977b), there has been little experimental investigation of analogical thinking in more complex problem-solving tasks. Some studies have examined transfer between homomorphic or isomorphic versions of puzzle problems, such as the "missionaries and cannibals" (Reed, Ernst, & Banerji, 1974) and Tower of Hanoi (Hayes & Simon, 1977) puzzles. These are relatively "well-defined" problems ... in which the initial conditions, legal operations, and goal state are explicitly specified. In contrast, anecdotal reports of the use of analogies typically involve problems that are much less well defined. The present study was designed to investigate the use of analogies between disparate domains as a guide to finding solutions for an ill-defined problem.

THE RADIATION PROBLEM AND ITS ANALOGIES

Our basic experimental procedure was to provide subjects with a story analogy, describing a problem and its solution, and then to observe how subjects used the analogy in solving a subsequent target problem. The target problem was Duncker's (1945) "radiation problem," which in our experiments was stated as follows.

Suppose you are a doctor faced with a patient who has a malignant tumor in his stomach. It is impossible to operate on the patient, but unless the tumor is destroyed the patient will die. There is a kind of ray that can be used to destroy the tumor. If the rays reach the tumor all at once at a sufficiently high intensity, the tumor will be destroyed. Unfortunately, at this intensity the healthy tissue that the rays pass through on the way to the tumor will also be destroyed. At lower intensities the rays are harmless to healthy tissue, but they will not affect the tumor either. What type of procedure might be used to destroy the tumor with the rays, and at the same time avoid destroying the healthy tissue?

There are several reasons why the radiation problem seemed especially suitable for use in a study of analogical problem solving. First, it has all the hallmarks of the kind of "ill-defined" problem for which an analogy from a remote domain might trigger a creative insight. The desired goal state is specified only at a relatively abstract level, and the permissible operations that might be used to achieve the goal are left very open ended. As a consequence, the possible solution proposals vary considerably. This made it possible to test for the use of analogies by attempting to influence the specific solutions that subjects would generate.

In addition, we were able to benefit from Duncker's analyses of the performance of subjects who worked on the problem without receiving an analogy. Duncker identified three broad categories of proposed solutions to the radiation problem: (1) reducing the intensity of the rays as they pass through the healthy tissue; (2) avoiding contact between the rays and healthy tissue; and (3) altering the relative sentitivity to rays of the healthy tissue and the tumor (e.g., by immunizing the healthy tissue or sensitizing the tumor). Our analogies were designed to guide subjects toward specific versions of the first two classes of proposals.

Our general aim in the present study, then, was to explore the process by which subjects use analogies between remote domains to generate problem solutions. Consequently, we wrote a series of stories far removed from the medical domain, each involving a military problem and its solution, which were analogous to the radiation problem.
[...]

A FRAMEWORK FOR ANALOGICAL PROBLEM SOLVING

It is important to develop a general conceptual framework within which specific issues concerning the role of analogies in problem solving can be formulated. What is meant by analogy, and how can an analogy be used to generate a problem solution?

In order to make our discussion more concrete we will consider the major story analogy used in the present experiments and the corresponding solution to the radiation problem. In the Attack-Dispersion story, a general wishes to capture a fortress located in the center of a country. There are many roads radiating outward from the fortress. All have been mined so that while small groups of men can pass over the roads safely, any large force will detonate the mines. A full-scale direct attack is therefore impossible. The general's solution is to divide his army into small groups, send each group to the head of a different road, and have the groups converge simultaneously on the fortress. The analogous solution to the radiation problem is to simultaneously direct multiple low-intensity rays toward the tumor from different directions. In this way the healthy tissue will be left unharmed, but the effects of the multiple low-intensity rays will summate and destroy the tumor.

At an intuitive level the parallels between the Attack-Dispersion story and the radiation problem are clear. Both situations involve an object that must be overcome, surrounded by objects that must be preserved. The target object in each case occupies a topographically central position in its environment. In each situation the protagonist has available a weapon with an effect proportional to the intensity or amount of the weapon that is used, and so on.

How might people represent these analogical relationships and use them to generate a solution to the target problem? This is not an easy question to answer. First of all, both the story and the problem must be read and understood. In attempting to describe this type of analogical problem solving we thus inherit all the problems associated with text comprehension. In particular, perception of analogy hinges on semantic knowledge and inference procedures. Since no general theory of language understanding is available, we must of necessity gloss over many important issues related to the understanding process. However, . . .there appear to be close ties between the concept of analogy and the concept of "schema," which has been widely applied in discussions of prose comprehension. In essence, both an analogy and a schema consist of an organized system of relations. Consequently, the framework for analogical problem solving presented here will draw its conceptual vocabulary from various schema-based models, as well as from Sternberg's (1977a, 1977b) model of component processes involved in analogical reasoning. We will first consider how analogy might be represented, and then how this representation could be used to generate a solution to a problem.

The Representation of Analogy

A system of representation for analogy must be able to describe a fundamental property of such relational systems, namely, that analogy may be defined at multiple levels of abstraction. For example, at a relatively low level of abstraction the Attack-Dispersion story and the radiation problem have a variety of corresponding details (e.g., small groups of soldiers correspond to low-intensity rays). At a more abstract level, the story and the problem both involve the goal of overpowering an object located in a region that must be preserved.

The multileveled nature of analogy can perhaps be understood in the context of Kintsch and Van Dijk's (1978) theory of prose representation. They argue that the understanding process may involve the iterative application of a set of inference rules that generate increasingly abstract "macrostructure" representations of a prose passage. These macrostructures essentially correspond to summaries of the passage at various levels of generality. In the case of a problem-oriented story such as the Attack-Dispersion story, an abstract level of macrostructure might state a general solution principle (e.g., to destroy a target when direct application of a large force is harmful to the surrounding area, disperse the attacking forces, and have them converge at the target). The process of extracting a solution principle might thus be viewed as a special case of the process of deriving macrostructures for a body of information. While much remains to be learned about how this process operates, the three specific inference rules proposed by Kintsch and Van Dijk (which they term "deletion," "generalization," and "construction") would seem readily applicable to the type of story analogies we are considering here.

Kintsch and Van Dijk emphasize that control processes are required to select a level of macrostructure analysis consistent with the person's processing goals. Similarly, we assume there is an optimal level of abstraction at which analogical relations may be represented in order to effectively guide the solution process. Indeed, an important empirical issue is to determine what factors influence this optimal level of abstraction.

We will now consider in more detail how an analogy between two relational systems might be represented, assuming an appropriate level of macrostructure has been derived. To pursue our example, Table [13.1] presents our own summary of the Attack-Dispersion story, as well as a summary of the radiation problem and its dispersion solution. These summaries are intended to reflect the major causal connections within both the story and the problem, and to illustrate the major analogical relations between them. The sentences in Table [13.1] are numbered to correspond to an approximate propositional analysis presented in Fig. [13.1]. Propositions from the story and from the radiation problem are matched to indicate analogical relations, and the propositions corresponding to the dispersion solution to the radiation problem (which a person would be required to generate) are italicized in both the table and the figure. Note that some of the propositions included in the story summary (e.g., proposition 11) are inferences, which are not directly stated in the original story. . . .

The notation in Fig. [13.1] consists of propositional functions, in which predicates are followed by one or more arguments (enclosed in parentheses). The arguments fill various semantic roles, such as agent, object, and location. Propositions may themselves serve as arguments, so in

TABLE 13.1

A Summary of Attack-Dispersion Story and of Corresponding Solution
to Radiation Problem (See Fig. 13.1)

Proposition number	
	Attack-Dispersion story
1–2	A fortress was located in the center of the country.
2a	Many roads radiated out from the fortress.
3–4	A general wanted to capture the fortress with his army.
5–7	The general wanted to prevent mines on the roads from destroying his army and neighboring villages.
8	As a result the entire army could not attack the fortress along one road.
9–10	However, the entire army was needed to capture the fortress.
11	So an attack by one small group would not succeed.
12	The general therefore divided his army into several small groups.
13	He positioned the small groups at the heads of different roads.
14–15	The small groups simultaneously converged on the fortress.
16	In this way the army captured the fortress.
	Radiation problem and dispersion solution[a]
1'–2'	A tumor was located in the interior of a patient's body.
3'–4'	A doctor wanted to destroy the tumor with rays.
5'–7'	The doctor wanted to prevent the rays from destroying healthy tissue.
8'	As a result the high-intensity rays could not be applied to the tumor along one path.
9'–10'	However, high-intensity rays were needed to destroy the tumor.
11'	So applying one low-intensity ray would not succeed.
12'	*The doctor therefore divided the rays into several low-intensity rays.*
13'	*He positioned the low-intensity rays at multiple locations around the patient's body.*
14'–15'	*The low-intensity rays simultaneously converged on the tumor.*
16'	*In this way the rays destroyed the tumor.*

[a] Italicized propositions summarise the target dispersion solution.

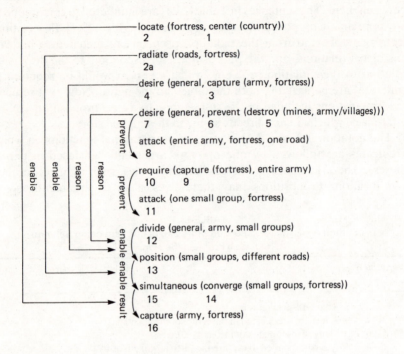

locate (fortress, center (country))
2   1

radiate (roads, fortress)
2a

desire (general, capture (army, fortress))
4   3

desire (general, prevent (destroy (mines, army/villages)))
7   6   5

attack (entire army, fortress, one road)
8

require (capture (fortress), entire army)
10   9

attack (one small group, fortress)
11

divide (general, army, small groups)
12

position (small groups, different roads)
13

simultaneous (converge (small groups, fortress))
15   14

capture (army, fortress)
16

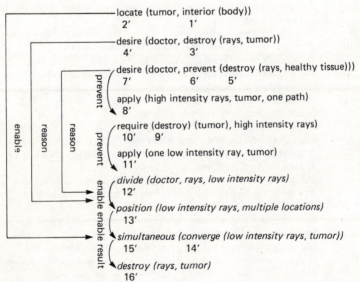

locate (tumor, interior (body))
2′   1′

desire (doctor, destroy (rays, tumor))
4′   3′

desire (doctor, prevent (destroy (rays, healthy tissue)))
7′   6′   5′

apply (high intensity rays, tumor, one path)
8′

require (destroy) (tumor), high intensity rays)
10′   9′

apply (one low intensity ray, tumor)
11′

divide (doctor, rays, low intensity rays)
12′

position (low intensity rays, multiple locations)
13′

simultaneous (converge (low intensity rays, tumor))
15′   14′

destroy (rays, tumor)
16′

FIG. 13.1 Analogical correspondences between the Attack-Dispersion story and the radiation problem.

several cases one proposition is embedded in another. We make no claims about the logical adequacy or completeness of the representation in Fig. [13.1]; indeed, many of the indicated arguments (e.g., "low-intensity rays") clearly could be further decomposed. However, separation of relations (predicates) and arguments serves to highlight the critical properties of analogy between remote domains: similarity of corresponding relations despite dissimilarity of corresponding arguments.

The notation in Fig. [13.1] has been augmented by labeled arcs that represent the major causal connections within the Attack-Dispersion story and the radiation problem. The labels are inspired by but not identical to the analysis of causal types offered by Schank and Abelson (1977). . . . Roughly, a goal can be a "reason" for an action; a state or action can "enable" a subsequent action; an action can "result" in a subsequent state; and a state or action can "prevent" a subsequent action. Again, the adequacy of this analysis is not really critical for our present purpose, which is simply to make salient the correspondences in causal structure between the story and the problem, particularly with respect to the target solution. Note that the labeled arcs are equivalent to higher-order predicates that embed numbered propositions as arguments.

The representation in Fig. [13.1] can be used to highlight a variety of properties of analogy, as well as some of the issues we have glossed over in constructing this representation. Fundamentally, an analogy consists of a mapping between two sets of propositions. Propositions are matched on the basis of similarity between the corresponding relations. Note that similarity need not imply identity. There need only be a consistent transformation that maps one set of relations onto the other. Boden (1977) gives the example of the Black Mass, which is based on systematic semantic reversals of the Catholic ritual. In the case of our story and problem, we wrote the summaries to maximize the similarity of the relations. Yet dividing an army (proposition 12), for example, is clearly not quite the same as dividing high-intensity rays (proposition 12′). To generate this aspect of the parallel solution the person would need to take account of the relevant differences between an army and rays, perhaps explicitly introducing multiple machines that each emit low-intensity rays. In order to map proposition 1 onto 1′ a person must have semantic knowledge of the relation between the meanings of "center" and "interior." Incidentally, note that we assume proposition 1′ is included in the macrostructure for the problem as an inference based on knowledge of where the stomach is located. In the case of propositions 16 and 16′, we assume the person will use semantic knowledge to transform the relation of "capturing" into the relation of "destroying," operating on the common semantic core (i.e., "overcoming") that links the two relations.

As Fig. [13.1] indicates, there is clearly a high degree of correspondence between the propositions of the story and of the problem. At the same time, the systems are not perfectly isomorphic. It is probably the case that analogies used to guide problem solving are generally incomplete in some respects. ... For example, proposition 2a in the Attack-Dispersion story, which states that many roads radiate outward from the fortress, has no parallel in the statement of the radiation problem. Note that in the story this proposition serves as an important enabling condition for the solution. The absence of any explicit mention in the radiation problem of multiple paths to the target object would presumably hinder generation of the dispersion solution.

For the above example it is plausible to argue that people must infer the fact that there are multiple potential "routes" to the tumor in the course of generating the dispersion solution, even though no such inference is represented in Fig. [13.1]. But in addition, Fig. [13.1] reveals at least one clear disanalogy between the story and the problem. In a complete analogy, there is a consistent mapping between pairs of arguments. That is, wherever argument A occurs in one relational system, argument A' occurs in the other. For example, in Fig. [13.1] the role the fortress plays in the story consistently maps onto the role the tumor plays in the problem. Note that the role of the army usually corresponds to that of the rays. However, this is not the case in propositions 5 and 5'. In the Attack-Dispersion story, sending the entire army down one road will result in destruction of the *army* (as well as neighboring villages) by *mines*; whereas in the radiation problem applying high-intensity rays to the tumor will result in destruction of the *healthy tissue* by the *rays*. In other words, the army and the rays do not fill corresponding semantic roles in propositions 5 and 5': rather, the army is the *object* of the process of destruction in 5, while the rays are the *instrument* of the destruction in 5'.

This example illustrates that degree of analogy in part depends on the level of abstraction at which the analogy is defined. In macrostructures slightly more abstract than those depicted in Fig. [13.1], the fact that an attack by the entire army is impossible would map onto the fact that direct application of high-intensity rays is impossible. At this level the roles of the army and of the rays correspond appropriately. However, the story and the problem are disanalogous at the more specific level depicted in Fig. [13.1] (i.e., the level of the *reasons* why the two respective courses of action are blocked). This observation suggests that for use in solving a problem the optimal level of abstraction for representing an analogy may be that which maximizes the degree of correspondence between the two relational systems. In many cases a very detailed representation will include disanalogous relations, while a very abstract representation will omit information about important correspondences.

The Process of Analogical Problem Solving

So far we have been discussing how analogical relations may be represented: we must now consider how this information might be used to generate a solution to a problem. For our story analogy and target problem the solution process appears to require three major steps.

1. A representation of the story analogy and of the target problem (i.e., its initial state and goal state) must be constructed, as described above.
2. The representation of the story must be mapped onto that of the problem. If the story and the problem are drawn from remote domains, as in our example, the correspondences between arguments will not be immediately obvious. We would therefore expect the mapping process to be initiated by detection of similar relations in the two systems. For example, the person might notice that propositions 2 and 2' both involve location. Accordingly, a mapping between the two propositions will be established. This will automatically establish a mapping between the corresponding arguments (i.e., the fortress and the tumor, the center of the country and the interior of the body). Once a few such correspondences have been detected, the mapping process may proceed in a more "top-down" manner, guided by expectations that previously mapped arguments will continue to play parallel roles. For example, having mapped propositions 2 and 2', the person might assume that 8 maps onto 8' because the role of the fortress should correspond to that of the tumor.
3. Finally, the person must use the mapping to generate the parallel solution to the target problem. This can be done by constructing a set of solution propositions for the target problem that correspond to the solution propositions of the story. For example, consider how proposition 12' might be generated on the basis of proposition 12. The mapping process will have identified the general with the doctor and the army with the rays. Accordingly, "doctor" and "rays" will be used to fill the argument slots corresponding to "general" and "army." In addition, the relation between the general and the army in 12 will be used to construct a parallel relation between the doctor and the rays in 12'. Thus the idea of the general dividing the army into several small groups will be transformed into the idea of the doctor dividing the rays into a number of low-intensity rays, initiating the dispersion solution to the radiation problem.

ISSUES AND EXPERIMENTS

A number of important questions arise within the framework of the process model we have outlined. A major issue, which we touched upon earlier, concerns the level of macrostructure at which the mapping process takes place. At one extreme the solution process might amount to abstracting a solution principle from the story and then applying it to the target problem. At the other extreme subjects might map the correspondences between the story and the problem at the most detailed possible level. It is possible, of course, that the mapping process may actually proceed partially in parallel on several different levels.

Even at a single level of macrostructure, there may be strategic variations in the degree of mapping that takes place during the solution process. For example, subjects need not derive the entire set of correspondences outlined in Fig. [13.1] in order to generate the dispersion solution. One possibility, which we will term the "solution-focusing" strategy, is that subjects attempting to apply the story analogy will immediately identify the solution propositions of the story. By doing the minimal amount of mapping required to match the arguments in these propositions with arguments in the radiation problem, the parallel solution could be generated. Subjects using the solution-focusing strategy might thus solve the target problem without entirely grasping the correspondences between the problem statements in the story and in the radiation problem.

Given the lack of empirical research on analogical problem solving, even more basic issues arise. We have sketched a model of how in principle a problem might be solved on the basis of an analogy. However, we do not know whether subjects could actually execute this kind of process for our story analogies and target problem. There seem to be at least three distinct ways in which subjects who have a relevant analogy available might nonetheless fail to derive the parallel solution to a target problem. The first and most basic is that subjects might be unable to successfully apply the story analogy even if they tried. Second, even if a story analogy is potentially useful, subjects might be unable to locate it in memory, especially if it had been encoded in the context of irrelevant distractor stories. Third, subjects might be able to retrieve a potentially useful analogy and yet fail to spontaneously notice its relevance to the target problem.

The experiments reported below were designed to explore these and related issues. [. . .]

EXPERIMENT I

Experiment I was designed to demonstrate that subjects can use an analogy from a remote domain as a hint for solving a problem. Subjects first read a story analogy, and then attempted to propose as many solutions as possible to the radiation problem. By varying the nature of the solution suggested by the story, we hoped to influence the likelihood that subjects would generate specific solutions to the target problem. Subjects' "thinking aloud" protocols were tape recorded and later analyzed as a source of evidence regarding the process of analogical problem solving.

Subjects in three experimental conditions read one of three stories about a military problem and its solution.... Table [13.2] informally illustrates the correspondences among the three stories and the radiation problem. The statement of the radiation problem (see Introduction) was worded so as to minimize obvious lexical or syntactic correspondences with the story analogies. The Attack-dispersion, Open Supply Route, and Tunnel stories all have identical first paragraphs describing the problem setting, desired goal, and the constraints on a solution. These aspects of the stories are analogous to the radiation problem, as discussed earlier (see Fig. [13.1]).

However, the stories differ in their second paragraphs, which state the general's solution to his problem. In the Attack-Dispersion story (described in the Introduction) the general divides his army into small groups and sends them simultaneously down different roads to the fortress. The analogous solution to the radiation problem is the "dispersion" solution: have multiple low-intensity rays converge at the tumor. This is a very effective solution, but one which subjects seldom generate spontaneously. Duncker (1945) reported that only 2 of 42 subjects arrived at this dispersion solution, and both were prompted by the experimenter. A basic difficulty that appears to block generation of this solution is that people do not spontaneously think of rays as having the property of "divisibility." [...]

In the Open Supply Route story the general discovers an unblocked road leading to the fortress, and sends the entire army down this open road. An analogous radiation solution is to direct high-intensity rays down the esophagus (or some other open passage, such as the intestines) to the stomach. This solution was generated relatively frequently by the subjects tested by Duncker (29% gave the open passage solution as opposed to only 5% who gave the dispersion solution). In the Tunnel story the general digs an underground tunnel and sends his army through it to the fortress. Analogous radiation solutions might be to operate to expose the tumor to the rays, or to insert a tube through the stomach wall and send rays through it to the tumor. Many of Duncker's subjects (40%) spontaneously suggested such solutions. However, such procedures to create an open route to the tumor involve operating, and hence conflict with one of the constraints imposed on the radiation problem (that it is impossible to operate). The Tunnel story is therefore a kind of "false analogy" to the radiation problem. That is, although the problem statements are analogous, the solution suggested by the story is inappropriate. If the analogy is

TABLE 13.2
Schematic Outline of Duncker's Radiation Problem Showing
Correspondences with Analogous Stories

Problem Statement	Radiation problem	Story analogies—Experiment I
Problem setting	Doctor has rays. Patient has tumor. Tumor in stomach, surrounded by healthy tissue.	General has army. Country has dictator. Dictator in fortress in center of country, surrounded by villages. Roads radiate from fortress like spokes on a wheel.
Desired goal	Destroy tumor with rays.	Capture fortress with army.
Problem constraints	High-intensity rays destroy tumor but also destroy healthy tissue. Low-intensity rays destroy neither tumor nor healthy tissue. Impossible to operate.	Entire army can capture fortress, but large group detonates mines on roads, destroying army and villages. Small group of men can pass safely over roads but can not capture fortress.
Solutions		
Type I	Reduce intensity of rays on way to tumor.	Reduce size of group traveling to fortress on one road.
Dispersion (Attack-Dispersion story)	(1) Many low intensity rays (2) From different directions (3) Simultaneously	(1) Many small groups of men (2) From different directions (3) Simultaneously
Type II	Avoid contact between rays and healthy tissue.	Avoid contact between army and mines.
(1) Open passage (Open Supply Route story)	Send high-intensity rays through an open route (e.g., esophagus).	General discovers road that is not mined, and sends entire army down this road.
(2) Operation (Tunnel story)	Make an incision in stomach wall, removing healthy tissue from path of rays, and apply high intensity rays to tumor.[a]	Dig tunnel under mines, and send entire army through.
Resulting goal state	Radiation of high-intensity reaches tumor. Tumor destroyed. Healthy tissue intact.	Entire army reaches fortress. Fortress captured. Army and villages preserved.

[a] Incision violates constraint.

nevertheless applied, subjects given the Tunnel story might be especially likely to momentarily disregard the problem constraints and propose an operation solution to the radiation problem.

Although the above analysis of the analogous relationships between various solutions to the military problem and to the radiation problem was initially based on the experimenters' intuitions, we will see below that subjects' ratings essentially confirm the validity of this analysis.

The primary prediction in Experiment I was that each story analogy would tend to increase the frequency of the analogous solution to the radiation problem, relative to the solution frequencies obtained for control subjects given no prior story. However, there are additional ways in which the story analogies might influence the solutions given to the target problem. First, note that the problem statements for all three stories contain all the enabling conditions (see Fig. [13.1]) for generating the dispersion solution (e.g., the central location of the fortress, the roads radiating outward, the fact that small groups can travel on the roads). Accordingly, subjects might spontaneously think of the dispersion solution to the general's problem, and then use it to generate the parallel solution to the radiation problem. If so, subjects given the Open Supply Route and Tunnel stories might also produce the dispersion solution more often than would control subjects.

It is also possible that giving subjects a story analogy may actually hinder the generation of nonanalogous solutions. That is, attempting to generate a parallel solution to the target problem may create a kind of "set" effect, so that other possible solutions (e.g., immunizing the healthy tissue to protect it from the rays) will not be discovered. If such a set effect is obtained, control subjects should produce more total solutions than experimental subjects, and in addition there should be qualitative differences between the solutions produced by control subjects versus subjects given story analogies.

[. . .]

[. . .] Subjects' protocols for the radiation problem were transcribed and scored for the presence of various types of proposed solutions, by two independent scorers. For this purpose any suggestion, even if it was eventually rejected by the subject, was counted as a proposed solution. The results of major interest concern the three types of proposals that are analogous to the solutions embodied in the story analogies—the dispersion solution, the open passage solution, and operation solutions. Table [13.3] presents the percentage of subjects in each condition who produced these various types of proposed solutions. The frequency of each solution was highest for subjects who received the relevant story analogy, i.e., the dispersion solution was most frequent for the Attack-Dispersion condition, the open passage solution was most frequent for the Open Supply Route condition, and operation solutions were most frequent for the Tunnel condition.

TABLE 13.3
Percentage of Subjects in Each Condition of Experiment I Who
Proposed Various Solutions to the Radiation Problem

	Proposed solution		
Condition	Dispersion	Open Passage	Operation
Attack-Dispersion story	100	10	30
Open Supply Route story	10	70	50
Tunnel story	20	30	80
Control	0	20	50

These differences in solution frequencies were most dramatic for the dispersion solution. All 10 subjects who were given the Attack-Dispersion story produced this solution, whereas not a single control subject did so.

In order to obtain ... evidence regarding a possible set effect, the frequencies of specific radiation solutions, other than those analogous to the various stories, were tabulated for each condition. The solutions examined were proposals to treat the healthy tissue directly, rather than altering the route that the rays take. Specifically, these solutions suggested decreasing the sensitivity of the healthy tissue to the rays (e.g., by a chemical injection, or building up a tolerance to the rays), or covering the healthy tissue with a barrier to protect it from the rays (e.g., by inserting a lead shield to protect the healthy tissue). Such solutions were produced by 30% of the subjects in the Control condition, 10% of the subjects in the Tunnel condition, and none of the subjects in the Attack-Dispersion and Open Supply conditions. While the numbers involved were too small to be statistically reliable, these results suggest that an analogy may tend to block generation of alternative types of solutions.

[...] The results discussed so far demonstrate that story analogies can play a major role in directing the problem-solving process. However, they reveal little about the process by which subjects arrive at an analogous solution. We therefore supplemented the quantitative analysis of solution types, ... with a more qualitative analysis of subjects' problem-solving protocols. Several aspects of the protocols were examined. Occasions when the experimenter prompted the subjects to use the story were noted, as were correspondences between the story and the target problem that subjects mentioned in the course of generating solutions. This analysis was, of course, constrained by the overall quality and quantity of the protocols. For example, some subjects insisted that talking aloud hindered their thinking, and consequently did not say very much. Rather than presenting an exhaustive analysis of all the protocols, we will therefore concentrate on particularly suggestive excerpts. While this type of protocol analysis has obvious limitations, it may at least provide some hints about the process of analogical problem solving, and in fact served in part to motivate subsequent experiments.

A major issue, raised earlier, concerns the degree of mapping subjects perform in the process of generating an analogous solution. Do subjects make use of detailed correspondences between the story and the target problem, or do they focus directly on the solution embedded in the story and attempt to apply it to the target problem? Of the 10 subjects in the Attack-Dispersion condition, 7 produced the dispersion solution without any prompt, and 3 produced it after being prompted to refer back to the story. In some respects the protocols for prompted subjects are potentially more informative, since what such subjects say is more likely to reflect an ongoing solution process, rather than the result of a process already completed. The protocols of 2 of the 3 prompted subjects suggested use of a solution-focusing strategy.

Table [13.4] presents an excerpt from the protocol of one of these subjects, S15. After the prompt to use the story, this subject clearly focuses on the solution of dividing up the army into groups and immediately generates the parallel solution to the radiation problem. There is no apparent mapping between the initial problem stated in the story and the target problem.

Notice also that the solution S15 proposes prior to the prompt involves the idea of applying many low-intensity rays. After the prompt, the subject produces the dispersion solution by augmenting this aspect of the earlier solution with the idea of sending rays from many angles. This pattern of gradual solution development was also evident in the protocol of another prompted subject in the Attack-Dispersion condition.

[...]

The details of the problem-solving process are less evident in the protocols of the seven unprompted subjects, since they expressed the solution all at once. Three of these subjects simply stated the solution and alluded to the usefulness of the prior story (saying, for example, "considering the problem before"). These subjects did not mention any specific correspondences between the story and the target problem, and hence their protocols were quite unrevealing with respect to the solution process.

However, two other unprompted subjects did spontaneously mention correspondences between the problems. Immediately after reading the radiation problem, S23 stated:

Like in the first problem, the impenetrable fortress, the guy had put bombs all around, and the bombs could be compared to the destruction of healthy tissue. And so they had to, they couldn't go in in mass through one road, they had to split up so as not to destroy the healthy tissue. Because if there's only a

TABLE 13.4
Portion of Protocol for S15 (Attack-Dispersion Condition)

Subject reads radiation problem.

S: Alright I, what I most, what I'd probably do is send in the ray at sufficiently high intensity and then taking the risk that the tissues, the healthy tissues that would be destroyed, could be repaired later on. Trying to relate this to the other problem, I could say that you could give multiple treatments of low-intensity ray. But from this problem it seems that they won't have effect on the tumor so . . . so I don't think that would work.

Later . . .

E: Okay. And as a last question can you give me a, tell me ways in which your solution would satisfy the constraints of the experiment?

S: What are the constraints of the experiment?

E: Okay, i.e., that the healthy tissue will not be destroyed, and the tumor will be?

S: Alright, in that way my first suggestion would probably not be the way to go at it. Because that way you're getting low intensity so it won't destroy the tissue and hopefully over a period of time the additive effect of low-intensity rays would kill the tumor. But from reading the article, I don't know if that would work or not, because it says that a low-intensity ray doesn't have any effect on the tumor at all. So I don't know. I don't know any other possible ways of doing it.

E: Would it help to possibly go back to the story and see whether you can apply that?

S: Well, that's what I was trying to do here. It says here he divides his army into different small groups. Okay, may . . . possibly. What they could do, but this is a whole new solution now, possibly what they could do is attack the tumor from a multiple of directions with lower intensity rays and then, since you're coming in from all different directions, the healthy, with small-intensity rays you're not going to be destroying the healthy tissue but you're, and they'll all converge at the point of the tumor which will hopefully destroy the tumor.

little bit of ray it doesn't damage the tissue, but it's all focused on the same spot.

[. . .]

It is clear in the above two cases that the subjects noticed some correspondences involving the initial conditions and constraints of the story and target problem. However, it is difficult to tell whether these aspects of the mapping process were instrumental in generating the analogous solution, or whether subjects simply mentioned the correspondences to justify the adequacy of the solution, after it had already been generated. In general it was not clear what particular correspondences were central to the solution process. However, several subjects alluded to the importance of the phrase "like spokes on a wheel." Recall that the existence of multiple routes is a critical enabling condition for the solution embodied in the Attack-Dispersion story, and it has no explicit parallel in the statement of the radiation problem. This aspect of the story analogy may therefore serve to generate the critical insight that it is possible to send rays from multiple directions. One illustrative example is the following excerpt from the protocol of S7 in the Attack-Dispersion condition, which begins immediately after the subject had read the radiation problem:

> Well, I already know the answer. I knew it when I read it. I might as well stop and say that. What you do is you have a bunch of rays that are weaker, and you point them so that they concentrate on one point. So you just have many different angles. It could not only be two dimensional, the analogy of the spokes on the fortress. But you could even have it three dimensional, so you could have a whole ball of spokes going in. And you would have a high intensity right at the tumor.

In addition, the protocols of all three subjects in the Open Supply Route and Tunnel conditions who produced the dispersion solution suggested that it was triggered by the idea of multiple converging routes. For example, immediately after S2 in the Open Supply Route condition read the problem, she expressed the idea of using a "circular approach" (which in her earlier story summary she explicitly related to the phrase "spokes on a wheel"). This idea then led to the multidirectional aspect of the dispersion solution to the radiation problem.

Two subjects in the Tunnel condition who produced the dispersion solution did so after first spontaneously remarking that the general might have sent his men down multiple roads. One other subject, in the Open Supply Route condition, also suggested the dispersion solution to the military problem, but failed to apply it to the radiation problem. [. . .]

Subjects' protocols also provided information about some of the difficulties they encountered in attempting to apply analogies based on the Open Supply Route and Tunnel stories. As we pointed out earlier, the open passage solution is not especially practical and some subjects may have thought of this solution without mentioning it. For example, S32 in the Tunnel condition gave the open passage solution as an afterthought at the very end of the interview, and also outlined the problems with it: that the esophagus is not straight, and that there would be "refraction off the esophagal walls, or absorption of the rays," which would destroy tissue. Three subjects attempted to overcome this difficulty by suggesting that a ray-proof tube through which the rays could be directed should be inserted down the throat.

In addition, the nature of the analogy suggested by the Open Supply Route story is somewhat different from that suggested by the other two stories. The solutions embodied in both of the latter stories suggest procedures that can be used to generate parallel solutions to the radiation problem (dividing the rays in the case of the Attack-Dispersion story, operating in the case of the Tunnel story). In contrast, the Open Supply

Route story only suggests that an existing open passage might be used. The subject must then search his memory to find a concrete example of such an open passage to the stomach (e.g., the esophagus). Applying the analogy thus involves two steps: mapping the abstract idea of an open passage from the story to the target problem, and then thinking of a concrete example of such a passage. The difficulty of applying the analogy may account for the fact that four of the seven subjects in the Open Supply Route condition who gave the open passage solution had to be prompted to use the story.

Table [13.5] presents a portion of the protocol for S19 in the Open Supply Route condition. This subject works through a rather detailed mapping of the correspondences between the story and the radiation problem. But while she clearly develops the abstract idea of finding an open passage, she fails in the attempt to think of a concrete example. The partial solution produced by S19 can be contrasted with the complete lack of success apparent in the protocol of S37 in the Open Supply Route condition:

> The only thing that is apparent to me is that the general had other information that he knew that one of the thoroughfares would be left open, and so he was able to use that. But, unless the doctor had some new information or some other treatment, I don't see any other applications from the first problem to the second problem.

TABLE 13.5
Portion of Protocol for S19 (Open Supply Route Condition)

E: It might help if you reread the instructions here. This part.

(S rereads radiation problem.)

S: Okay, so what was the first problem? The spokes of the wheel—right?

E: Right.

S: So the center fortress deal would be the idea of the tumor. That's . . .

E: Okay.

S: And then the spokes that blow up a little would be like the healthy tissue that blows up a little bit. And so with that one the guy had one route that was gonna do it. I guess in this one that's what you have to do is find the one route that would work.

E: Okay.

S: And, I think, and not use the other ways.

E: Okay. What would that be?

S: That would mean we have to find one approach that was going to get to the tumor without getting the healthy tissue. And I don't see how you could do that. Cause it's not—it doesn't seem like it's the same thing.

E: What doesn't seem like the same thing?

S: Well the idea that road, with a road its possible to have one road unguarded but without, in your body there's always going to be, unless the tumor was right on the outside, there would always be some tissue you would have to go through to get to it.

TABLE 13.6
Portion of Protocol for S24 (Tunnel Condition)

E: If you read your instructions, it says that this story might give you some hints . . . What are you thinking?

S: Well, I remember that the main way they solved this problem was they dug under the fortress and went around it. So, possibly in this situation, you could go around the healthy tissue. I don't know how you'd do that . . . I see an analogy, it's not real clear.

E: Why isn't it clear?

S: Because when I picture healthy tissue in my mind, healthy tissue all over and, you know, just like a tumor in between all this healthy tissue. But here, the mines they're on top near the surface of the ground, so they can, you can dig under those and you won't really have any problem. But here no matter where you go, like a circle around the healthy tissue . . . maybe an operation.

E: Except that one of the constraints of the experiment says that you can't operate.

S: Okay, that's not possible . . . maybe . . . I was thinking that maybe you could give intervals of high intensity, but I don't know, that still would probably destroy the healthy tissue.

E: Can you think of anything else? . . . Is this problem, the previous story, is that distracting?

S: (mumbles) Again, I'm looking for an analogy between the two. And kind of set up the same problem and solve it the same way, but I don't know if I can or not.

E: So, can you think of any other possibilities?

S: (long pause) . . . No.

Notice that S37 appears to have mapped the story and the target problem at a very abstract level of macrostructure, so that the perceived analogy (the general had new information, so perhaps the doctor might also) was too vague to yield a specific solution proposal for the radiation problem.

In the case of the Tunnel condition four of the eight subjects who generated operation solutions received a prompt to use the story before they did so. Some subjects may have been reluctant to suggest an operation solution because they were aware that it violated a constraint given in the problem statement. An excerpt from the protocol of S24, presented in Table [13.6], illustrates the kind of difficulty encountered in this condition. The protocol suggests that the subject was quite carefully mapping components of the story onto components of the radiation problem. However, the subject was unable to generate a satisfying parallel solution to the target problem.

The overall impression created by the problem-solving protocols is that the generation of analogous solutions involves a conscious process of mapping correspondences between the story and the target problem. The degree of mapping required seems to vary a great deal. Sometimes mapping was done in considerable detail, particularly if the subject was having difficulty producing a parallel solution. In other cases noticing one or two major points of correspondence seemed sufficient to generate the solution. In some instances, particularly for dispersion and open passage solutions, aspects of the solution were clearly generated in sequential steps.

Experiment II was designed to provide additional information about the degree of mapping required to produce a solution on the basis of story analogy.

EXPERIMENT II

For Experiment II, a new story, the Parade-Dispersion story was generated. This story retained the critical enabling conditions for the dispersion solution (centrally located fortress, multiple roads radiating outward), but in other ways was substantially disanalogous to the radiation problem. (Table [13.7] presents a schematic outline of the Parade-Dispersion story). In the parade story, the general is not trying to attack the dictator in the fortress, but rather to stage a parade that meets the dictator's specifications. The constraint of the mined roads has been removed. In the Parade story, the procession of soldiers to the fortress directly constitutes the goal state, whereas in the attack story the similar movement of troops is simply the means by which the final goal (capturing the fortress) can be achieved. Thus, even though the surface description of the solution is the same in both stories, the solution contexts differ.

TABLE 13.7
Schematic Outline of Parade-Dispersion Story

Problem statement	
Problem setting	General has army. Country has dictator. Dictator in fortress in center of country, surrounded by villages. Roads radiate from fortress like spokes on a wheel.
Desired goal	Produce impressive parade that can be seen and heard throughout entire country.
Problem constraints	Sending entire army down one road fails to produce impressive parade. If parade fails to impress dictator, general will lose his rank.
Solution	
Dispersion	Divide up parade so that each part of country sees part of parade. Use (1) Many small groups of men (2) From different directions (3) Simultaneously
Resulting goal state	Parade seen and heard simultaneously throughout country. General preserves his rank.

TABLE 13.8
Percentage of Subjects in Each Condition of Experiment II Who
Proposed the Dispersion Solution to the Radiation Problem

| Condition | Dispersion solution | | | |
	Complete	Partial	Total	N
Attack-Dispersion story	57	19	76	47
Parade-Dispersion Story	31	18	49	45
Control	8	0	8	50

In Experiment II, subjects were divided into 3 conditions. In the two experimental conditions, subjects received either the Attack story or the Parade story, and were then asked for possible solutions to the radiation problem having been told that the [preliminary] story might contain some hints for solving the problem. In the control condition, no initial story was given, subjects being asked simply to solve the problem in the radiation story. The results are summarized in Table [13.8].

[. . .]Unlike subjects in Experiment I, subjects in Experiment II were not prompted to fully explicate their solutions. As a result, a number of subjects produced incomplete versions of the dispersion solution. In order to be scored as a complete dispersion solution, three features had to be present in the proposal: (1) the rays are applied to the tumor from different directions, (2) at low intensity, and (3) simultaneously. A partial solution had to contain at least the first feature, the critical element of dispersion. However, partial solutions might omit features 2 and/or 3. [. . .]

The basic results of Experiment II are ... extremely clear. First, subjects can readily use story analogies to guide their attempts to solve the radiation problem, even without feedback from the experimenter. Second, the effectiveness of analogies in prompting a specific solution is a matter of degree. In particular, a story with a problem statement analogous to that of the radiation problem (the Attack story) was more likely to trigger the dispersion solution than was a story with a problem statement less related to that of the radiation problem (the Parade story). This was true even though both stories embodied similar setting information and solution statements.

Our central concern in the experiments reported so far was to determine if people can use an analogy to generate a solution to a target problem, and to investigate how analogical problem solving proceeds. Consequently, we simplified the subjects' task in several important ways. First, subjects were always allowed to reread the story analogy at any time, so that their performance would not be limited by memory factors. Second, the story was always presented alone, so that subjects would have no problem identifying the relevant analogy. Third, subjects were always explicitly told to use the story as an aid in solving the target problem. This hint was quite nonspecific; at no time were subjects told the nature of the analogous relationship between the story and problem. Nevertheless, the hint eliminated the need for subjects to spontaneously notice the possible analogy.

In many cases of everyday problem solving in which an analogy could help, the person would have to spontaneously notice the correspondence between the target problem and some analogous problem, either of which might be stored in memory. The two experiments reported below begin to investigate the effect of such additional processing requirements on analogical problem solving.

EXPERIMENT [III]

In Experiment [III], two 'distractor stories' were given to all subjects along with the Attack-Dispersion story. These stories were intended to be as disanalogous to the radiation problem as possible while being matched for length and maintaining the basic problem-with-solution format.

The critical point in Experiment [III] was that while all subjects were given the radiation problem to solve after having studied the three preliminary problem stories, only half the subjects were given the instruction that 'one of the stories you read will give you a hint for a solution to this problem'.

The results of this experiment were striking. [...] Whereas 92% of the subjects in the Hint condition produced the dispersion solution, only 20% (3 out of 15) of those in the No Hint condition did so. ... Furthermore, 2 of these 3 subjects gave only partial solutions (as defined in Experiment II), and indicated that they did not consider using the stories. It is therefore possible, and in fact rather likely, that only 1 of the 15 subjects spontaneously noticed the critical analogy and successfully applied it to produce the dispersion solution.

EXPERIMENT [IV]

The results of Experiment [III] demonstrated that subjects can identify a relevant story analogy encoded into memory in the context of distractor stories, and can use the analogy to generate a solution to a subsequent target problem. However, when the experimental instructions did not provide a hint that the stories might help to solve the target problem, subjects seldom noticed or used the analogy. This suggests that the process of analogical problem solving is neither automatic nor invariably applied by college students as a conscious strategy. The knowledge acquired in the context of the story recall phase of the experiment seemed to be encapsulated in such a way that its pertinence to the problem-solving task was not recognized.

An important question is whether this type of encapsulation of experience is more or less absolute, or whether there are factors that would make a relevant analogy more likely to be noticed even though it was initially encoded in a recall context. Experiment [IV] modified the design of Experiment [III] in order to examine two such possible factors. First, the total memory load was reduced by eliminating the two distractor stories from the recall phase; and second, in one condition the story analogy was presented *after* subjects had read and begun to work on the radiation problem. The latter condition can be viewed as an experimental analog of a situation in which a person "stumbles upon" relevant information in the course of working on a problem, as is often reported in anecdotes describing the "Eureka" experience of creative thinkers.

Table [13.9] presents the percentage of subjects in each condition who produced the dispersion solution during the various steps of the procedure. There was no evidence that the manipulation of presenting the problem prior to the story analogy (Story Second condition) increased the probability that subjects would notice or use the analogy. In the Story First condition, 41% of the subjects gave the dispersion solution on their first attempt following recall of the story; while in the Story Second condition, 35% of the subjects produced this solution immediately after reading the story. One subject in the Story First condition gave a partial solution; all other solutions were complete. For the Story First condition we cannot clearly separate subjects who used the story to produce the solution from those who may have produced it spontaneously (as did those subjects in the Story Second condition who gave the dispersion solution prior to seeing the story). However, of the seven subjects in the Story First group who gave the dispersion solution immediately after story recall, six reported that they used the story to help solve the problem. If we accept these reports at

TABLE 13.9
Percentage of Subjects in Experiment [IV] Who Produced Dispersion
Solution at Each Step of the Procedure

Condition	Before story	After story (no hint)	After story (with hint)	Never	N
Story First	—	41	35	24	17
Story Second	10	35	30	25	20

face value, it appears that the percentages of subjects in the two conditions who spontaneously noticed and used the analogy were identical (35% in both conditions). The percentages of all subjects who reported that it occurred to them to use the story were also similar across the two conditions (47% in the Story First condition, 40% in the Story Second condition).

GENERAL DISCUSSION

The present study provides an experimental demonstration that a solution to a problem can be developed by using an analogous problem from a very different domain. Our results substantiate anecdotal descriptions of the role that analogical thinking may play in creative problem solving, and at the same time provide some information about the mental processes involved in analogical problem solving. The results of Experiments I and II indicated that there is considerable variation in the degree of mapping required to generate an analogous solution. In particular, the intermediate frequency of dispersion solutions produced in Experiment II by the Parade story, which was only partially analogous to the radiation problem, supports two important conclusions about the mapping process involved in analogical problem solving. First, subjects in the parade condition were much more likely to generate dispersion solutions than were control subjects. Thus it seems that subjects can often generate an analogous solution even though a complete mapping between aspects of the prior story and the target problem is impossible. In such cases it seems that a solution-focusing strategy may be sufficient to produce the parallel solution. Second, the Parade story was not as effective as the more completely analogous Attack story in prompting the dispersion solution. This suggests that subjects can also perform a more detailed mapping between the problem statements of the story and of the target problem, and that these additional correspondences are sometimes critical in determining whether the subject arrives at the analogous solution.

However, the types of correspondences between the two problem statements that are most critical in developing a solution are not entirely clear. Numerous subjects in our experiments commented on the importance of the reference in the story to roads radiating outward "like spokes on a wheel." Intuitively, this phrase seems to elicit a spatial image that represents those essential aspects of the dispersion solution that can be applied to both the military and the medical problems. Even though the stories and the target problem were always presented verbally in our experiments, the problems essentially describe spatial relationships. Our use of a propositional representation to describe the correspondences between the stories and the radiation problem does not preclude the possibility that some form of analog representation plays an important role in the mapping process. For example, the mapping process may in part depend on interpretive procedures that are applied to a mediating spatial image. Further research is needed to explore the role of spatial representation in analogical problem solving.

It is clear that our understanding of the use of analogies in problem solving remains severely limited in many important respects. We certainly need to be cautious in generalizing on the basis of the present study, which used only one target problem and a very limited set of story analogies. While it seems reasonable to expect that comparable results would be obtained with other ill-defined "insight" problems, for which a solution hinges on a small number of critical inferences, this remains to be demonstrated.

It is still less clear whether analogies can be used in a similar fashion to help solve more "computational" problems, for which the solution consists of a series of discrete steps. Reed et al. (1974) were unable to demonstrate positive transfer between two homomorphic "river crossing" problems, except when the correspondences between the arguments of the two problems were described to subjects. In addition, most subjects in the Reed et al. study reported making little or no use of the first problem when solving the second. It is possible that the mapping process required in such multimove problems places excessive demands on memory capacity. [. . .] In addition, it is possible that people are able to use analogies more easily in solving some computational problems than in solving others. For example, Hayes and Simon (1977) have demonstrated positive transfer between isomorphic versions of the Tower of Hanoi puzzle, another computational problem. Clearly much remains to be learned about the influence of problem characteristics on problem solving by analogy. In addition to investigating the effects of problem type, we need to learn more about the ways in which the use of analogies may interact with other strategies (e.g., means–ends analysis) used in problem solving.

Noticing and Accessing Potential Analogies

A number of important questions for future research involve the closely related issues of the spontaneous noticing of analogies, and the accessing of potential analogies stored in memory. The results of Experiments [III] and [IV] suggest that one of the major blocks to successful use of analogy may be failure to spontaneously notice its pertinence to the target problem. When subjects were not told to try to use the prior stories to help solve the radiation problem, only a minority succeeded in generating the analogous solution. This decline in transfer performance cannot be attributed to faulty encoding of the story analogy, since most subjects were able to produce the analogous solution once they were given a hint to apply the story. Also, the problem of spontaneous noticing was not limited to stories previously encoded into memory. In the Story Second condition of Experiment [IV], many subjects failed to notice the relevance of the story even though they had to read, memorize, and recall it *after* beginning to work on the target problem.

[. . .]

Why should subjects so often fail to notice the relevance of a story analogy to a target problem when a hint to use the story is not provided? One might argue that this result is not particularly surprising, since the story was presented in a different experimental context (a story recall experiment). The difficulty of the recall context may be related to the problem of identifying the optimal level of abstraction for representing an analogy, as we discussed in the Introduction. A recall task, with its emphasis on memory for specific wording, may lead the person to represent the story at a level of macrostructure too detailed to maximize its analogical correspondence with the target problem. A hint to use the story may lead the person to derive a more abstract level of macrostructure, better suited for the problem-solving task.

But in any case, the issue of how analogies are noticed is a very general one. A potential analogy may often be encoded in a very different context from that in which the target problem appears. Indeed, the basic problem in using an analogy between remote domains is to connect two bodies of information from disparate semantic contexts. More generally, successful transfer of learning generally involves overcoming contextual barriers. This may not be easy; for example, it is all too common for a student to fail to notice the relevance of knowledge acquired in one class to a problem encountered in another.

The problem of how analogies are noticed is closely related to the issue of how analogies are accessed in memory. Noticing that information in memory is relevant to a target problem is part of the process of retrieving an analogy. These problems were side-stepped in Experiments I–II, since subjects received a hint to use the story analogies and were allowed to reread them at any time. The problem of memory access was greatest in Experiment [III], in which the relevant story analogy was memorized in the context of two irrelevant distractor stories. Subjects in this experiment seemed to have little difficulty in identifying the appropriate story in memory, and applying it to the target problem, as long as they were instructed to do so. However, subjects may have performed this task by simply testing each of the three stories to see if it suggested a solution to the target problem. Such a strategy would presumably be impractical in most everyday problem-solving situations, where virtually any piece of information in memory might potentially afford a useful analogy.

How might potential analogies be accessed in memory? Is the memory search process directed, and if so, how? At one extreme the problem solver may not actually search memory at all; rather, he or she may simply "stumble upon" an analogy. That is, after a piece of knowledge has for some reason become the focus of attention, the person may spontaneously notice its analogous relationship to a problem yet to be solved. It also seems plausible, however, that people may sometimes locate useful analogies in memory on the basis of a conscious search process. It may be possible to use a representation of the current problem as a retrieval cue for accessing analogous problems. Perhaps in some cases the person first begins working on a problem and arrives at an abstract characterization of a potential solution, as we discussed in Experiment I. This solution representation might then be used to retrieve an analogous problem with that type of solution, which could then be used to help generate a more concrete solution to the target problem. The latter possibility is related to the solution-focusing strategy discussed in connection with Experiment I. A better understanding of how analogies are retrieved and noticed is clearly essential in order to effectively teach the use of analogies as a heuristic strategy for problem solving. . . .

The Generality of the Mapping process

The mapping process involved in the use of analogies may play a role in a variety of cognitive skills. Using an analogy involves mapping the representations of two (or perhaps more) instances onto one another. Similar processes may also be involved in *abstracting* the relational structure common to a set of particular instances. In the domain of problem solving, for example, a person who encounters several analogies to the radiation problem might eventually derive a schema for "dispersion-type" problems. This schema would presumably be structured much like a concrete instance of a dispersion problem (cf. Figure [13.1]), except that the predicates and arguments would be more abstract. A person equipped with such a general schema could then solve new dispersion-type problems by mapping them directly onto it. These observations suggest that similar mapping processes may be involved in three distinct but interrelated activities: (1) comparing one instance to another; (2) deriving a schema for a class of instances; and (3) comparing an instance to a general schema.

Note that the above description of the role of mapping potentially applies not just to problem solving, but to a wide range of cognitive skills requiring concept learning and classification of instances. Such skills are involved in tasks that vary a great deal in terms of both complexity and cognitive domain. For example, the mapping of correspondences between relational structures is involved in the use of schemata for story under-standing (Rumelhart, 1975), frames for scene perception (Minsky, 1975), and scripts for understanding of social behavior (Abelson, 1975). Such structures all serve to describe our ability to deal with novel instances of familiar situations. Theories in each domain must explain how abstract structures can be derived from a set of instances, and how instances can be related to each other and to abstract structures.

If similar mapping processes are involved in analogical problem solving and other cognitive skills, then the study of the use of analogies to solve problems has implications that extend to other domains. We mentioned at the beginning of this paper that an analogy may often serve as a model to guide the development of a new theory. In a similar fashion a theory of analogical problem solving might serve as a useful model in developing theories in other areas of cognition.

REFERENCES

Abelson, R. P. (1975) Concepts for representing mundane reality in plans. In D. G. Bobrow & A. Collins (Eds.), *Representation and understanding: Studies in cognitive science*. New York: Academic Press.

Boden, M. (1977) *Artificial intelligence and natural man*. New York: Basic Books.

Duncker, K. (1945) On problem solving. *Psychological Monographs, 58*, (Whole No. 270).

Hayes, J. R., & Simon, H. A. (1977) Psychological differences among problem isomorphs. In N. J. Castellan, Jr., D. B. Pisoni, & G. R. Potts (Eds.), *Cognitive theory*, [*Vol. 2*]. Hillsdale, N.J.: Lawrence Erlbaum Associates.

Kintsch, W., & Van Dijk, T. A. (1978) Toward a model of text comprehension and production. *Psychological Review, 85*, 363–394.

Minsky, M. (1975) A framework for representing knowledge. In P. H. Winston (Ed.), *The psychology of computer vision*. New York: McGraw-Hill.

Reed, S. K., Ernst, G. W., & Bannerji, R. (1974) The role of analogy in transfer between similar problem states. *Cognitive Psychology, 6*, 436–450.

Rumelhart, D. E. (1975) Notes on a schema for stories. In D. G. Bobrow & A. Collins (Eds.), *Representation and understanding: Studies in cognitive science*. New York: Academic Press.

Schank, R., & Abelson, R. P. (1977) *Scripts, plans, goals, and understanding*. Hillsdale, N.J.: Lawrence Erlbaum Associates.

Sternberg, R. J. (1977a) *Intelligence, information processing and analogical reasoning: The componential analysis of human abilities*. Hillsdale, N.J.: Lawrence Erlbaum Associates.

Sternberg, R. J. (1977b) Component processes in analogical reasoning. *Psychological Review, 84*, 353–378.

VII CONCLUSION

14

Twelve Issues for Cognitive Science

Donald A. Norman

HUMAN INFORMATION PROCESSING: THE CONVENTIONAL VIEW

When I first began the study of psychology, I was interested in mechanisms. The task seemed straightforward enough—difficult, yes, but well defined. The human is an animate being, functioning in the environment. The human has certain biological facets, physical facets, intellectual facets. The basic conceptualization went like this: Intellectual processes are the result of the operation of several separable systems; sensory-perceptual systems, central processing (thought), memory, and response output (motor control). Sensory transducers feed a steady stream of information about the environment to some central processing structures where that information is analyzed, interpreted and fed to a response system which controls body movements and speech sounds.

Considerations of this sort led to the view—the reasonably well accepted view in psychology—of the human as composed of separable subsystems of information processing mechanisms: perceptual systems (including pattern recognition), motor or output systems, memory systems, and systems for internal reasoning and deduction, which includes thought, problem solving, and language. A summary of the components and a rough sketch of their interactions is shown in [Fig. 14.1], which might be considered to be a modern updating of the conventional flow chart of the human information processing system. The figure summarizes what is known today about the "Pure Cognitive System," the system built around pure cognitive functioning, with a physical symbol system as its central component.

Different workers might put more weight on one aspect of this system than on another, but on the whole, this has come to be a fairly well accepted view of things. I will not review for you the history of this and other approaches to the study of the human information processing system, but I will discuss some aspects of it. Basically, I believe that although this view is accurate, it is but one of many posssible views. Taken alone, this view is both inadequate and misleading.

In recent years I have become more and more dissatisfied with the conventional view of information processing. The source of the dissatisfaction was not obvious: each of the components of [Fig. 14.1] seemed reasonable, and although one might (and did) argue about the details, the powerful arguments for physical symbol systems seemed persuasive. The problem seemed to be in the lack of consideration of other aspects of human behavior, of interaction with other people and with the environment, of the influence of the history of the person, or even the culture, and of the lack of consideration of the special problems and issues confronting an animate organism that must survive as both an individual and as a species, so that intellectual functioning might perhaps be placed in a proper perspective. These considerations have accumulated until they finally have forced themselves upon me. The human is a physical symbol system, yes, with a component of pure cognition describable by mechanisms of the sort illustrated in Fig. 14.1. But the human is more: The human is an animate organism, with a biological basis and an evolutionary and cultural history. Moreover, the human is a social animal, interacting with others, with the environment, and with itself. The core disciplines of cognitive science have tended to ignore these aspects of behavior. The results have been considerable progress on some fronts, but sterility overall, for the organism we are analyzing is conceived as pure intellect, communicating with one another in logical dialogue, perceiving, remembering, thinking where appropriate, reasoning its way through the well-formed problems that are encountered in the day. Alas, that description does not fit actual behavior.

[. . .] Let me illustrate [the approach I will be taking] by several examples. One is a brief description of an airplane accident, another the view of classroom behavior. These two examples are followed by some general discussion of human functioning and then by a re-evaluation of the role of pure cognition. I conclude that there is more to human intelligence than the pure cognitive system, and that a science of Cognition cannot afford to ignore these other aspects.

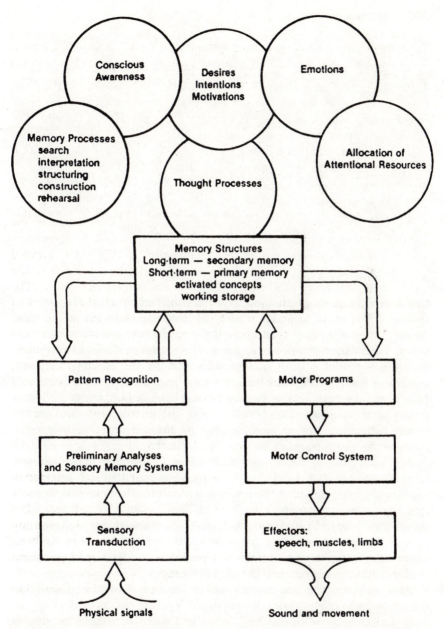

FIG. 14.1. A modern version of the conventional flow chart of the human information processing system. The basic components are a series of processing mechanisms that take in information about the environment, perform general central processing operations, and control motor output. The central processing is complex, with various sources of knowledge interacting with one another, controlled by an as-yet little understood processing structure which allows for some simultaneous operation, self awareness, consciousness of some of the processes. The stuff in the central part of the figure is sufficiently vague as to allow for a large number of interpretations of its nature.

Tenerife

In March of 1977, two Boeing 747 airliners collided on a runway at Tenerife, in the Canary Islands. The crash killed 582 people. What caused the accident? No single factor. The crash resulted from a complex interaction of events, including problems of attentional focus, the effects of expectation upon language understanding that combined with an inability to communicate effectively over a technically limited communication channel when there were major difficulties in language (although all involved were speaking English), the subtle effects of differences of social structure among the participants, the effects of stress, economic responsibilities and social and cultural factors upon decision making. All in all, it is a fascinating—if horrifying—story for Cognitive Science.

A view of the Classroom

Consider the classroom situation, especially the early grades of school. The teacher has a point to make, a body of information to get across. This aspect of teaching has been receiving considerable attention in recent years. The teacher must construct a mental model of student knowledge, match the model of the student with that of the desired endpoint, determine some strategy for presenting the information not yet currently held by the students, and go forth and teach. [Figure 14.2] shows a possible model of the teacher. Don't worry about the details, just think of the model as an attempt to summarize how the teacher determines the appropriate way to transmit the topic matter to the class.

The individual students must themselves be represented by models similar to that of [Fig. 14.2] except complementary in that they respond to the new information about the topic matter and construct mental memory structures to accommodate them. Each student has some knowledge and as the student interacts with the teacher, the student knowledge is altered and enriched in appropriate ways. If questioned by the teacher, the student can apply the new knowledge in order to answer the query, thereby providing feedback to the teacher about the state of learning.

Alas, anyone who has actually taught in a classroom (especially an elementary school classroom) knows that this description provides only the most idealistic view of the real behavior. Some of the description is appropriate, but there is much more happening. In some classrooms, it would be difficult to find any evidence that teaching—in the sense just described—was ever taking place. The students are in a social setting, interacting with one another, acutely aware of each other and of the overall classroom behavior. Individual students tailor their behavior for the other students to some degree, sometimes entirely for the other students. The

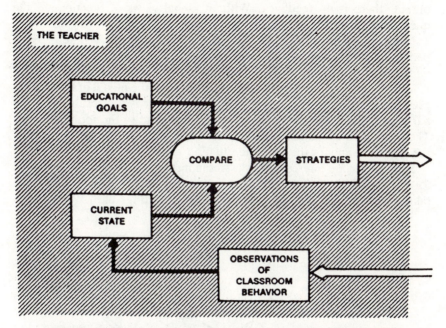

FIG. 14.2   An information processing model of the teacher. Starting with educational goals, the teacher compares those goals with the current state of classroom behavior and knowledge and uses an instructional strategy appropriate to the situation. The teacher continually monitors classroom behavior and modifies the instructional strategy, or the knowledge being taught accordingly. This is a feedback model of instruction. The "current state" implies, among other things, a model of student knowledge and behavior. This model of a teacher is common to modern instructional theory (including my own). It is probably necessary, but by itself, it fails to be useful in the prediction of classroom behavior.

behavior of the teacher and the individual students is responsive to the events of the classroom, but the classroom events are the results of the combination of behaviors of the teachers and the students.

Cybernetics and Behavior.   Cybernetics. A term connotating engineering models of servomechanism systems, the sort of systems one would expect for motor control, or for homeostatic body functioning. Why do I introduce it here?

I use the term "cybernetics" to mean a feedback system, one in which the operation of the system depends upon interaction with the environment. This is what Norbert Weiner meant when he coined the term. The concept has been lost from most of cognitive studies, in part because of the lack of study of output and of performance (more on this later). Without output, there is no feedback. Without global views of functioning, the question of the role of feedback does not arise.

Much social interaction can be viewed as a cybernetic system. Each person is responsive to the environment. Each person is a human information processing system, consisting of something like the components of [Fig. 14.1], each behaving something like the model of the teacher presented in [Fig. 14.2]. But the overall behavior is the result of all the participants, and the participants, in turn, respond to the total behavior. The overall view is something like [Fig. 14.3]—a view that works for both the classroom and for the Tenerife situation as well.

Suppose we are interested in classroom instruction. In this case we need to understand classroom interaction, the classroom behavior. We must take a view that is something like that shown in [Fig. 14.3]. We need to

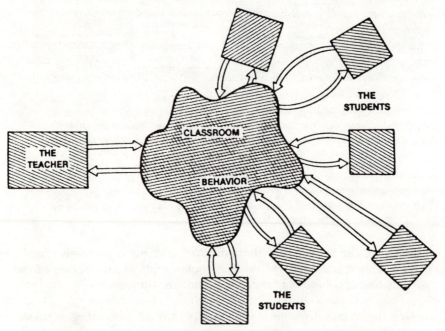

FIG. 14.3. The classroom behavior is the result of a combination of interactions. Each student responds to the behavior of the classroom, as well as to the internal goals of satisfying other students, the teacher, and self needs. So too with the teacher. The teacher and students are all modeled by something akin to [Fig. 14.2], but understanding of their behavior requires understanding of the entire interaction. The classroom is a system of individual cybernetic actors. (This basic picture of interaction applies to a variety of situations in addition to the classroom. Only the labels need be changed.)

understand the several different interactive themes that are simultaneously active within the classroom: the social interactions among the students, the sociolinguistics of their language use, the status differences among the students and between students and teacher. These all color the use of language and participation. Even the seating pattern and room arrangement will turn out to matter.

Obviously one also needs to know of the motives that drive the teacher, the lesson that is to be taught, the time constraints that must be obeyed, the kind of classroom interaction the teacher desires, and the kind that the teacher will tolerate.

Now, if one wishes to understand the particular responses of the teacher or of an individual child to a particular classroom event, then it is going to be necessary to have an information processing view of the person, somewhat of the form of [Fig. 14.2]. But the model is only going to be useful if it is coupled with an understanding of the several simultaneous (and possibly conflicting) goals and motivations of the various participants.

My point is not an indictment of any particular approach to the study of learning and teaching. On the contrary, it is a statement that all approaches are necessary. The information processing psychologist who studies the transfer of knowledge from teacher to student is contributing some understanding of the classroom situation. The person who studies the sociological influences upon the students' behavior and their tolerance to classroom discipline is also contributing some understanding, of an entirely different kind. My argument is that the situation is not going to be understood until all these different points of view are combined, for the overall classroom behavior is a result of all these forces, no one more fundamental than another.

How Much Does Cognitive Science Know?

I am struck by how little is known about so much of cognition. The crash at Tenerife and the interactions of the classroom are but two examples of the complex interactions of cognitive factors that can play important roles in our lives. But there are much simpler examples.

Memory. I have studied memory for years, yet am unable to answer even simple questions about the use of memory in everyday life. Mental activity; the study of thought processes has concentrated upon logical, systematic behavior, one step at a time. What about the processing deeply buried within the subconscious where it can go on without awareness for hours, days (months?).

Slips, Freudian and otherwise.   People make slips of the tongue, slips of action. Some are undoubtedly easy to explain: confusions, lack of knowledge, or obvious sources of the error. But others require much more subtle analyses, involving the nature of memory and retrieval, activation and stress, or conflicting simultaneous thoughts. Freud had a theory, one that I suspect is much more appropriate than Cognitive Scientists tend to give credit today. At least Freud did worry about the relationships among emotions, conscious and subconscious events (we would say "processing"), and how the subconscious is manifested in behavior.

Performance.   Consider the highly skilled typist, producing over 100 words per minute, about 10 keystrokes per second. Or the professional pianist playing 25 notes per second in a Chopin Nocturne. Motor skills are fascinating aspects of our behavior, little understood, little studied (in comparison with, say, language). How does one hit a baseball that is travelling at great speed, or steer a speeding automobile through narrow spaces, or control a large crane, making precise movements at the end of a boom a hundred meters long with controls that seem to have little relevance to the actions being performed?

Language.   If you think we understand language, well, how about real language, the language between two people in casual conversation? By the rules of formal language, such language is often ungrammatical and it should be unintelligible. Indeed, as an inveterate eavesdropper on the conversations of strangers (in the name of Science, of course), I can attest that one-minute fragments of other people's conversations are unintelligible and remarkably free of content. The conversants would not agree. They have established sufficient bonds that they can relax the normal constraints of language. Gesture, timing, intonation can carry as much weight as the formal content of the words. This observation is not meant to be a surprise: We are all aware of the phenomenon. But not as scientists: we do not understand how.

You will not be surprised if I tell you that we understand little of the interactions of social groups, or of society, or of cultures, especially of the mechanisms of that interaction. You might be surprised if I claim that these factors play a large role in everyday behavior, even in performance on our abstract tasks within the laboratory. Perhaps one reason that our theories of the separable components of information processing say so little about real world activities is the neglect of social and cultural factors, among other things.

One goal of this paper is to convince you that the study of cognition requires the consideration of all these different aspects of the entire system, including the parts that are both internal and external to the cognizer. (By "internal," I mean the knowledge, the processing mechanisms, the rules, strategies, and control mechanisms. By "external" I mean the environment, the society, culture, and the interaction of all these with one another.) Of course no one can study everything all at the same time, but I argue that we cannot ignore these things either, else the individual pieces that we study in such detail will not fit together in the absence of some thought about the whole.

ON THE DIFFERENCES BETWEEN ANIMATE AND ARTIFICIAL COGNITIVE SYSTEMS

Intelligence, thought, cognition—these are central topics in the study of Cognitive Science. So let us start by considering the elements of a cognitive system. Suppose we concentrate on the intellectual functioning—what are the essential elements of a cognitive system? Let me go through the arguments of the necessary components, starting with a reasonably traditional view (I will end quite differently). The basic picture of the human information processing structure, in its modern format, has been presented as [Fig. 14.1].

Now consider, if you will, an intelligent artificial system, one that might be the goal of your favorite robotologist. What does an artificial system need? Obviously there are several possible answers. If we consider only the *Pure Cognitive System* (henceforth, PCS), then we see obvious differences in structure between natural and artificial systems, between electronics and biology. Nerve cells convey their signals through electrical potentials, by chemical transmission. They are affected by biological chemicals (hormones, nutritive fluids, transmitter substances). And natural systems have wiring diagrams that are not yet understood, that seem to be adaptive, that have billions of interconnections. But despite the obvious differences, there are no obvious differences at the level of functional mechanisms. Presumably, the biological system has memory structures, perceptual structures, and so on, and in principle, if we wish to and knew enough we could build artificial systems whose operations mimicked the biological ones. We would need to learn a considerable amount more than we currently know about the functioning of such a system, but the "in principle" point is what is critical for those of us who pursue the study of psychological mechanisms.

But wait. The difference between natural and artificial devices is not simply that they are constructed of different stuff; their basic functions differ. Humans survive, get nourishment from the environment, protect themselves against physical insult, form families and societies, reproduce

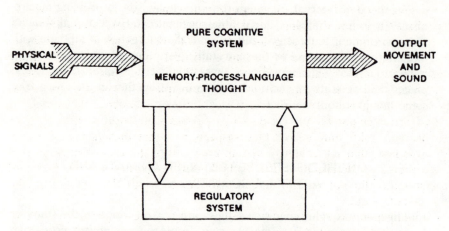

FIG. 14.4.   To the Pure Cognitive System of [Fig. 14.1] we must add the
properties of the Regulatory System. In this view of things, the Cognitive
System dominates. This view is an obvious one, but probably wrong.

themselves and protect and educate the young. Much of this is handled
with the aid of biological structures that I will call the *Regulatory System*
(RS). Consider how the RS interacts with the cognitive system—something like [Fig. 14.4] emerges.

Consider the implications of [Fig. 14.4]. (Yes, even such a simple
diagram does have implications.) Dangerous situations require immediate
attention, immediate response. If potential danger is to be discovered
quickly, there must be continual monitoring of possible sources of
evidence. Moreover, when danger is detected, then the organism must be
alerted to the problem and it must allocate sufficient resources to deal with
it. It is easy to understand how this might be done when dealing with things
like changes in body states, such as temperature, blood sugar level or
fatigue. Environmental situations that lead to pain or otherwise send
sensory signals that can be monitored are also easy to understand with the
framework shown in [Fig. 14.4].

The issues are not so simple when we consider how to respond to events
that must be interpreted: dangerous heights, the sight of a wild tiger, fire,
the sound of an explosion, or the airline pilot's announcement that two
engines have failed. For these events, perception, knowledge, and language must be called into play—essentially, all the mechanisms of the Pure
Cognitive System. But these interpretations must operate with immediacy,
interrupting whatever primary task was going on. The problem here is that
it takes the cognitive system to do the interpretation for the maintenance
system, thereby allowing the maintenance system to interrupt the cognitive
system. It can't work.

We need to rethink the organization implied in [Fig. 14.4]. Maybe the PCS is not the pinnacle of human functioning. It is comforting to think so, that the focal point is PCS, with the RS serving to maintain both the body and the PCS. This egotistical point of view is especially nice for intellectuals, but it doesn't hold up. It is always dangerous to invent and then to rely on biological principles and evolutionary causation, but it is also useful. Did the evolutionary sequence that produced superior cognitive systems do so to permit professors to exist, to publish, to hold conferences? One suspects not, that the regulatory system was first, that the cognitive system grew out of the requirements of that system. To determine that a limb should be withdrawn from a painful stimulus did not require much cognition: to avoid the situation in the first place did.

The point is simply that the functions and the requirements of animate systems include the problem of survival, and that this problem requires a regulatory system of considerable complexity, one in which considerable cognitive power is required. And so, the cognitive system is apt to be the servant of the regulatory system, not the other way around, as shown in [Fig. 14.5]. Emotional systems might very well be an interplay between the two, so that perceptual analysis (done by the PCS) might at times cause the RS to create the necessary emotional arousal to alert the PCS.

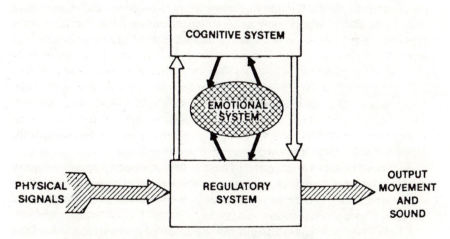

FIG. 14.5. The Regulatory System is here given primacy over the Pure Cognitive System. Compare with [Fig. 14.4]: the basic format is the same, except that sensory inputs and motor outputs now leave and enter RS rather than PCS. An emotional system stands between. And the relative sizes of the boxes that symbolize the systems have been changed to mark the change in emphasis.

If the RS dominates, with the cognitive system its servant, interesting implications follow. Perhaps PCS is a myth, with intellectual thought an outgrowth of the use of biological function for purposes somewhat foreign to the original need. Cognitive systems might be the result of the generally increasing demands of the regulatory system for an intelligent component. Perhaps when the cognitive side reached some critical mass, it then possessed sufficient computational power to have its own existence and to establish its own goals and functions. But only afterwards, grafted on, if you will, to the functions of supporting one's own life.

What about emotions? Are they superfluous to cognitive functioning? Most of us—and I include myself in the "us"—would prefer to believe this. Contemporary theories of cognitive functioning—no matter the discipline—seem to be theories of pure reason. Emotions have to do with something else, perhaps an evolutionary carry over from an earlier time when the demands upon human functioning were different. Well, the novelist, the playwright, the clinical psychologist and psychiatrist know differently. If I am correct in my assertion that the cognitive system is subservient to the regulatory system, with pure cognition an artificial situation grafted on to a biological organism, then emotions play a critical role in behavior.

A summary of these arguments about the nature of cognitive systems in general and of animate cognitive systems in particular is presented in [Table 14.1]. I believe that we should reconsider the functioning of human processing. Some things will not change: our observations and theories will still apply. But I suspect some aspects will change in fundamental ways. I cannot now tell you what will change and what will not: we must wait and see.

SOME ISSUES FOR COGNITIVE SCIENCE

The arguments of the preceding pages suggest that we must broaden the issues considered by the discipline of Cognitive Science. In fact, twelve major issues attract my attention. These twelve are neither independent of one another nor equal in importance. I do claim, however, that these twelve are among a core group of issues along which we must progress if our field is to make substantive advances.

I believe in the value of multiple philosophies, multiple viewpoints, multiple approaches to common issues. I believe a virtue of Cognitive Science is that it brings together heretofore disparate disciplines to work on common themes. My reason for discussing these twelve issues is the hope that I can focus some efforts upon them. I introduce and discuss these issues from my own perspective, which is primarily that of a

TABLE 14.1
Essential Elements of Cognitive Systems: In General, and in Animate Organisms

All Cognitive Systems

All cognitive systems, animate and artificial, must have the following:
A way of receiving information about the world: receptors
A way of performing actions upon the world: motor control
Cognitive processes, which include:
a means of interpreting and identifying information received by the receptors
a means of controlling the actions to be performed
a means of guiding the allocation of cognitive resources when more needs to be done than can immediately be done (this can be derived from the fact that a finite system must have finite resources)
a memory for the history of actions and experiences
These cognitive processes imply that:
because resources are finite, there will be times when more is being attempted than can be accomplished; some means of resource allocation (attention) will be required
because there will be synchronization problems with events in the environment and internal events, buffer (short-term) memories are required
There must be basic operations, an interpreter, and some feedback mechanisms that can observe the effect of operations upon the world and change accordingly
There must be some way to devise plans and then to monitor their operation; this requires levels of knowledge—meta-knowledge
For intelligent interaction, there must be a model of the environment, of one's self, and of others
There must be learning, changing one's behavior and knowledge in fundamental ways (as opposed to simple adaptation), and this will probably require a system capable of inferring causality, inter-relations among concepts and events, and self-observation

Animate Systems

A major difference between animate and inanimate systems is that an animate system maintains itself, protects itself, regulates its own operation, and reproduces itself. A newly born organism requires considerable physical, biological, and educational maturation, which takes place through a protracted time course of infancy, childhood, and adulthood. The organism at birth differs from adulthood;
It is smaller, both physically and in the amount of its cognitive (neural) structure;
It has less knowledge;
Its regulatory system is not fully developed.
An animate system must survive, which means it must be alert for unexpected occurrences: its regulatory and cognitive systems must interact. The regulatory system is a homeostatic system, designed to maintain life. It must interact with the cognitive system, for interpretations are required of the situation and actions are required to maintain homeostasis, comfort, and safety.
An animate system has goals, desires, purposes. The system is motivated to perform some activities. There must be a means of selecting "interesting" and goal-related tasks from among those that could possibly be done, controlling the amount of effort devoted to that task, and scheduling the initiation and termination of the various activities. Long term goals and issues related to survival receive dominance, although the mechanisms for accomplishing these may not be part of the self-awareness of the organism.

psychologist interested in the workings of the mind. I treat the twelve briefly. My intention is to raise them, not discuss them in detail: that is done elsewhere. Alternative points of view are possible, welcome, and necessary.

Issues Are Not Levels

The issues are topic matters that are to be studied. They are not the names of disciplines nor prescriptions for methods of study. Each issue should be addressed from different directions, yielding different levels of explanation.

When we come to describe the mechanisms of cognition, the explanations should be couched at several different levels. The psychologist talks of functional mechanisms and of behavior, the neuroscientist talks of cells and neural systems. The anthropologist and the sociologist each have their levels of analysis. Linguists, philosophers, and computer scientists each view cognition from their special perspectives, each different, yet complementary. I believe that the complete science must have all of these different levels represented. We need to know about the neurological and biological basis for animate cognitive systems, about the mathematical and philosophical basis for cognitive systems, about the mechanistic basis for artificial systems. But that is not the point of this paper. The issues I discuss are not statements about the philosophy or level of approach. Rather they are issues, or problem areas, that should be considered.

The Twelve Issues

I give you the following issues:

Belief systems	Emotion	Learning	Performance
Consciousness	Interaction	Memory	Skill
Development	Language	Perception	Thought

"What a strange list," you must be thinking. Not what you expected. Emotion? Skill? On the same level as language and memory? Aren't learning and memory and skill and performance all the same, or at least highly related? What about motivation, or representation, or whatever your favorite topic? Wait, I will clarify some of the problems (though not all). Remember, these 12 issues are ones that I see as key to the development of a science of cognition. Not all are recognized by everyone as being relevant. Not all are thought to be important. Some are well studied, but not normally thought to be a part of cognition. Some issues are seen as simply subsets of others. I disagree: all are essential.

A BRIEF TOUR OF THE TWELVE ISSUES

Belief Systems

I start with Belief Systems, accidentally the first in my alphabetized list of issues, but deserving of primacy under other criteria as well. For belief systems mark the merger of the traditional domain of cognitive science—the study of knowledge—with the domains of those who study real world interaction of humans—the anthropologists, the social psychologists and the sociologists. This issue could perhaps more easily be called "knowledge," or perhaps, "world knowledge." I do not use these labels in order to emphasize the merger of several different classes of knowledge, including culture, belief, and world knowledge of several sorts. The basic concept here is that we acquire a lot of knowledge over our lifetime which then colors our interactions with others, with the environment, and even our internal processing. A major component of anthropology and sociology is concerned with the examination of these belief structures.

Cultural knowledge is that special subset of general knowledge that is passed on from generation to generation, taught in the family, or in the schools, or (more commonly) not so much taught as experienced. Styles of dress, social interaction, rankings of social groups, interaction patterns including conversational (discourse) rules, social deference, and other patterns are included here. The physical shape of the environment is altered through culture. The style of buildings, paths, transportation—our technology.

The belief systems go beyond obvious cultural interactions, however. They carry over to such things as rules for memory and thought. You will come to believe these statements more the more you believe that thought and memory are done through reference to real world experience. Suppose that logical inference is normally done by setting up a mental model of a concrete analogy to the problem, using experience to guide the solution of that concrete analogy, then interpreting the result for the problem at hand. If this is the case, then belief systems are of critical importance in determining the basis for much of thought.

Similar statements can be made about memory, perception, problem solving, the interpretation of texts and the conduct of dialogues, legal negotiations, and so on, and on, and on. Many of you are familiar with delusional belief systems that result from mental abnormalities (paranoia being the most fashionable to discuss, for it seems most directly tied to the development of a rich, delusional system, self consistent in its own way, but a great danger to the possessor).

So, belief systems are important, both as interesting items of study in their own right but also as important determiners of much of the rest of cognitive behavior. At the moment, the tools for formal analysis of such structures are just being developed. There is much talk among cognitive anthropologists and sociologists of scripts and schemas, of story grammars, and representational issues. I have an obvious interest in this direction of work, having myself urged the importance of the study of representation and the utility of the study of structured memory units (schemas). The major issue, though, is not yet the one of representation. Rather, we must first lay out the development of the problem itself, examine the nature of belief systems in general, and determine what the implications are for cognitive behavior. My brief excursions into this area have left me impressed with how much my own hidden belief structures influence my "pure" logical inference, memory processes, and social interactions. I suspect that we will find that more of our behavior is thus determined, not less.

Consciousness

"Everyone knows what attention is." So said William James in 1890, and so too have I said repeatedly in my courses and lectures on attention. But the statement is false, quite false. We really do not know about attention, to a large extent because we do not know about consciousness. Studies of attention have restricted themselves to a small segment of the phenomena of which James wrote:

> It is the taking possession of the mind, in clear and vivid form, of one out of what seems several simultaneously possible objects or trains of thought. Focalization, concentration, of consciousness are of its essence. It implies withdrawal from some things in order to deal effectively with others (James, 1890, Vol. I., p. 403–404).

Consciousness, under which I include the issues of conscious and subconscious thought, the problem of self awareness, attention, the control structures of cognition, the formation of intentions. Here too are such issues as the phenomenological states of awareness, states of consciousness. Hypnosis: a powerful force, potentially a powerful tool for the investigation of consciousness, but little understood, not sufficiently well explored.

It should not be necessary to talk about consciousness to a group concerned with cognition. But consciousness is a peculiar stepchild of our discipline, agreed to be important, but little explored in research or theory. There are legitimate reasons for the relative neglect. This is a most difficult topic, one for which it is very difficult to get the hard, sensible evidence that experimental disciplines require. We have little idea of the real nature of consciousness, of the functions it might serve, of the nature of the subconscious. We are just beginning to get a glimmer of the phenomenology of consciousness, of different states of awareness and different phenomenological experiences (though most of this comes from nontraditional sources).

It is exactly the description given in the quote from James that we do not understand, cannot understand until we come to a better appreciation of the working of the mind, of the several simultaneous trains of thought that can occur, of the differences between conscious and subconscious processing, and of what it means to focus upon one train of thought to the exclusion of others. What—who—does the focussing, what happens to those other trains of thought as they are excluded? (Some, I am certain continue silently, unheeded, as subconscious processes that may later interrupt to again force conscious attention to themselves.) And what does it mean to have *conscious attention*? Can there be attention that is not conscious? What—who—experiences the result of conscious attentional processes?

Some of these issues seem to result directly from the properties of an animate cognitive organism. An animate organism can not afford the luxury of concentrating entirely upon a problem until it has been completed. Animate organisms must be multiple-minded, data-driven by environmental events, ever ready to capitalize on the accidents of the world, or to avoid the unexpected dangerous spots. The tasks we assign ourselves to do are often long and complex ones, things which we are incapable of completing at one sitting. We have finite cognitive resources and these must be deployed in some manner that is effective. We can't be entirely data-driven, else the steady flow of information from the sensory system would completely occupy our attention: we must be able to exclude the excludable, to concentrate upon that which is most important (or interesting) at the moment. Subconscious processing [also] seems essential to functioning. Whatever the special properties of consciousness, they are not needed by all mental processes. [. . .]

Glimpses into the role of conscious and subconscious processing can come from several sources. Hypnotic experiences offer one method, and they can be performed with some rigor in the experimental laboratory. Experiences of subconcious problem solving or memory retrieval are often experienced and talked about, and there is some possibility that they too can be explored experimentally. Studies of attention are, of course, another possible route, one that has been under active exploration. And there are the errors that people make, slips of the tongue, slips of action, another source of information about subconscious processes and their relationship to conscious ones, to thoughts and motives and intentions. Experiential literature is relevant too, although it must be approached with caution, separating out the description of the experience from the interpretation of that experience, something the experiencer may not be able to do as well as an external observer.

Development

A child is not a small-sized adult, simply lacking in experience, in physical development, and in knowledge, waiting for its head to be filled with the mindstuff of an adult. As adults, we have a wide range of skills, enormous amounts of detailed, specialized knowledge, well established belief systems. We are not just more than children, we are different.

The study of development is well established, of course, hardly in need of suggestions or advice. [. . .] But in the study of adult cognition there seems to be the implicit assumption that once we come to understand adults, children will simply be seen to be at various stages along the pathway towards the adult. Perhaps. But perhaps also that the complexity and experience of the adult will forever mask some properties. Automatic behavior masks the underlying structure, pushing things beneath the conscious surface to the inaccessibility of subconscious processes. Well established belief and knowledge systems mask their content.

Much of cognitive behavior could be studied best through the developmental cycle, with the history of the development leading to better understanding of the adult. Animate organisms take very long times to reach adulthood: the human is learning new concepts throughout the entire life span. Language learning goes on through the late teenage years, and vocabulary learning never ceases. We are fundamentally organisms that learn, that develop over time. By ignoring this aspect of behavior and concentrating on the static phases we may miss the keys to understanding.

Emotion

And what is the role of emotion in the study of cognition? We leave it to the poet, the playwright, the novelist. As people, we delight in art and in music. We fight, get angered, have joy, grief, happiness. But as students of mental events, we are ignorant of why, how.

Emotion. Is it a leftover of a primitive alerting system, or is it a sophisticated set of states reaching its highest pinnacle in the human? Earlier I argued in the direction of the latter point of view. Now, I simply remind you of the issue. The study of emotion is an important field, with important findings and implications for the study of cognition. We cannot ignore our biological heritage, ignore our emotional states. Geschwind (1980) ... [has emphasised] the fundamental role that emotion plays in biological organisms, and of the close relationship between the neurological structures thought to be important for emotion and those thought to be important for memory. Indeed, there is some experimental evidence for state-induced memory retrieval, so that we remember best events whose emotional content matches our current state: sad events are best remembered while sad, happy ones while happy. Geschwind suggested that some neurological control structures have dual activations, one from below— from the emotions, [and] one from above—the intellect. We smile, cry, and laugh from emotional signals: our attempt to mimic these acts from intellectual desires or upon receipt of a verbal command to do so recreates neither the true emotion, nor the same motor actions. An observer can often tell which behavior is real, which synthetic.

Interaction

Human beings are social organisms. Our intelligence does not operate in isolation, but rather in conjunction. We interact with others, we transmit knowledge through cultures.

We supplement our intelligence with social interaction, by our use of the environment, through the construction of artifacts: reading and writing ...; machine transportation; communication methods that operate over distance (signalling devices, mail services, telegraph, phone, vision); machines for commerce, for other essentials of life; and machines for computation. The interactions that result become a fundamental aspect of our behavior. In some sense our intelligence has become partially externalized, contained in the artifacts as much as in our head. ("I don't need to know that," we say, "I just need to know ..."—choose one: "who to ask," "where to look," "where to go to find out," "that it is known,")

My major concern here is social interactions, but the issues of interaction share properties, whether it be with person, society, machine. We need to have mental models of the people (and things) with which we interact, for communication depends strongly upon mutual use of shared knowledge, shared understandings. Without a good model of the digital-chronograph-stopwatch-calendar-timer-watch, remembering which buttons to push for what is a hopeless task. With a good mental model ("good" does not mean the "true" model, just a consistent one), the buttons make sense and the use is facilitated. Without a good mental model of our conversational partners, the conversation does not make progress. "Where is the empire state building?" the answer depends upon why the question was asked, in what part of the world it was asked, and how much the questioner needs to know.

Much of the study of cognitive processes has been the study of the isolated person. Much of the study of interactive groups has been of the dynamics of the situation, or of the behavioral aspects of the group. To my knowledge, little has been done to combine these efforts, to examine the individual cognitive processes as they are used within interactive settings. But, because the normal mode for the human is to interact, the studies of memory and language and problem solving and decision making in isolation address only one part of the mechanisms of human cognition.

[...]

Language and Perception

I include these two issues to remind us that they exist, to dispel any illusion that I have forgotten them. But I do not wish to discuss either language or perception, primarily because they are of such central importance that they have already received sufficient emphasis. Actually, the emphasis is itself a problem. There is a tendency to identify the study of Cognitive Science with the study of these two topics (and within perception, with visual perception). I believe this to be mistaken, a view that is both wrong and unfortunate. Even language and perception themselves are complex topics, with many different aspects of cognition interwoven together. Like all of the issues within Cognitive Science, these different aspects support one another, enriching the performance of one domain through the knowledge and characteristics of the other domains. I do not believe we can solve the problems of interpretation of language and of perception until we have made substantive progress on the other 10 issues of Cognitive Science.

Learning

Learning. Recognized by many as a key issue. Still eluding us. In the early days of psychology and in the construction of artificial devices for intelligent behavior, learning was the core topic of study. Machines were constructed that were to learn through their interactions, perhaps to acquire broad, general intelligence as a result. Psychologists developed global theories of human and animal behavior, often built around such fundamental learning principles as "the law of effect" or "associative properties of learning and memory." It all has come to nought. Today, the study of learning is not considered a central part of either psychology or artificial intelligence. Why? Perhaps because the understanding of learning requires knowing about problems of representation, of input (perception), of output (performance), and of thought and inference. It is only recently that we began to understand these issues with appropriate depth.

We spend much of our lifetimes learning: in a sense, we learn from everything we do. If learning is not yet understood, it is because there is more to it than the simple accumulation of knowledge. Accumulation is indeed one form of learning, but there are other things that must be done. One fundamental mode of learning is that of restructuring one's knowledge, reformulating the very basis of understanding of some topic as a result of new concepts and new experiences. Then there is the tuning of behavior, the fine sharpening of adequate skills and understanding to that of the expert, smooth, efficient, effortless.

There has been remarkably little study of learning—real learning, the learning of complex topics, the learning that takes months, even years to accomplish. . . . I have estimated that experts at a task may spend 5,000 hours acquiring their skills: that is not such a long time; it is $2\frac{1}{2}$ years of full-time study, 40 hours a week, 50 weeks a year. Not much time to become a professional tennis player, or computer programmer, or linguist. What goes on during that time? Whatever it is, it is slow, continuous. No magic dose of knowledge in the form of pill or lecture. Just a lot of slow, continual exposure to the topic, probably accompanied by several bouts of restructuring of the underlying mental representations, reconceptualizations of the concepts, plus many hours of accumulation of large quantities of facts.

The relative importance of learning is well understood and often stated. We know how important learning is for the child, and how important the developmental sequence from child to adult. Most of us are professional educators. Surprise, then, that so little is known about learning (and so little about the complement, teaching). And in this case, the lack is, in part, from lack of trying. People talk fondly of computer programs that will start with some fundamentals and acquire all the knowledge needed by some natural sequence of learning, experiencing the environment in which it must function. Very little effort gets spent at studying what it would take to accomplish this, perhaps because there is implicit realization that the task is harder than it might seem. Perhaps the sober realization that a newborn infant takes 25 years to become a fledgling professional, perhaps 5,000 hours of practice and training after the fundamentals have been acquired. Who wants a computer program that can't perform well for the first 25 years of fulltime running. . . . And so the study and understanding of the learning process remains at a miniscule level. Pity.

Memory

Do not be impressed by all that is presumably known about the psychology of memory. Less is known than you might think.

Research on the properties of memory has several important functions, some obvious, some not so obvious. For one, it must be obvious that human memory is central to human cognition, and that in general, memory systems are central to cognitive systems (that PCS again). But the complexities of retrieval from a very large memory store are not well appreciated. In Computer Science, the real difficulties of memory retrieval have not yet been faced.

How does one find the information required to answer a question when the form of the question was not anticipated at the time of acquiring the information? Not possible with artificial systems today, a commonplace occurrence with people. And how is the desired information recognized once it is found if it wasn't known in the first place? If I seek the name of a long-lost colleague and retrieve the name Isaac Newton, how do I reject that as the name I seek when I do not know the sought-for name? This example provides its own clue to the solution, but the general case is not so simple. How do we remember stories, events, experiences? More to the point, how do we retrieve them when least we expect them?

Memory has some other puzzles. We recognize the meanings of words in tenths of seconds (as in reading), yet may take hours or days to retrieve one of those words when we seek it for use in a sentence. And what is it that keeps the memory search going for those hours or days, while conscious thought proceeds in other directions, when the need for the word may have long passed? Current events bring to mind previous experiences, not always in any obvious fashion. It is a well accepted statement that memory is associative, that memory structures are organized into some form: networks, concepts, prototypes, basic levels, schemas, frames, units, scripts. How? We need to understand the representation of knowledge, including the process that operate upon the representation. What is motor memory like, or image, or spatial information?

Associations among memory concepts have the immediate suggestion that somehow there is the equivalent of wires interconnecting memory structures. A little thought indicates that the notion of wires (neurons) simply will not do. That implies much too much knowledge of the wire (or its biological equivalent) that is to snake its way among the already existing stuff to the spot some distance away that might correspond to the new stuff (hold with me for the moment the belief that memories are stored in places). Alternatives to wires are not easy to find, the major candidate being numbered, labelled places (don't worry about numbers: just realize that each place must have a unique name). Then, the association between two memory structures is done by giving each one the unique name of the other, trusting to the existence of some clever machinery that can get from one place to another if only it has this name. This problem—I call it the "address problem"—is fundamental to the organization of any large scale associative memory. [. . .]

But wait a minute. Why is it that I assume that memories are stored in places. Can't they be distributed in space? [. . .] They can. Essentially there are two different classes of memory structures: place memories (the sort I have just described) and additive memories, memory structures which superimpose particular memories on top of one another, relying on various schemes to extract the relevant information. [. . .] These memories offer, for free, content-addressable storage and retrieval, but pose their own host of problems. There has not yet been sufficient research on additive memory structures.

And finally, but of great importance, there are the functional properties of the memory system that have received some attention: Short-term . . . working memory, activations in memory. Then there are various uses of memory: strategies for organizing, strategies for retrieval, rehearsal, the repeating over and over again of an item in temporary memory in order to maintain it while—while what?—while other operations can get done on it, I suppose. Is there one temporary memory? Many? Any? How is stuff represented in permanent memory, in working memory? Images? Propositions? I stop. I could go on indefinitely, but these issues are well known.

Performance

Performance, too long neglected, now just starting to receive its due attention. The problem of output, of performance, of motor control. The human hand is a marvelously complex instrument, with 27 bones, controlled by over 40 muscles (most of the muscles being in the forearm, connected to the fingers through an intricate set of tendons). The high-speed typist or musician moves the fingers with intervals of less than 100 msec., fingers simultaneously moving in different directions for different targets, with different time schedules for their time of tapping the target key (or string). Interesting errors arise in these high-speed operations, errors indicative of control structures: the doubling error in typing in which the wrong letter of a word is doubled, as when "look" becomes "lokk"; the alternation error, similar in spirit to the double in which "these" might become "thses"; the transposition error, in which two neighboring letters exchange positions so that "music" gets typed as "muisc," almost always occurring across hands as if the difficulty resulted from a synchronization problem between the hands, hardly ever within hands. And once mis-synchronized, the hands can continue, smoothly, wrongly, as in my transformation of "artificial" into "artifical" in the typing of the draft of this paper, each "i" coming one position early. The control process for going from perception of rough draft to the rapid movement of the fingers that produces the final copy is immense, involving synchronization of looking, perception, reading, motor programming, and feedback.

Consider handwriting, simple on the surface, complex in the details. A set of orthogonal muscle control systems, with intricate timing relationships (50 msec timing pulses, so some say). Handwriting can be thought of at many levels: organization of the ideas, determination of the words, physical organization of the words on the page, control of the letters, with individual motions of various sorts—micro motion to make the individual letters, macro motion to shift the palm across the page ..., the global motion to place the hand on the page or move it when returning to a new line or adjusting the placement of words on the page. Each level controlled, perhaps, by different parts of the cognitive system, for the control of the precise timing signals that create the letter segments would seem to be a different problem than determining during what part of the word the palm may shift, which is in turn different from the backup required to dot the i's, cross the t's, or the large shift required when, say, deciding to set things off indented with a large gap from the preceding line.

The motor control programs are non-trivial in character, their set up being as much a cognitive function as is reading, or perceiving, or talking. They take time—longer with longer or more complex motor sequences. They can be interfered with by simultaneous acts. They require long periods of training.

With all the muscles to control, with so many degrees of freedom possible because of the numerous joints and the flexibility of the body, the computation of the proper motion of each antagonist muscle pair seems beyond possibility. It probably is. Bernstein (1967), the Soviet investigator of motion, argued for complexes of motor control, systems in which one controls ratios and higher level parameters, the local computation available at the spinal cord and lower taking care of the local translations into muscle commands.

Huge hunks of the brain are devoted to motor control. The cerebellum, a marvelous device, seems dedicated to the function, as is the motor cortex. With so much of the brain dedicated to motor control, it seems unthinkable that this issue should be divorced from the study of higher mental processes. The sensory systems and the motor control systems are intimately linked, closely related neurologically. Probably closely linked psychologically.

The problems of performance are real, they require understanding of computational issues of considerable sophistication, and they interact with perceptual and thought processes in fundamental ways. It is possible to argue that much of our knowledge of the world resides in our knowledge of the procedures that interact with the world, that the perceptual-cognitive-motor schemas are unitary memory constructs, and the separation of one from the others destroys the whole.

Skill

Skill? Why is not skill the same as learning, or performance, or memory? Isn't skill simply expert performance?

Skill. A combination of learning and performance. But more than that, perhaps a fundamental aspect of human cognition. Suppose that our biological heritage developed by means of specialized subsystems for specialized behavior. Maybe skills are independent pockets of knowledge, with independent knowledge sources, computational resources, even independent brain and body structures. Maybe, maybe not. As usual, I suspect the truth is somewhere in between: we are neither general purpose computational devices, all knowledge and abilities being treated alike, nor are we highly specialized subsystems, each independent of the rest. In fact, let me call separate skills "separable," as opposed to "independent." We cannot ignore the specialization of function of an evolving biological creature, and so the issue of whether we have separable skills is an important one, with major implications for theories of human cognition.

Skills, specialized subsystems of knowledge and of performance. The expert at a task performs differently [from] the non-expert: the statement is correct, but misses the essence of the difference. The expert performer is qualitatively and quantitatively different [from] the non-expert. Bartlett (1958), in his book on thinking, stated that a major difference between expert and non-expert performance was timing. Experts had lots of time. They did their tasks easily, smoothly, without apparent effort, and with plenty of excess time. The expert tennis player is there before the ball. The expert pilot flies "ahead of the plane." The difficult looks simple. The non-expert is always scurrying, barely able to cope, rushing from this to that. With the non-expert, the difficult task looks difficult.

There are other differences, differences in perspective. Consider what happens when you first learn to drive an automobile. The instructions you receive emphasize the actions and the mechanics: hold the steering wheel this way, synchronize foot (for clutch) and hand (for gearshift) that way. As you progress, the point of view changes. Now you are turning the wheel, not moving your hands clockwise. Then you are turning the car, later you are entering that driveway. Eventually, when a truly expert driver, you drive to the bank, go shopping. The differences in the qualitative feeling of the performance are great. At the expert level, you may no longer be aware of all the subsidiary operations that you perform:

you look at the driveway, form the intention to enter, and the car obediently follows suit. Driving the car becomes as natural as walking, the car becoming as much a part of the body's controlled appendages as the limbs.

Thought

It is hardly necessary to state that the study of cognition should include the study of thought. The concern, though, is not that thought should be included, it is with how the inclusion should go. You may have thought we know a lot about thought. I claim not: what we do know is important, but primarily restricted to that part of the thought process available to conscious awareness—and as long as we lack knowledge of consciousness, we will lack a complete understanding of the role of conscious thought.

A question to be debated seriously is how much thought can be studied in isolation, as if it were a pure, abstract activity, divorced from special knowledge or special mechanisms. The mathematics of thought does indeed have this character, and as that mathematics has been used for models of human thought, it has tended to yield the vision of the human as a general purpose computational device.

But what if we are not so general, if our thought processes are designed for world interaction, with mental models of experiences being the major reasoning method, with limited ability to hold formal constructions in mind while we perform abstract operations upon them. I believe that too much emphasis has been given to possible formal properties of human reasoning, not enough to informal, experiential based models of reasoning. Take care, though, with this argument. . . . We must have some class of a general physical symbol system as a basis for much of cognition. We may be specialized, but we can also be general, learning new abilities, reasoning through novel situations, planning. [. . .]

The environment plays an important role in thought. We solve some problems by imagining the environment, solve others by using the environment. Micronesian navigators evidently use the outrigger of their canoe as a sort of analog computer which, when coupled with star positions and rate of passage of water past the canoe, can be used to aid precise navigation for hundreds of miles, out of sight of land much of the way (Hutchins, 1979). We use external aids ourselves, such as pencils, papers, drawings, even the placement of objects on a table. The computer is, in some sense, an artificial extension of our intellect, invented by humans to extend human thought processes. Just as we no longer need to master the art of memory because of the ease of writing, and just as we may no longer need to master arithmetic because of the availability of the calculator, or calligraphy because of the typewriter, we may perhaps forego some forms of thought once small portable computers become commonplace. (Hopefully, thus freeing ourselves for higher levels of thought processes.) Here is not the place for social commentary on these changes, just notice of the heavy dependence our culture places on technological aids to thought processes.

AFTERTHOUGHTS

Is There a Thirteenth Issue?   "You left out an issue," my readers rush to tell me, "why do you not have X?" The answer to some extent must be arbitrary. The division of Cognitive Science into 12 issues is idiosyncratic. My list is meant to cover the important principles and phenomena, to be those things that must be included in the study of cognition. The important point, therefore, is not whether my divisions are correct, but whether I have complete coverage. Have I left out anything? Among the various suggestions I have received, one stands out: motivation.

Motivation, the Thirteenth Issue?   What makes something interesting? Why do I sometimes watch a television show when I pass by an active set, even when I do not wish to? [...] For years I studied learning, concerned about the proper way to present material to improve a student's understanding. I studied many things, including proper organizational structure of the material, various instructional strategies, the making of detailed models of teacher, of student, and of topic matter. Yet none of these variables seemed to be as powerful as the one I did not study: changing the motivation of the student. Why is it that we do some tasks easily, readily, while others, seemingly no different, repel us, requiring huge amounts of self discipline to start, and then to finish? Interest and motivation seem intimately linked, the issues seemingly more complex than can be provided by simple analysis of missing knowledge structures or recourse to concepts such as the overall goals of a person. Note too that the desire to do something is not the same as being motivated to do that thing: I may want to do something, but find it difficult to force myself to do it. I may wish not to do something else, yet find it difficult to stop myself. [...]
  [...] Motivation can make the difference between learning or not, decent performance or not, what one attends to, what acts one does. Once, it was a leading topic in psychology, although oftentimes linked to emotion: [...] Is motivation a thirteenth issue?
  I think not. I believe motivation to result from a combination of things, from one's fundamental knowledge and goal structures, partially from emotional variables, and partially from decisions about the application of mental resources. Hence, the phenomena of motivation come from various

aspects of several issues: Belief Systems, Emotion, and Consciousness. Moreover, and more important, I am not convinced that there is a single phenomenon of motivation (if there is, it should indeed be afforded the special status of an issue). Rather, I believe it to be a complex of things, some biological, some cultural, some emotional, some the result of conscious goals and intentions, other subconscious. Motivation is indeed important, worthy of serious study, and a major determiner of our behavior. I believe, however, that it is a derived issue, composed of different aspects of the others.

IMPLICATIONS FOR COGNITIVE SCIENCE

The fact that I can write such a paper, ask such questions, complain with some reasonable specificity, is a positive sign about the emergence of a new discipline. It is a sign of progress that things are sufficiently well understood that the list of non-understood topics can be prepared.

The major results of my concerns should probably be in the education of new researchers, education at the advanced levels. It is here that I think my points best made, for it is within the education of ourselves and our students that the wider implications and wider aspects of our field ought to be acknowledged, discussed, considered. I would certainly not want my 12 issues to become 12 examination questions or 12 reading lists. I wish Cognitive Science to be recognized as a complex interaction among different issues of concern, an interaction that will not be properly understood until all the parts are understood, with no part independent of the others, the whole requiring the parts, and the parts the whole.

REFERENCES

Bartlett, F. C. (1958) *Thinking*. New York: Basic Books.
Bernstein, N. (1967) *The co-ordination and regulation of movements*. New York: Pergamon Press.
Geschwind, N. (1980) Neurological knowledge and complex behaviours, *Cognitive Science*, 4, pp. 117–133.
Hutchins, E. (1979) *Conceptual structures in pre-literate navigation*. Unpublished manuscript. La Jolla, California: Program in Cognitive Science, University of California, San Diego.
James, W. (1890) *Principles of psychology*. New York: Holt. (Reprinted New York: Dover, (1950).

Author Index

Subject Index